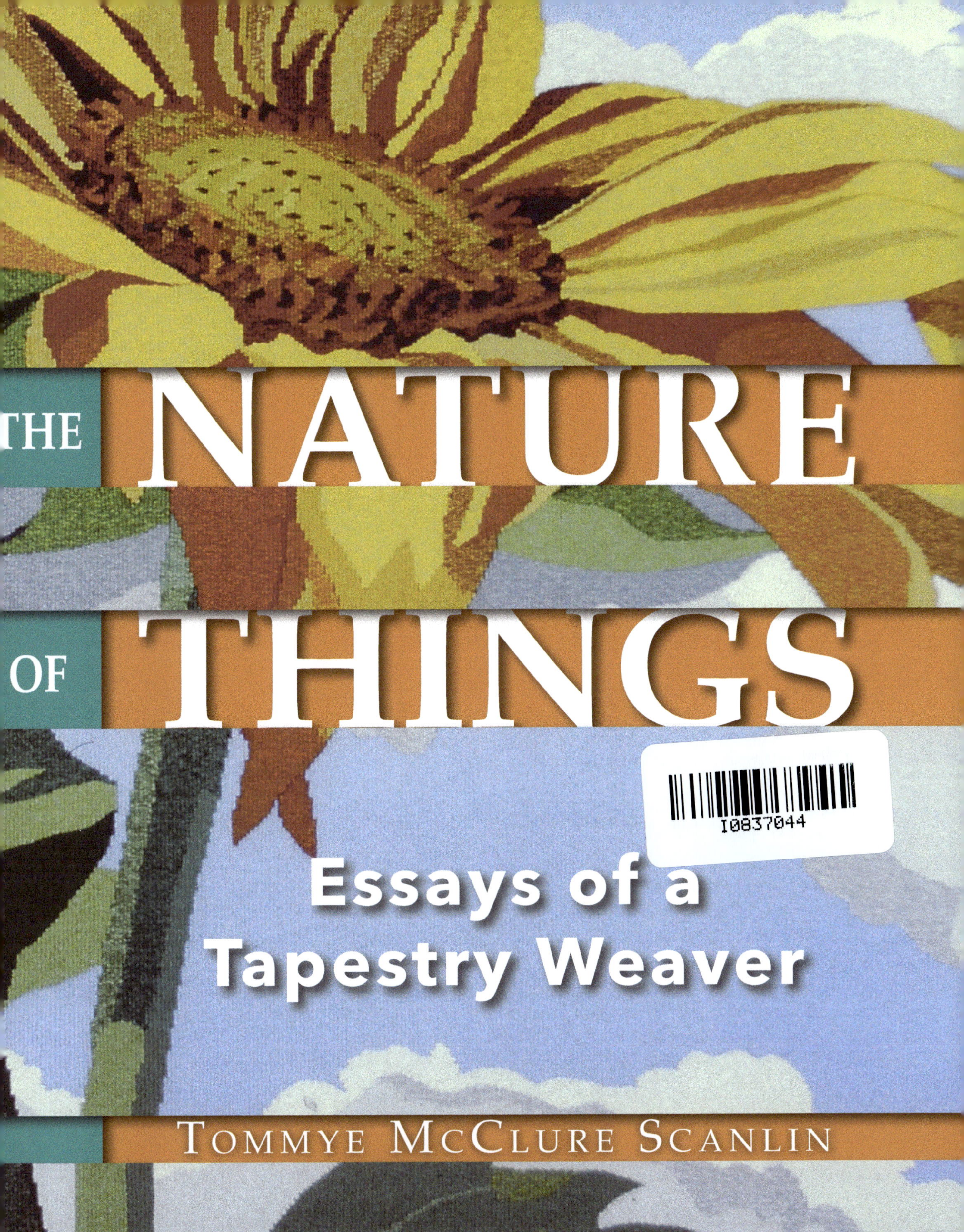

THE NATURE OF THINGS

Essays of a Tapestry Weaver

TOMMYE MCCLURE SCANLIN

THE NATURE OF THINGS

Essays of a Tapestry Weaver

Tommye McClure Scanlin

Published by:
University of North Georgia Press
Dahlonega, Georgia

Printing Support by:
Lightning Source Inc.
La Vergne, Tennessee

Book design by Corey Parson.

ISBN: 978-1-940771-72-4

Printed in the United States of America
For more information, please visit: http://ung.edu/university-press
Or e-mail: ungpress@ung.edu

To my husband, Thomas E. Scanlin.

I'm very grateful for his support and encouragement. Thomas dealt with the day-to-day realities of home responsibilities when I traveled to teach workshops, participated in artist residencies, attended conferences, or studied for months on end at Penland School of Craft and at West Dean College. Thomas has believed in me from the first time we met—and I am a better person (and artist) because of him.

After we have finished here,
the world will continue its quiet turning,
and the years will still transpire,
but now without their numbers,
and the days and months will pass
without the names of Norse and Roman gods.

Time will go by the way it did
before history, pure and unnoticed,
a mystery that arose between the sun and moon
before there was a word
for dawn or noon or midnight,

before there were names for the earth's
uncountable things,
when fruit hung anonymously
from scattered groves of trees,
light on the smooth green side,
shadow on the other.

—Billy Collins

Contents

Foreword

by Philis Alvic

Tommye Scanlin is an artist who has chosen tapestry as her medium of expression. Why would an artist choose weaving in the first place, and then a technique that requires considerable advance planning and many hours of execution? Why would an artist not choose the faster process of painting the subject? Besides being much faster, the painter is allowed to easily change from the original idea as the work progresses. As a weaver myself, I understand the seduction of textiles. Light reacts much differently to the yarn surface than it does to paint. Light is absorbed by yarn, creating a richness and depth. With yarn, and particularly the wool that Scanlin uses, the colors are intensified.

Tapestry is a weaving process where the design is built up row-by-row, inserting yarn for short distances across the row as the image dictates. Scanlin uses a traditional approach where she makes a cartoon—a detailed drawing of her subject—which is mounted behind the warp or upright threads on the loom. In her essays she describes in detail how she comes to the images she uses in her work. The preparation for her tapestry work builds on her love of walking in the woods and perceiving the small things in her surrounding that combine to make it a fulfilling experience. She photographs and draws her subject. The photograph is the reference, while the drawing is a method of understanding the dynamics of the item and the relationship of its parts and to the ground or space behind the item. Drawing is an aid to seeing. Only through drawing with repeated capturing of the image does an artist come to know why there was initial attraction. From her writings, we learn that Scanlin enjoys this process of becoming acquainted with her subject before she even begins to develop a composition for her piece.

Occasionally she will test an image by producing a small tapestry. While these are finished works in themselves, it allows for further understanding of the object and a trial of yarns and color.

Composition is how objects relate to one another within the frame of the piece. The artist is conscious of the viewer and how the eye will travel over the work. Scanlin is particularly interested in how the figure floats above the ground and the negative shapes created when the ground is outlined by the edge of the object. Often the ground is not a single surface, but made up of shapes itself that either echoes the object or contrast with it. None of this happens by chance, but is worked out in successive drawings until the design is deemed complete. Then it is transferred to a detailed drawing, which is the cartoon.

All the time when working on the composition, the artist is aware of how color will interact with the shapes and the special dynamics as different colors find different planes within the composition space. A tapestry artist, even one who dyes her own yarn, is limited by yarn colors. This is a challenge that a skilled artist like Scanlin meets by sometimes combining two different colors—using them as one thread—and sometimes by actual weaving techniques.

While most elements of the composition are fixed, any weaver is very aware of what happens during the weaving process. Are edges of the figures coming together properly? Are colors in the correct intensity and proportion? Is the surface tension consistent to insure a flat finished piece? And the multitude of questions that the artist and the craftsman deal with in construction. For the most part, these are not issues that come from a checklist, but from experience gathered over time. An artist understands when things are working and adjusts when needed.

The work of an artist is solitary for the most part. Especially for a tapestry weaver, constructing a piece involves many hours alone. Those of us who choose this path know that there is a certain gratification in the repetitive work, where the body develops a rhythm in the sequence of tasks. However, there are many other requirements in the life of an artist. Finishing pieces after they are cut from the loom, applying for exhibitions, keeping up a webpage, shipping or transporting work to shows, teaching opportunities—to mention just a few of the things that take a weaver away from the loom. One often wonders at the time it takes to manage a career in relationship to the time of actually producing the work. Years ago, I saw a documentary about the sculptor, Henry Moore. The major fact that I took away from it was that he had a personal curator. Unfortunately, for most of us in the arts, we are our own curator, secretary, publicist, packer, social media manager, equipment maintainer, and general all around repairperson.

I keep an extensive calendar to manage the different parts of my life and to prove to myself that I've actually accomplished something during the day. Several years ago, Scanlin came up with the idea of weaving a calendar. Really, it was weaving something each day as a way of centering herself as a weaver, when other chores consumed most of the day. Over subsequent years and more calendars, she has imposed more structure with a view to the final outcome.

Many artists are very bad at articulating what they do and why they do it. The slow process of weaving provides lots of opportunity for thought. In this collection of essays, Scanlin lets us into the thought process that she goes through in investigating a visual idea, and then developing it into a woven tapestry. She shows unusual insight into her own process.

Philis Alvic is an artist, weaver, and writer. She has exhibited her complex woven wall textiles in over 300 juried and invitational exhibitions. Alvic has written *Weavers of the Southern Highlands* (University Press of Kentucky, 2003), *Crafts of Armenia* (USAID/IESC Armenia, 2003), and over 100 magazine articles. As a short-term consultant for crafts development and marketing, she has worked on projects in fourteen different countries. Alvic is a founding member of the Kentucky Craft History and Education Association and is the on the Board of Weave A Real Peace.

Preface

A few years ago as I was preparing a presentation about my work, it occurred to me that my primary source for inspiration has always been found in the world in which I grew up—the fields and valleys of the Southern Appalachian Mountains. I credit my mother, Hazel Teague McClure, for being my first guide to the beauty these surroundings hold. She would often describe the latest wildflower found on an afternoon walk. After she died, the flower identification book I'd given her came back to me. In it, I found her notes sprinkled throughout the margins of the pages, noting where and when she'd spotted particular flowers.

Both my sister and I were raised with her expectation to simply do the best we could in whatever we wanted to pursue, and each accomplishment was celebrated with us. My sister and I chose different paths, both in the teaching field. She loved sports and became an early childhood physical education teacher. I loved art and became an art teacher. Mother was proud of both of us.

My journey to becoming an artist began simply and has taken modest paths. I haven't traveled extensively to experience a wider world. Most of my years have been spent close to the mountains where I grew up. Every day, I still find something to see and wonder about and to respond to in a visual way, maybe in a photograph, a sketch, a painting, or a tapestry. There is a beauty in the limits of place and time. Maybe Dorothy from *The Wizard of Oz* said it best: "There's no place like home." And so I wanted to write to describe the small things that I've found where I've lived for almost my whole life and the artworks that came from those observations.

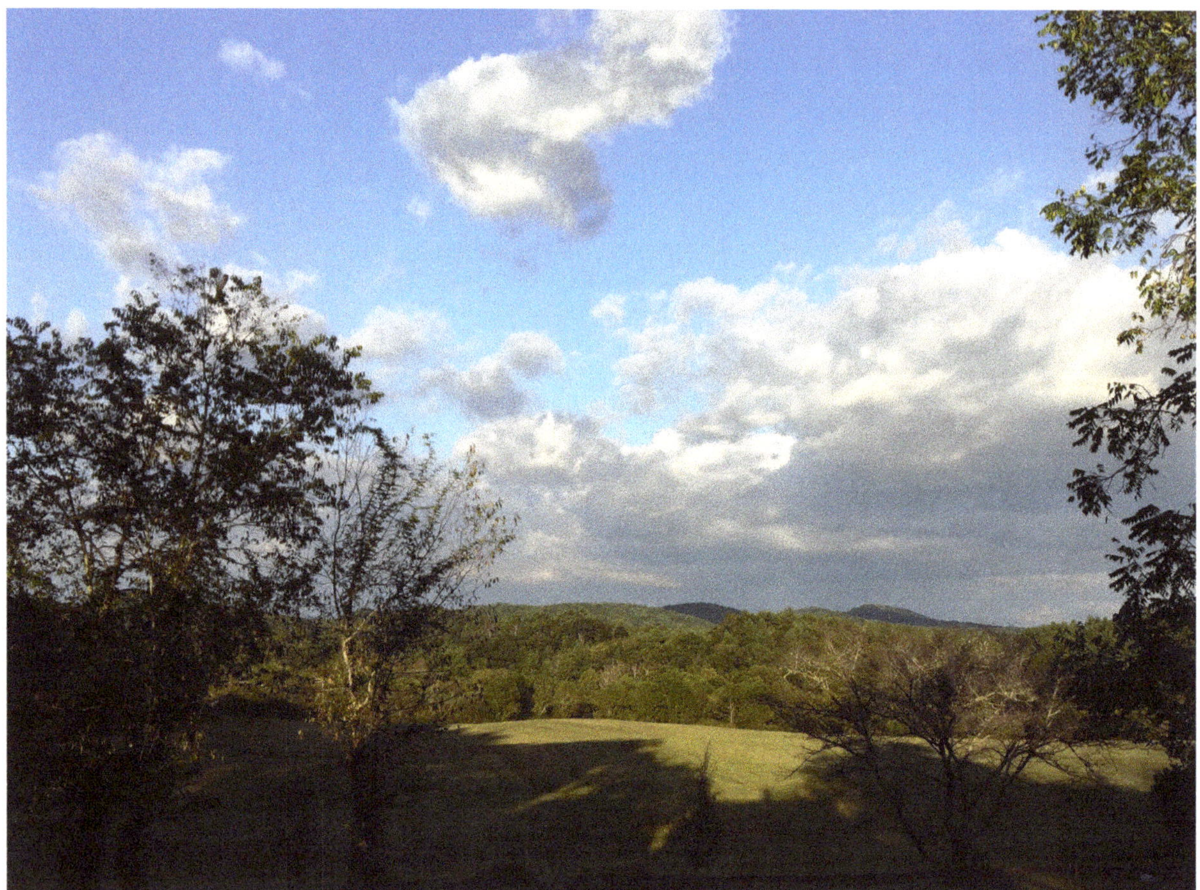

Figure 0.1
Brasstown valley, a few miles from home.

Along my way, many people have been my guides. There are several to whom I am especially grateful for what they shared with me. I owe much to Bob Owens, my first art teacher, and, later, colleague at North Georgia College. Edwina Bringle, my first weaving teacher at Penland School of Crafts, nudged me along for years. Archie Brennan and Susan Martin Maffei are my tapestry gurus.

Noel Thurner and Patrick Horan have shown me how to see and be part of the natural world in ways I never imagined. Their dedication to preserving many hundreds of acres in Western North Carolina for posterity through conservation efforts is inspiring.

Authors Nancy Peacock and Carol Polsgrove read my drafts and gave insightful suggestions about my attempts to describe what I experience in the natural world and hope to represent in my artwork. Tapestry artists and writers Molly Elkind, Sarah Swett, and Pat Williams read later versions and made kind comments. Sharon Hall, wonderful writer and friend, gave great advice. Fran Porter and Beth Rickert, whom I've known since early college days, have also read my assorted essays along the way and encouraged me to keep on with it. I thank them all for their support.

Photographs of inspiration sources leading to the making of tapestries are important in this book. I've made most of the nature photos with either a point-and-shoot camera or a smart phone. Tim Barnwell has photographed my completed tapestries for many years. I'm grateful to Christopher Dant, Assistant Professor of Photography in the Department of Visual Art at the University of North Georgia, for working closely with me during the last stages of pulling this book together. His photographs of the visual research I've done for several bodies of work have been helpful to document the multiple directions I sometimes take ideas before winding up at the end with a tapestry.

I've had guidance and encouragement as my ideas came together from Jillian Murphy, Assistant Managing Editor, and Bonnie (BJ) Robinson, Ph.D., Director, of University of North Georgia Press. It was a chance meeting between Jillian and Philis Alvic at an Appalachian Studies Association conference that led to my asking Philis to write the Foreword. Philis Alvic's writings about weaving have informed me for decades and I'm honored that she's contributed words to this book.

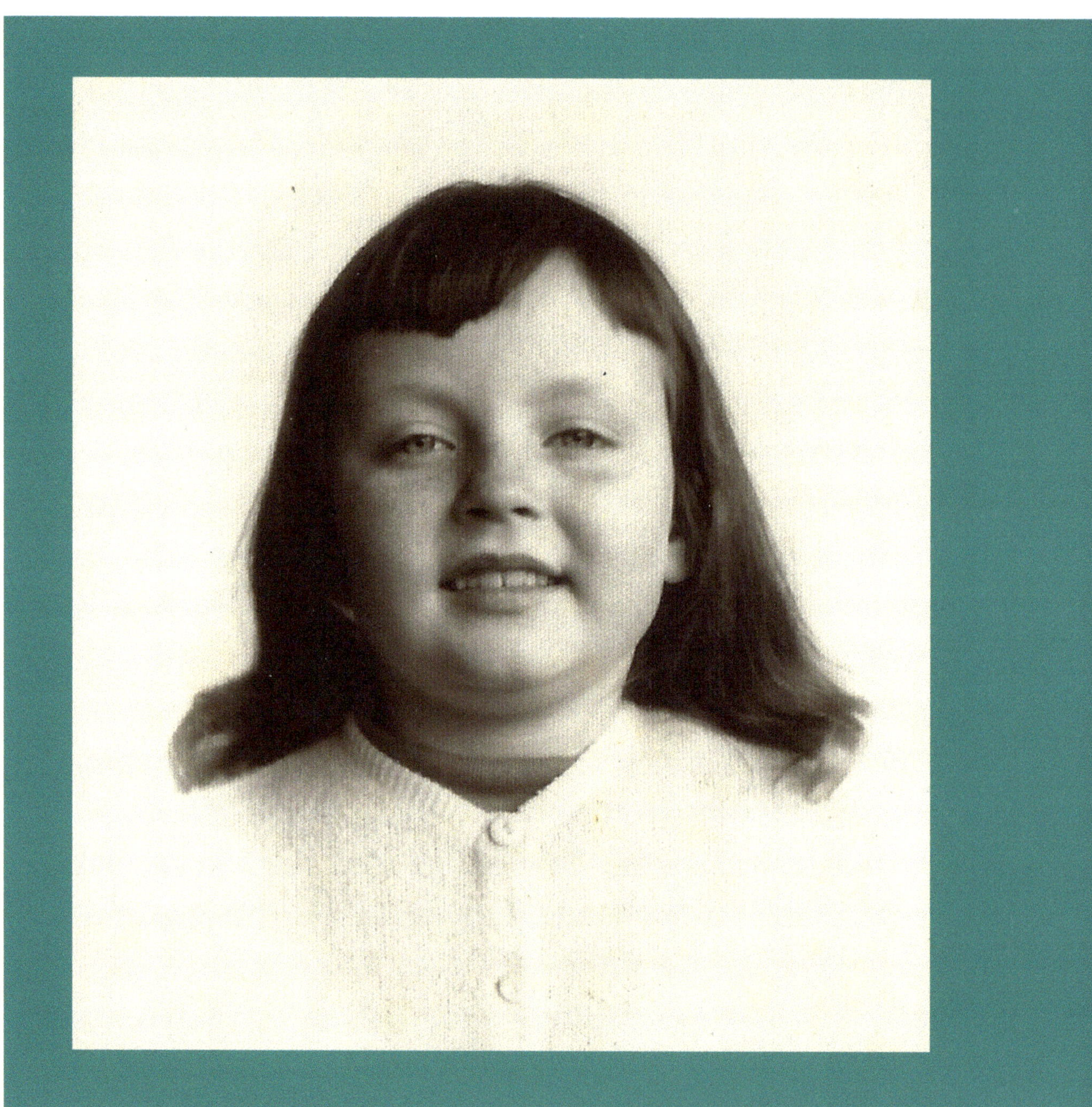

Figure 1.1
Tommye—second grade photo
(photographer unknown)

1

Once Upon a Time
An Introduction

Once upon a time I wanted to be an artist. Along the way from there to now I found my way to tapestry weaving.

As long as I can remember, I've wanted to draw pictures. As a child, I heard others say I was the "class artist," and that encouraged me to think I could be a real artist when I grew up. What I thought an artist did was pretty limited since there wasn't an art program in the rural North Georgia schools I attended. Even so, kids in our class happily cut out stenciled holiday decorations for each season that we then colored with crayons and taped to windows and doors. We drew with pencils on our lined notebook paper to illustrate reports. And in our spare time, several of us girls drew horses and pretty dresses while some of the boys filled pages with elaborate battle scenes between cowboys and Indians.

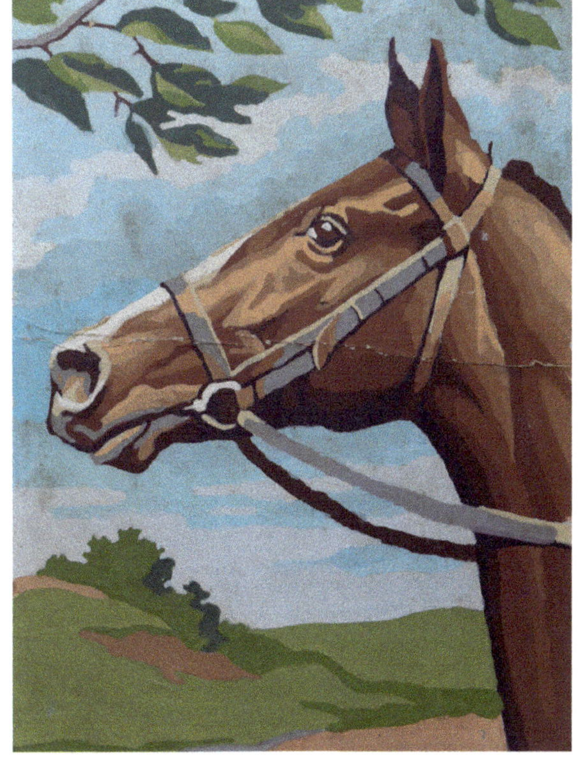

Figure 1.2
Paint by numbers horse
(photo by Christopher Dant)

One Christmas, under the tree I found the Jon Gnagy (1907–1981) *Learn to Draw* kit that included a pad of manila paper, some sticks of charcoal, and the book of art lessons. I drew every example in the book many times over and used notebook paper once the drawing paper ran out. The next year, Santa brought a couple of paint-by-number sets, and how exciting those were! I loved to fill in the printed outlines on the canvas board with a brush loaded with that juicy, heady smelling oil paint. Drawing with charcoal and painting with oil paint—those were things an artist did, I decided.

I received encouragement for my artistic "talent" from family, friends, and teachers all through my early years in spite of no art classes being offered at school. By high school, the idea that I might actually become an artist had a strong hold on me. I was even offered a modest art scholarship at a private college. As tempting as that offer was, because of the family's limited financial means, it wasn't enough. Instead, after high school graduation, I enrolled at North Georgia College (NGC) in Dahlonega where

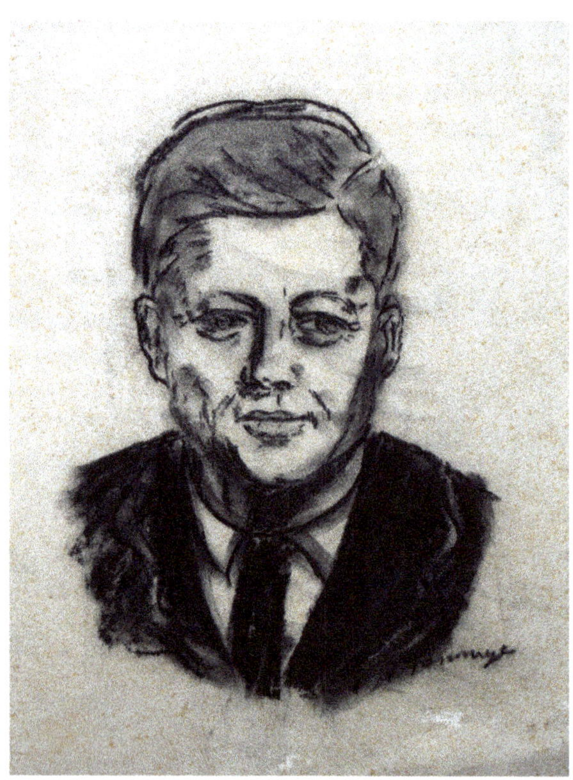

Figure 1.3
Early drawing: John Kennedy
(photo by Christopher Dant)

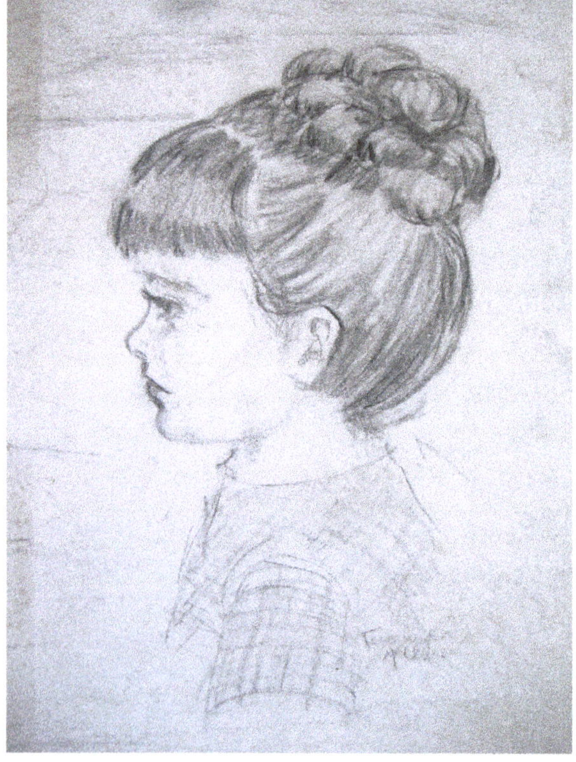

Figure 1.4
Early drawing: Janie
(photo by Christopher Dant)

I was given a scholarship with the provision that I would major in education and agree to teach for several years in a public school in Georgia. Being enrolled in an education degree program was not at all my first choice since I'd held dreams of studying art in college. But the reality was that I needed financial assistance to attend school.

As it turned out, one of the prerequisites for the elementary education major at NGC was an art education class. In that course, I encountered Bob Owens (1939–2004) who became my first art teacher, unofficial advisor, and mentor. Bob had been at NGC for just a few years and was teaching several studio, art history, and art education courses. His dream was to establish an art degree program at the college, a goal he accomplished in 1971 when the Department of Fine Arts was formed, with Bob as the first head.

The art education course I took in the fall of 1966 was my first opportunity to have art instruction, and I was so ready for it. I began to discover a world of art making that was more complex and wonderful than I had imagined. Being in that class confirmed for me that making art must indeed be part of my life. After the required art education class was finished, I continued to fill my electives with the other assorted classes Bob offered. He soon learned I was disappointed to be locked into the field of elementary education by financial necessity and that I really wanted to study art. Bob recommended I consider transferring to another school to major in art education—an option I didn't even know existed when I entered college—and continue to fulfill the scholarship requirements that way. His advice opened a new path for me. I transferred to the University of Georgia (UGA) and in 1969 completed an undergraduate degree for teaching art at elementary, middle, and high school levels.

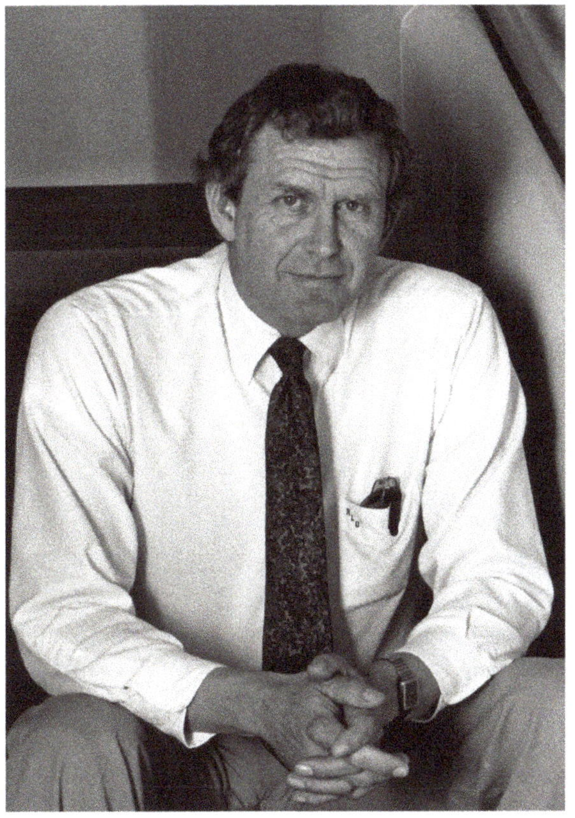

Figure 1.6
Bob Owens
(photo by Hank Margeson)

After graduation, I began teaching high school art classes and, in the first summer break, immediately began working toward a Master of Art Education from UGA. Although I would have preferred a Master of Fine Arts (MFA) degree program with more concentrated studio time, I was given a grant that covered some of the tuition costs by the school system where I was employed. Still, I loved it all. Art filled my life. I found myself in my early twenties teaching high school art classes, taking art courses in the art education graduate program during summers, and making art.

I enjoyed my years of teaching middle and high school art classes, and I was thrilled when Bob invited me to apply as a faculty member in the new Fine Arts Department at NGC. Thus, in 1972, I became his colleague at the college and continued for decades to benefit from his insightful mentoring about both the making and teaching of art.

Once I was employed at NGC, my desire to seek an MFA came back into the picture. Indeed, it was a required degree if one wished to move up the promotion and tenure ladder at the college. The program I chose was at East Tennessee State University where there was a strong tradition in weaving instruction. I attended ETSU in the summers of 1976 to 1979 and taught at NGC during the academic years between. In 1979–80, I was given a leave of absence from NGC to complete the required year of residence at ETSU and completed the MFA in 1980.

I'm forever grateful for the circumstances that allowed me to meet the man who became my mentor when I was nineteen years old and that I was willing to take his advice for my future path in the field of art education.

2

The Making of a Teacher

I guess it's ironic that someone who said she didn't want to be an education major in college spent the better part of a lifetime going into classrooms and standing in front of students. Young ones, old ones, and all ages in-between.

Although I didn't know it at the time, it wasn't really teaching that I was resisting when I entered college as an elementary education major. Instead, I feared that making art wasn't going to be part of my future. Yes, I now know that one can be an artist while occupied with another job for their livelihood. At the time, I just couldn't see how that was possible.

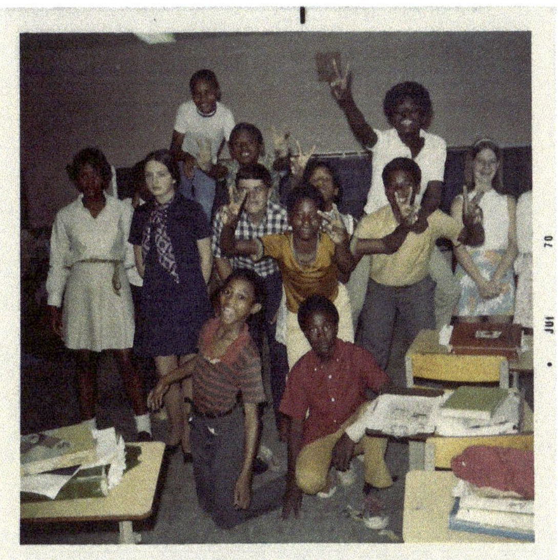

Figure 2.1
Fair Street School, 7th grade art students, 1970

The art education program at UGA that Bob guided me to opened the way to be intimately connected to the making side of art. Not only were art education theory and practice courses part of the curriculum but also studio classes were required. Those were most important to me.

The three years I spent in middle and high school art classrooms right after graduation offered many pieces of the larger teaching puzzle I began putting together. Each day,

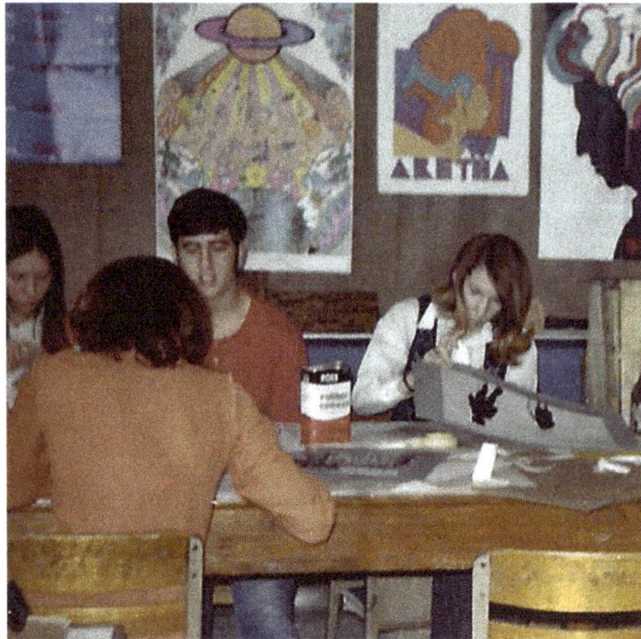

Figure 2.2
Gainesville High School art class, 1970

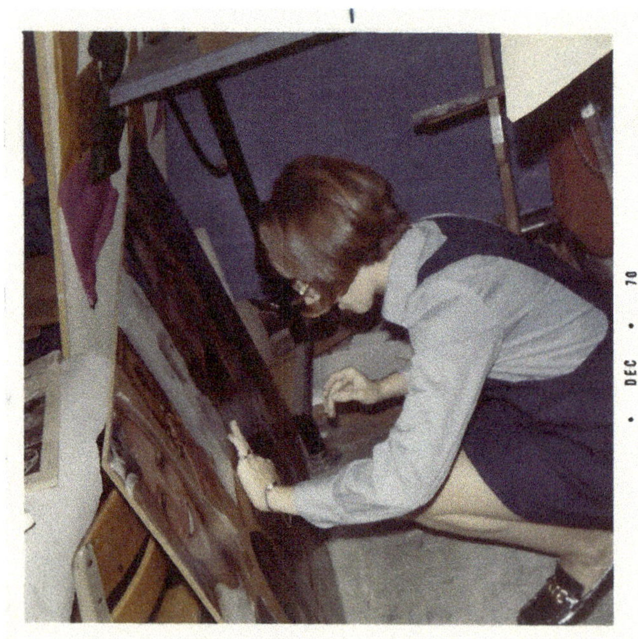

Figure 2.3
Gainesville High School art student, 1970

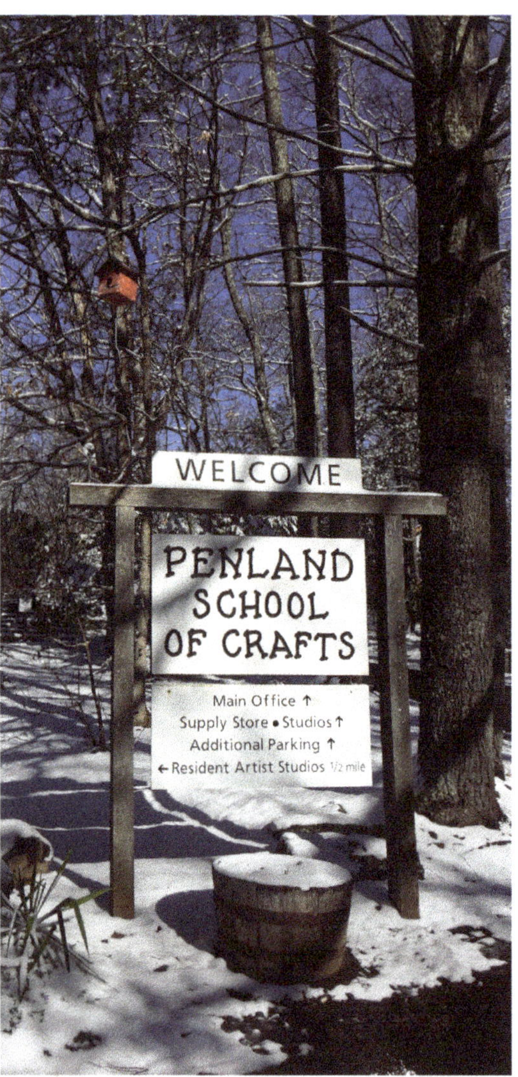

Figure 2.4
Penland sign, 1975

I faced teenage students who were either eager to jump into art making or unsure and afraid to try things. Then there were the few goof-offs, the kids who were putting up with the system while they did as little as they could to get by.

I began to see that almost anyone could become motivated to make something in the art class, depending on the approach I used when presenting the project. I also realized that I needed to say the same thing in different ways. Some students could easily see what to do with a demonstration. Others had to have both demo and verbal instructions. A few only needed to refer to a handout. Some would rather plunge right in and try their own way.

I learned how to plan on the fly to quickly explain or show in different ways. Soon, I wasn't afraid to adapt and to be patient. I figured out how to be attentive to the whole room, even if it seemed I was only watching or listening to one person.

Looking back on my teaching style, I realize that most of it didn't come from the classes in art education in the university degree program. Instead, much of what I understand about teaching came from having a few exceptional teachers as my role models. Each of those had calm, patient

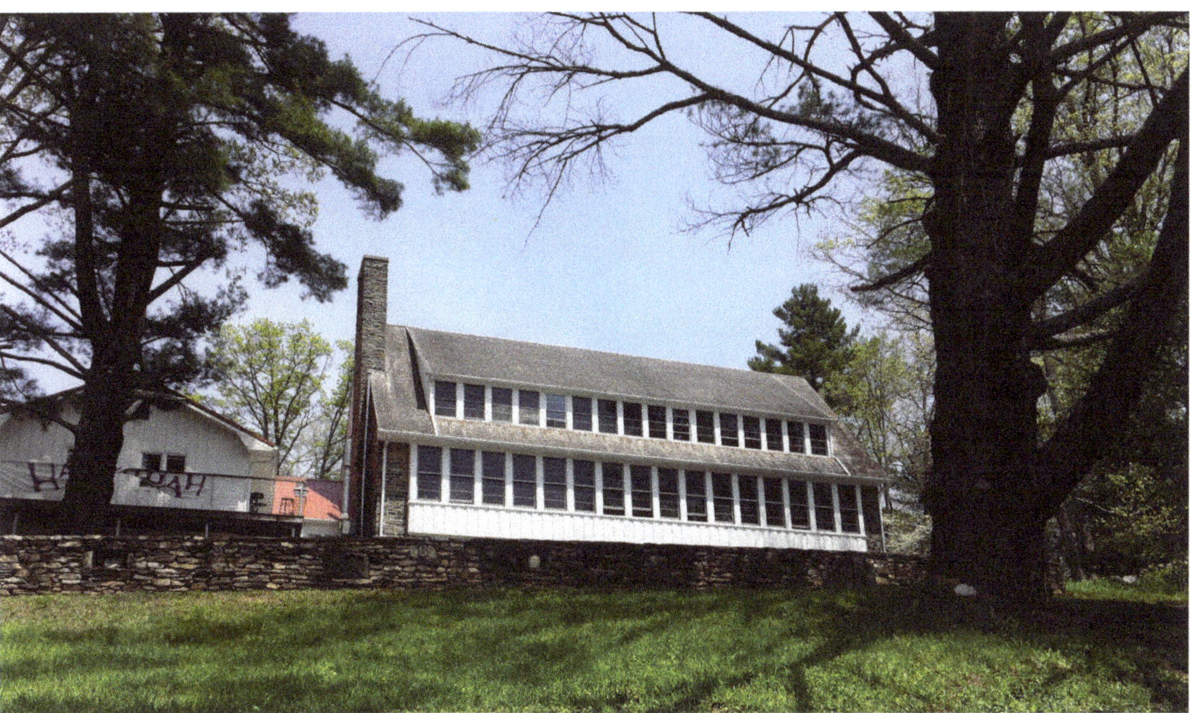

Figure 2.5
Penland—Lily Loom House, 1975

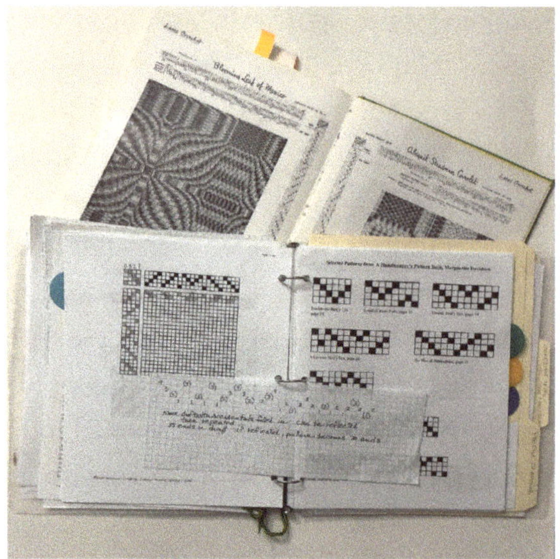

Figure 2.6
Weaving drafts in Davison book and later examples of drawdowns

ways that showed how they cared about both their students and the processes of conceptualizing and making art.

Bob had opened my eyes to the field of art education when I was his student at NGC. Later as his colleague, I saw his teaching style from a different perspective. It became clear that Bob took himself and what he was doing very seriously. Art making *and* art teaching were both important to him, and he knew the same could be true for others. His advice to transfer to a school with an art education degree option was life changing for me. Over the years I knew Bob, I came to realize that he guided and advised many

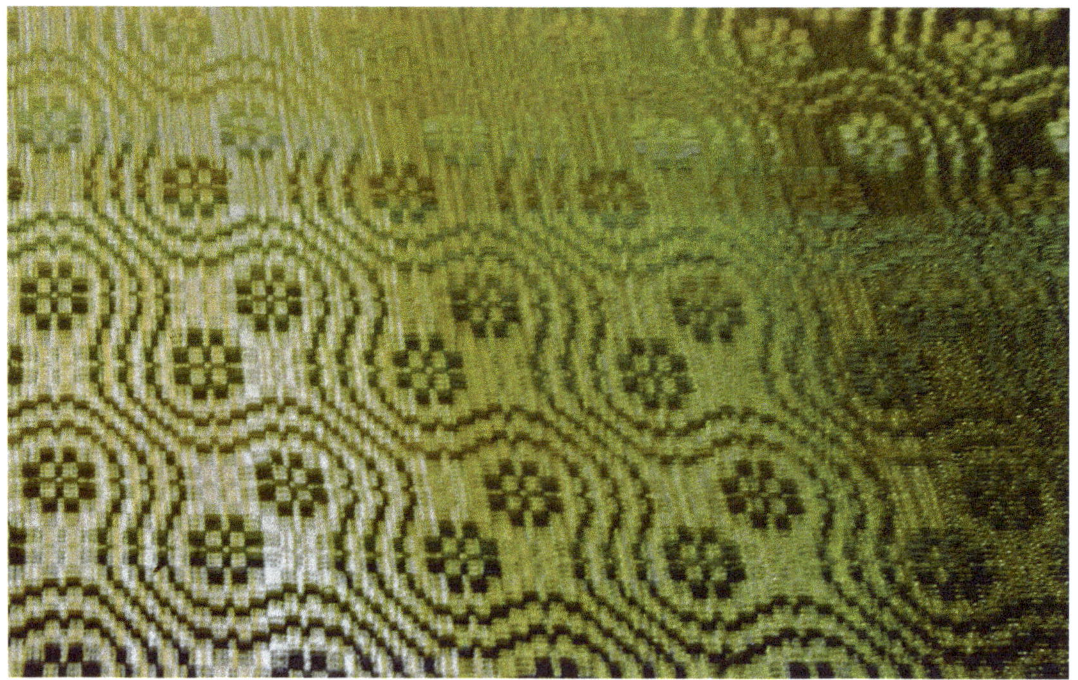

Figure 2.7
Penland–Scanlin weaving: Cat Track and Snail Trail overshot, 1975

others in equally life-changing decisions.

I saw how he approached any situation, often coming up with solutions that were most beneficial for everyone concerned. I also began to appreciate how Bob could dream—how he could envision the arts enhancing the lives of the larger community of north Georgia and beyond—and how hard he worked toward that goal.

Maybe what I gained most from Bob was confidence. He always thought I could do it, whatever the "it" happened to be. Even when I was uncertain of my abilities, his unwavering belief that I would work hard and get the job done often gave me the push needed to begin and then to follow through to the end of the task. His faith in me helped me realize I had persistence. Under his guidance and encouragement, I grew in self-reliance and self-confidence in my art making abilities and my teaching skills.

I was fortunate to encounter another remarkable teacher early in my career when I enrolled in a three-week weaving class at Penland School of Craft in the summer of 1975, knowing only that it was open to all skill levels. The instructor was Edwina Bringle (b. 1939). The class included those who had been weaving for many years. Other classmates were totally new to it. Several were like me, mostly self-taught weavers with some knowledge we'd cobbled together from here and there. Edwina was able to direct each of us in various weaving techniques to fit our needs.

In my case, I was curious about weaving drafts. Those are the shorthand notations that can be used to create diagrams for the patterns that will happen when a loom is set up in different ways.

To help me understand weaving drafts Edwina pointed out a classic book that I hadn't encountered before: Marguerite Porter

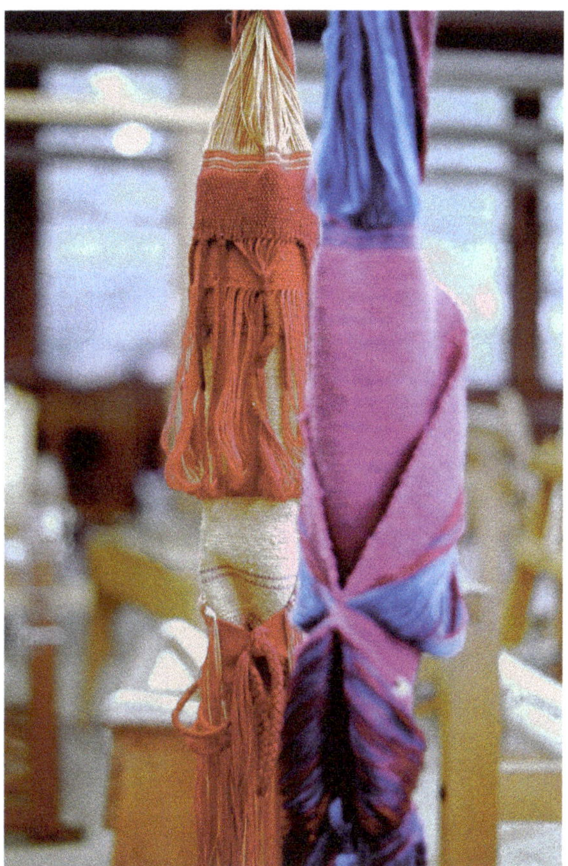

Figure 2.8
Penland–Scanlin weaving: double weave sculptural hanging, 1975

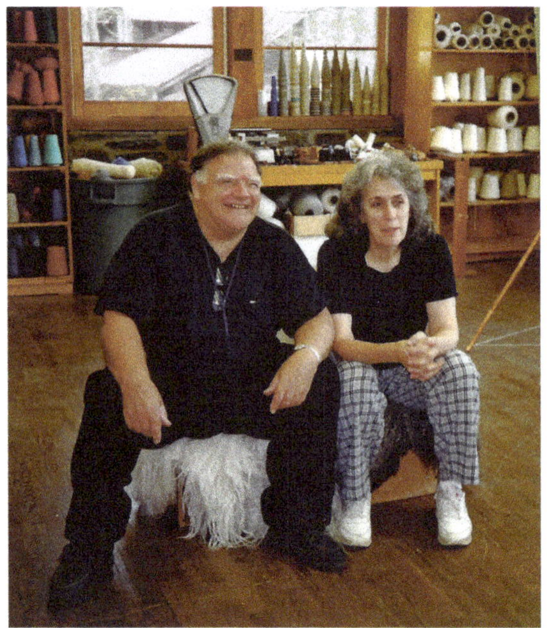

Figure 2.9
Archie Brennan and Susan Martin Maffei, photo during Penland Concentration, 2000

Davison's (1887–1953) *The Handweaver's Pattern Book* (1950); she also showed me how to read the code contained in the drafts. In that early book and with Edwina's guidance, I discovered for the first time traditional, and seemingly complicated, patterns called overshot. With this weaving method the weft threads could float across the surface of the warp in places, to be stitched down with a background thread that was woven almost simultaneously. I thought this technique offered amazing freedom at the loom. In the class, I made two weavings from overshot threading drafts, using a wide variety of colors and textures rather than the traditional materials associated with the method.

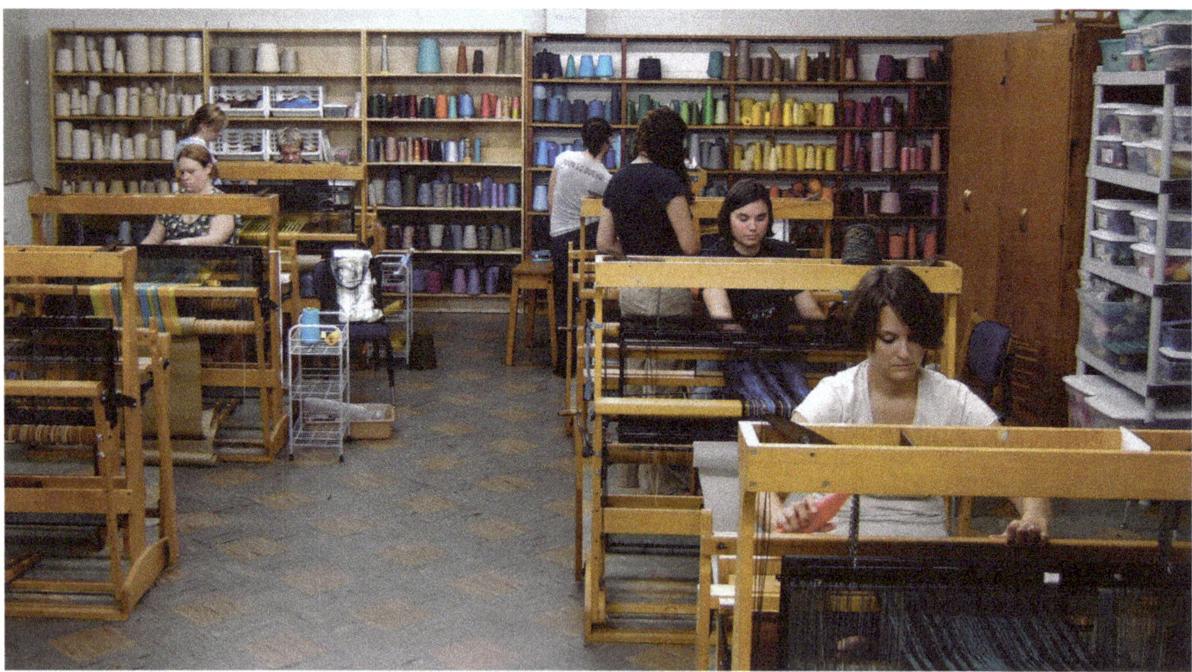

Figure 2.10
North Georgia College & State University, weaving class, Fall 2007

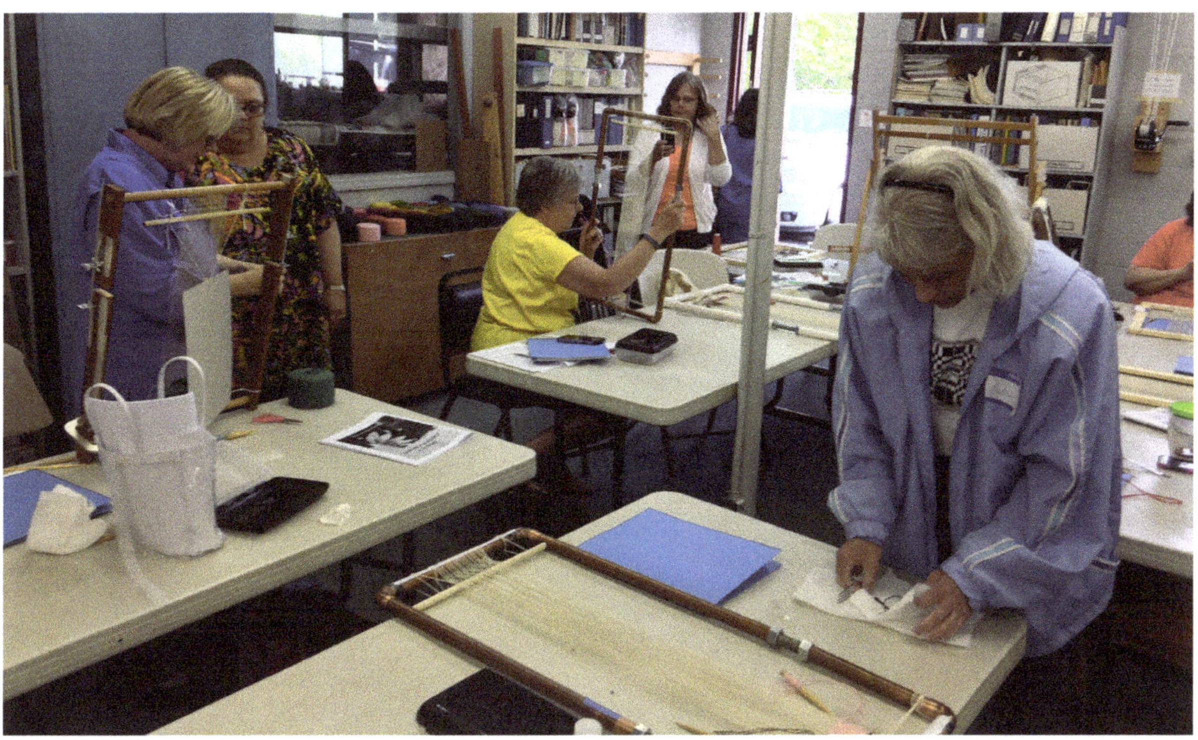

Figure 2.11
Appalachian Center for Art and Craft, Norris, TN, weaving workshop 2016

She also suggested how to set up the loom to allow for weaving in multiple layers, one on top of the other. Magic? So it seemed as I experimented with methods of double weave to create tubes and interchanged layers of the fabric.

The three weeks at Penland under Edwina's guidance were transformative. She provided not only sound weaving instruction but also an example of a master teacher who could lead each person in different ways. For those who needed specific guidance in selecting projects to weave, she gave them that. Others had their own agenda for what they wanted to weave, and she listened, watched, and let these students be, helping if needed. And for those like me who wanted to go in lots of directions, seeking new things to learn about the structure and possibilities of weaving, she led the way to the resources we'd need to figure things out on our own. And she always answered any questions along the way for anyone.

Two others whom I consider as teaching mentors are Archie Brennan (b. 1931–d. 2019) and Susan Martin Maffei (b. 1947). I've had many accomplished tapestry instructors, but it's the guidance of Archie and Susan that

I follow most in my tapestry making. I met them in 1994 at Harrisville, New Hampshire when they led a weekend retreat sponsored by the Tapestry Weavers of New England. They expertly answered questions about tapestry technique, and both gave individual attention to every student several times each day. Archie had an illuminating way of discussing tapestry as a process, and his thoughtful musings about the reasons for both historical and contemporary tapestry making gave me much to think about. That initial workshop experience with Archie and Susan convinced me I needed to study with them whenever possible, and so I have many times over the past decades.

I spent three years teaching art in high school and the next twenty-eight years at North Georgia College (later North Georgia College & State University) as a professor in the Fine Arts Department. I carried the examples of *how* to teach from Bob, Edwina, Archie, and Susan with me every day when I stood before students.

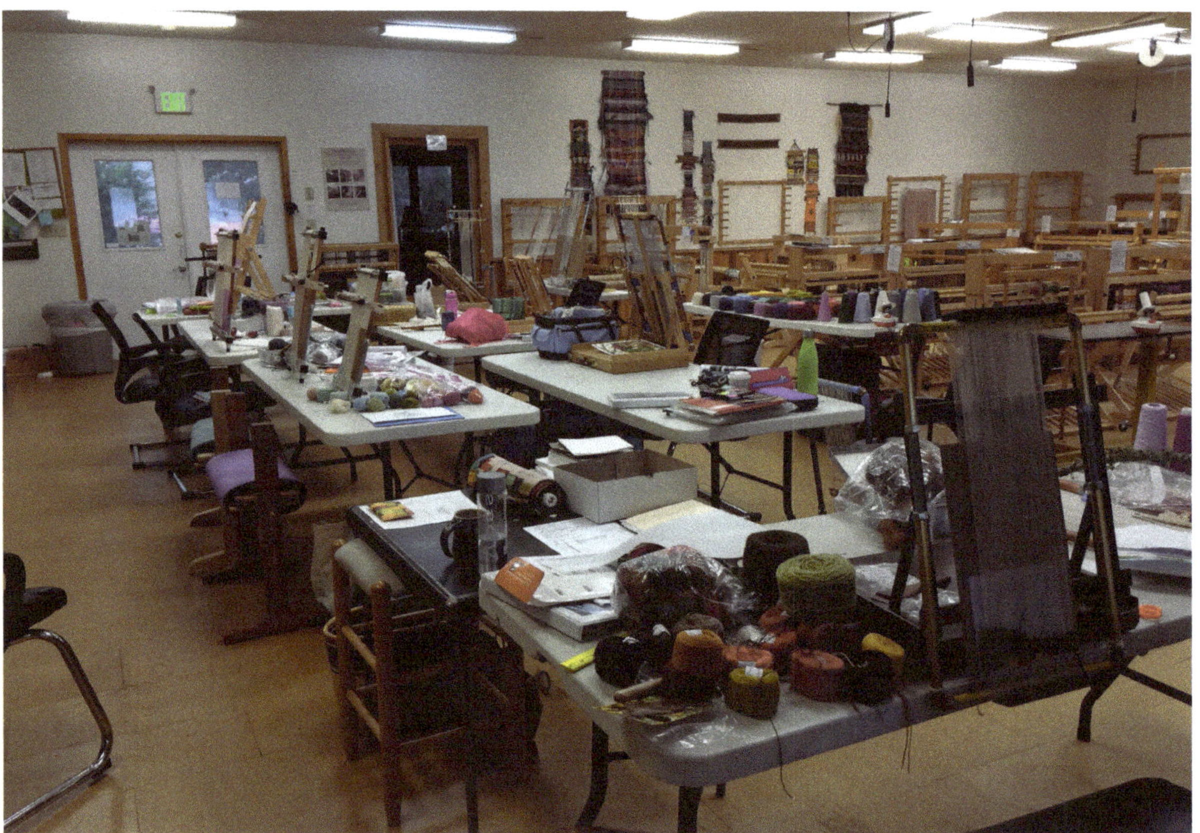

Figure 2.12
John C. Campbell Weaving Studio, 2017

After retiring from full-time employment at the institution that is now the University of North Georgia, I've continued to be a workshop instructor for weavers' groups and at craft schools. I walk into each new teaching experience filled with a sense of anticipation about where the journey we're about to embark upon will take us—even if it's only a few days we'll be spending together, immersed in the wonders of image making and tapestry weaving.

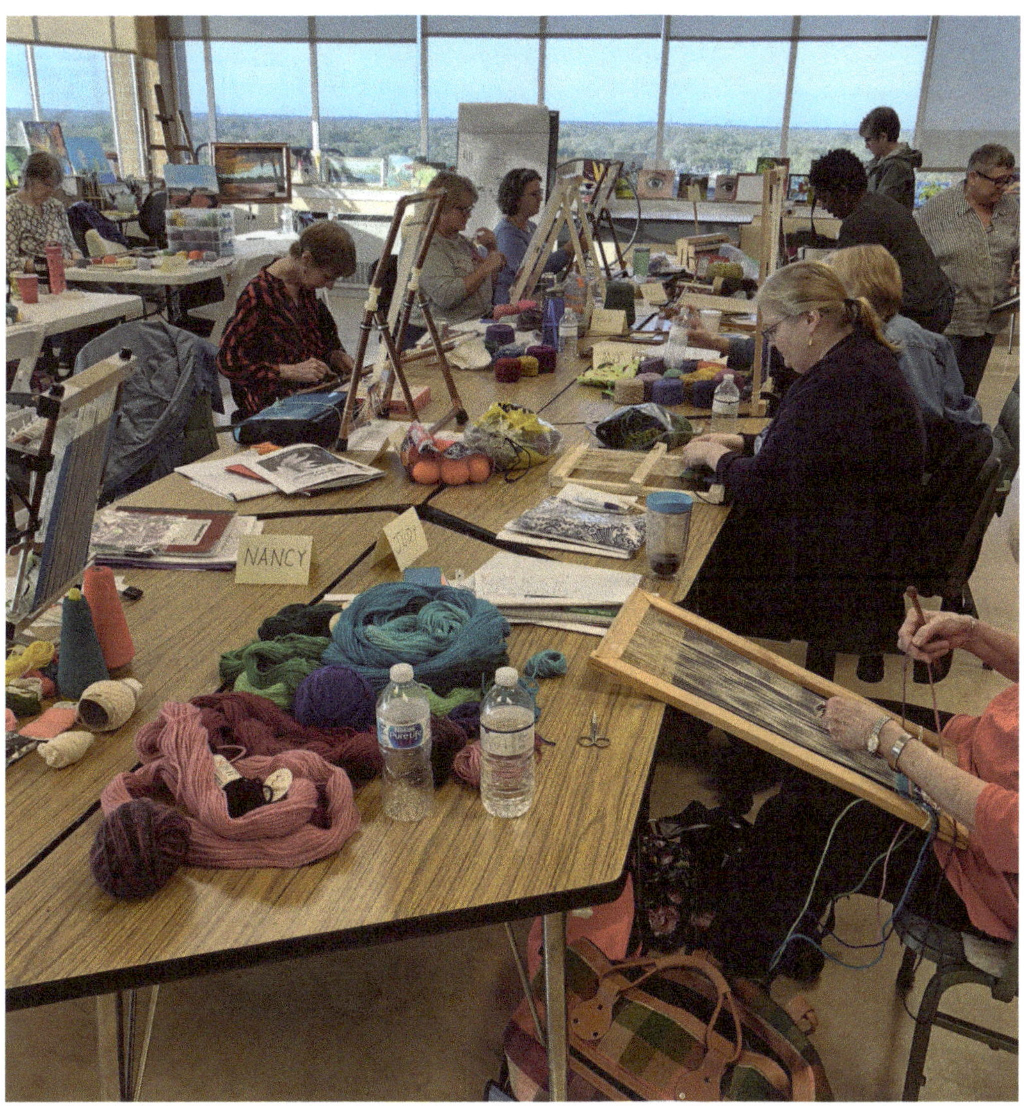

Figure 2.13
Weavers of Orlando workshop, Winter Park, Florida, 2018

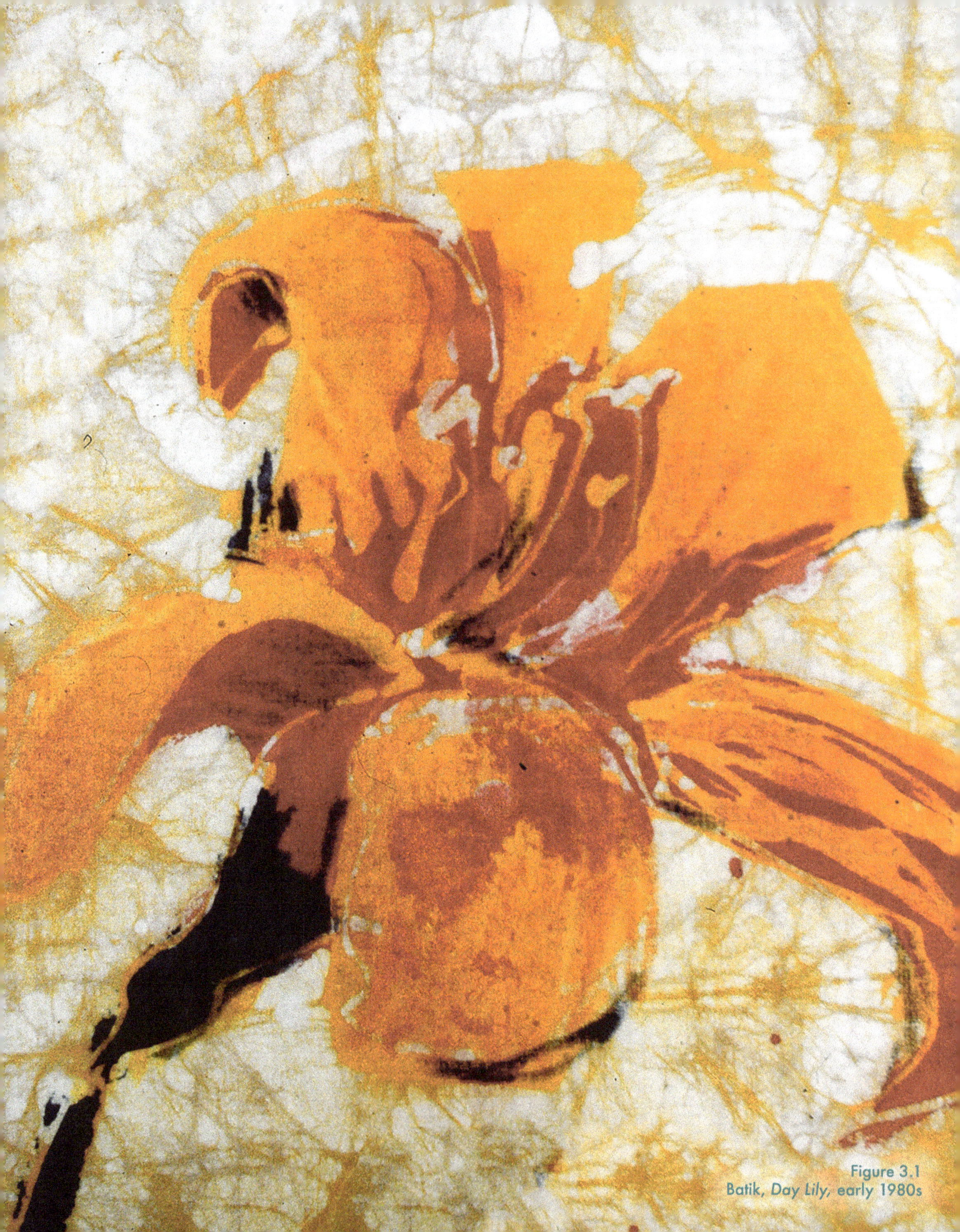

Figure 3.1
Batik, *Day Lily,* early 1980s

3

Finding the Way to Tapestry

I've mentioned that there wasn't art instruction in the schools I attended in my youth so my early art making experiences were limited. The Jon Gnagy *Learn to Draw* kit introduced me to charcoal, and most of the drawings I made in high school were done with that medium. As a college student at NGC and UGA, I was introduced to other visual art forms that offered many more ways to create images.

I began to understand that fabrics and fiber could be artistic disciplines with a variety of methods and techniques. Of course, quilts were familiar because we had many of those at home, made by women in the family. I also knew about weaving on a loom but didn't know anyone who did the craft. Discovering that there were contemporary artists working with fabric and fibers in creative ways was a revelation, and I wanted to explore this newly-discovered creative avenue as much as possible.

My career as an art educator was proceeding, first as a high school teacher and soon as a college instructor. My interests in fiber and fabric grew in those years as I shared what I was learning with students by developing lessons in various fiber and fabric techniques. In my first years of teaching, my students and I plunged into fabric dyeing and surface design techniques. We tried things like batik (where hot wax is used on fabric to protect areas from dye and then later removed) and hand printmaking methods for applying designs to fabrics. We tried stitchery and also constructed large, freeform crocheted and wrapped sculptural hangings. I learned how to make simple frame looms, first so that students could do a project, but quickly I became fascinated with the process itself. Of all the fiber and fabric techniques I tried, it turned out that weaving became my passion.

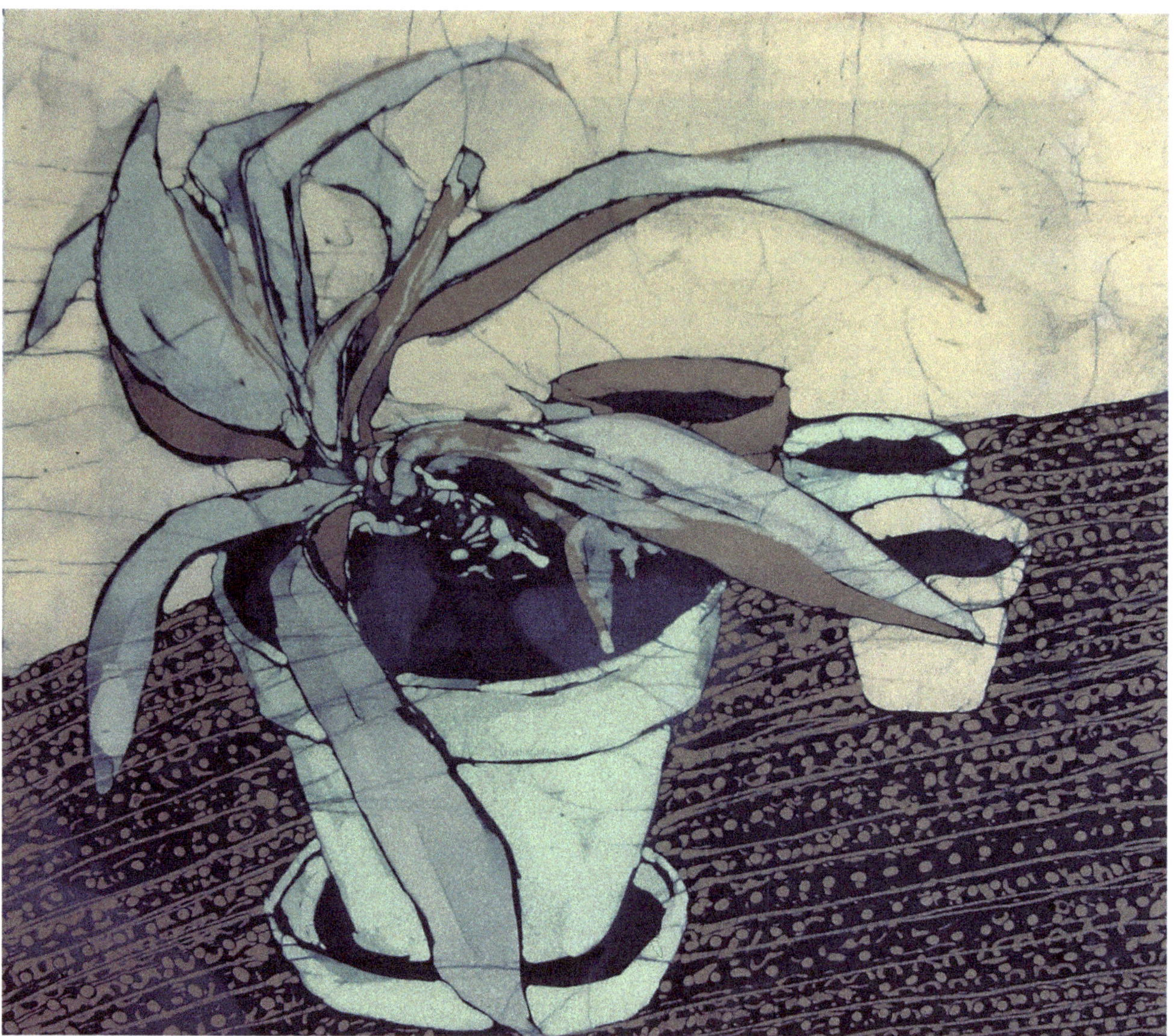

Figure 3.2
Batik, *Potted Plant*, early 1980s

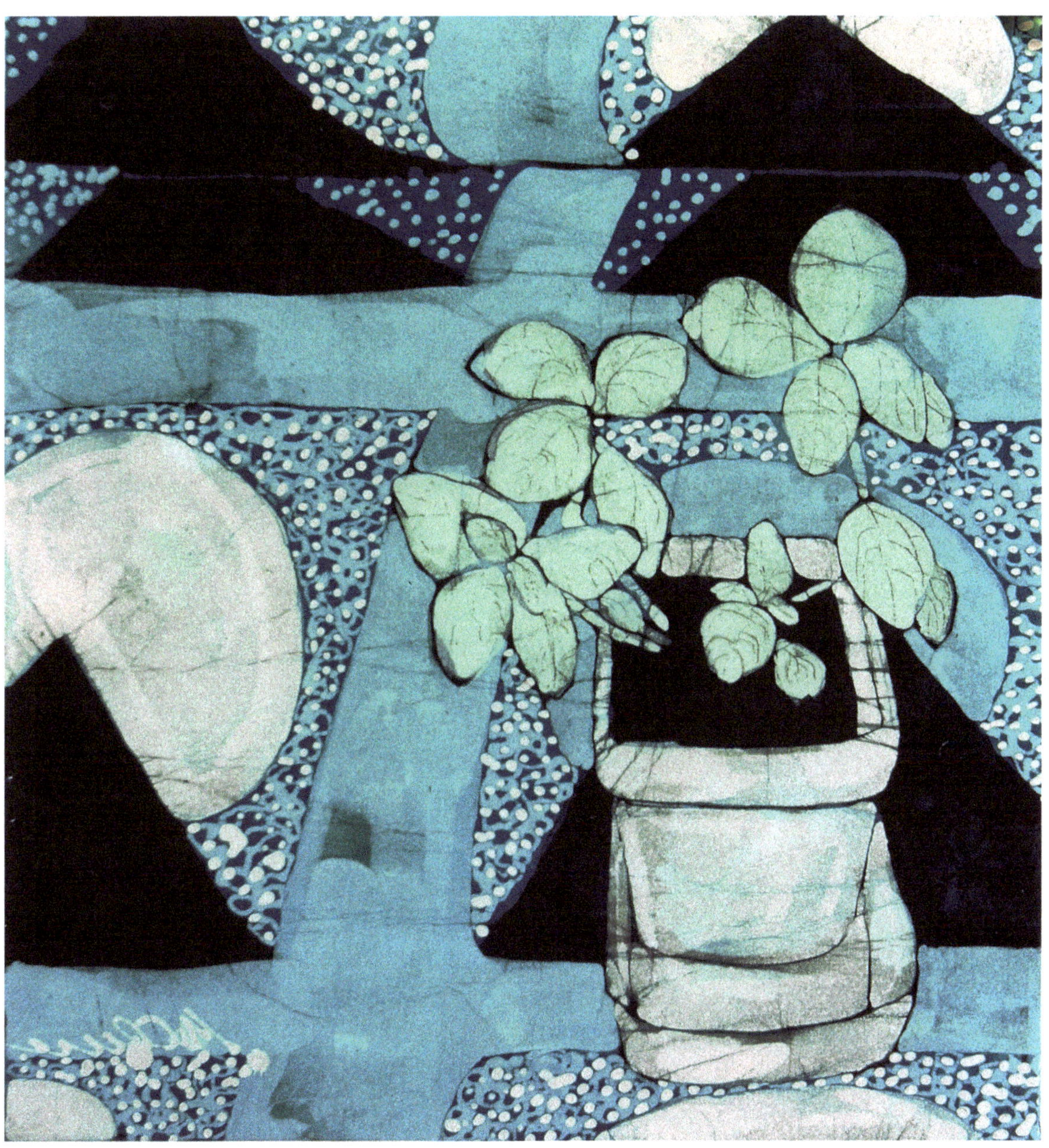

Figure 3.3
Batik, *Potted Plant and Quilt*, early 1980s

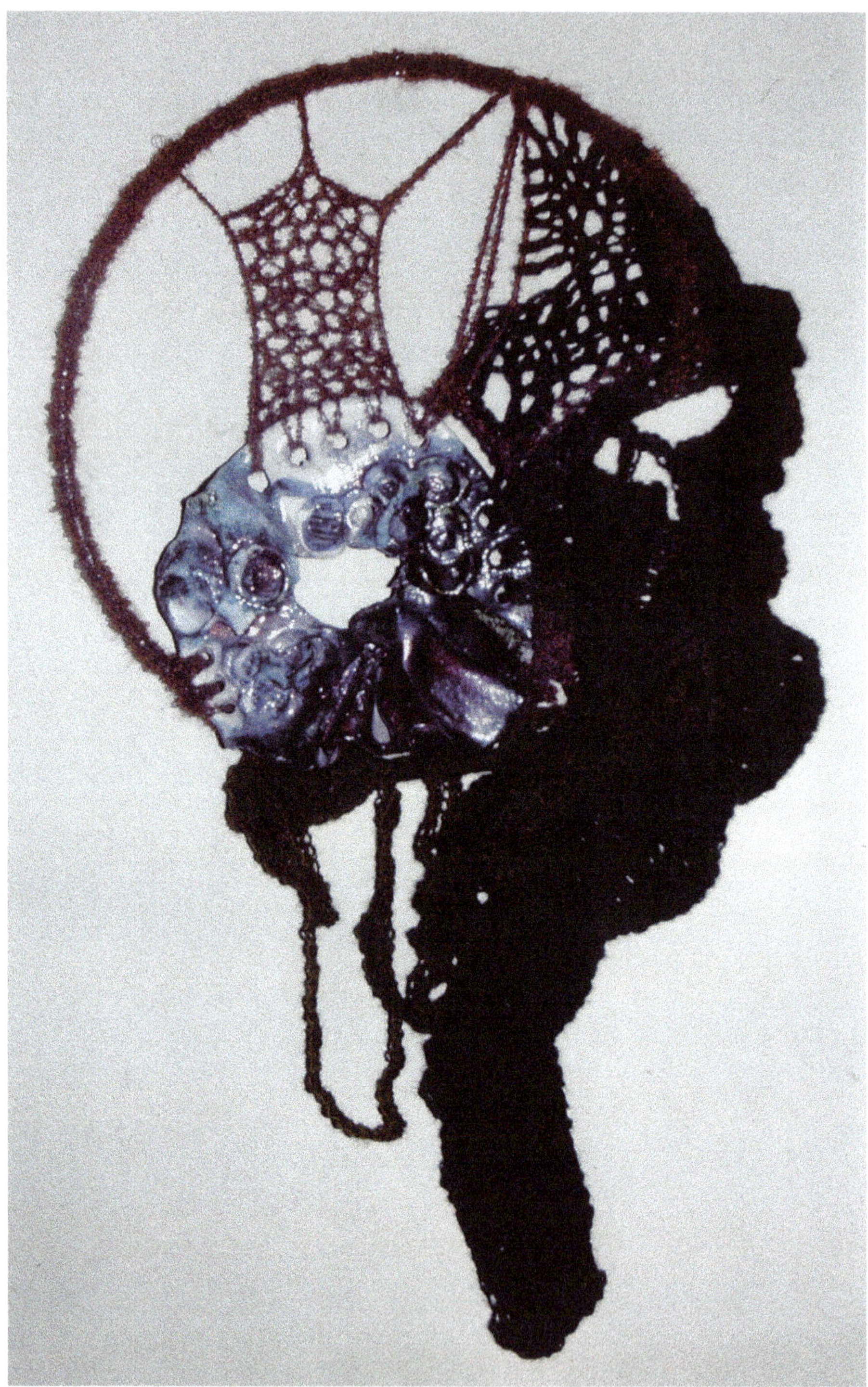

Figure 3.4
Crocheted hanging, wool and clay, mid 1970s

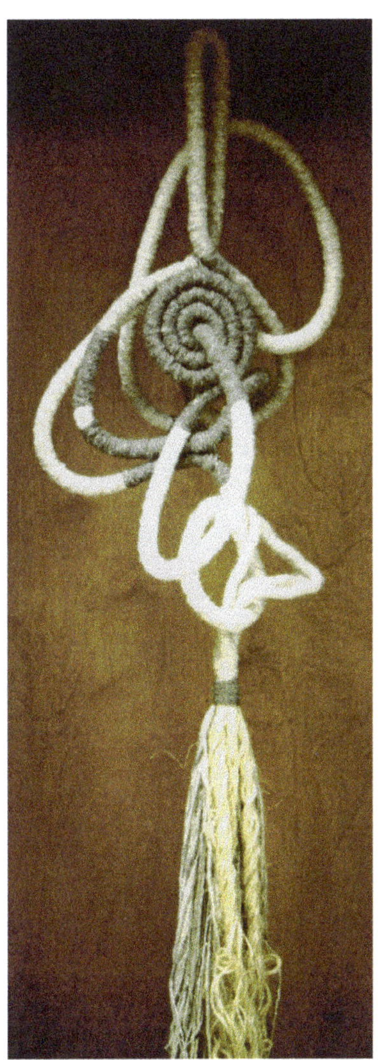

Figure 3.5
Wrapped and coiled hanging, mid 1970s

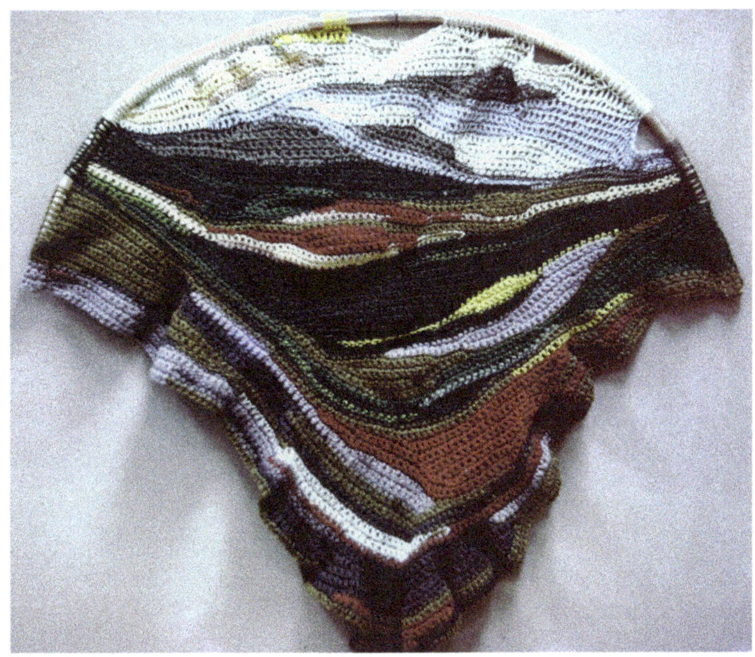

Figure 3.6
Crocheted hanging, wool on copper pipe form, mid 1970s

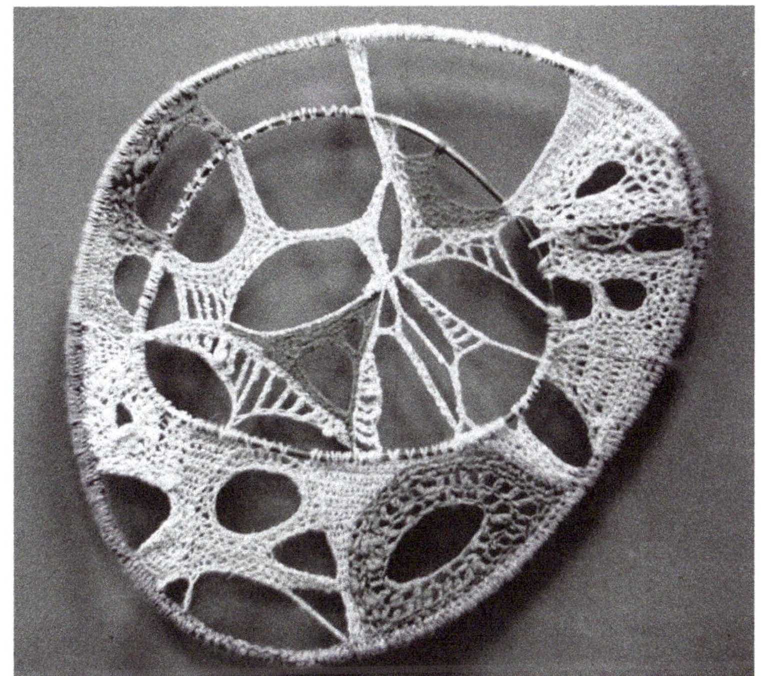

Figure 3.7
Crocheted hanging, handspun wool on copper pipe form, mid 1970s

I began to exhibit weavings, mostly functional things like scarves, rugs, and table linens. Those were interesting to design and make, but the desire to create images continued to pull me. I began to search for weaving methods through which that could be done. I even ventured briefly into tapestry weaving. I was fascinated that yarn could be used to make pictures as the cloth was woven, but tapestry making was so tedious. The ability it took to do it well also seemed to elude me. I didn't believe I had the discipline to achieve the skill needed to become fluent with the technique. Even so, my desire to be a tapestry weaver kept growing. Then, in one remarkable year, those doubts were thrown aside, and I stepped firmly onto the tapestry path.

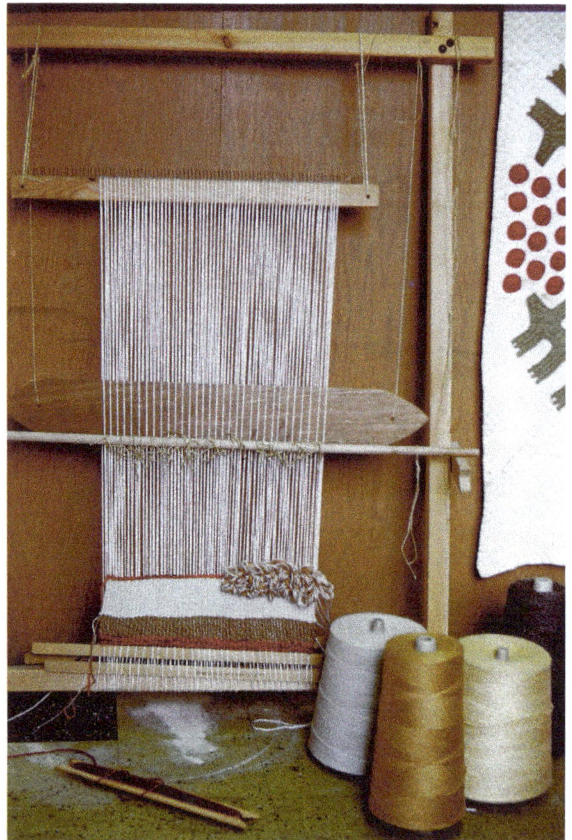

Figure 3.8
Frame Loom at NGC, 1972

The year was 1988. I was forty years old and had been teaching art at high school or college for almost twenty years. In those decades, I had exhibited drawings and paintings as well as some weavings, but none of those media and methods felt completely right. Something was lacking. Then, several remarkable circumstances all happened within a few months of each other and changed my artistic life forever.

That summer, I attended a weavers' conference in Chicago. While there, I saw an extraordinary exhibit called *World Tapestry Today*. I was enthralled as I gazed at the tapestries. I'd previously only seen a few large, old tapestries hanging in museums but not many contemporary tapestry pieces, designed and woven by the artists. In this exhibit of fifty recent tapestries by artists from around the world, it wasn't just the imagery of the pieces that moved me, it was also the cloth itself. I loved the densely-packed fabric, the way the surface absorbed the light and made the colors rich and vibrant. So much more dynamic than painted color, I thought.

The next day, I came across representatives of American Tapestry Alliance (ATA)

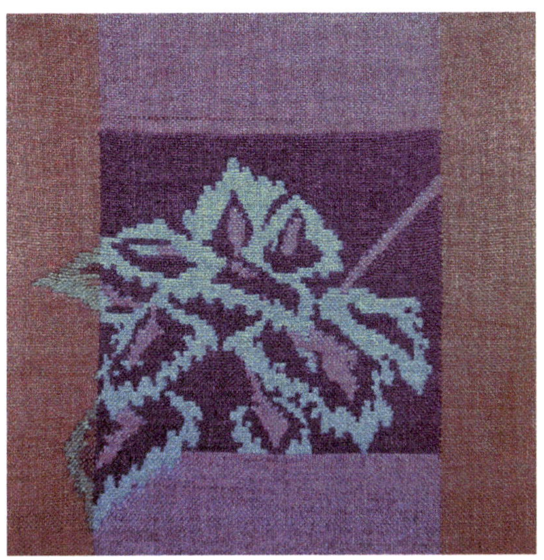

Figure 3.9
Double weave pick up, *Coleus*, early 1980s

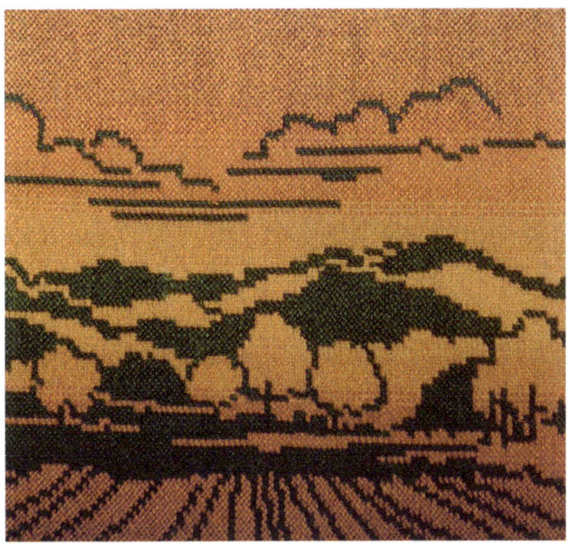

Figure 3.10
Double weave pick up, *Fall Fields*, early 1980s

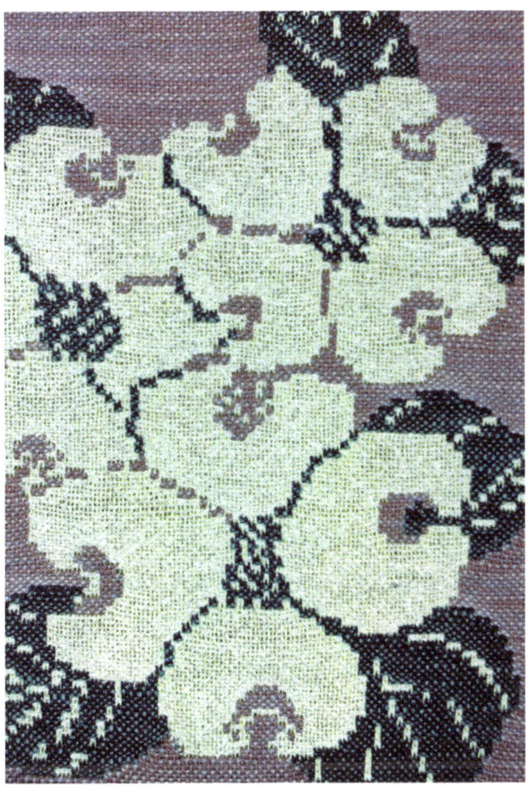

Figure 3.11
Triple weave pick up, *Dogwoods*, mid 1980s

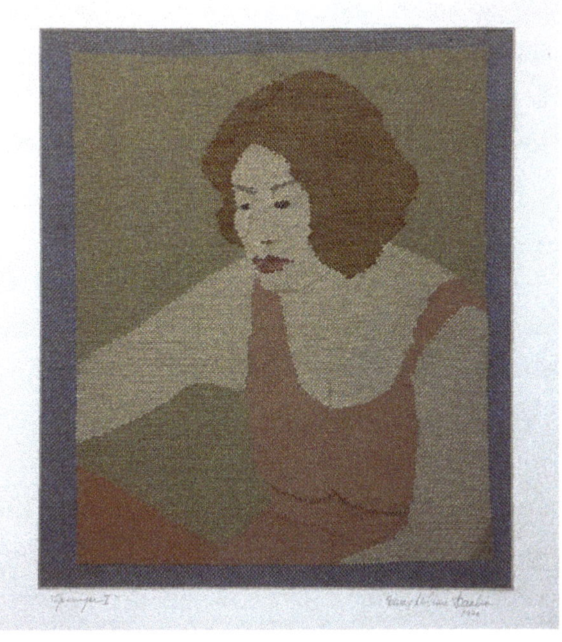

Figure 3.12
Inlay weave, *Jennifer I*, late 1980s

at their promotional booth among the vendors at the conference. ATA had sponsored the tapestry exhibit that had just made such an impact on me. I bought the catalog for the exhibit and joined the organization, hoping that the association would provide insight into the next steps I must take to become a tapestry weaver.

Shortly after returning from the Chicago conference, I learned that someone in a weavers' group wanted to sell a large tapestry loom because she was moving to a smaller apartment. She was asking only a few hundred dollars for it—a bargain and one I could afford on my modest teacher's salary. The loom moved into my apartment, and I was excited to get started.

So many things came together in those few months that kept directing me to tapestry. I knew I must finally make the effort to learn the technique—or I should stop saying I wanted to be a tapestry weaver. And so I went to work.

I began with a couple of videotapes as well as a how-to book of tapestry techniques. After a few years of self-study, I sought out workshops from master weavers to expand my knowledge of both historical and contemporary tapestry making. The more I wove, the better my skills became. With each small piece, I felt increasingly comfortable with how to position the yarn and pack it into place. I learned to adapt my design ideas into images that could be made within the constraints of the woven medium—to make them "weaverly." And I wove tapestries.

By the early 1990s, I was exhibiting and even selling a few tapestry pieces. When I retired from full-time teaching in 2000, an opportunity arose to have an eight-week session at Penland School of Craft with Archie and Susan, the master weavers I'd learned so much from previously in several shorter workshops. It was a remarkable opportunity for a longer study with them and perfectly timed, as my studio time was soon to take precedence over my teaching.

Drawing and painting continue to be part of my practice, but, since 1988, I have regarded tapestry weaving as my artistic medium. When one of my earliest pieces was included in the gallery section of a 1995 *Handwoven* magazine, I said: "Tapestry is a medium allowing the freedom to create almost endless variations of line, shape, and color. Tapestry is demanding, consuming, and rewarding, and I feel I am at last home in weaving."[1]

Now, over fifty years since my first "real" art class, I still want to be an artist. And three decades after beginning to weave tapestries, I still find it to be a challenging medium in which to work. In spite of those challenges, the beautiful surface quality of traditional

---

1 "Tapestry Gallery," *Handwoven*, May/June 1995, 71.

handwoven tapestry still draws me. I know that my childhood heart's desire to be an artist is truly being fulfilled with every pass of the yarn when I weave tapestry.

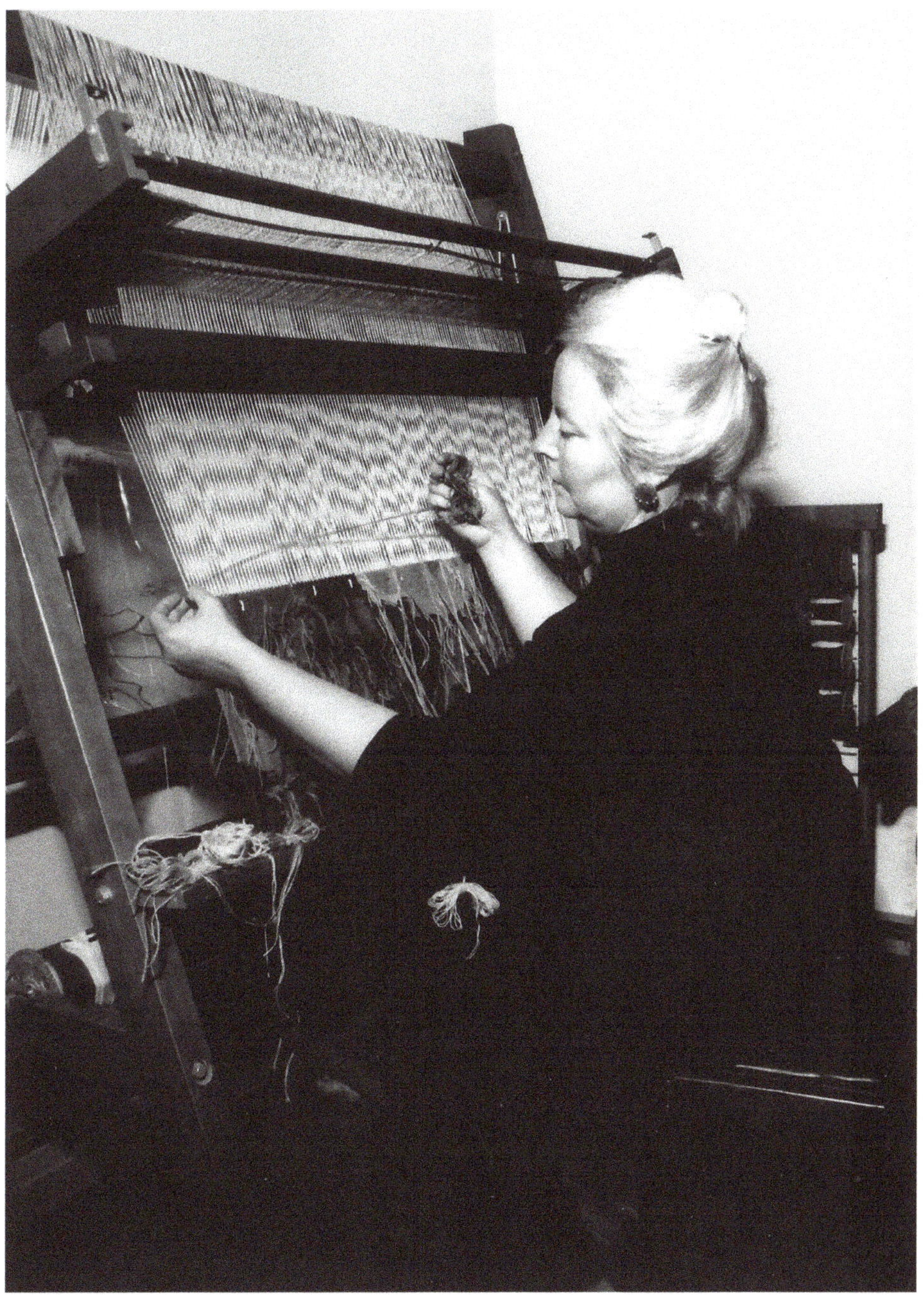

Figure 3.13
Tommye weaving with tapestry loom, 1989

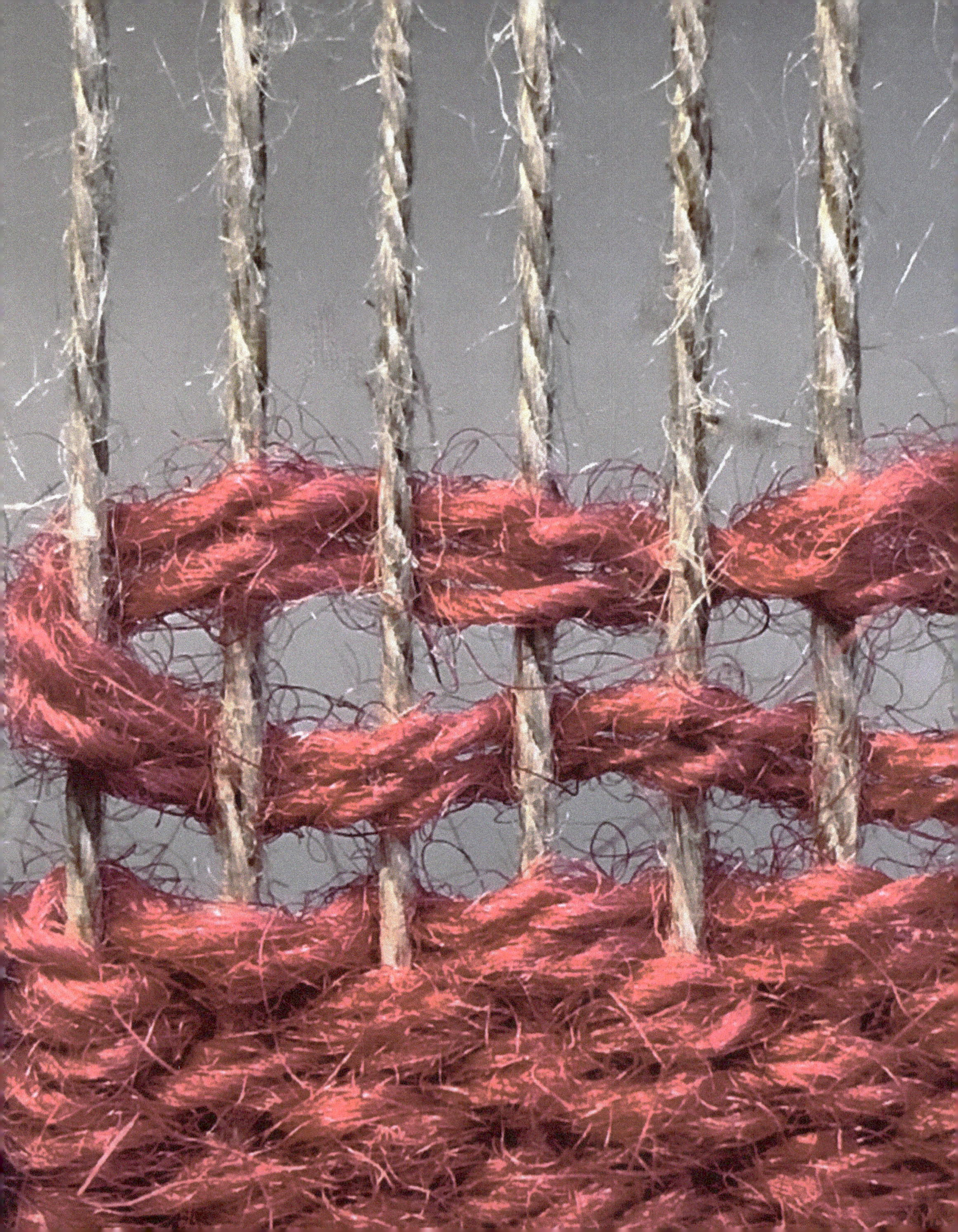

4

Tapestry: A Closer Look

> I work in a minor art form. Tapestry is an indulgent, elitist, economically farcical, and frequently boring 20th century activity. It's astonishing that the craft still survives today, and I know that I find particular delight in the required degree of preplanning and the order of growth, slowly and erratically from one edge.[1]

Those words, at the end of Archie Brennan's artist statement in the "World Tapestry Today" exhibition catalog, shocked me. Now, after having been a tapestry weaver myself for several decades, I can certainly attest to all he said. The comment about its being a frequently boring activity is one I definitely relate to when I'm still weaving a piece that's been on the loom for months and the end seems to be nowhere in sight.

Archie also clearly described what keeps me absorbed with tapestry making. It *is* delightful to engage in the stages of preplanning needed—from concept to design development—then preparing the loom, and finally actually doing the weaving. It builds up, bit by bit, from the bottom edge to the top of the piece. Days pass as the weft slowly but

1 *World Tapestry Today,* (Chiloquin, Oregon: American Tapestry Alliance, 1988), 54, 74. Published in conjunction with a world-touring exhibition of the same title organized by the American Tapestry Alliance, U.S.A., in collaboration with the Victorian Tapestry Workshop, Melbourne, Australia. The exhibit was shown in seven venues in four countries between May 1988 and June 1989.

Figure 4.1 (opposite)
Plain weave detail showing weft and warp

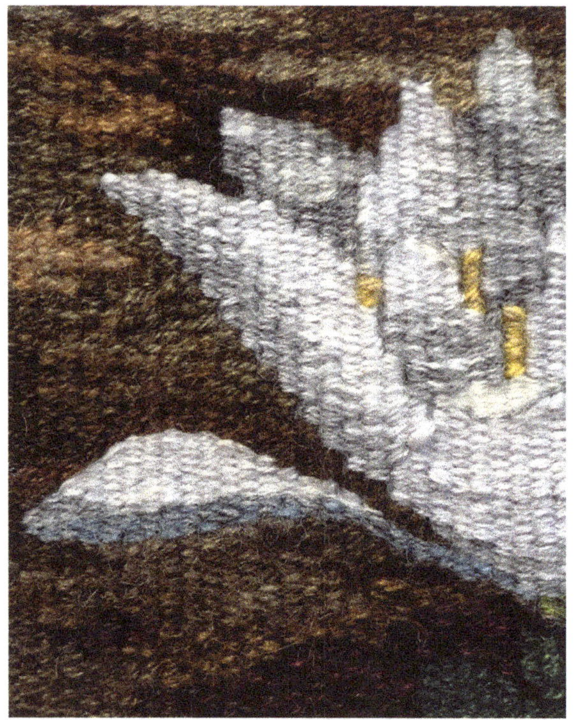

Figure 4.2
Detail of section of a tapestry showing discontinuous weft area used to make shapes.

surely fills the warp threads until at last the tapestry is woven.

When I talk to people about what I do as an artist, I realize that tapestry is a word we often use metaphorically. "The rich tapestry of life," someone may say when trying to describe wide-ranging experiences. If using the word in reference to cloth, there's also sometimes a bit of confusion about how tapestry is made. Several kinds of textiles, from stitching (like the Bayeux Tapestry), Jacquard woven cloth, and even printed fabrics are sometimes called tapestry. However, *handwoven* tapestry is both the method by which it is made as well as the resulting pictorial fabric.

Let me briefly describe the structure and the process of handwoven tapestry,

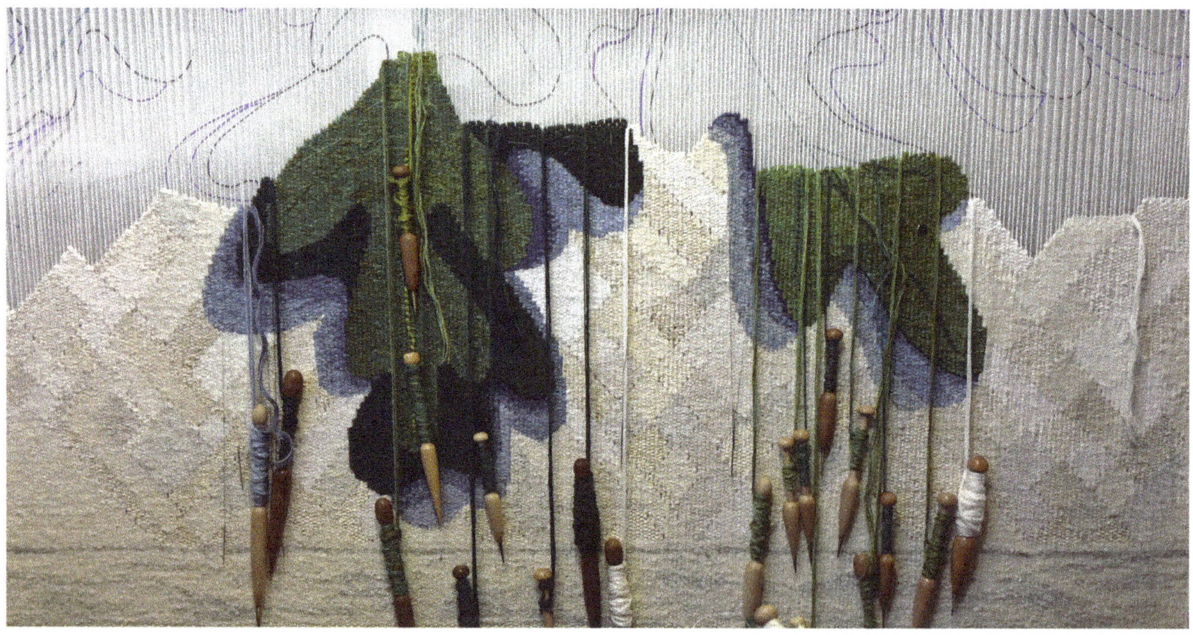

Figure 4.3
Detail of tapestry in progress showing the cartoon behind the warp.

beginning with the two basic components: warp and weft. The warp is the thread that's placed on a loom, and the weft is woven into the warp. Handwoven tapestry is usually defined as being a *plain weave structure that is weft faced and uses discontinuous wefts* to make designs. So what does that mean?

Plain weave is the simplest weave structure of all: first, the weft goes over and under alternate warp threads in one direction along a row and then is packed

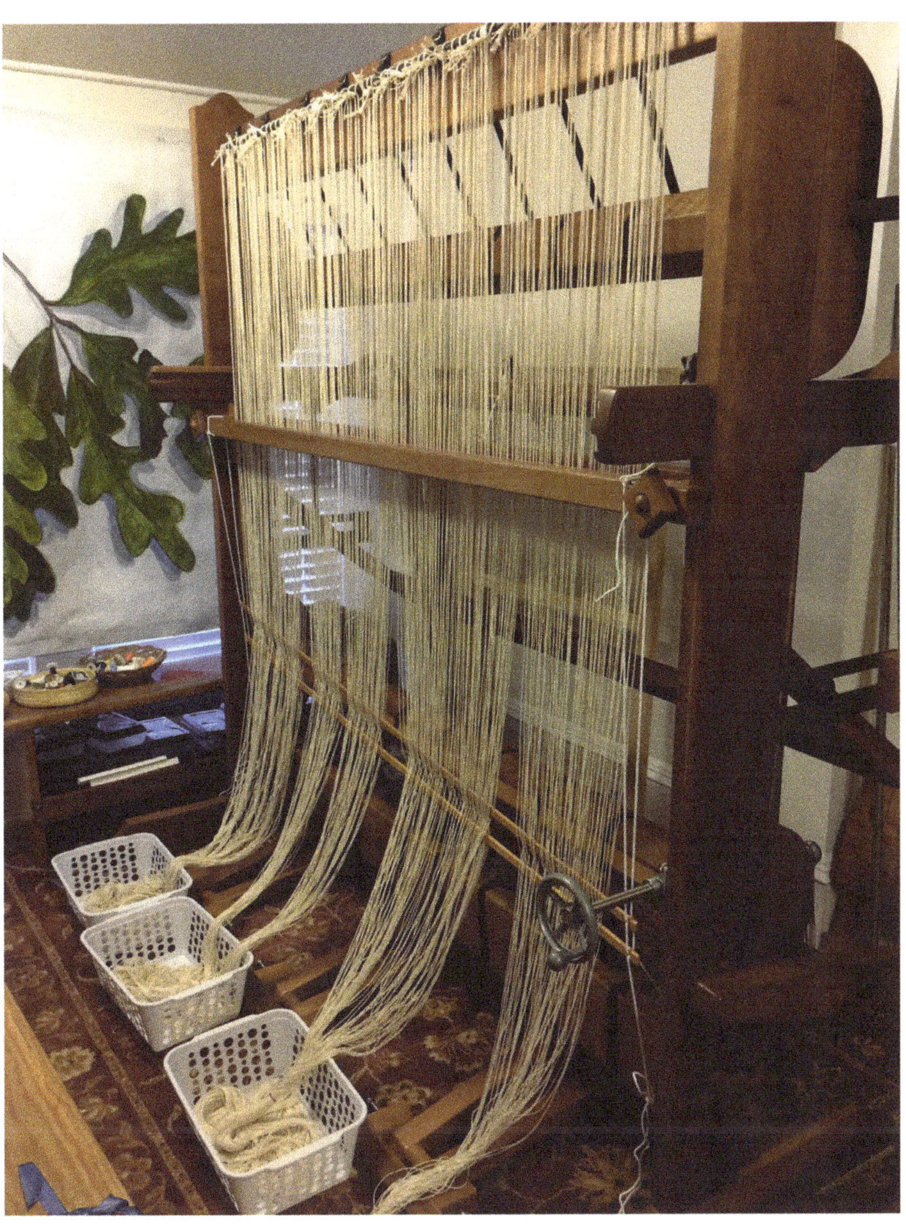

Figure 4.4
Winding the warp onto the tapestry loom; painting as reference hangs at the side.

down into place. The weft takes the opposite path on the return row. Because different colors may be used in each row as the design is created, the weft is discontinuous. When the warp is totally covered by the weft, it's described as being weft faced.

Both the cloth and the image are made as the tapestry is woven. This is different than creating an image with painting. For instance, to place a dark shape near the top of a tapestry design I would have to build up to it in the weaving—I can't simply weave it there beforehand like I could do by painting a dark shape on a canvas anywhere I wanted it.

Throughout history, many handwoven tapestry techniques and traditions have developed around the world. The sorts of images woven in tapestry are also a product of different customs, cultures, and time periods. For instance, in the Americas, the weavings of ancient and contemporary Native weavers are well documented and appreciated.[2] Kesi tapestries, dating from as early as the Tang Dynasty in China were made with fine silks woven into intricate imagery.[3] Tapestries woven in Europe in the twelfth through seventeenth centuries—the Medieval, Renaissance and Baroque periods—filled walls of castles and churches. The largest of these, the Apocalypse Tapestries, were made up of multiple panels and woven between 1373 and 1382. The entire set covers 338 feet in length and is over fourteen feet high.[4]

The European tapestries commonly were designed by an artist to be executed by skilled craftsmen/weavers. This tradition continues to a lesser extent today in a few remaining tapestry studios, like the Dovecot Tapestry Studio in Scotland, the International Center of Aubusson Tapestry in France, and the Australian Tapestry Workshop in Australia.[5]

When creating a tapestry, one often follows a full-size design, called a "cartoon." This may outline every shape to be woven or be a simple line drawing that's interpreted as the tapestry progresses. Some tapestry artists also work without a cartoon, creating their designs as the weaving develops.

The designer of a tapestry may also be the weaver, and, since the 1960s, many people around the world have found this artistic medium to be a rewarding one in

2 Kate Peck Kent, *Navajo Weaving: Three Centuries of Change* (Santa Fe: School of American Research Press, 1985).

3 Michael Sullivan, *The Arts of China* (Berkeley: University of California Press, 5th ed, 2008), 247, 248.

4 Joseph Jobé, ed., *Great Tapestries: The Web of History from the 12th to the 20th Century* (Lausanne, Switzerland: Edita S.A. Lausanne), 46.

5 The Australian Tapestry Workshop in Melbourne; Dovecote Tapestry Studio in Edinburgh; the West Dean Tapestry Studio near Chichester; and the Cité Internationale de la Tapisserie Aubusson in France are among the best-known tapestry studios currently engaging skilled weavers to interpret the designs of other visual artists.

which to work.[6] Several organizations have been formed to promote and encourage artist/weavers by mounting exhibits, providing workshops, and publishing newsletters and journals.[7]

For my work, drawings, paintings, or photographs are references and are modified as needed when making the cartoon. The next task is to prepare a warp and set up a loom. Threads used for warps must be strong and able to hold up to fairly tight tension; strong cotton seine twine or linen serves that purpose well. These are measured out and wound onto the top beam of the loom. The warp threads are then tied in small groups to the bottom beam of the loom, and then spread out evenly before the weaving may begin. The stages of loom preparation are usually completed in a few days; the process of actually weaving the tapestry may take months. I often use wool weft and sometimes supplement that with small strands of linen or cotton. The cartoon is used as a guide for the weaving and is attached behind the warp threads by temporarily stitching it to the tapestry as it progresses.

The initial design source, whether photograph or painting, is the basis for color choices, and I often combine more than one strand of yarn in the weft bundles to create a nuance of hue. The weft colors are reminiscent of the colors in the design source, but I don't attempt to replicate them exactly.

After the weaving is completed and taken off the loom, there are many more steps before the tapestry is ready to be displayed. The many hundreds of tail ends of weft threads are clipped, and the piece is given a hanging method, often a mounting frame or a hanging bar.

I find every stage of weaving a tapestry to be both physically and mentally engaging. Although my thoughts may occasionally wander along with music or an audio book, I have to snap right back to the reality of the tapestry as my eyes and hands demand the attention to detail and process. This is part of the complexity of the simple plain weave of tapestry that continues to both amaze and delight me each day.

---

6 Courtney Ann Shaw. *American Tapestry Weaving Since the 1930s and Its European Roots.* Exhibition catalog (College Park, Maryland: The Art Gallery, The University of Maryland. 1989).

7 American Tapestry Alliance, British Tapestry Group, and Canadian Tapestry Network are among those membership organizations.

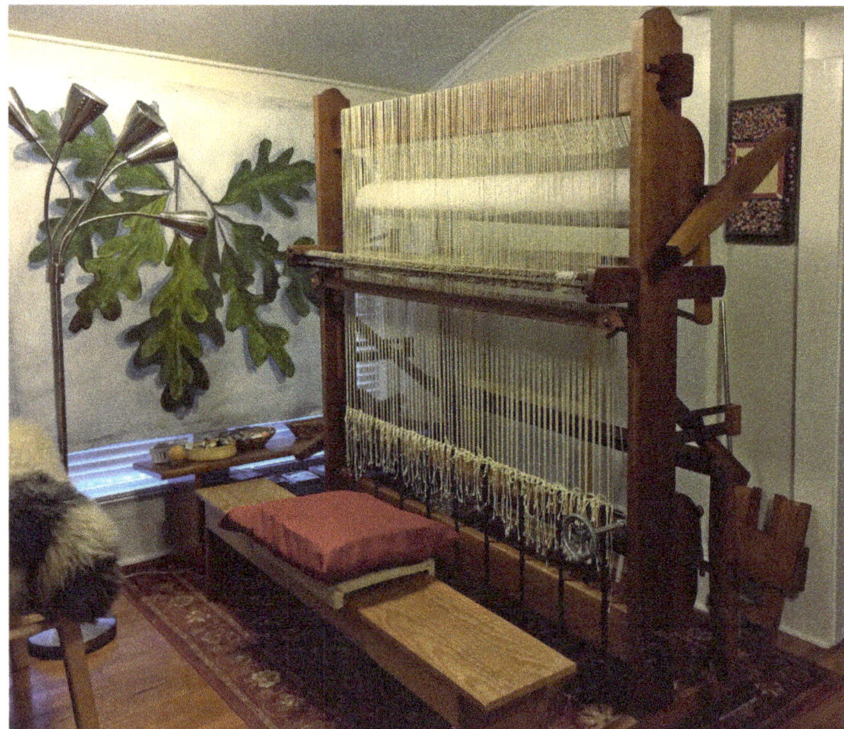

Figure 4.5
Warp is tied in place and tapestry is ready to begin.

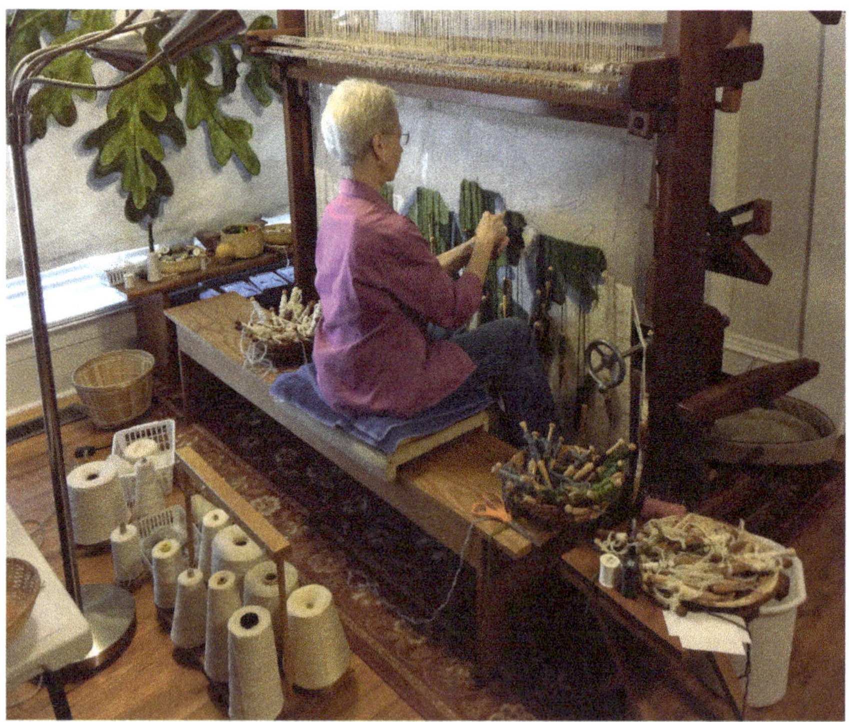

Figure 4.6
Weaving is underway.

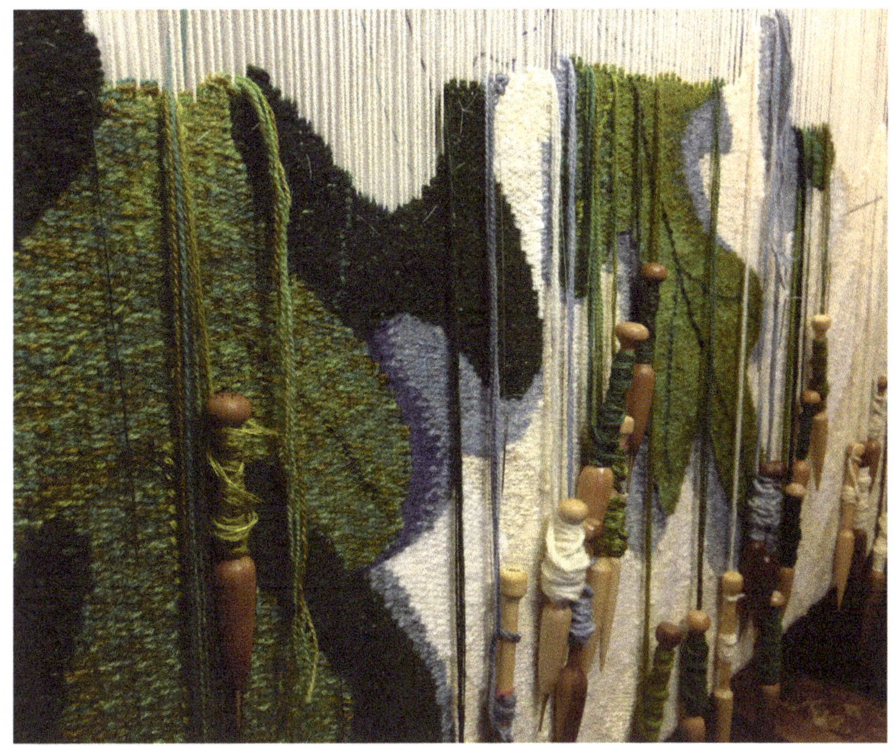

Figure 4.7
Bobbins show weft yarns and woven areas. The thin white stitches near the top edge of the weaving are there to hold the cartoon close to the weaving area.

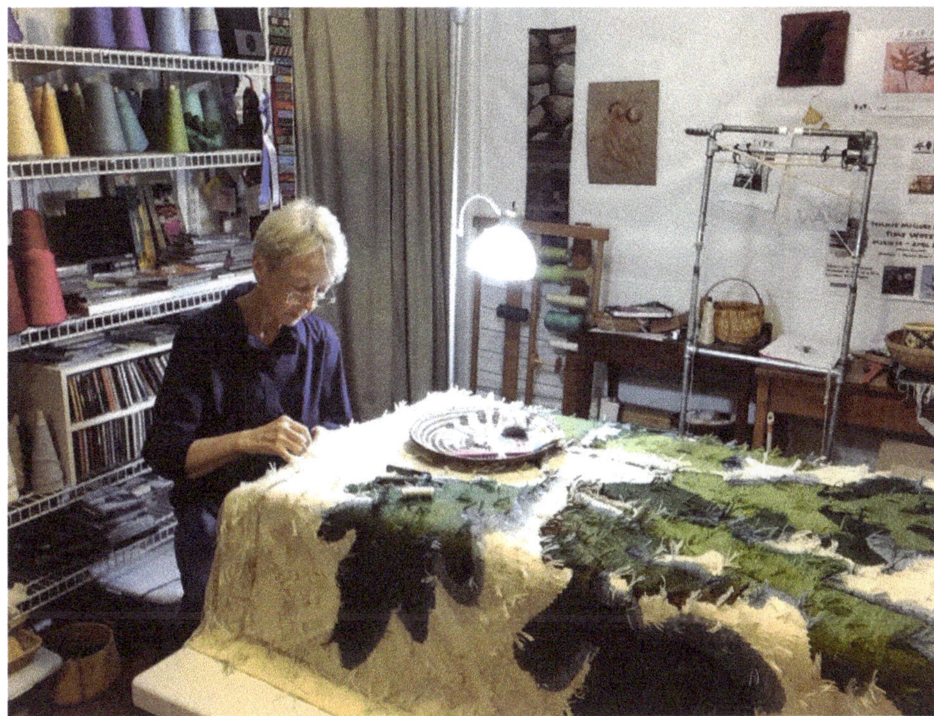

Figure 4.8
After the tapestry is woven, finishing steps remain to clip weft ends and prepare the piece for hanging.

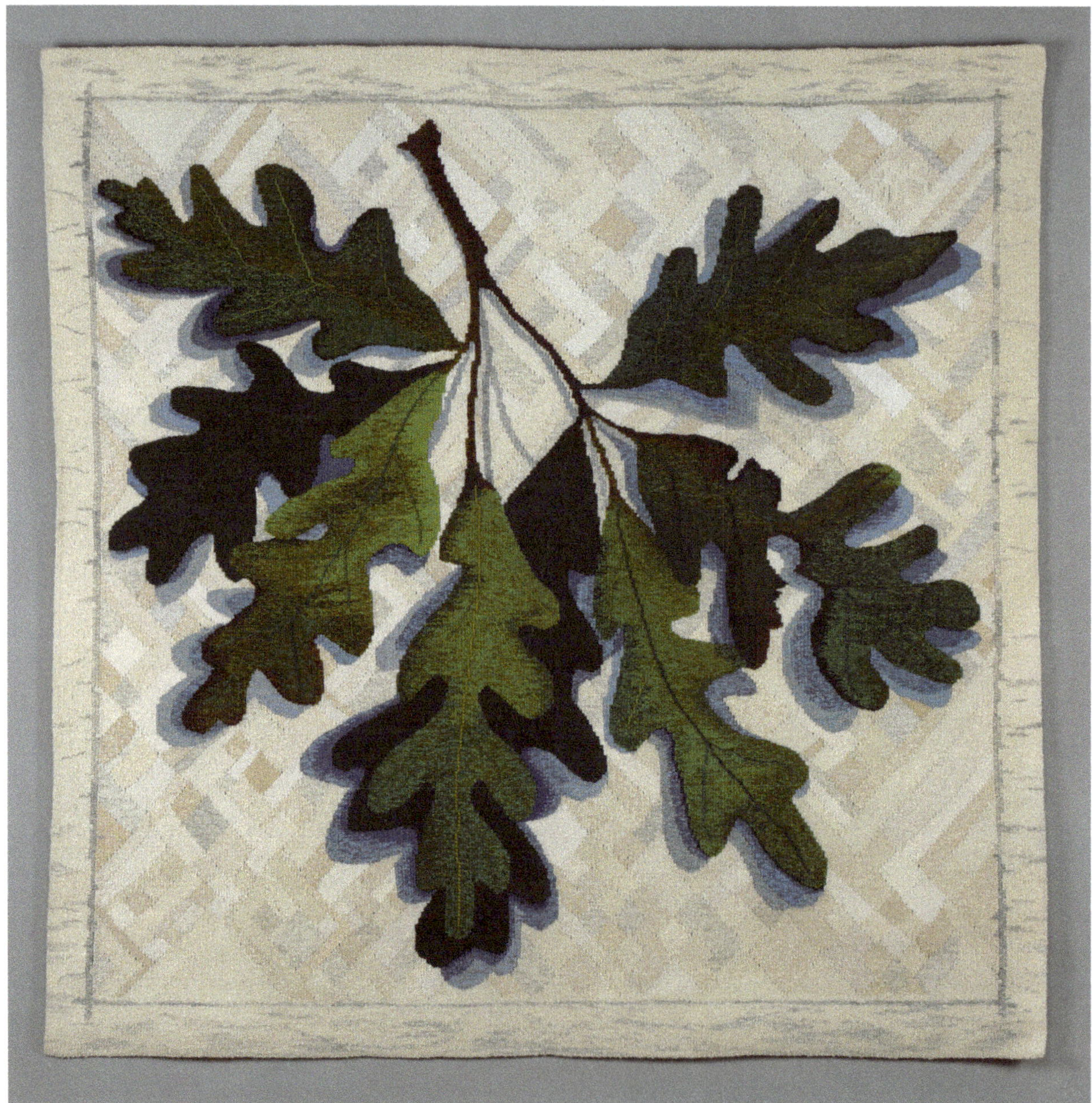

Figure 4.9
Oak Leaves, 60 inches by 60 inches by 1 inch, completed in 2016
(photo by Tim Barnwell)

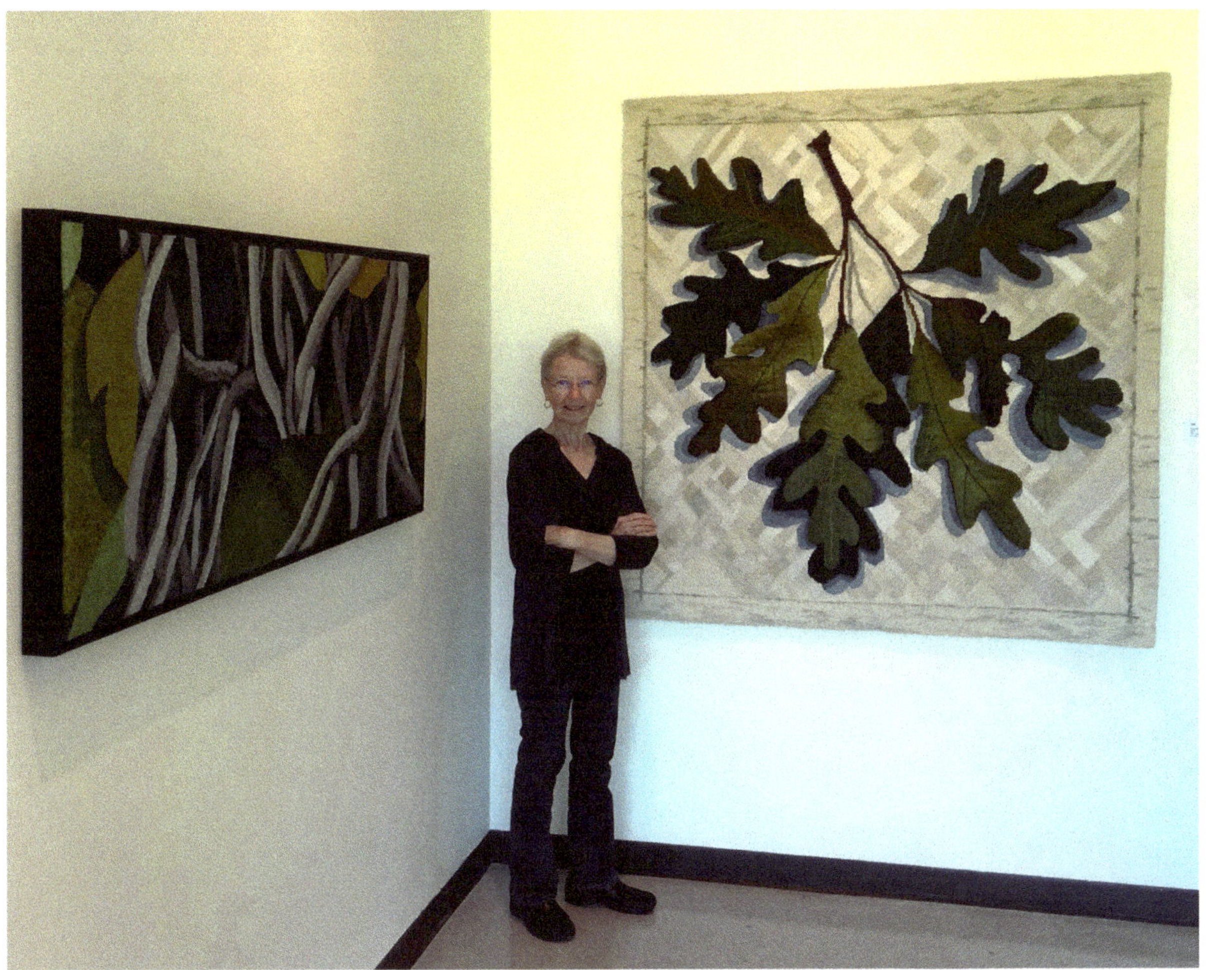

Figure 4.10
Scanlin stands with two tapestries at the Smith-Williams Gallery, Piedmont College, exhibited in "View from the Mountain," a one-person show of her tapestries inspired by nature. (photo by Thomas Scanlin)

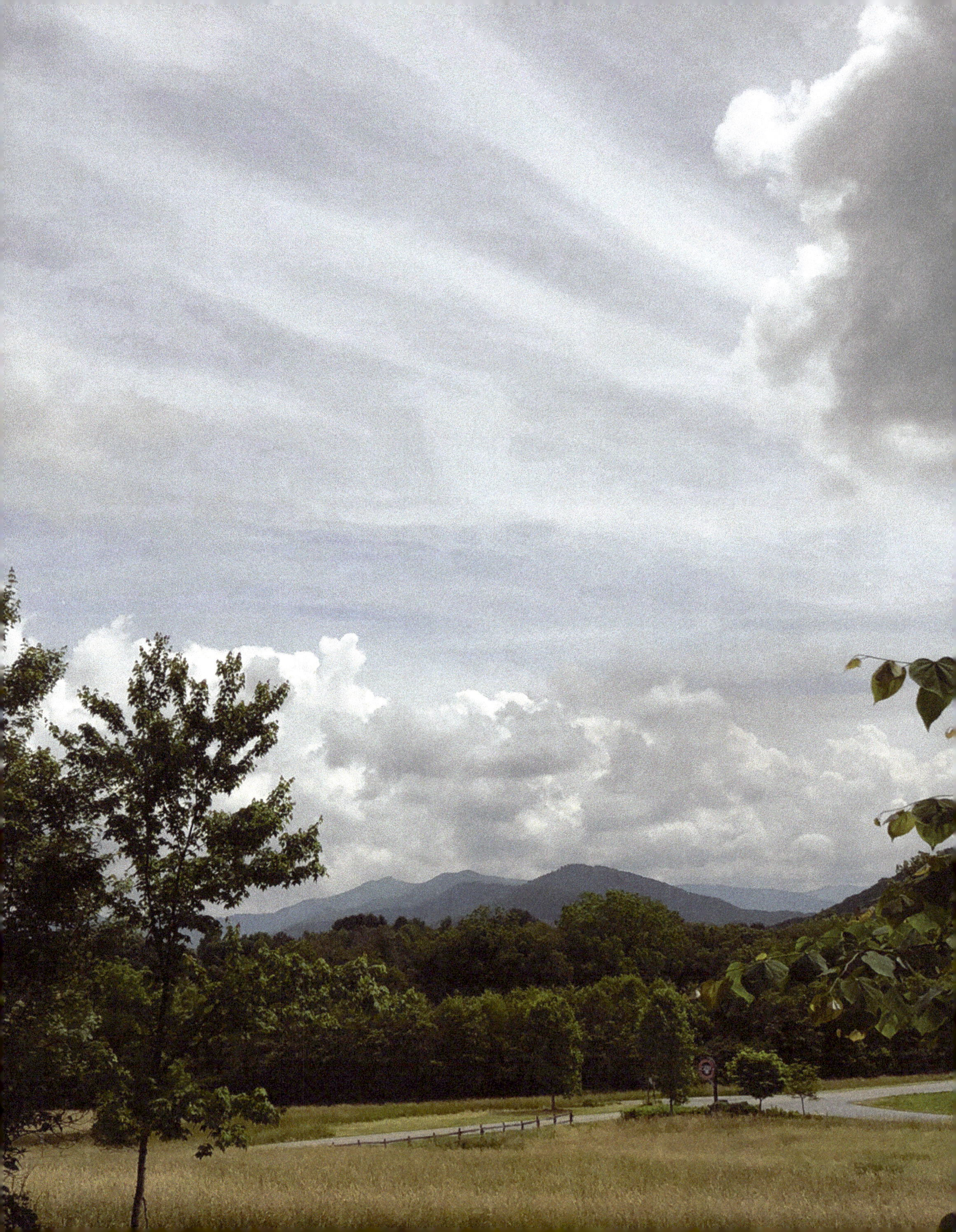

5
Seeking Inspiration

Designs. Where do they come from? What will spark an idea that will develop into a tapestry? I continue to find myself challenged to discover ways to tap into a creative process and find inspiration for art making. I search for ideas and, once I find them, I'm then confronted with how to turn those ideas into artworks.

Early on, I realized I was especially drawn to the work of artists who used the natural world as subjects. Some of the artists whose work strongly called to me were Dutch still life painters and their images filled with lush and vibrant plants, Vincent van Gogh's (1853–1890) turbulent views of the world, Charles Burchfield's (1893–1967) watercolors depicting symbolically the scenes and the sounds of nature, Georgia O'Keeffe's (1887–1986) beautiful celebrations of small things, and Alex Katz's (b. 1927) massively enlarged views of grasses, flowers, or trees.

Poems by Billy Collins (b. 1941) and Wendell Berry (b. 1934) expressing their encounters with nature also moved me. Emily Dickinson's (1830–1886) writings held eloquent insights into her observations of the natural world that went far beyond simple descriptions. Quotes like Byron Herbert Reece's (1917–1958) "I know a valley green with corn where Nottley's waters roil and run. . . ."[1] find their way into my thoughts when I walk in the woods or fields of North Georgia.

1 Byron Herbert Reece, "I Know a Valley Green With Corn," *A Song of Joy and Other Poems* (Atlanta: Cherokee Publishing Company, 1985), 84.

Figure 5.1 (opposite)
Valley view from John C. Campbell Folk School, Brasstown, North Carolina

I've hoped to learn from visual artists and writers how to look beyond surface appearance in my search for the essence of something. Observation is the first step in that direction. The next step is to in some way record what I've noticed.

For years, I've used small sketchbooks in which to make quick visual notes of what's around me. It might be small details of art works I see in a museum, clouds viewed from airplane windows, or even interiors of waiting rooms at doctors' offices or car repair shops. Although the sketches usually don't become parts of tapestries I weave, doing them keeps my eyes and hands at work. Sharpening one's observation and making visual responses are critical parts of the creative process.

Before the arrival of digital photography, I took hundreds of print photos and slides to record bits of the world around me. Now, I have thousands of digital photo files on several hard drives. My portfolios are stuffed with countless drawings and paintings, and there are stacks of sketchbooks on the shelves.

In my ongoing quest for inspiration, I once thought the answers to all my questions about inspired creativity surely were in a book—I just needed to find the right book.

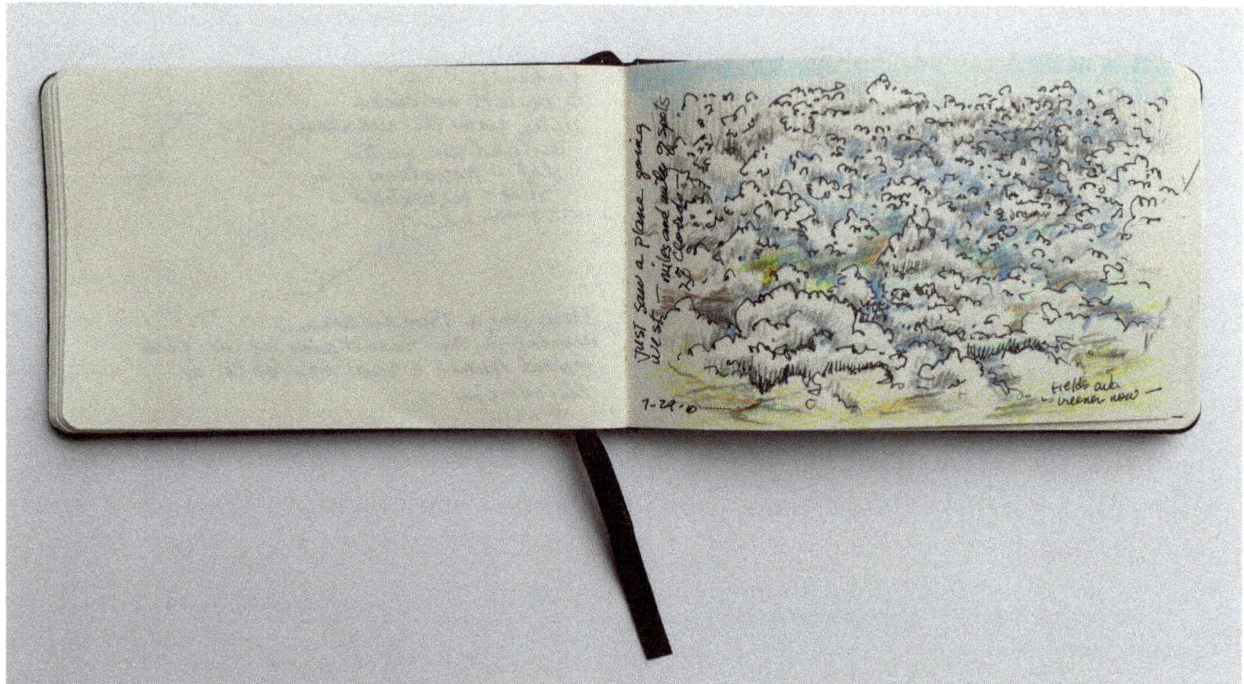

Figure 5.2
Clouds, sketch from plane window (photo by Christopher Dant)

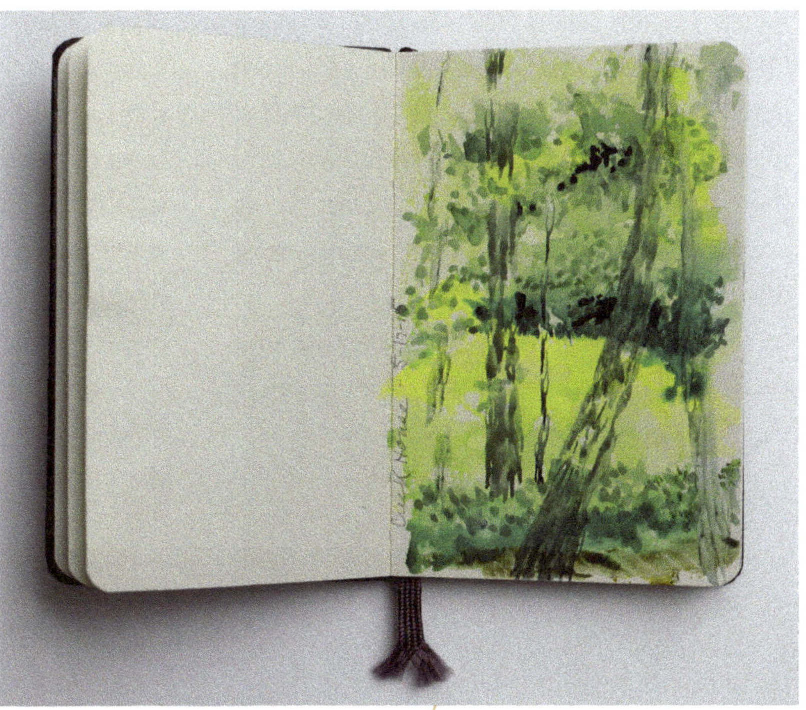

Figure 5.3
View at the creek house,
watercolor sketch
(photo by Christopher Dant)

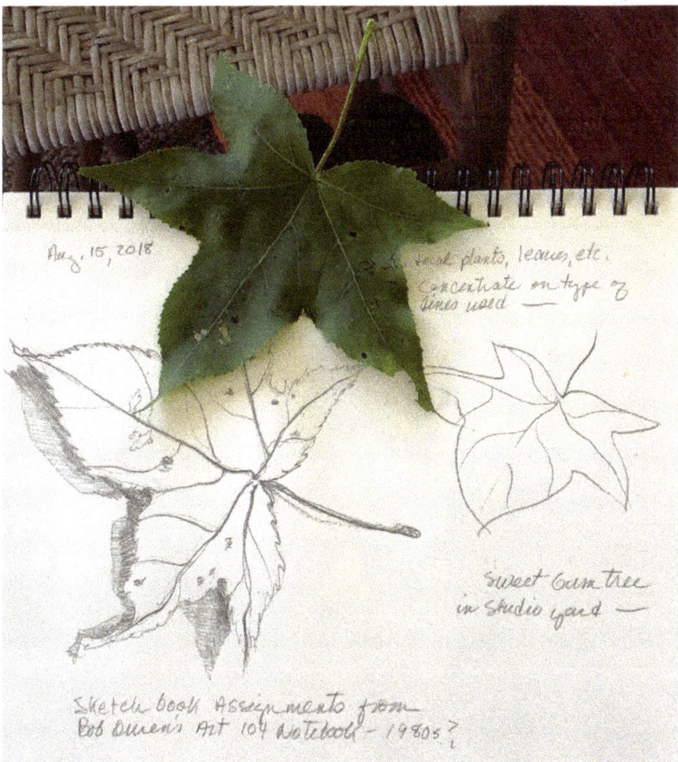

Figure 5.4
Sketch of sweet gum leaf

When I came across *The Mind's Best Work* (1981) by D. N. Perkins (b. 1942), I hoped it held the secret of how to come up with novel ideas. What I learned from Perkins was that there isn't a secret, magic formula for "being creative." Instead, creativity results most often from work.[2]

The process of first digging for ideas and then developing them further in creative ways may be painful or joyful or even sometimes boring—but always must take the form of action. Writers often say: "You have to show up every day..." and I've found that to be true in my visual work. I have to make the effort to discover the potential that lies in assorted ideas and images I generate every day. Every darn day.

Over the past decades, I've learned that I must look, draw, paint, take photographs, read, ponder, write, and weave every day. It

2 D. N. Perkins, *The Mind's Best Work* (Cambridge, MA: Harvard University Press, 1981).

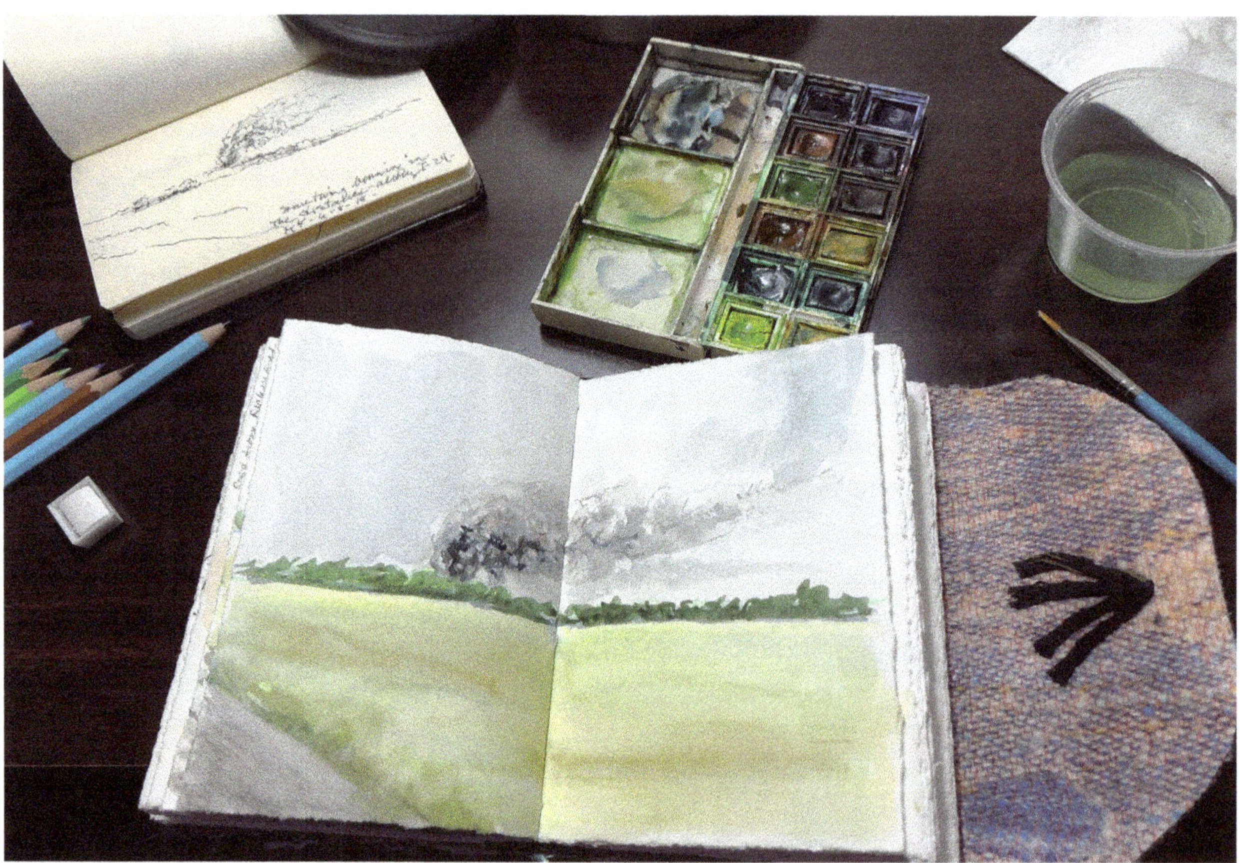

Figure 5.5
Two sketchbooks with scenes viewed from the car window while on a road trip with my husband. The motel room became a temporary art studio.

may turn out that I can only devote fifteen minutes to the activity, whatever it turns out to be. But if those few minutes are missed, then I know I may lose momentum. Once that happens, I may find myself in a negative cycle of self-doubt and un-productivity.

I finally understand that reading a book will not "make me creative." However, the author may lead me to things I haven't tried before. Two books, *The Artist's Way* (1992) by Julia Cameron (b. 1948) and *Drawing on the Artist Within* (1986) by Betty Edwards (b. 1926), have been especially helpful.

Cameron describes a sort of stream-of-conscious writing she calls "morning pages" in which one writes three pages daily, by hand and without editing or even rereading. I began the suggested practice in 2009, and now an important part of my morning ritual is sitting down with a cup of coffee, my favorite fountain pen, and a spiral bound notebook to write out three pages. I've found this habit is a great way to combat the niggling anxieties of my life by getting them out of my head and down onto the pages.

Cameron's book offers many other ideas for enhancing creative practice, but the daily writing suggestion has been the most valuable for me. In the morning's written rambles, I may replay events of the previous day, record dreams, jot down ideas about ongoing tapestries, or make notes for classes I'll be teaching soon. Even without reading

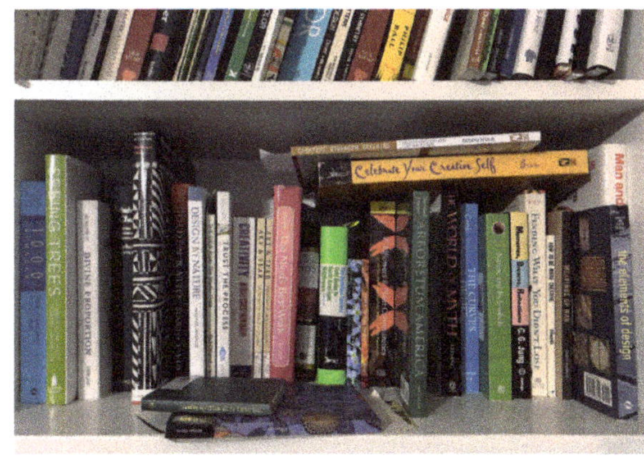

Figure 5.6
Bookcase with a few of the creativity titles, including *The Mind's Best Work.*

what I wrote in the pages, being faithful to this practice has enhanced my art making—and my life in general—by helping me to both sort out negative thoughts and generate positive ones.

In addition to the notebooks filled with morning pages, I use other journals to reflect on ideas for new work, a tapestry in progress, or anything else that happens to wander through my mind. Unlike the morning pages that I never revisit, I do refer back to these journals. I often find the writing helps me understand the concepts I want to convey more clearly. I sometimes work out design problems I may be encountering in a tapestry that's underway by writing them down and considering several possible solutions.

Betty Edwards's book *Drawing on the Artist Within* presents many visual exercises to also encourage creativity. One of these is an idea of quick gesture drawings from photographs, and, at the time I was reading her book, I was stalled in designing a new composition—maybe this would be a way to break through the block, I thought. She suggests using several small sheets of paper, a group of photos, a drawing tool, and a timer to be set for one minute. Next, draw loosely and quickly, using only a minute for each sketch. The tapestry design I wanted to do was based on fiddleheads emerging from the forest floor in the spring, and I had many photos to work with.

Following Edwards's suggestion, I set the timer for a minute and chose a different photo for each quick sketch. The short time demanded working quickly with less concern for detail. This way, I saw the energy of the spiraling movements of the fiddleheads and swiftly responded in the gesture drawings. Several of the dozen or so images made in the session became initial stages of larger and more detailed compositions I used in a series of tapestries.

I continue to look to other artists and writers for motivation—even though I know most of the answers I seek really lie within. I understand that the best creative solutions for my artwork will only come through the resolve I have to be an artist. Again, I've found that it's essential for my artistic practice to make a daily effort of some sort.

That daily effort may sometimes be quite mundane, as when I'm organizing things in the studio, attending to emails, updating my artist statements and resumé, or making applications for exhibits. But then there are the exhilarating times when I'm immersed in planning a design for a future tapestry, trying many solutions before finally deciding upon the right one for the piece.

Quiet and meditative days come next, those in which I'm actually weaving—many, many of those days will pass before I'm ready to cut the tapestry off the loom and move to the finishing stages. All of these things and more are parts of the creative process that fill my life as a tapestry artist.

Finding sources of inspiration and ways to sustain a flow of creative energy are distinct challenges for me. Yet I'm rewarded in many ways when I show up every day to do the work. To listen for the echo of the creativity that is within each of us, just waiting to be heard.

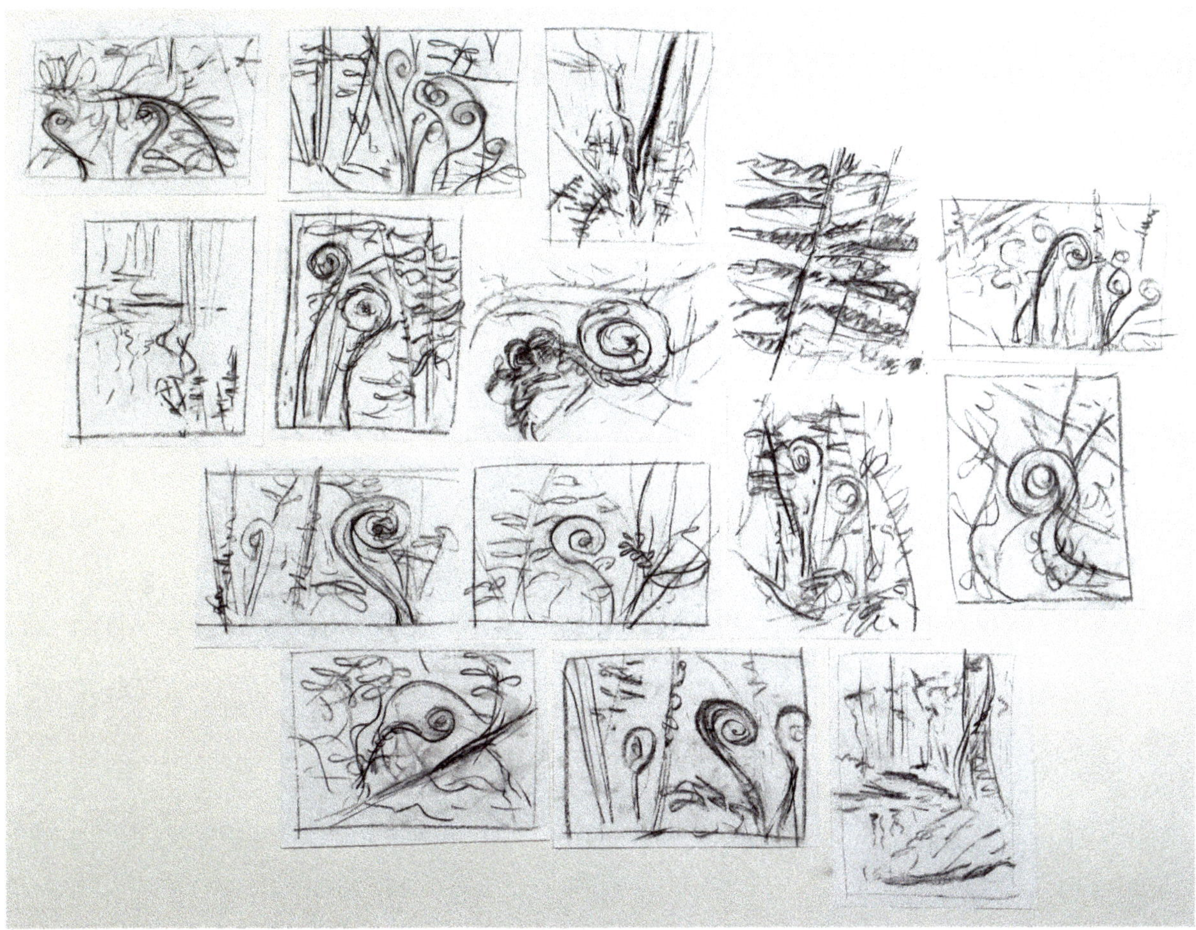

Figure 5.7
Fiddlehead gesture drawings based on Betty Edwards's book, *Drawing on the Artist Within*. (photo by Christopher Dant)

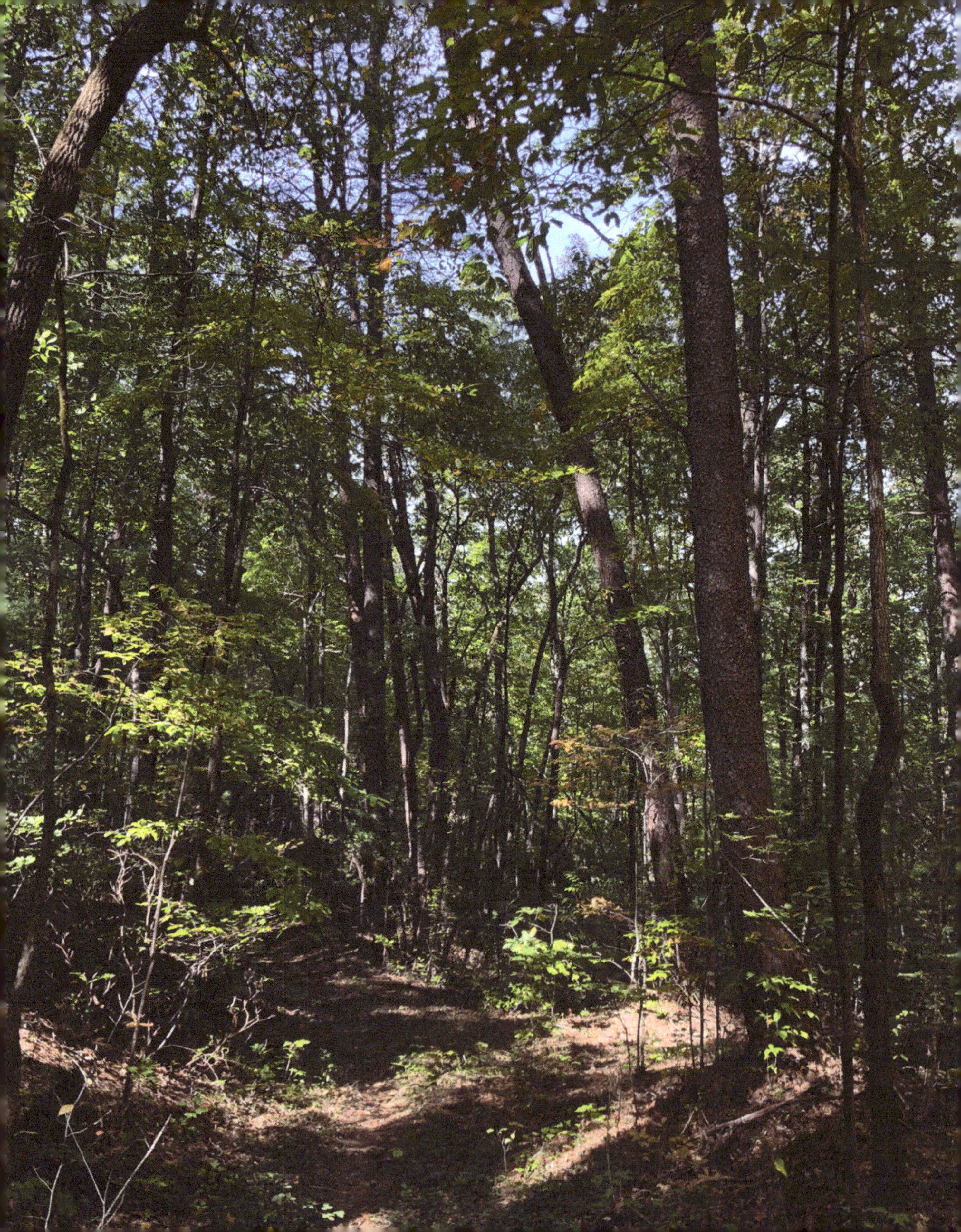

6

Time Out to Take a Look

Walking in the woods delights me—but I'm not a bold hiker. I don't seek the wild places for my walks; instead, joy from these walks comes when I'm on land that is familiar and safe.

I most often take to the woods on the gentle ups and down of trails in Northeast Georgia and Western North Carolina. Walking among the trees, I'm sobered to realize that as large as many of the trees are, they are relatively new growth in the woods. These now are only a fraction of the millions of acres of the Southern Appalachia forests that were clear-cut in the late 1800s and early 1900s to feed the demand of the logging industry. Chris Bolgiano (b. 1948) writes, in *The Appalachian Forest: A Search for Roots and Renewal* (1998), that serious tree cutting began around 1880 and, by the peak year of 1909, there were four billion board feet of hardwood lumber taken from the forests of Maryland to northern Georgia.[1]

Meandering hikes offer plenty to contemplate anytime of the year. One of the things I wonder about is what a walk in these woods would have been like 200 years ago. So different in many ways, and yet it would have been much the same in others. The trees would have been huge like the few that remain in old growth forests like the Joyce Kilmer Memorial Forest in North Carolina. No contrails from passing jets would be seen or four-wheelers heard. But when I walk amidst the canopy of leaves in summer, the buzz of insects and the melody of

1 Chris Bolgiano, *The Appalachian Forest: A Search for Roots and Renewal* (Mechanicsburg, PA: Stackpole Books, 1998), 72, 80.

Figure 6.1 (opposite)
Woods walk

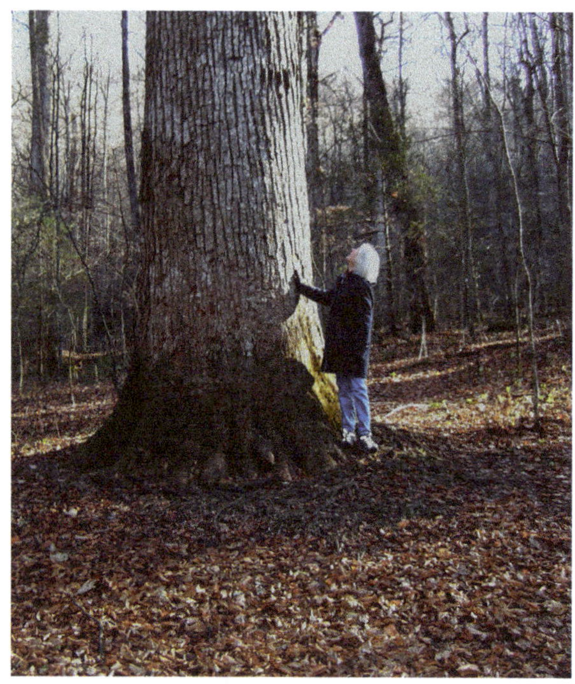

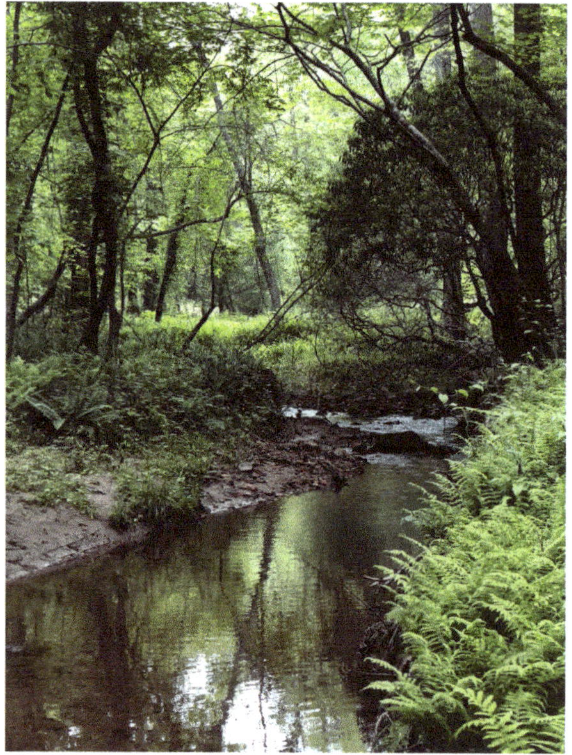

bird song fill the air—just as they surely did in the 1800s. In late October and November, the brilliant colors of fall visually shout against the bluest skies in the world. In the winter, my feet crunch in the frost covering the ground, and my breath precedes me on the trail. My heart hurts from the sublime beauty of the fresh, new greens of spring.

There are places in these gentle mountains where I go as frequently as I can. One of those is a house nearby that's set along a small creek. My husband and I often go there in the spring or fall as the seasons are changing. While my husband sits on the porch, listening to the water flow by as he reads, I walk in the woods to collect images. I always have a camera along as I ramble. Over the years, I've taken thousands of photographs trying to capture something of the essence of things that attract my eye. I also often take along a sketchbook, camping stool, and watercolors.

In April and May, I wander along the creek and discover fiddleheads pushing through the leaf litter or scramble up the steep hillside nearby to capture a few photographs of flame azalea and rhododendron. In late October, I sit on the porch and make

Figure 6.2 (top)
Visiting Joyce Kilmer Memorial Forest
(photo by Thomas Scanlin)

Figure 6.3 (bottom)
Creek view

drawings of tree trunks surrounded by the blaze of fall color. Several tapestries have been based on images created in times like these.

I also love to visit the wooded acres in western North Carolina owned by friends. Their property has waterfalls, streams, and a pond in front of their cabin where otters occasionally swim and ducks visit on their migrations. I've spent countless days at their place walking in the forest on small trails through the mountain laurel and hemlocks. Many times, I've sat in those woods near Sapphire, North Carolina, with sketchbook and watercolors.

I've collected feathers from the turkeys and admired the exotic breeds of chickens that my friends raise. Their organic garden and orchard yield luscious vegetables and fruit to enjoy both as subject matter for artwork and for delicious meals. Many of my tapestry ideas have begun with images made in those surroundings, and I continue to be moved by our friends' approach to living gently and mindfully on the land. Their property has been placed into a conservation

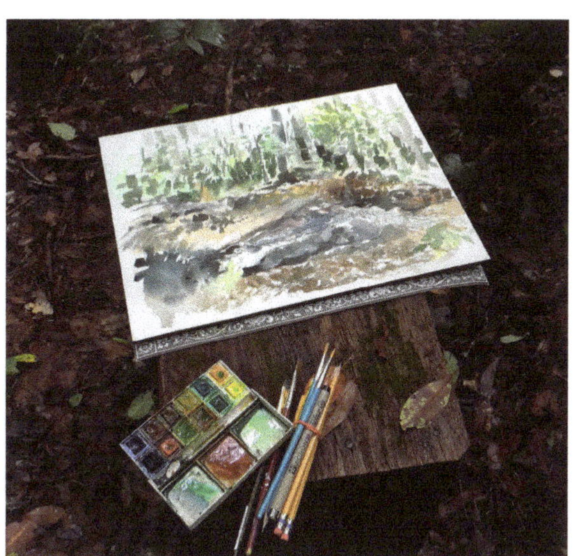

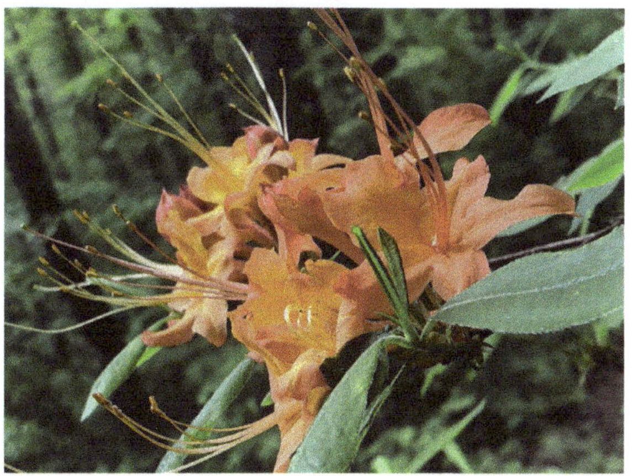

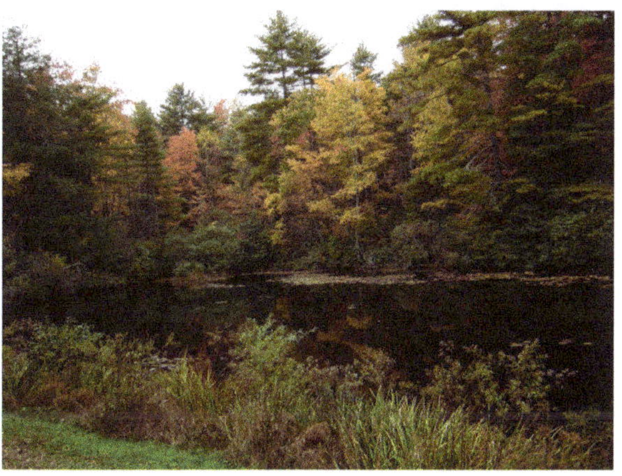

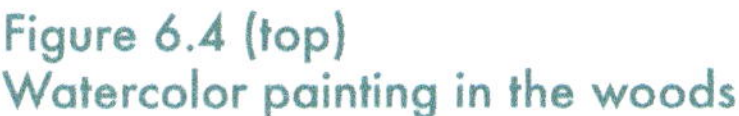

Figure 6.4 (top)
Watercolor painting in the woods

Figure 6.5 (middle)
Flame Azalea

Figure 6.6 (bottom)
Sapphire, pond view

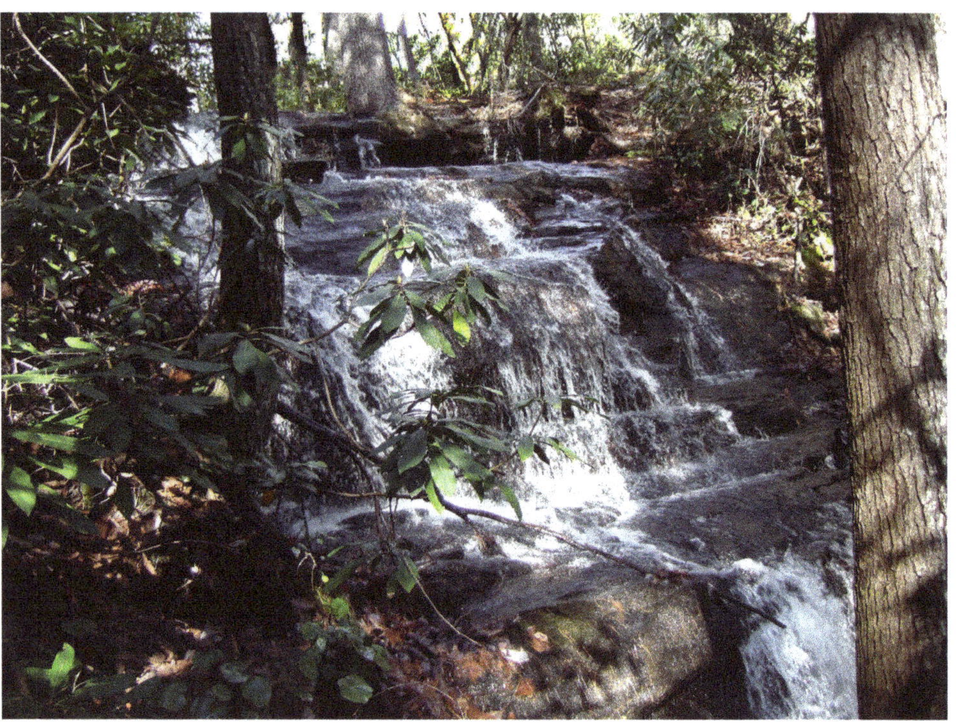

Figure 6.7
Dorothy's Falls

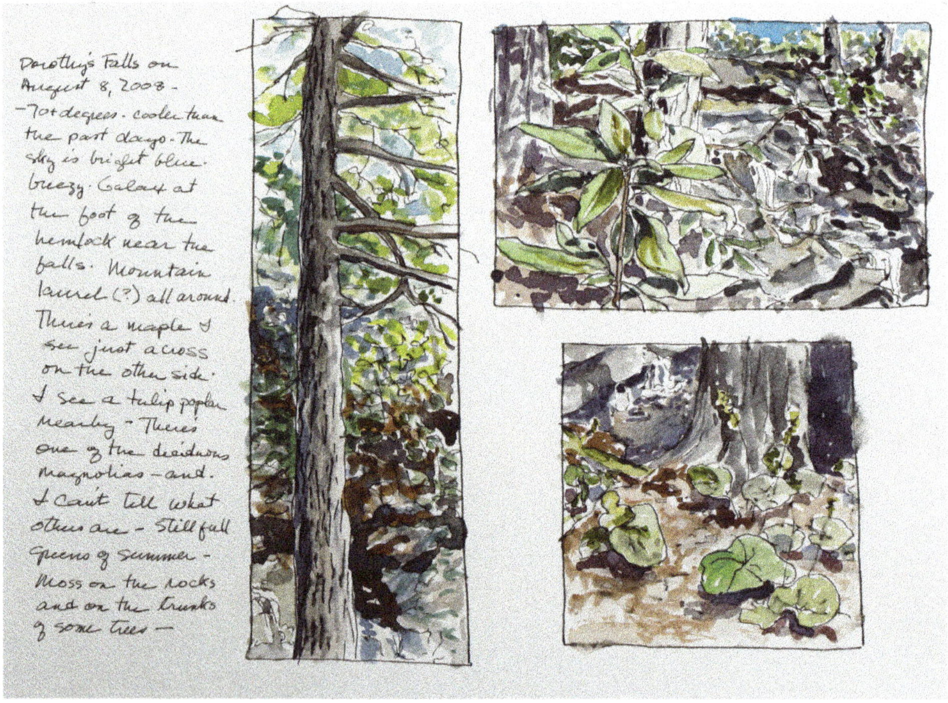

Figure 6.8
Dorothy's Falls
watercolor sketch
(photo by
Christopher Dant)

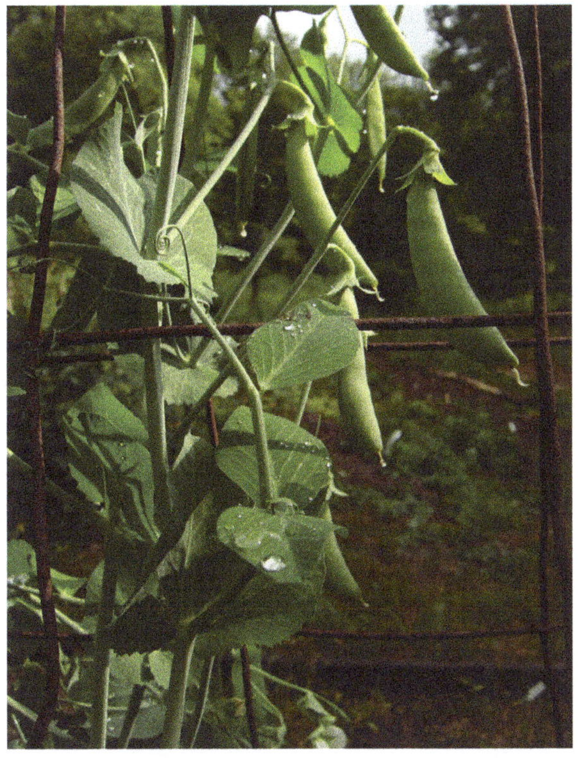

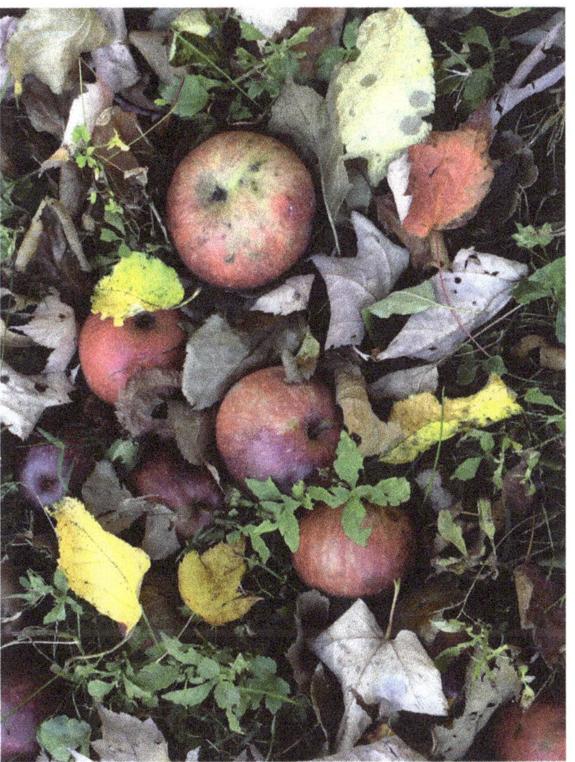

easement so it will be preserved to inspire others for generations to come.

The old saying, "Can't see the forest for the trees" certainly applies to my way of experiencing the woods. I like to be surrounded by trees as I walk in the pattern of light and shadow that plays through the limbs. But the details I find in the forest are what really interest me.

I become entranced by the intricacy of fungi and lichens growing on tree bark and limbs. The dull oranges and warm browns seen amongst the leaf litter amaze me with variety. The difference in the bark of various tree species is fascinating. And then there's the color of leaves in the fall—how can there be so many varieties of yellow, orange, red?

At waterfalls, I study the path of the water as it makes its way through the stones, my ears filled with the splash of its tumble. Sometimes I count the number of leaves in a cluster that's fallen to the ground, wondering if there's a Fibonacci number in the three, five, or eight leaves attached to one branch. And what about the size variations within the maple leaves that I see—alike and yet different? Look at the tenderness of the petals of a tulip poplar flower that's fallen to the ground. Feel the stickiness of the stamen of the flame azalea.

Figure 6.9 (top)
Sapphire, NC, peas in the garden

Figure 6.10 (bottom)
Sapphire, NC, Yates apples—windfall

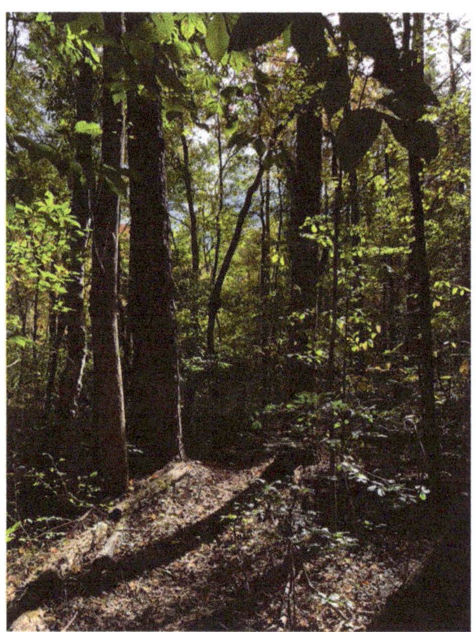

Figure 6.11
Woods walk with light and shadow

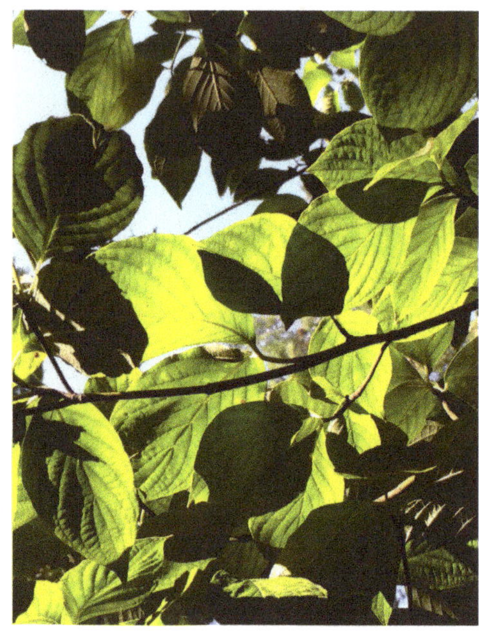

Figure 6.12
Dogwood leaves, light and shadow

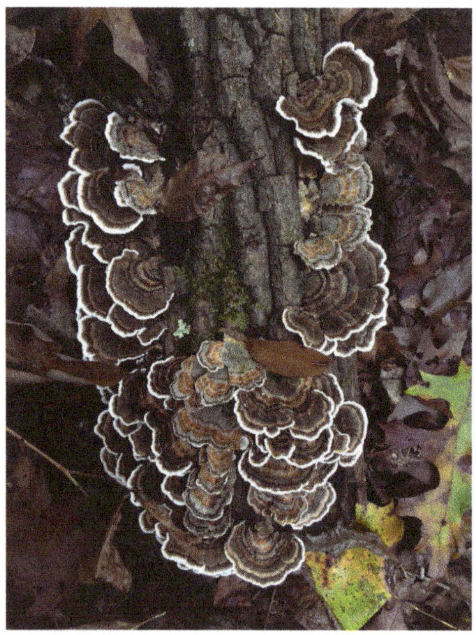

Figure 6.13
Turkey Tail fungi on tree bark

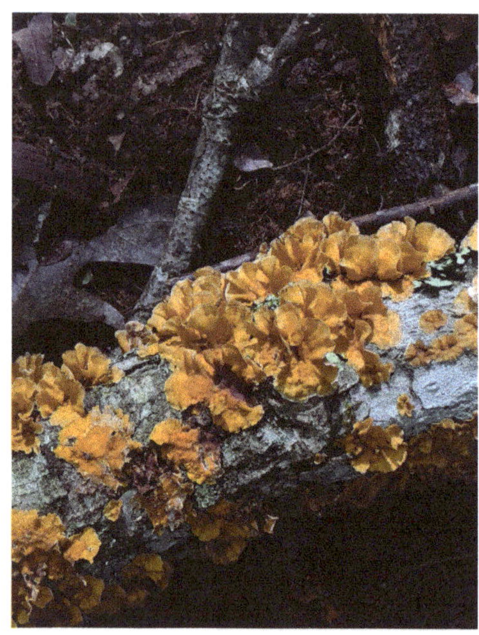

Figure 6.14
Chicken of the Woods fungi on tree limb

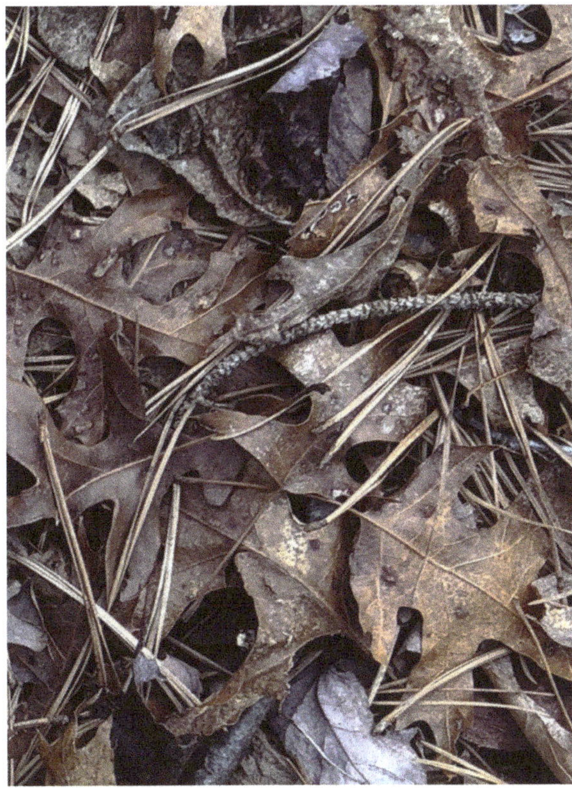

Figure 6.15
Leaf litter

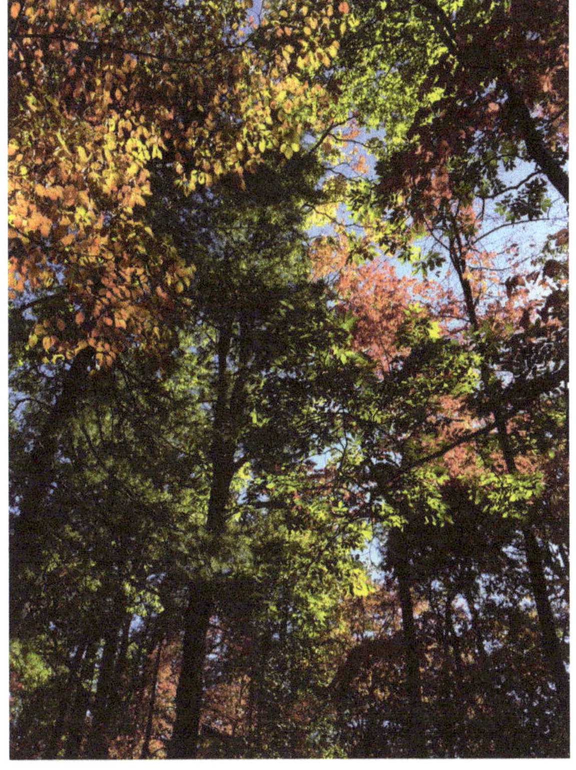

Figure 6.16
Fall leaves

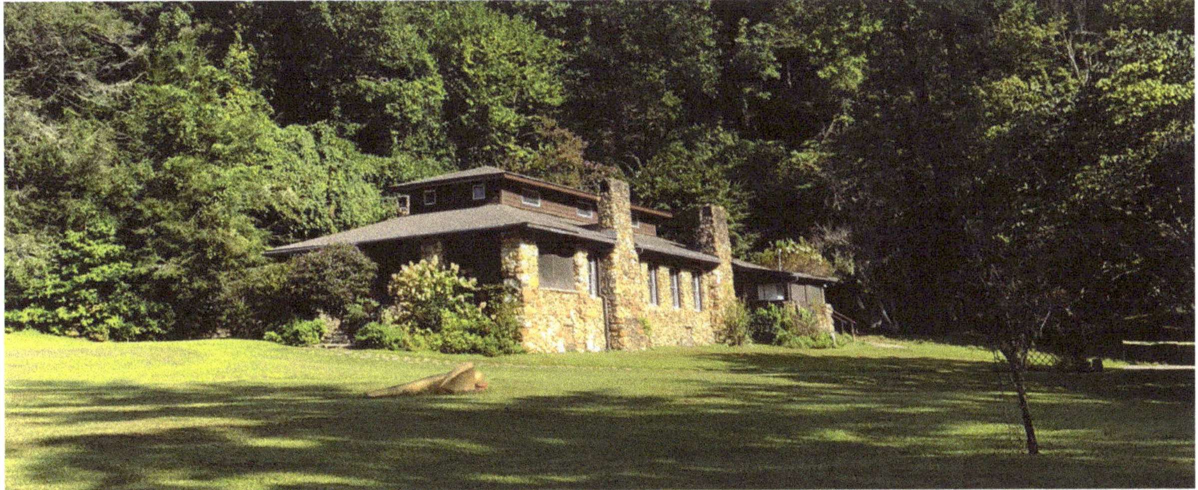

Figure 6.17
Hambidge: Rock House

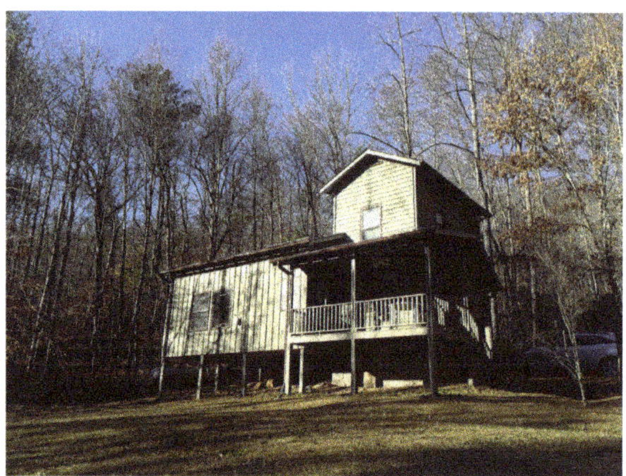

Figure 6.18
Hambidge: Fisher Studio

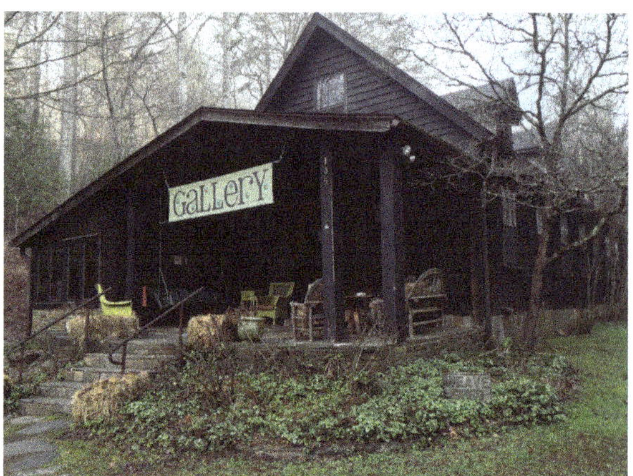

Figure 6.19
Hambidge: Weave Shed Gallery

As I roam through the woods, I wonder how I might possibly represent some of the beauty I'm observing. I know the images I'm capable of making will only dimly represent what I see and feel. I realize that noticing is the first step of many I'll take on the way from a fleeting observation to finished tapestry. Many hours of making and refining images are ahead of me as I attempt to create a tapestry that will contain an essence of the place, the time, and my feelings of the experience, brief though it may have been.

Sometimes I feel the need to spend several weeks of quiet and solitude immersed in a place to observe and make visual responses. I call these "time-out" experiences. Two restorative environments for those times are the artist retreats of the Hambidge Center and the Lillian E. Smith Center; coincidentally, both are located in Northeast Georgia in Rabun County.

The Hambidge Center has a long history as an artist retreat. Mary Hambidge (1885–1973) moved to the several hundred wooded acres along Betty's Creek in the 1930s. She was seeking a place to continue the work she had been immersed in with Jay Hambidge (1867–1924) as he studied the art of the Greeks and developed theories of Dynamic Symmetry. In Greece, Mary Hambidge had discovered weaving and spinning. Between her arrival in North Georgia after Jay Hambidge's death and the late 1950s, Mary Hambidge worked with the local mountain weavers and spinners to produce hand-dyed and woven fabrics that were sold in New York City as products of The Weavers of Rabun (1935–1950s).

In the later years of her life, Mary Hambidge began to welcome artists to spend time at the tranquil mountain property. *Mary Crovatt Hambidge: Whistler,*

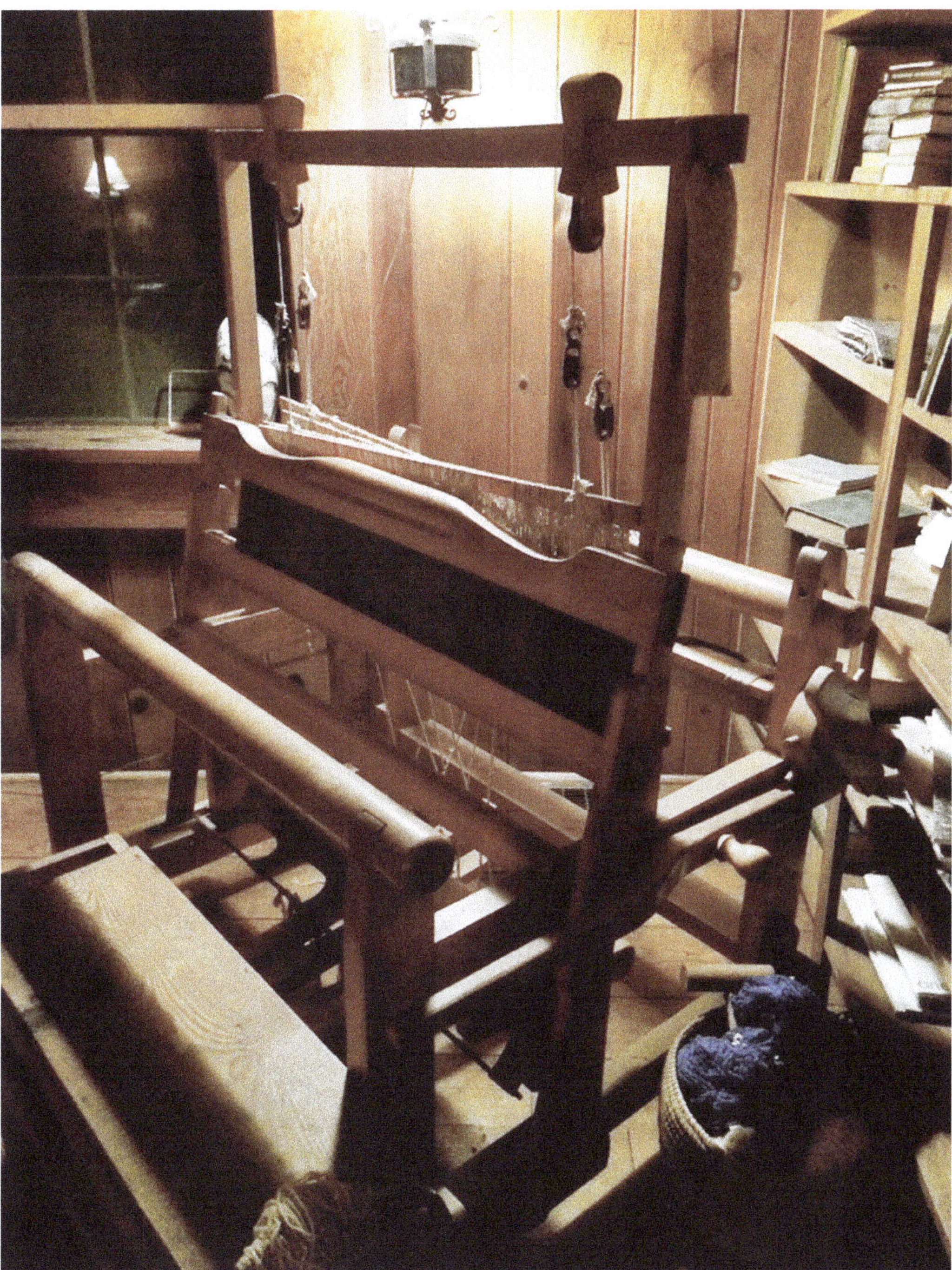

Figure 6.20
Hambidge: Mary Hambidge's loom

Wanderer, Weaver, Utopian is a documentary film released in 2017 that gives a fascinating look at Mary's life.[2]

Soon after her death in 1973, the Hambidge Center became a retreat dedicated to nurturing artists in all fields and from around the world, fulfilling Mary's dream for a haven of creativity.[3]

Hambidge residents stay in one of the nine cottage-studios that are scattered throughout the 600 acres. Artists spend their days with art making or hiking the surrounding wooded trails; in the evening, everyone gathers at the Rock House to share a meal and conversation.

The Hambidge Center has played a significant role in my development as a teacher and artist. In the 1980s, I taught a few workshops in the Weave Shed where we wove on the very same looms used decades before by the Weavers of Rabun. Times change, and now the Weave Shed holds a gallery and office. The old looms, with the exception of Mary's personal one, are stored away.

I first applied for an artist residency at Hambidge in 1994 and have been fortunate to be a returning Hambidge Fellow frequently since then. I've walked the trails on the property and collected many photographs of the landscape and details within it. I've drawn, painted, read, written, and designed and woven tapestries while there. Several of the artists whom I met at the Hambidge Center have become long-time friends.

Being at Hambidge offers treasured occasions for days immersed in the natural world. Likewise, so does another nearby artist retreat center: the Lillian E. Smith (LES) Center.

Lillian Smith (1897–1966) was a contemporary of Mary Hambidge; both were born in the late nineteenth century and also lived in the same county in rural North Georgia during much of their adult life. Did they know each other? Probably. But their goals in life were different. While Mary sought utopian artistic ideals; Lillian was dedicated to social justice. She was driven by the struggles for civil rights and wrote passionately about the inequities found in American society, particularly in the South.[4]

The Lillian E. Smith Center, now owned and managed by Piedmont College, is located on 150 acres of wooded land at the base of Screamer Mountain near Clayton, Georgia. Three cottages accommodate musicians, researchers, visual artists, and

2 Hal Jacobs, *Mary Hambidge: Whistler, Wanderer, Weaver, Utopian,* a documentary film, http://www.hjacobscreative.com/mary-crovatt-hambidge-documentary/

3 Philis Alvic, *Weavers of the Southern Highlands* (Lexington, KY: The University Press of Kentucky, 2003), 96–112.

4 Hal and Henry Jacobs, *Lillian E. Smith: Breaking the Silence*, a documentary film, https://vimeo.com/270713166

writers during the residency season that runs from early spring through late fall. Two of the cottages are the former homes of Smith's relatives where they spent their retirement years, and each cottage retains many of the books, memorabilia, and furnishings from their occupancy.

Since 2010, I've returned to the LES Center at different seasons of the year. In the spring, I've walked the trails to find tender new growth appearing all around. I've felt the hot, sticky days of summer and rushed inside as a popup thunderstorm approached, as they frequently do in the mountains. In October and November, the glory of changing leaf colors fills the forest. Coat, cap, and scarf add warmth to an early

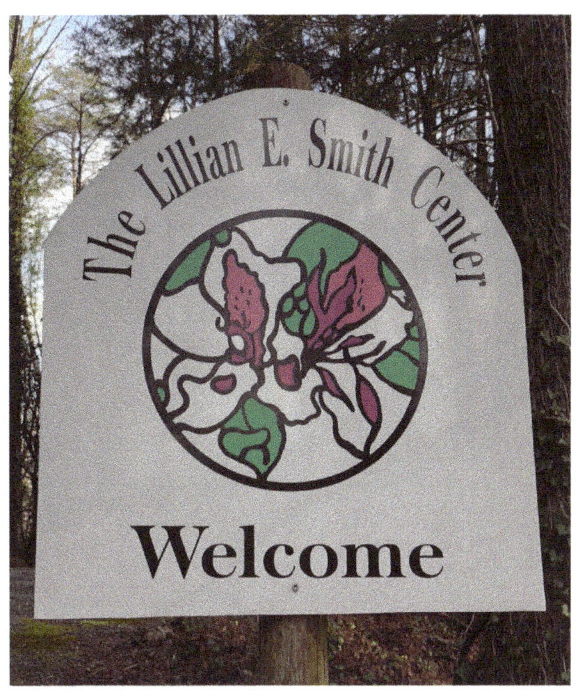

Figure 6.21
Lillian E. Smith Center (LES) sign

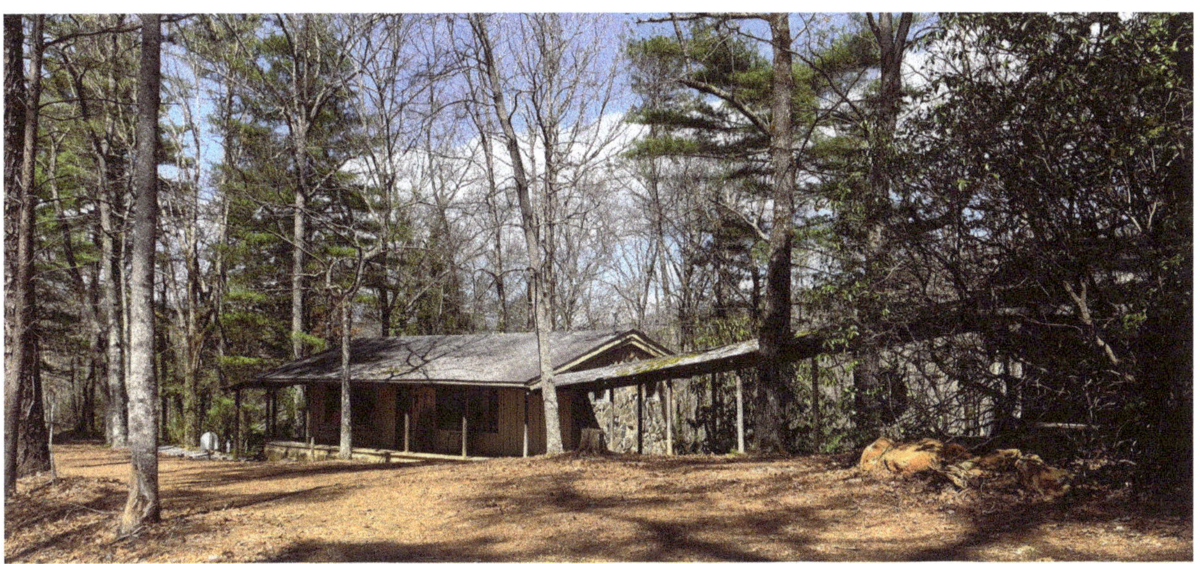

Figure 6.22
LES: Peeler Cottage

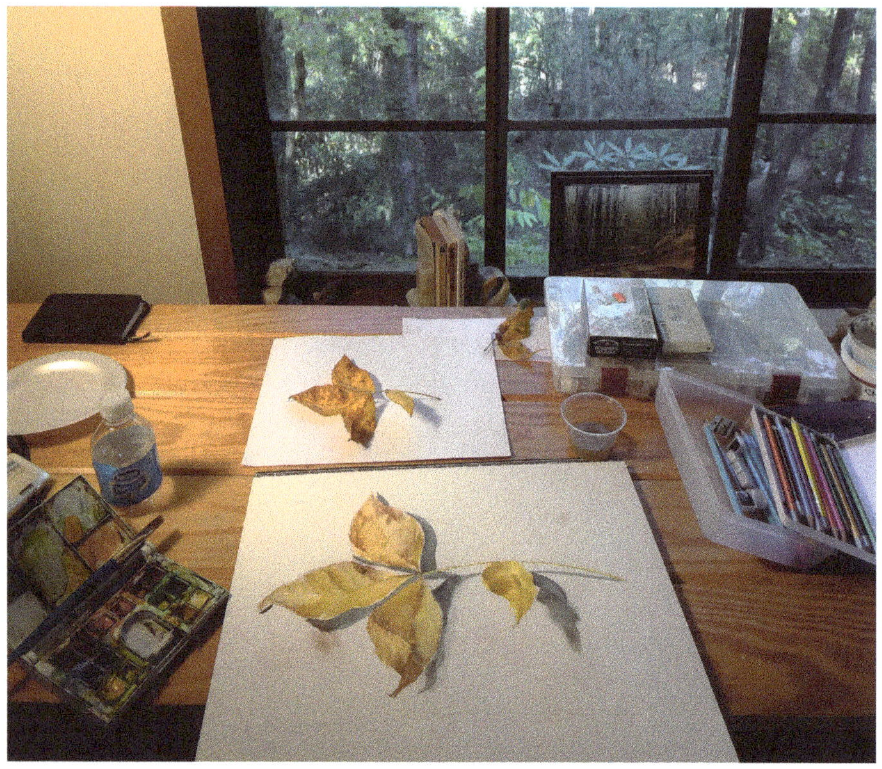

Figure 6.23
LES: Painting in the cottage during a residency

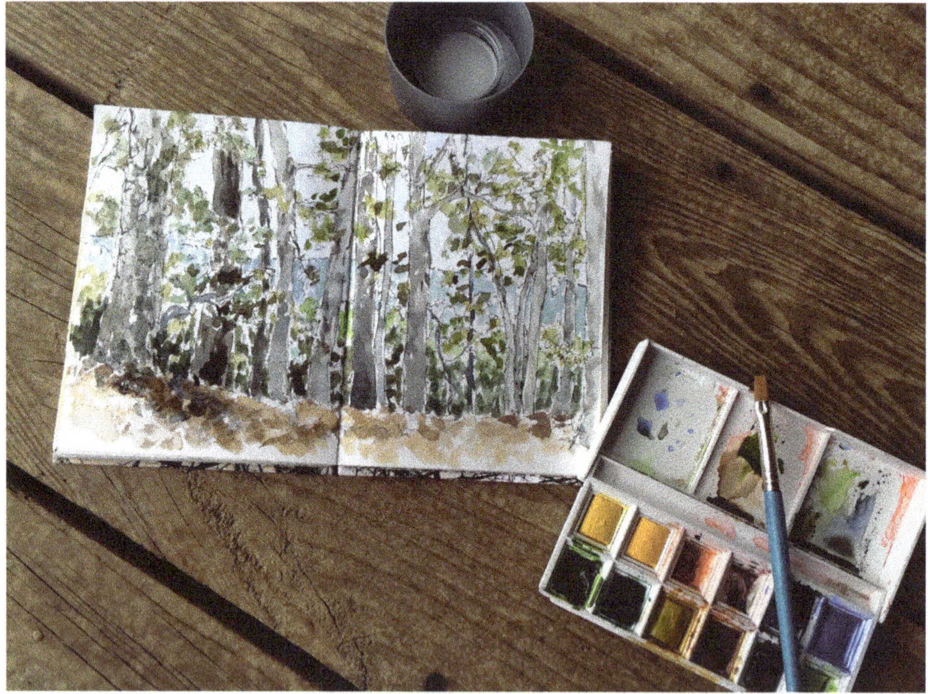

Figure 6.24
LES: watercolor of the view from the porch during a residency

morning walk in March when I see trunks and limbs of trees forming filigree patterns in the dawn.

At the LES Center, I've made many visual studies, some of which have later become the designs for tapestries. The rocking chair on the porch at Peeler Cottage lends itself to spending late afternoon hours sketching the view. I've written in my journal, planned classes, completed manuscripts for articles, and developed conference presentations. I treasure each stay I've had there. In 2018, in the hope that others may likewise benefit from a stay at the Center, my husband and I began sponsoring a two-week residency for a visual artist.

Taking time out from my normal life routine to concentrate on observing and responding is very important to me. Sometimes it's the design qualities I notice that are foremost. Maybe it's the pattern of light and dark among the leaves, or the positive-negative placement of stones in a creek, or the intervals among the tree trunks in the forest that catch my attention.

In other instances, it might be an expressive aspect that moves me. What do the light and shadows across the road suggest? Maybe the ephemeral shape of a shadow being cast by a single flower signifies a particular moment of time. The stacked stones of a chimney ruin cause me to wonder how I may render those

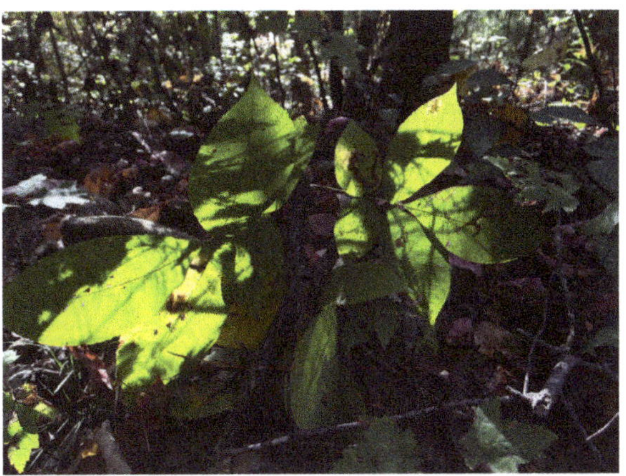

Figure 6.25
Light and shadow among hickory leaves in fall

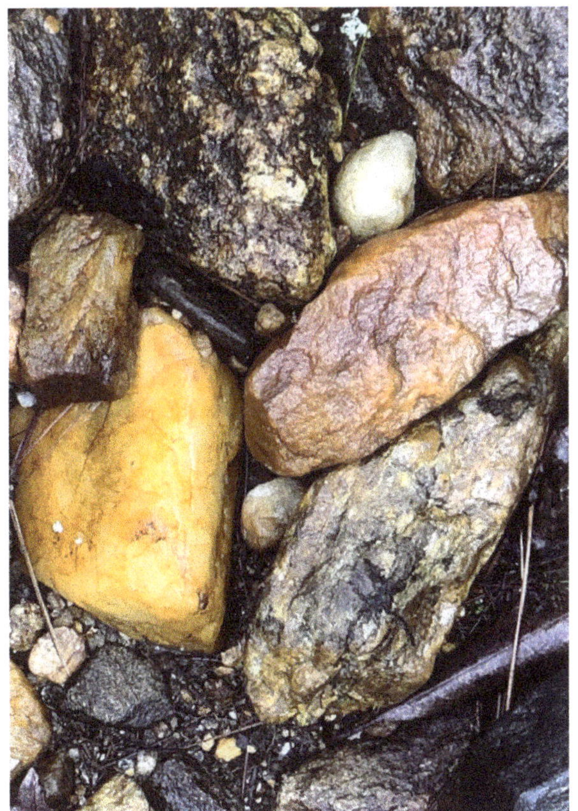

Figure 6.26
Creek stones

to suggest stability, permanence, or even eternity. Being removed from the demands of daily life and engaged in the "time out" mode encourages me to fully explore and make visual responses in ways I might not otherwise do. Essentially, it allows me time for the serious work of play.

The observations I make while on retreat—recorded as photos, sketches, paintings, and journal notes—later come together in my home studio. Months will go by as I finalize a design and then weave a tapestry inspired by the interlude of quiet retreat. The woods and valleys of the Blue Ridge Mountains of Southern Appalachia give me a wealth of subject matter to contemplate. My hope is that something of the sense of wonder and gratitude I hold for the nature of things breathes through the spirit of the tapestries I weave.

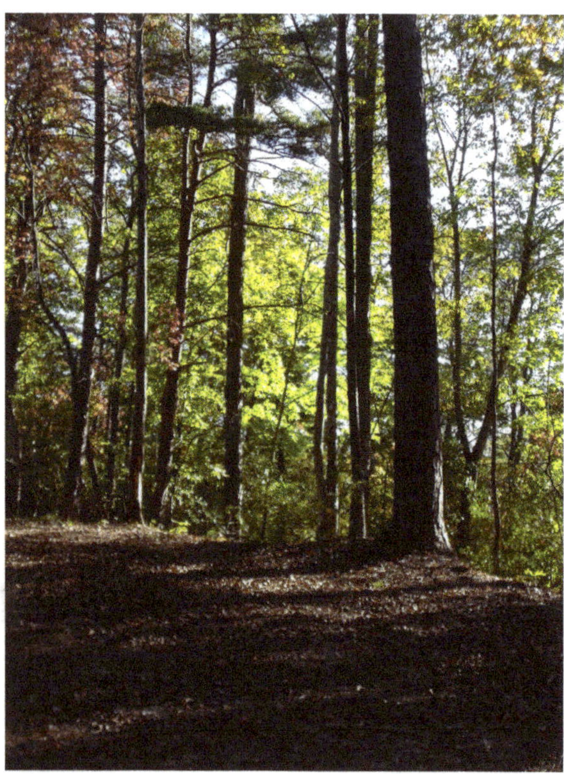

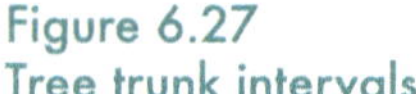

Figure 6.27
Tree trunk intervals

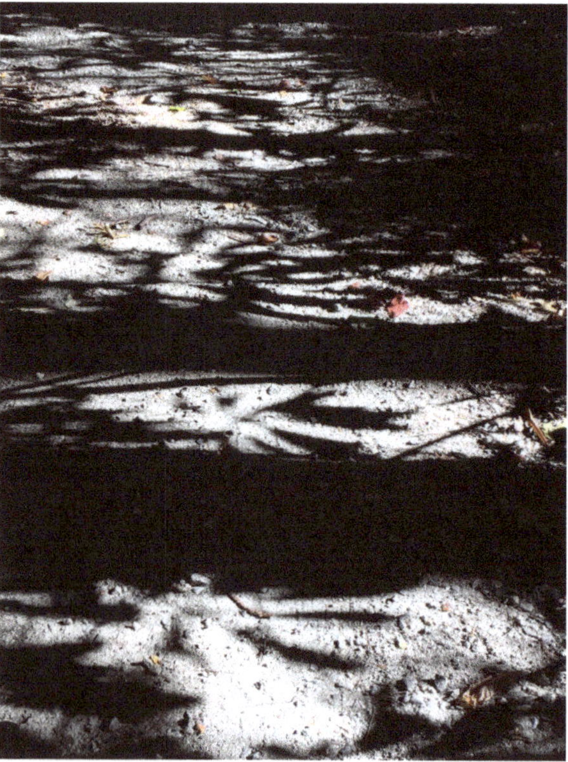

Figure 6.28
Shadows of mountain laurel across the road at LES Center

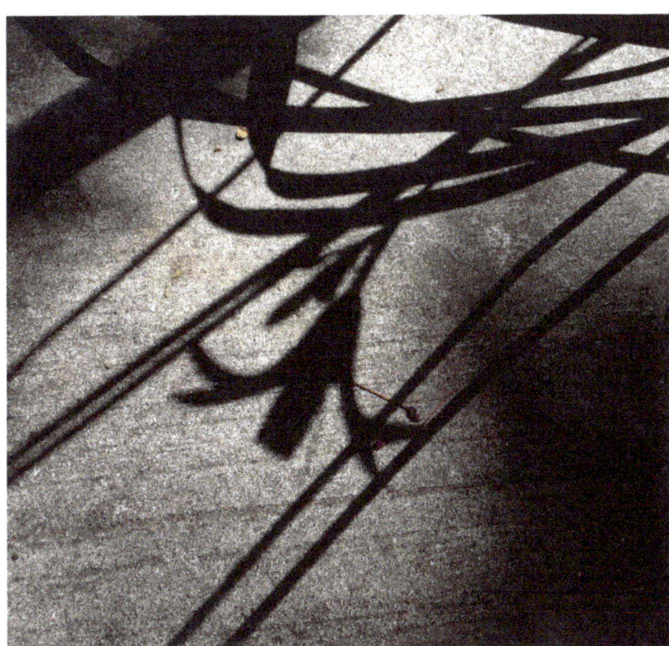

Figure 6.29
Day lily shadow

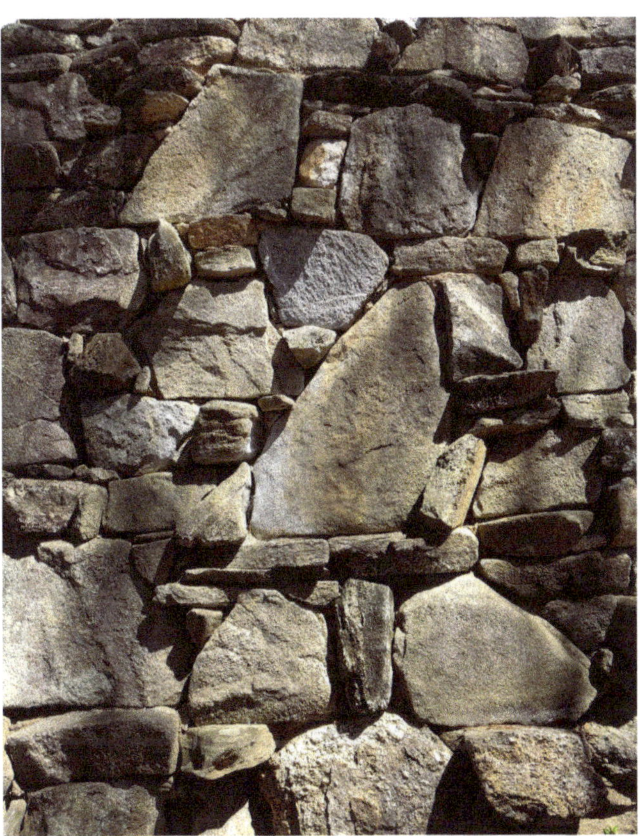

Figure 6.30
Stacked chimney stones at LES Center

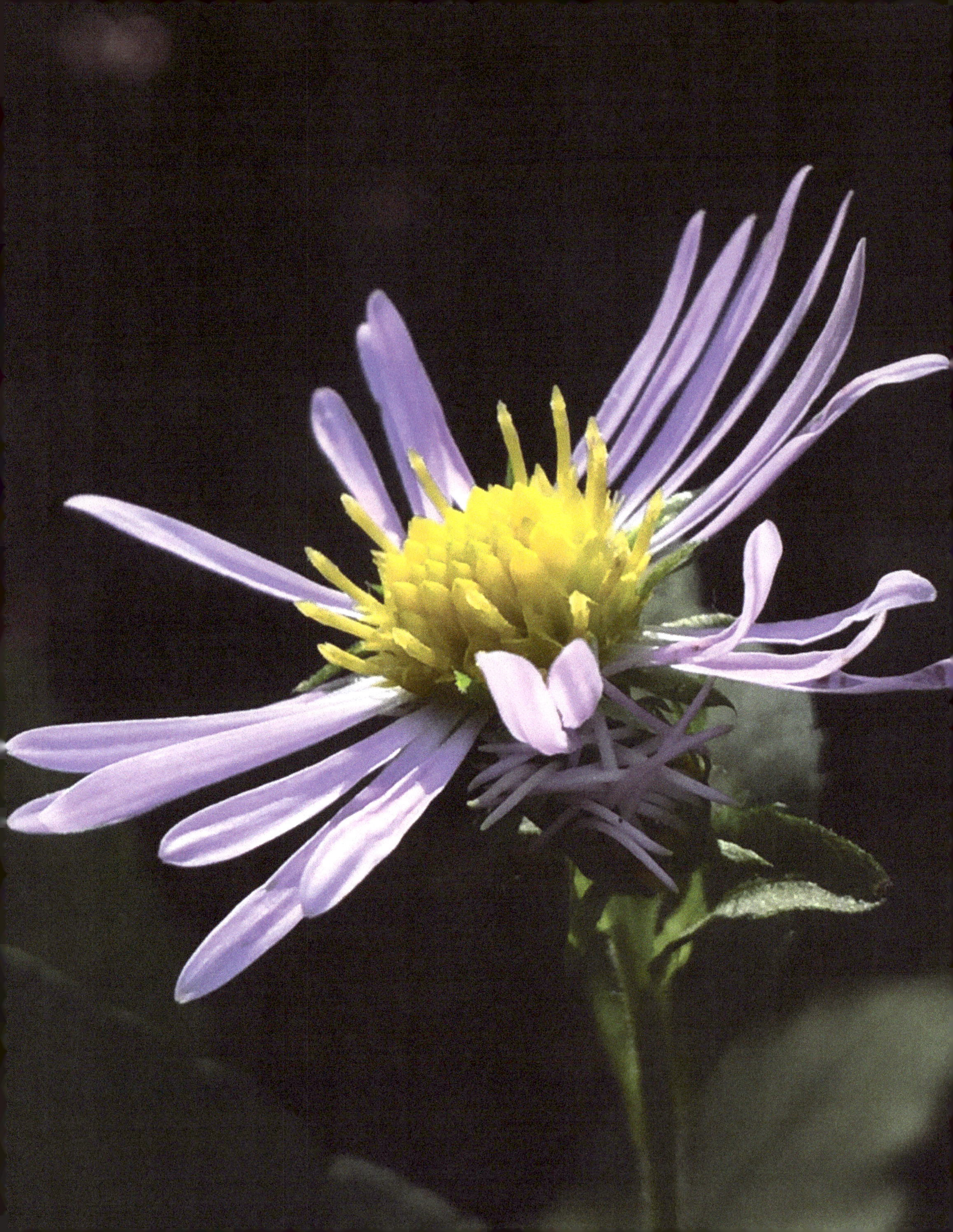

7
Small Things

Intimate features of the world around us: those are found in the exquisite details of small things. The trees rather than the forest are what I see at first. But then I want to look even closer. I'm constantly amazed by the similar shapes of the thousands of leaves on the oak tree in the yard. Yet every one of those leaves of the same tree have subtle variations. Pattern and repetition abound in nature's forms—but with remarkable variety within the sameness.

My fascination with small things includes leaves and flowers, stones and sticks, feathers and fiddleheads—and anything else I discover as I walk in the woods. I collect things. I pick up stones. I photograph moss and lichen. I sketch the Pink Lady's Slipper that's just appeared.

For many years, I've rendered these small things by drawing or painting them. As I turned to tapestry as my artistic medium, I realized that my ability to weave images was rudimentary. I knew that I needed to do many tapestries to improve my proficiency, and I also wanted to use subjects that were meaningful to me. I've always enjoyed seeing the variety in shapes and colors of flowers, so they became my first subjects. I'd say, "Flowers don't care if I make a bit of mistake with their shapes as I weave them—people would."

Beyond the familiarity and forgiveness the subject gave my designs, they were also experiments with color, shape, variety, and contrast in compositions. I enjoyed zooming in on the subject so that the positive and negative shapes of the flowers and the background areas became interesting. I simplified shapes and made the colors bold. I've now woven

Figure 7.1 (opposite)
Aster

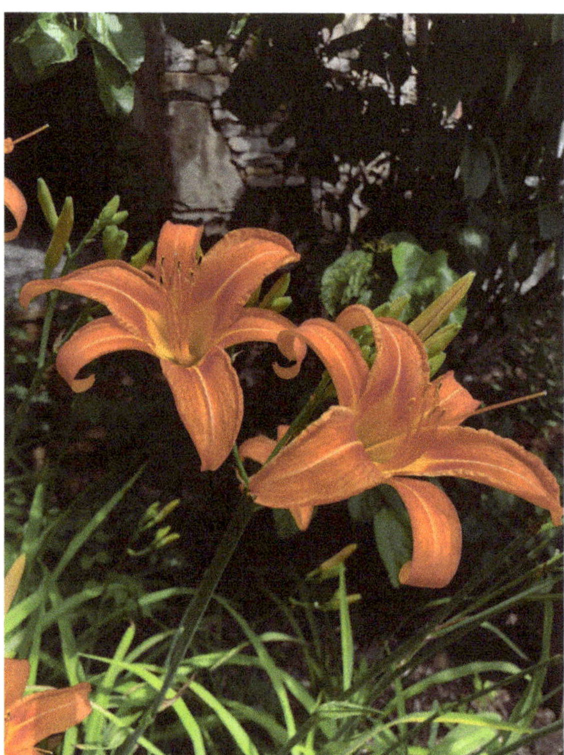

Figure 7.2
Day Lilies

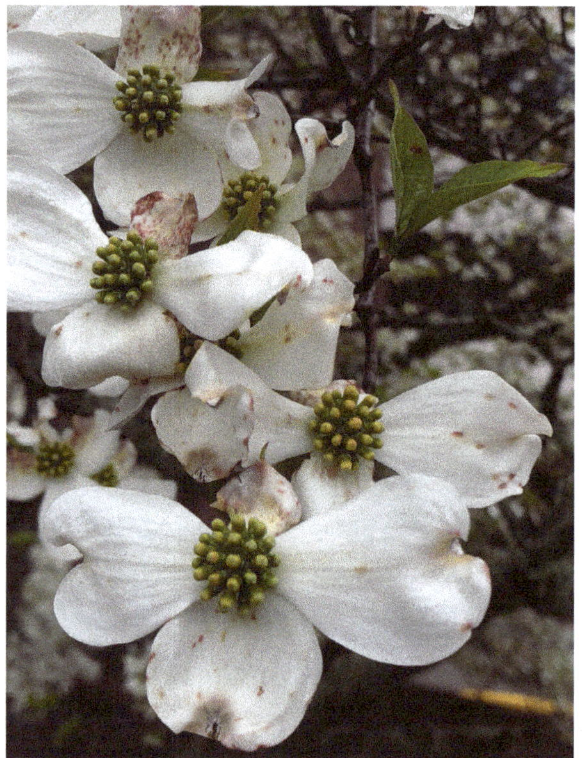

Figure 7.3
Dogwood

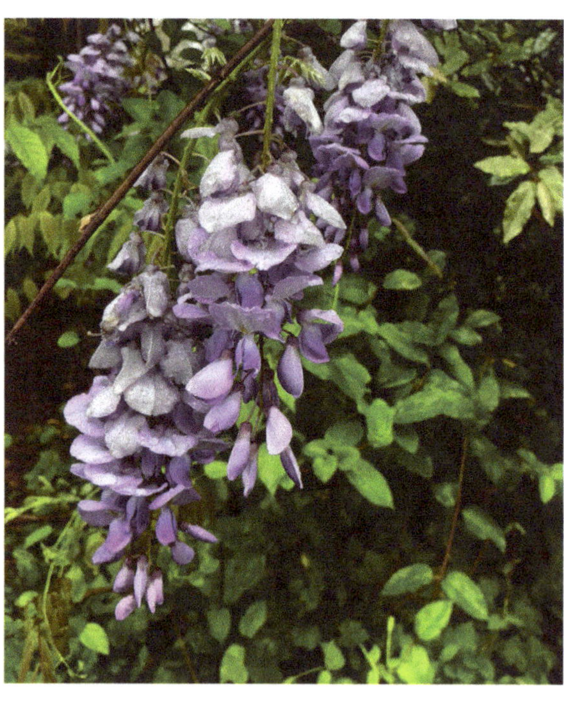

Figure 7.4
Wisteria

flowers galore: Althea, Aster, Black Eyed Susan, Bloodroot, Camellia, Carolina Lily, Coneflower, Daffodil, Fire Pink, Jack in the Pulpit, Magnolia, Orchid, Pink Lady's Slipper, Star Gazer Lily, and more. These became subjects of tapestries of small, medium, and large sizes. All of these tapestries have been a pleasure to weave—after all, who doesn't enjoy seeing flowers?

Even though I started using floral forms as subjects because of the forgiving nature of their shapes in designing, I've found weaving them to be a solace because they are so comforting in many ways. They also represent contrasts of meaning. Flowers are given in both times of joy and sorrow. They fill a bride's bouquet and cover her casket at the end.

Artists have long used flowers symbolically. In the Netherlands, they often appeared along with other items in "vanitas" paintings of the early seventeenth century as an example of the transience of life.[1] And so it was in 2001 that I turned to a flower subject for a tapestry in an attempt to ease some of the despair I felt when the United States invaded Afghanistan after the September 11 attacks.

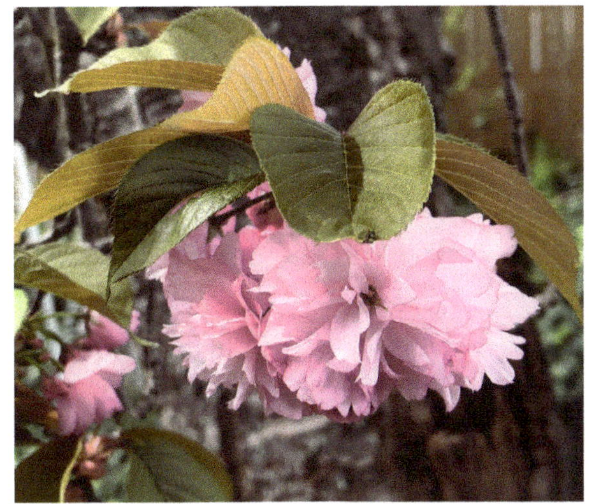

Figure 7.5
Cherry blossom

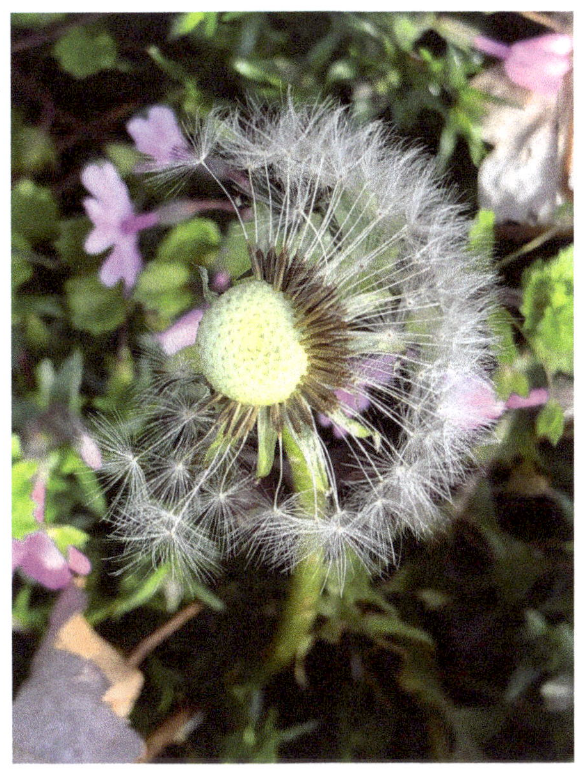

Figure 7.6
Dandelion

1 Marilyn Stokstad. *Art History*, rev. ed. (New York: Harry N. Abrams, 1999), 800.

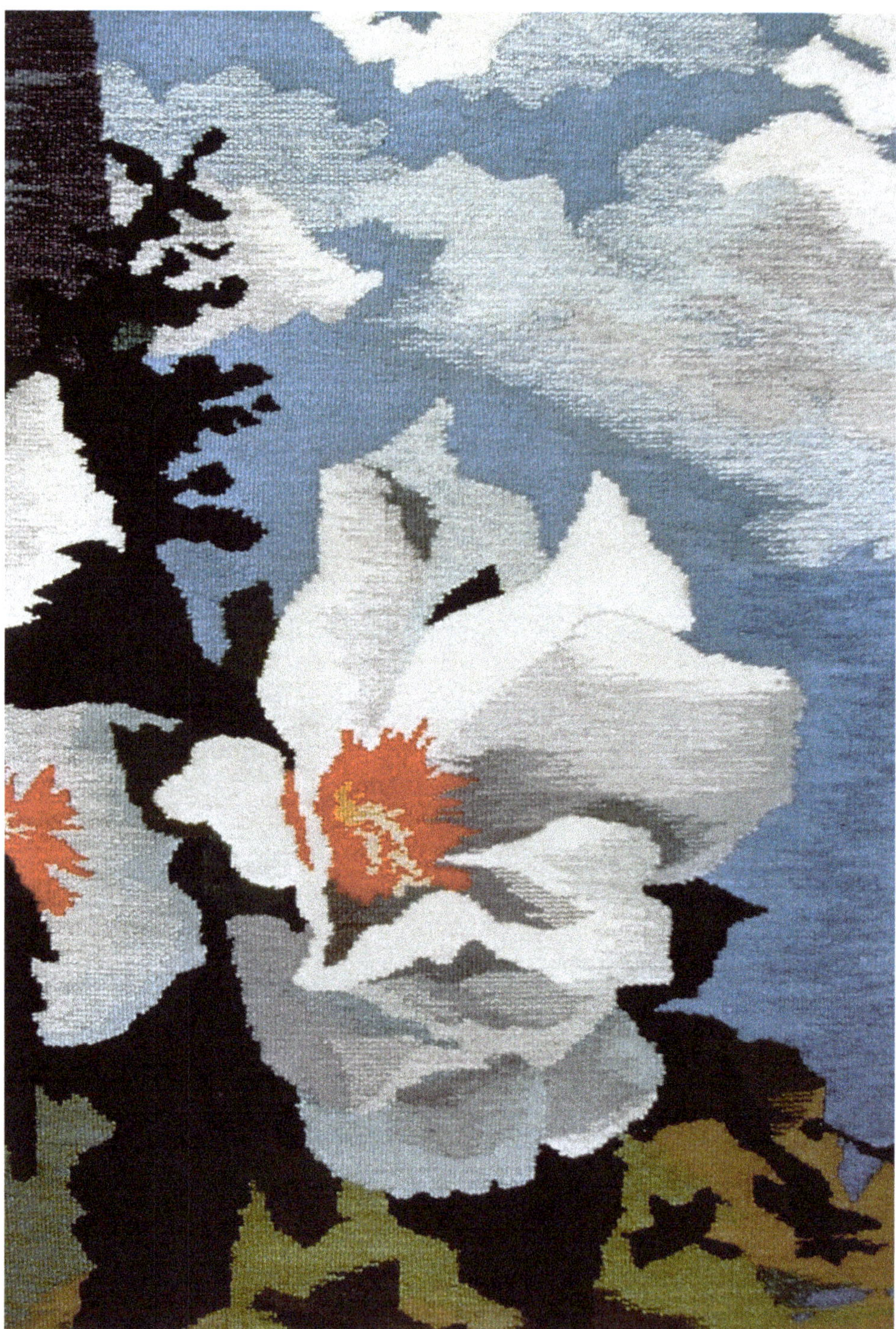

Figure 7.7
Althea, 56 inches by 38 inches, 1989

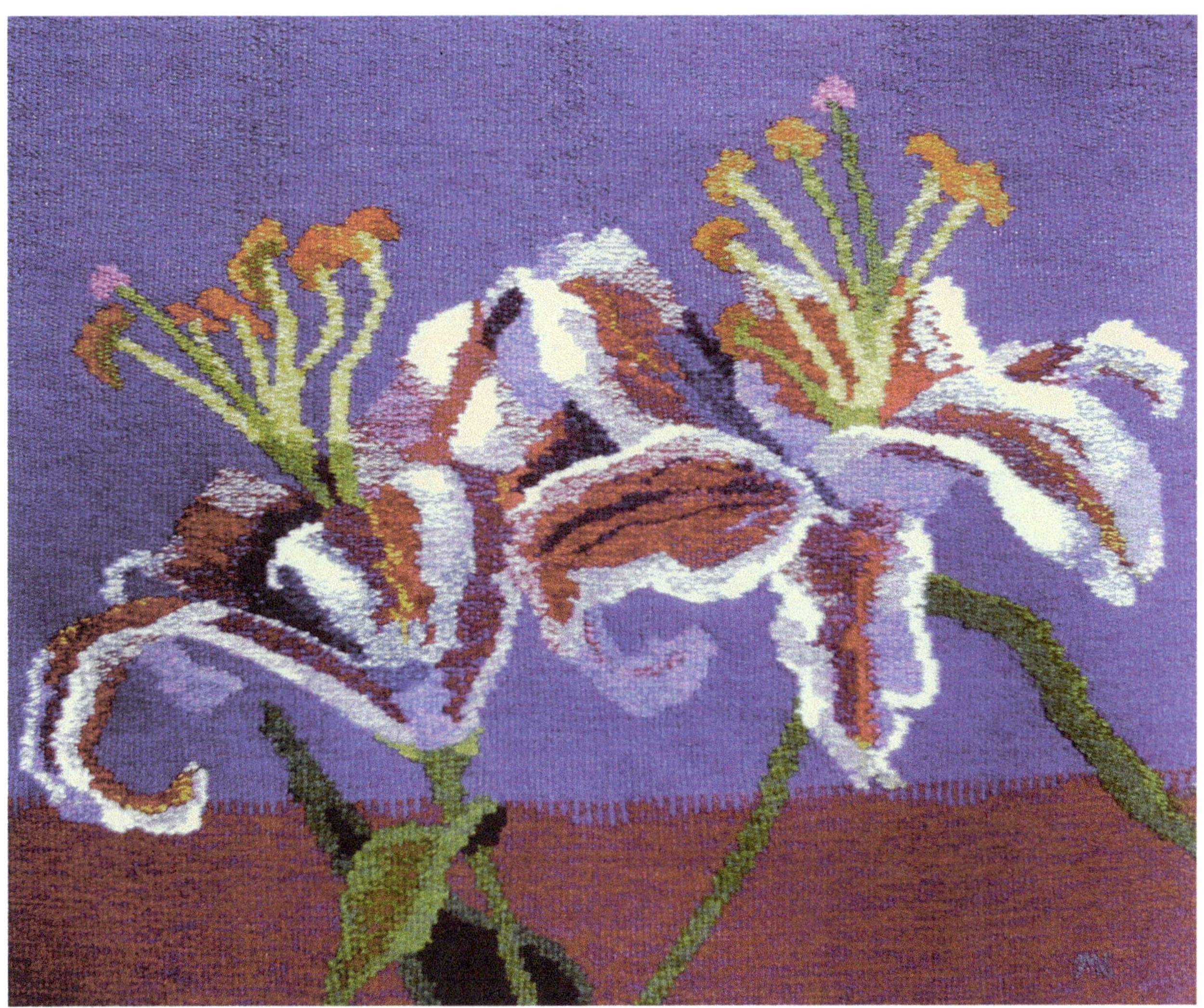

Figure 7.8
Stargazer, 36 inches by 40 inches, 1991

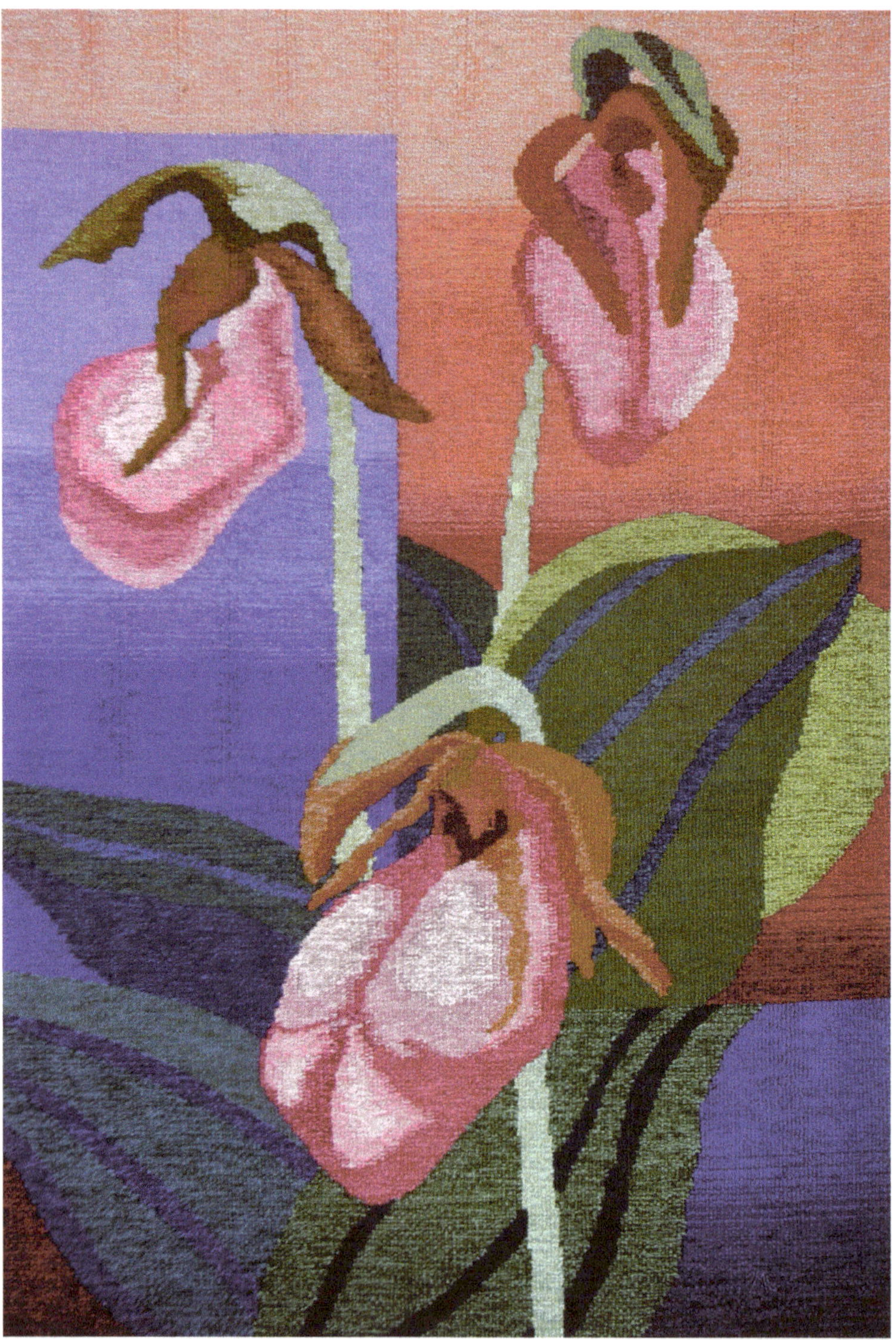

Figure 7.9
Pink Lady's Slippers, 60 inches by 40 inches, 1992 (photo by Michael Woods)

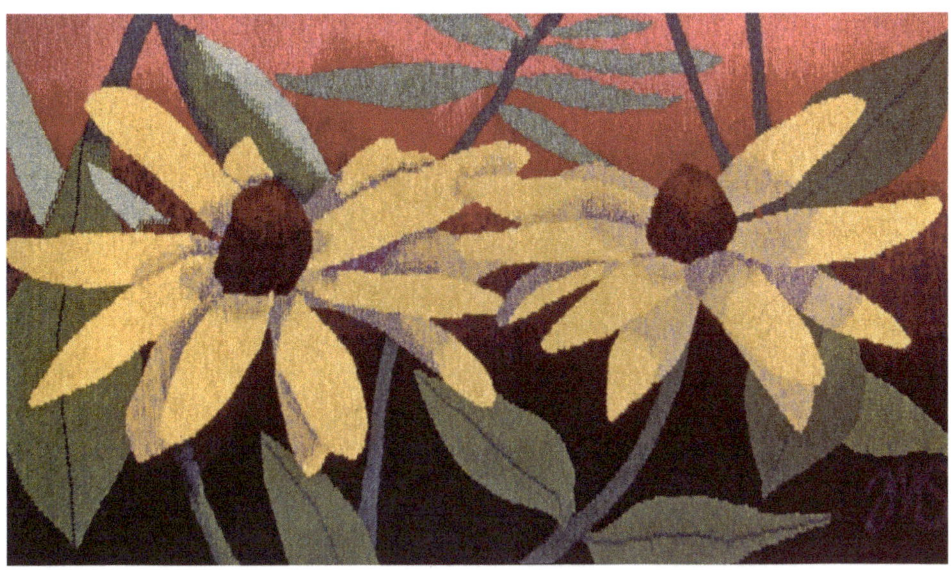

Figure 7.10
Black Eyed Susans, 38 inches by 64 inches, 1992 (photo by Michael Woods)

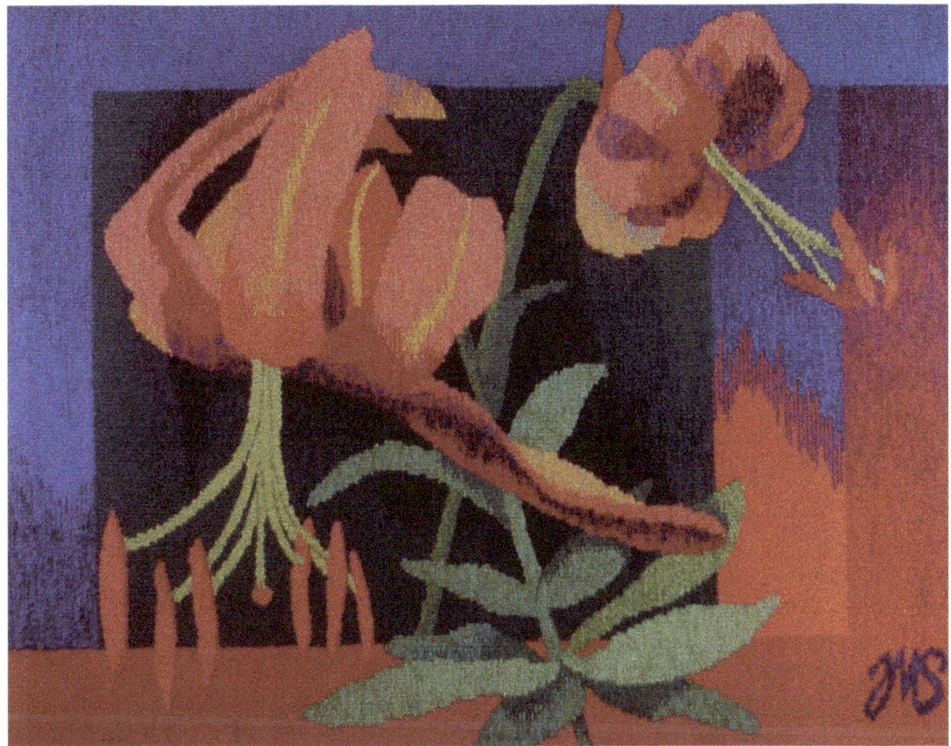

Figure 7.11
Carolina Lilies, 30 inches by 38 inches, 1992 (photo by Michael Woods)

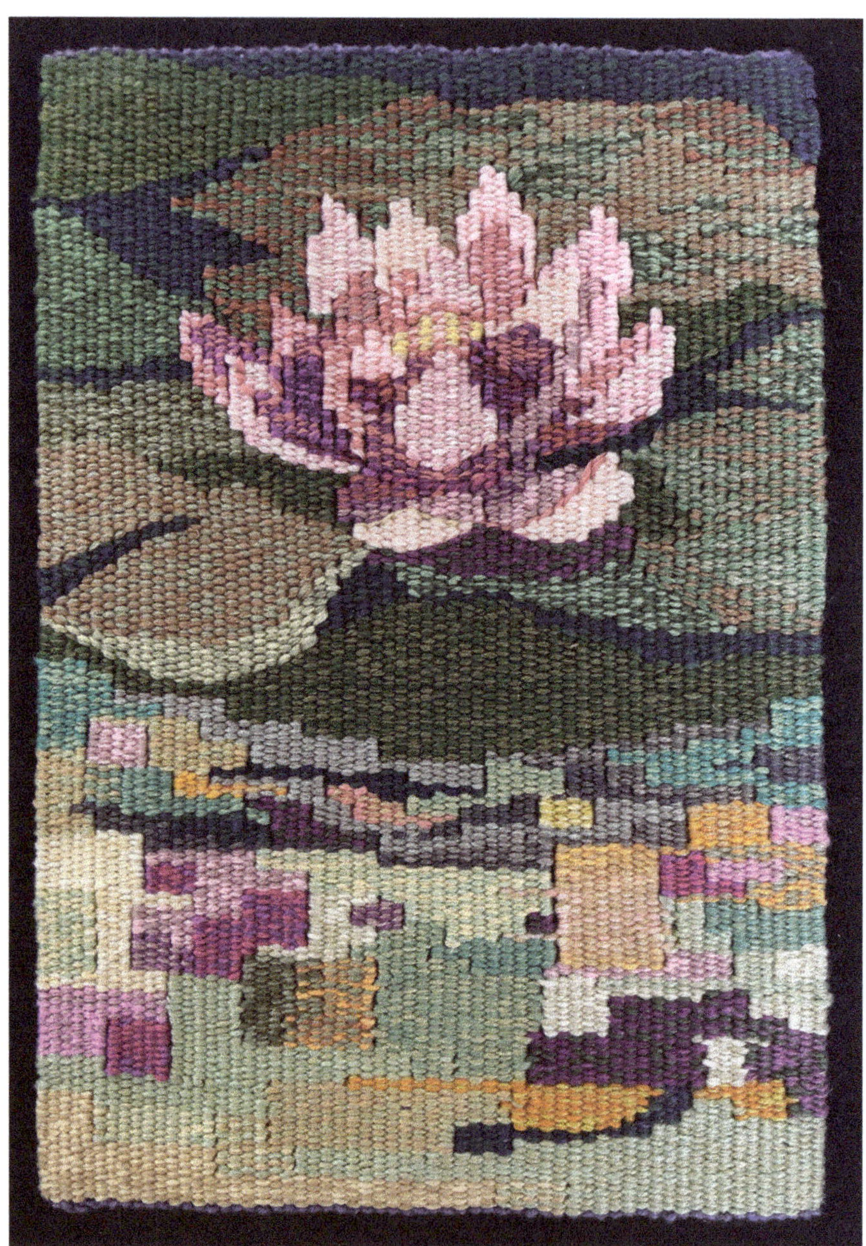

Figure 7.12
Water Lily, 9 inches by 5 inches, 2000 (photo by Tim Barnwell)

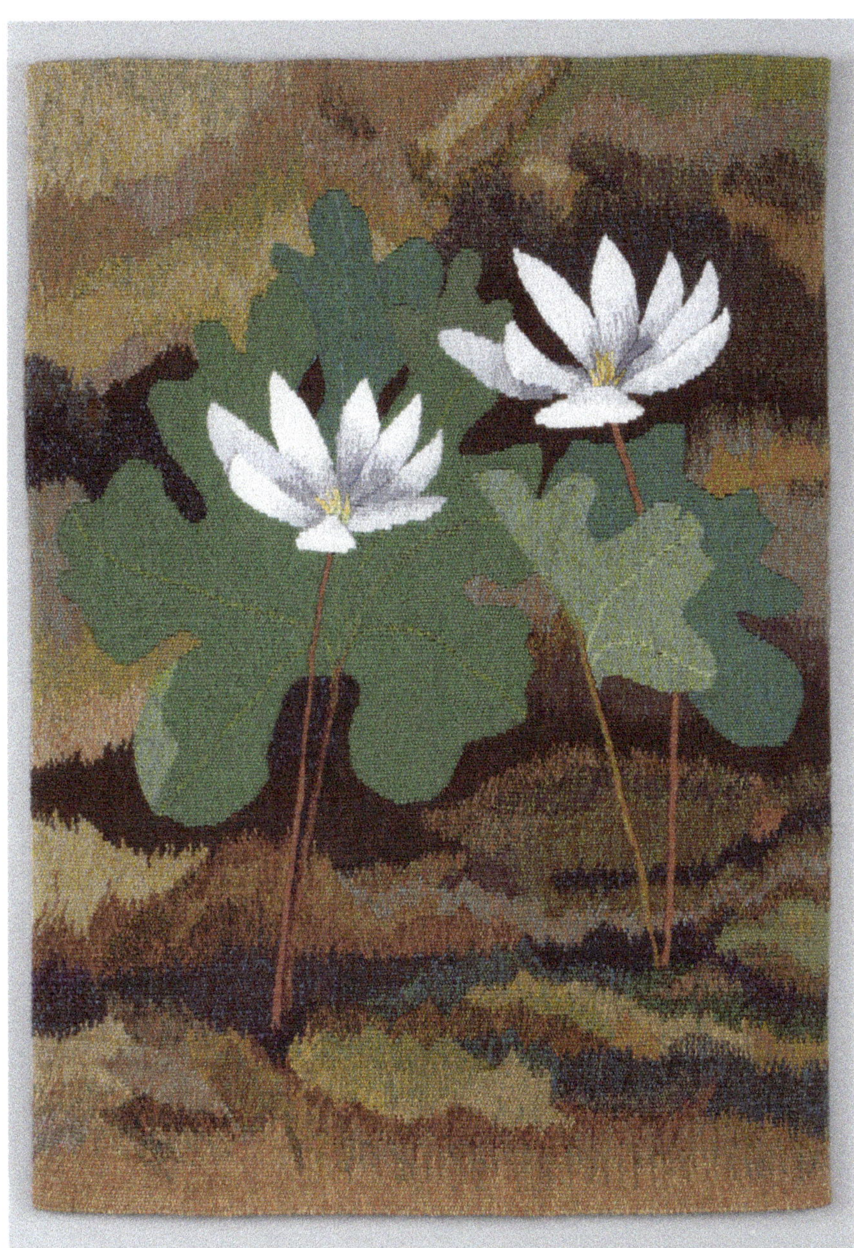

Figure 7.13
Secrets, 26 inches by 18 inches, 2015 (photo by Tim Barnwell)

The composition of the tapestry was based on a photograph I'd taken earlier in the year of a tall sunflower with a bright blue sky and white clouds surrounding it. I chose that photo to work from because all I could think whenever I looked at it was, "Sunflowers leap to the sky; they don't care about war."

The tapestry became almost five feet high and over forty inches wide, with the sunflower dominating the design. The shapes of the flower, leaves, and shadows on the stem were all simplified and stylized. The intense blue of the sky held bold clouds. Even though the finished tapestry was bright, colorful, and exuberant in appearance, it was a covert political commentary. Yes, an obscure statement, to be known only if I decided to mention it. The fact was that weaving this piece had been a way in which I dealt with my mental distress about yet another war in which thousands would die. That grief was embedded into the threads, day by day, as I wove.

Over the months as the tapestry grew on the loom, the war went on. And in their season, sunflowers returned once more to leap for the sky.

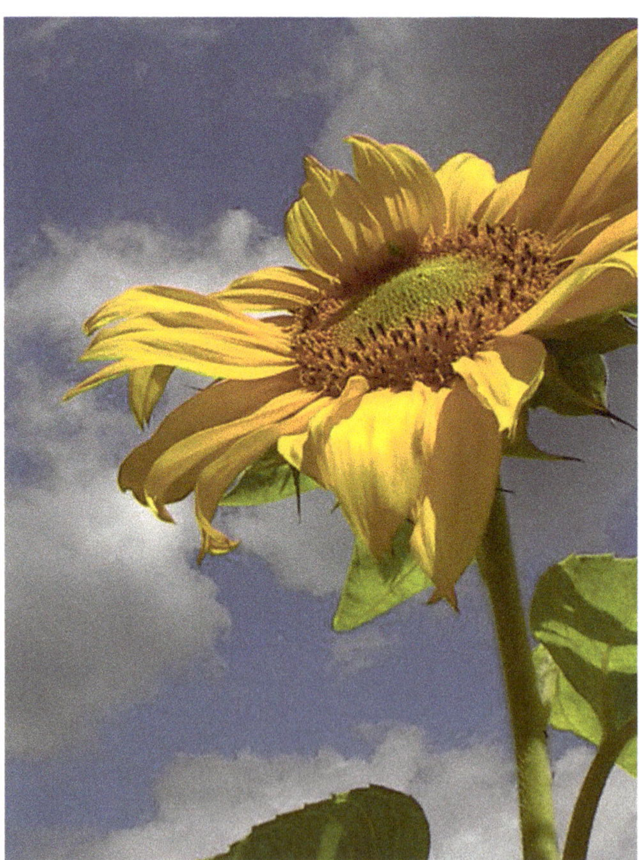

Figure 7.14
Photograph from which the tapestry *Sunflower and Sky* was designed

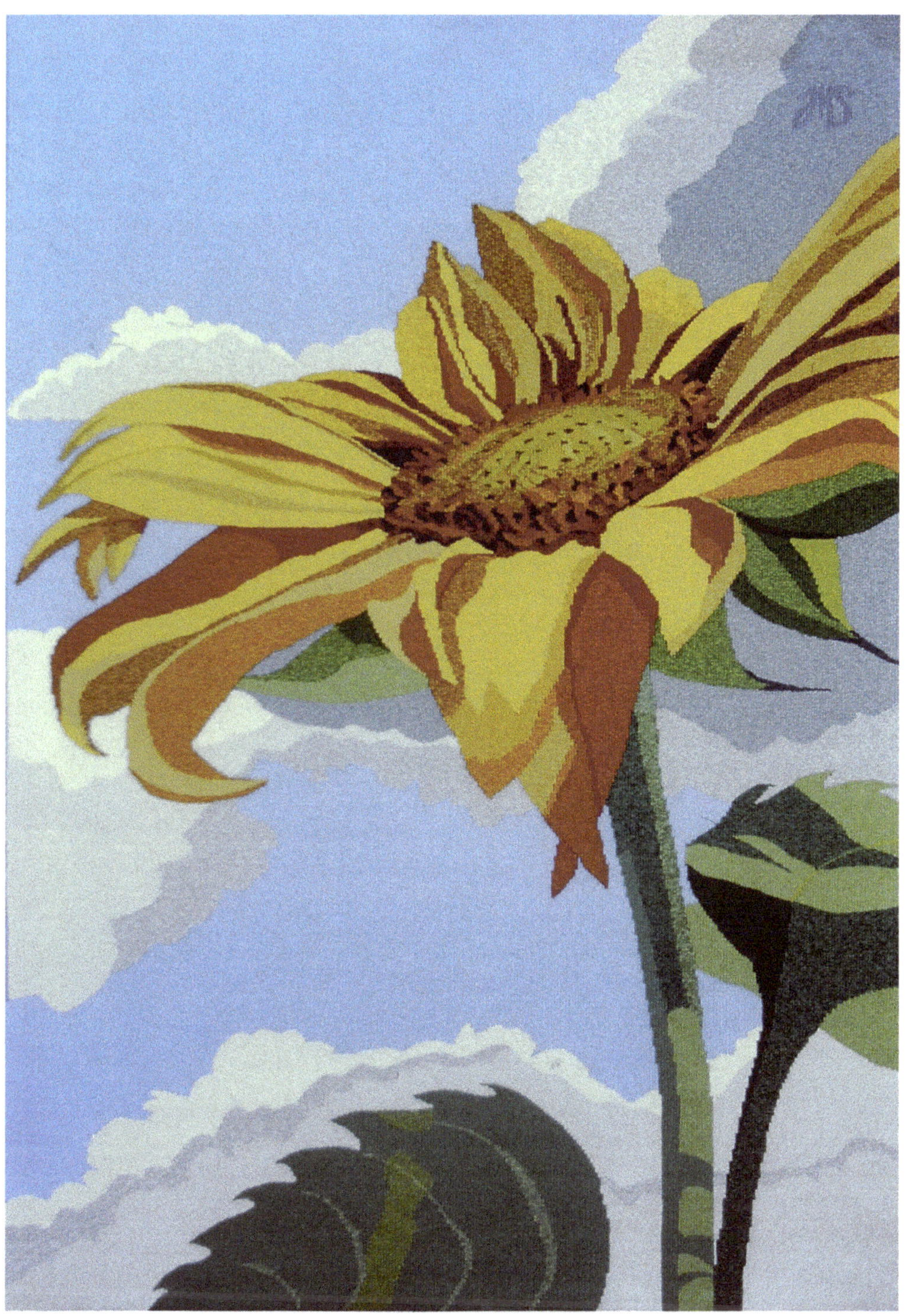

Figure 7.15
Sunflower and Sky, 38 inches by 64 inches, 2001 (photo by Paul Dunlap)

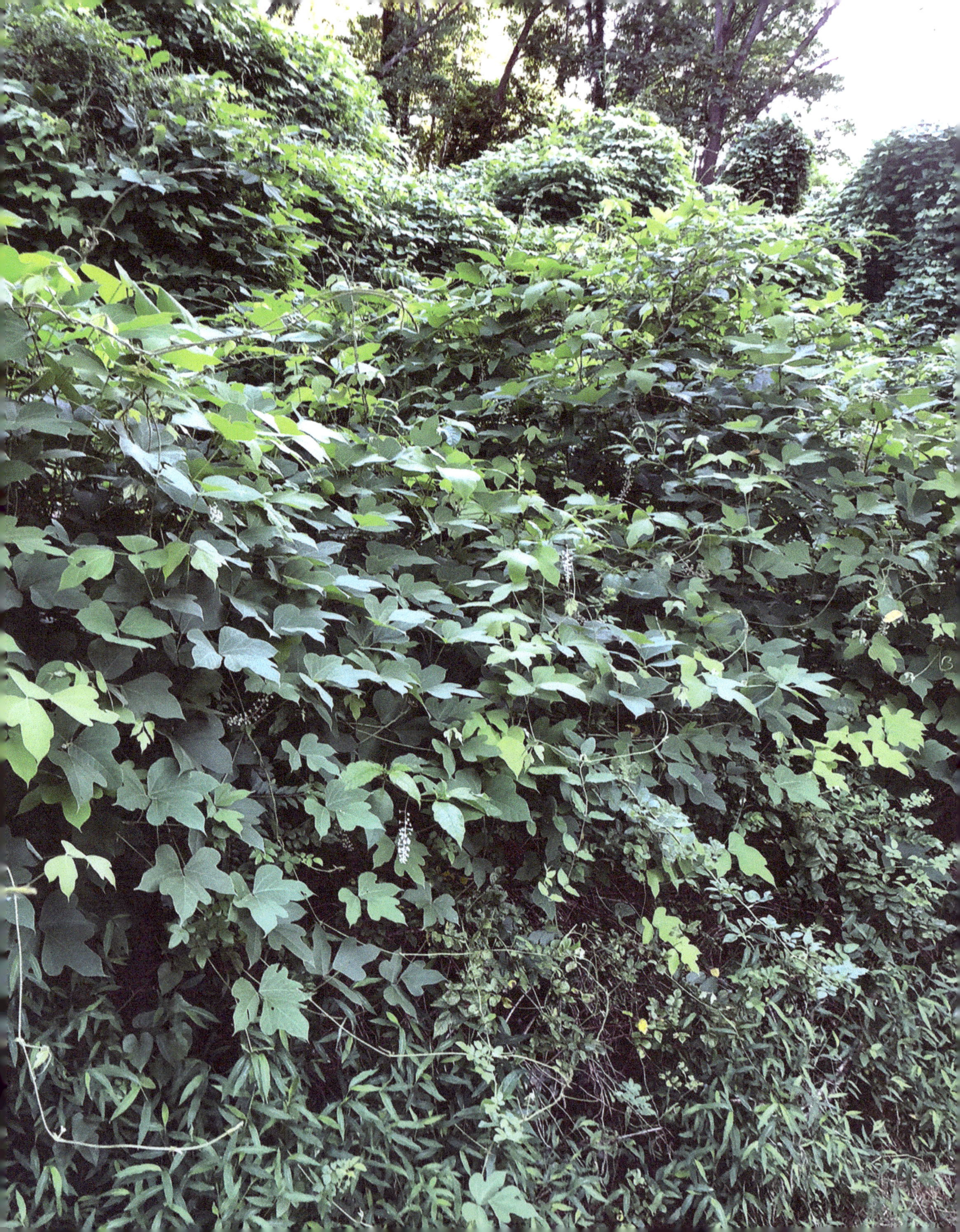

8

Kudzu: Enveloping Green

The color green has played a role in my tapestries for many years. I live surrounded by the hue because here in the north Georgia mountains, green is gloriously represented in many variations in all seasons. In the spring, there are the tender yellow-greens of young leaves appearing. Those soon turn into mature leaves exhibiting the intensity of summer's deep, rich emerald-like greens. In the fall, one finds the clear blue-green of hemlocks and other evergreens contrasting with the flame of fall color in deciduous trees. The brittle, robust deep green of holly enlivens the cold gray of winter. Mosses wax and wane in an array of greens with the effects of moisture in all seasons.

Often when I'm thinking of the beauty of the landscape found in valleys and mountains of the Southern Appalachians, my thoughts turn to examples of mankind's interventions in the natural world—many times with sad results. One instance of man's intrusion into nature was the introduction of *Pueraria montana* into the United States.[1] This is the Kudzu plant, now widely found in the South.

Kudzu was introduced to the U.S. from Japan in 1876 at the Centennial Exposition in Philadelphia, Pennsylvania. Originally touted as a solution for erosion control, Kudzu responded beyond expectations. The dense growth held back erosion, as hoped, but was soon

1 "The Growing Problem of Kudzu: An Exploration of Issues and Solutions," University of North Carolina at Chapel Hill http://kudzusolutions.web.unc.edu/

Figure 8.1 (opposite)
Kudzu in summer on South Park Street in Dahlonega

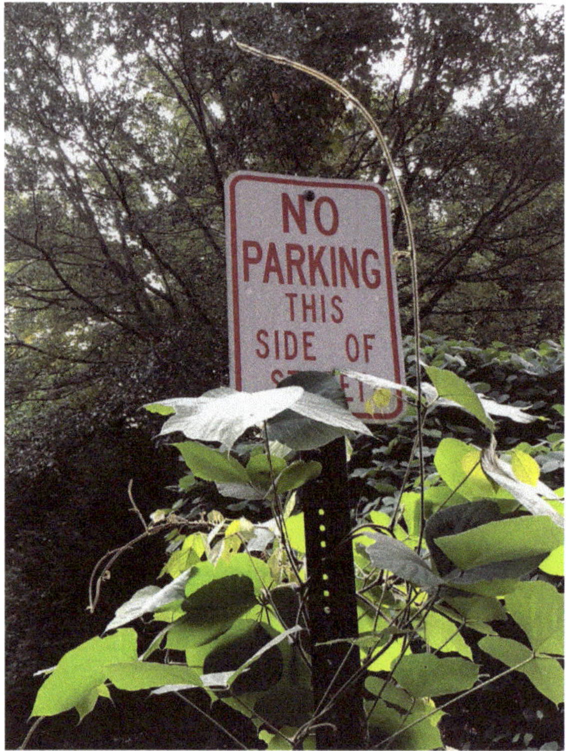

Figure 8.2
Kudzu overtaking a "No Parking" sign

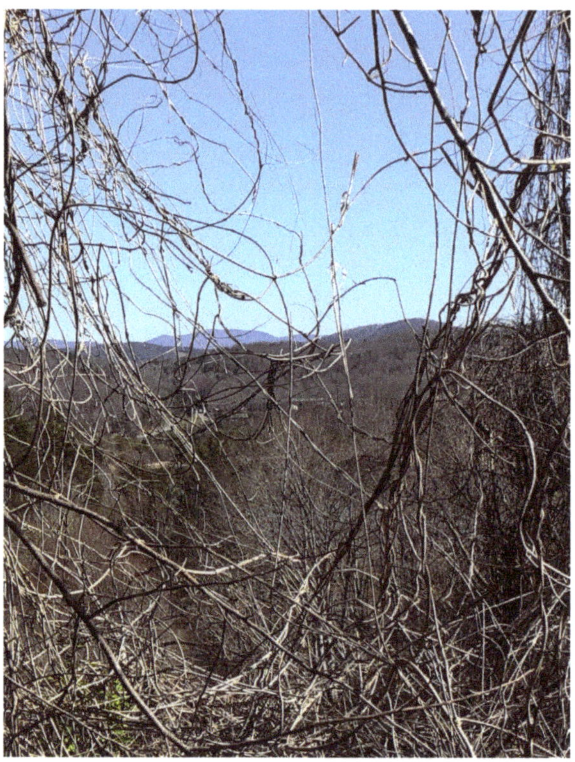

Figure 8.3
Kudzu shows a tangle of vines in the winter's dormant state

creeping over and enveloping many parts of the landscape.[2]

By the mid-twentieth century, Kudzu had spread extensively, especially throughout the Southeast where climate conditions were good and natural predators almost nonexistent. Kudzu has proven to be extremely hard to eradicate or even keep in check. Take a drive today on many roads in the Southeast in the summertime and you'll often see mounds of thick Kudzu plants that have climbed over, around, and through anything in their path. Even in its dormant state in winter the entwined vines can be impressive. In fact, I can walk just a few blocks down the street from my home near downtown Dahlonega and see trees filled with hanging vines of Kudzu. In its jumble, it creates intricate patterns of lush green leaves as it builds dense networks of vines and holds hidden secrets of beautiful flowers and seedpods.

For years, I've been fascinated with the visual effects of Kudzu, which I viewed as

2 Janet Lembke, *Despicable Species: On Cowbirds, Kudzu, Hornworms, and Other Scourges* (New York: The Lyons Press, 1999).

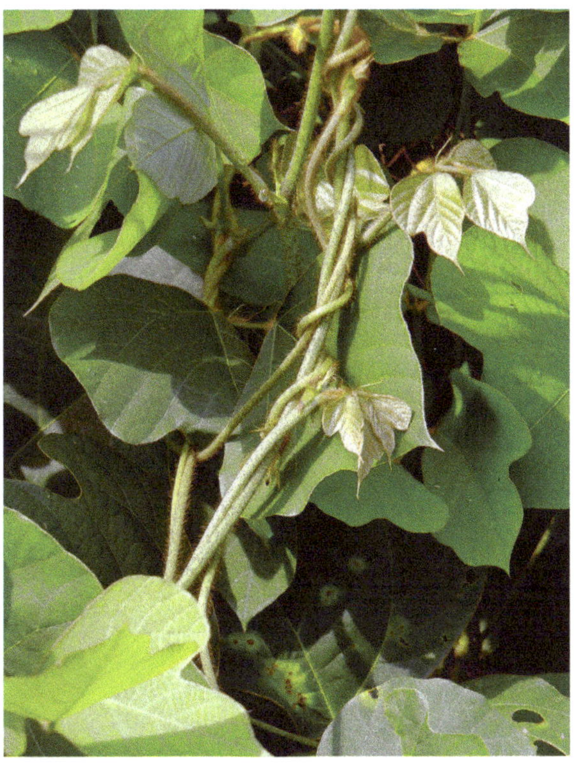

Figure 8.4
Kudzu—young leaves and vines, detail

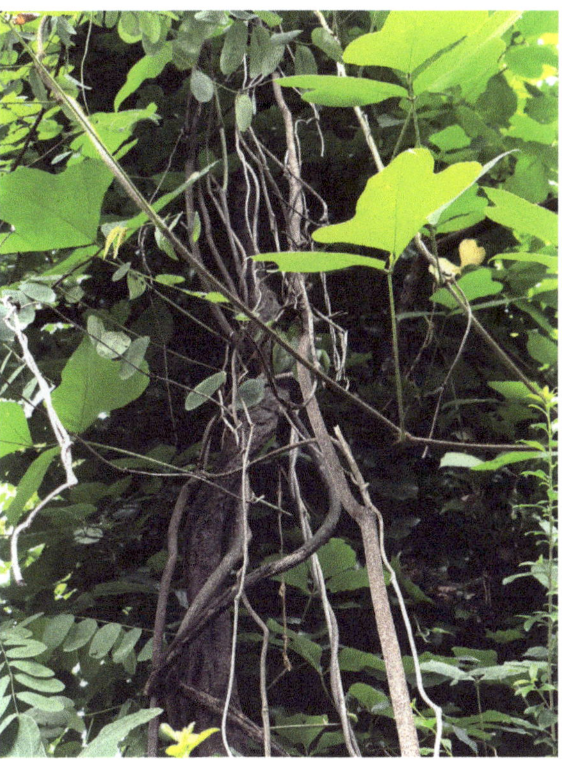

Figure 8.5
Kudzu leaves and vines, detail

nature's version of the massive sculptural fabric wrappings made by environmental artists Christo (1935–2020) and Jeanne-Claude (1935–2009).[3] A few years ago, I decided to use Kudzu as a subject for tapestry. This caused me to look more closely at the plant than I ever had before as I sought images, first by making photographs and then sketching from those. What came from the exploration were two tapestries: *Life Force* and *Kudzu: Bad Seed.*

Life Force was designed from a graphite drawing that zoomed in on a jumble of vines and leaves. With the tapestry, I wanted to illustrate the all-encompassing nature of the plant and the remarkable rapidity of growth. For the cartoon, I cropped the drawing to show an even closer view and then enlarged it to twenty-four inches high by sixty inches wide. At that scale, the close-up view, woven in a limited palette of greens and grays, gave the viewer a feeling of being tangled up in the foliage.

3 In Christo and Jeanne-Claude's 1968–1969 work, *Wrapped Coast*, one million square feet at Little Bay, Sydney, Australia, was wrapped with erosion-control fabric: https://christojeanneclaude.net/projects/wrapped-coast

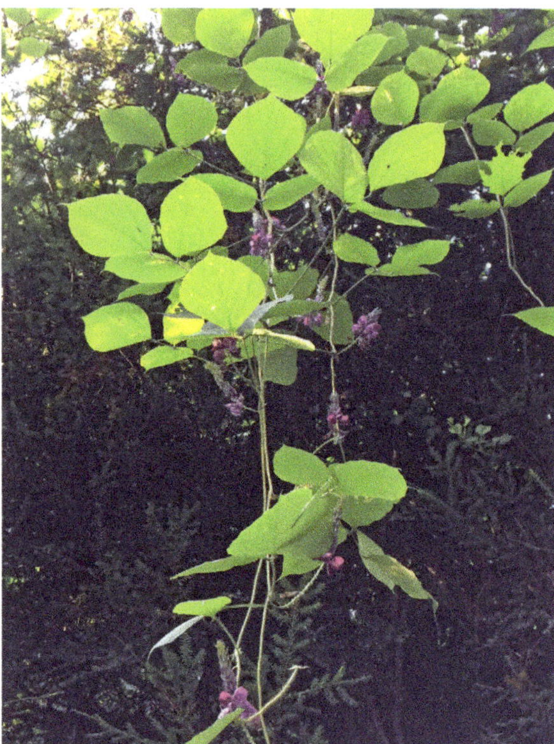

Figure 8.6
Kudzu vine and flowers

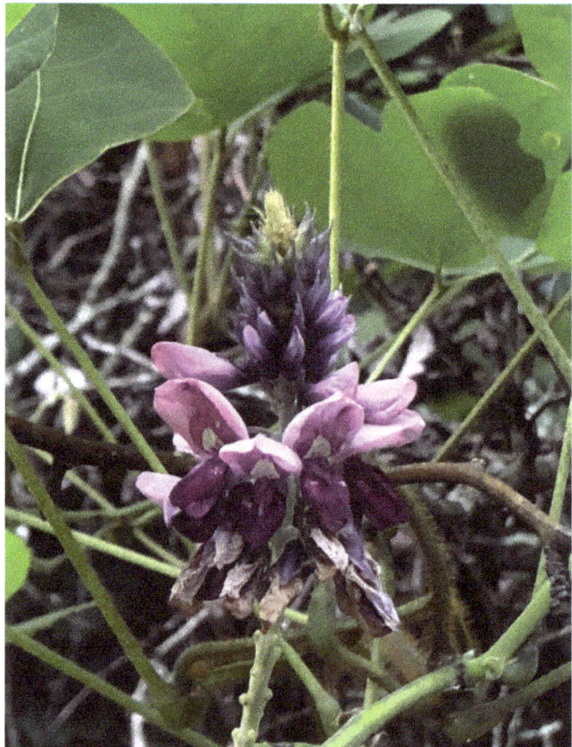

Figure 8.7
Kudzu flower, detail

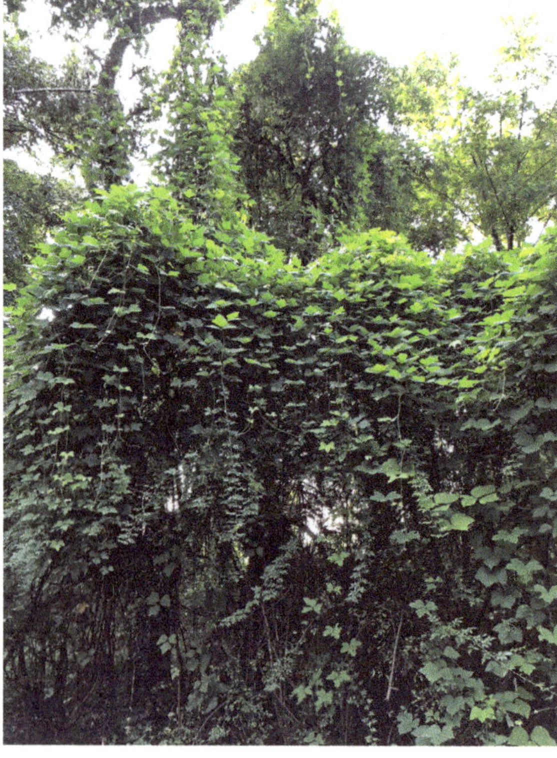

Figure 8.8
Hanging masses of Kudzu vines covered with leaves resemble environmental wrappings by artists Christo and Jeanne-Claude.

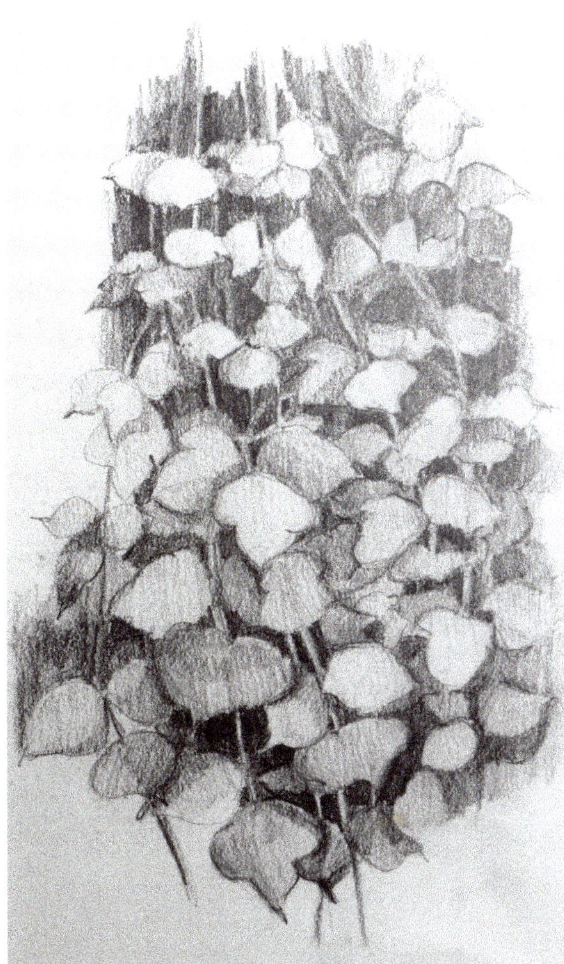

Figure 8.9
Kudzu, drawing of mass of leaves, graphite
(photo by Christopher Dant)

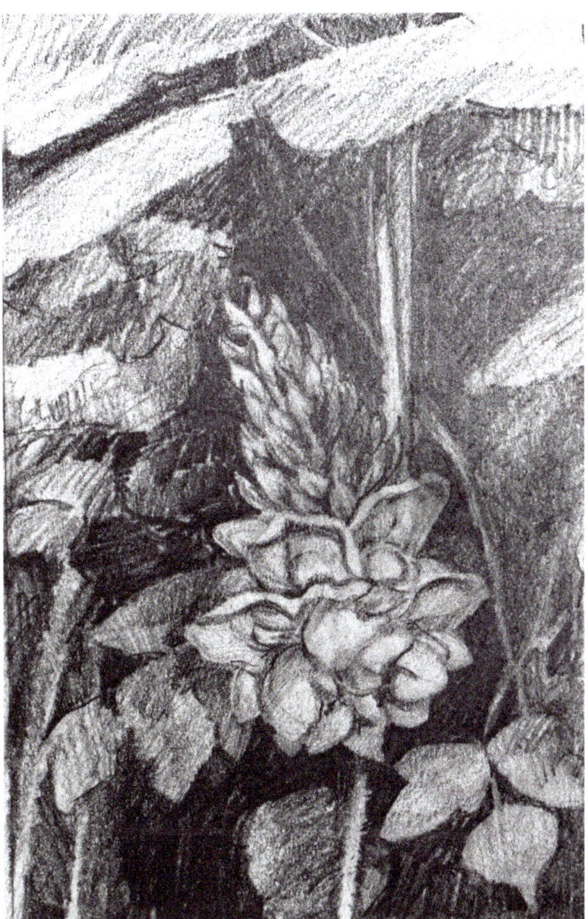

Figure 8.10
Kudzu, drawing of flower, graphite
(photo by Christopher Dant)

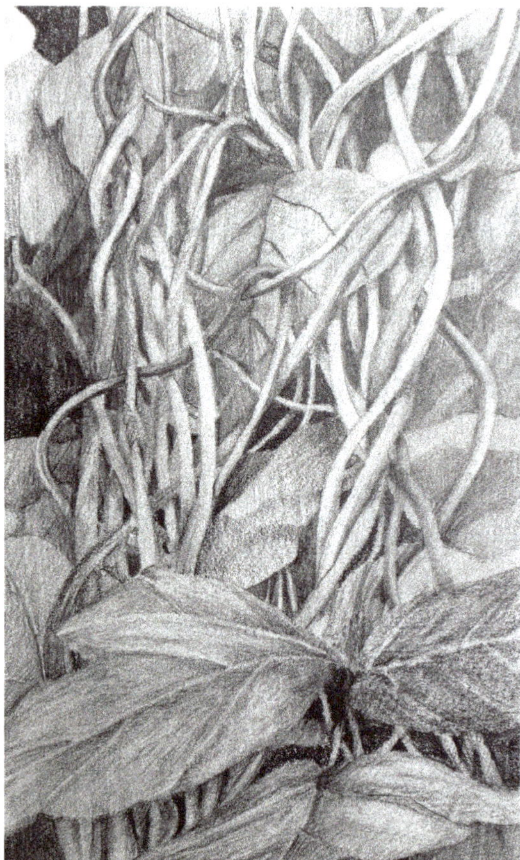

Figure 8.11 (left)
Kudzu, drawing of vines and leaves, graphite. A detail of this became the design source for the tapestry *Life Force*. (photo by Christopher Dant)

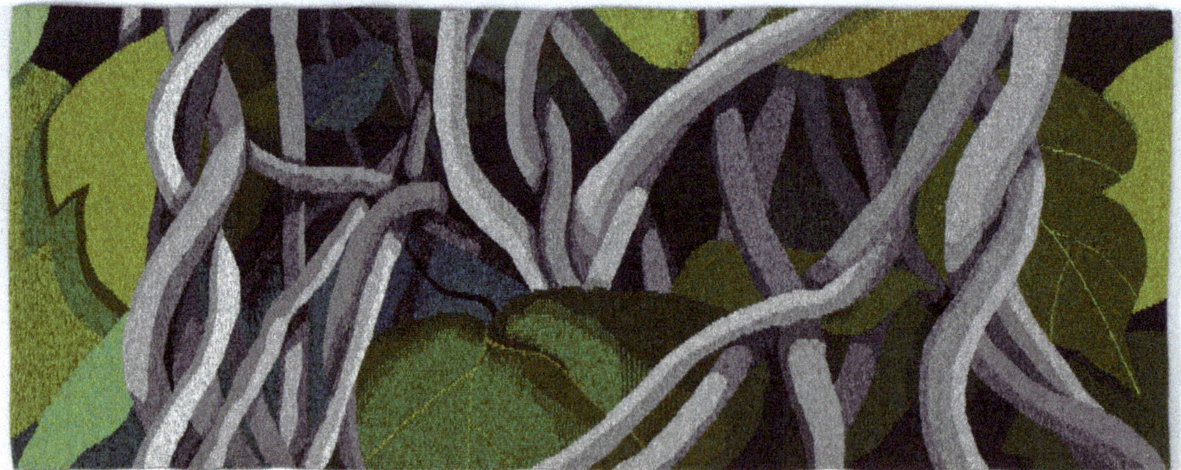

Figure 8.12
Life Force, 24 inches by 60 inches, 2010 (photo by Tim Barnwell)

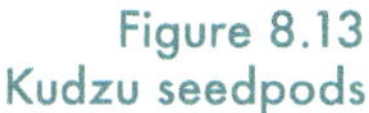
Figure 8.13
Kudzu seedpods

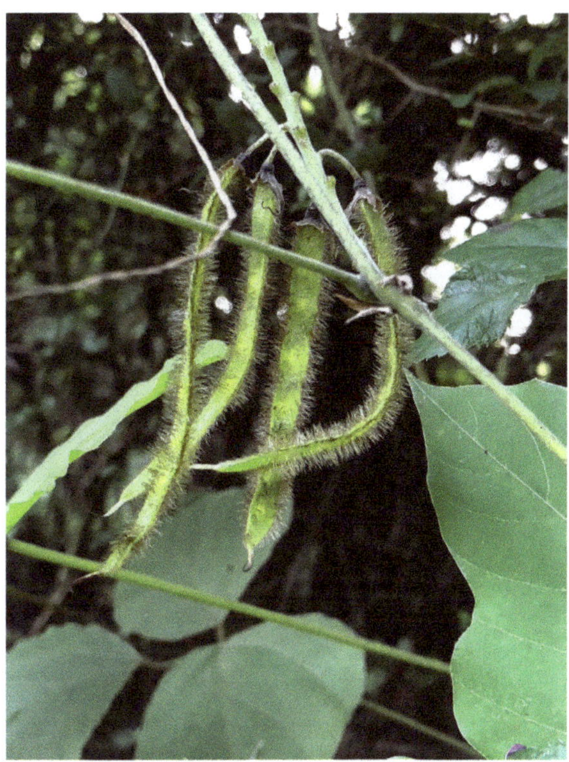

A second tapestry, *Kudzu: Bad Seed,* was about another aspect of the plant. Although Kudzu primarily propagates through runners from the roots, it does produce seeds. Those are found in the seedpods that develop from the delicate sweet-scented purple flowers found amongst the leaf-filled vines. They are just a few inches in length and tucked up into the larger leaves, making them hard to spot unless you're looking closely. In the tapestry, the seedpods became a dominant feature. Leaves were symbolized by a background pattern of repeating diamond shapes woven in many different greens. Those represented a few of the thousands of leaves that Kudzu displays in summer. The title was chosen to acknowledge the way the invasive plant is now regarded throughout the South.

I know that I've just scratched the surface of design potential with this ubiquitous plant in these two tapestries. Much more about Kudzu, including amazing photographs as well as a documentary film, is noted at several websites.[4]

4 Max Shores, film maker and professor, http://maxshores.com/the-amazing-story-of-kudzu/ and his 1996 documentary: https://www.youtube.com/watch?time_continue=17&v=BoAetCE_vmY

Jack Anthony has a gallery of kudzu photographs he's taken through the years: http://www.landscapesbyjack.com/Photography/Kudzu/

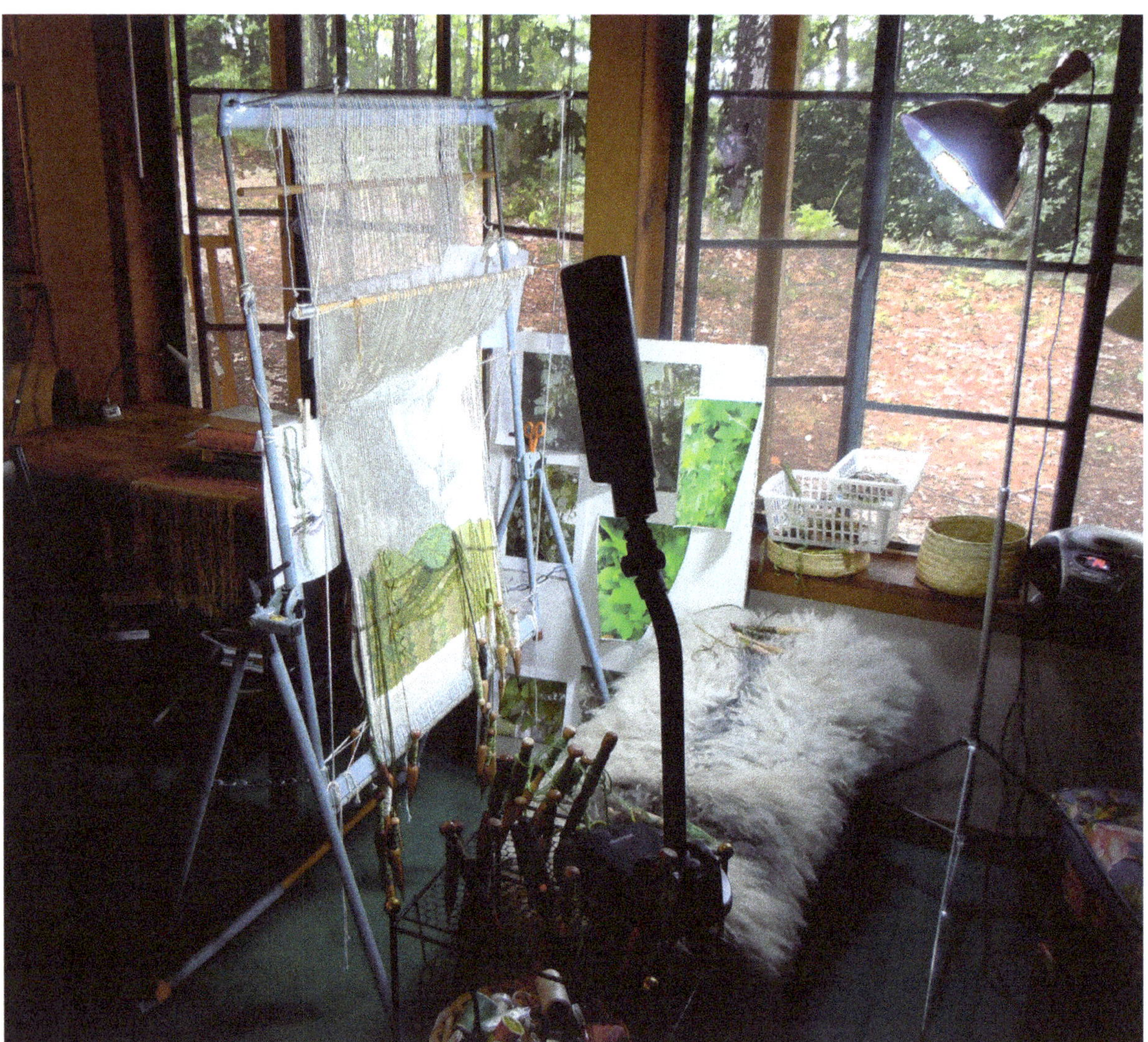

Figure 8.14
The tapestry *Bad Seed* was woven on a portable frame loom. I worked on it while at an artist residency at the Lillian Smith Center in 2010.

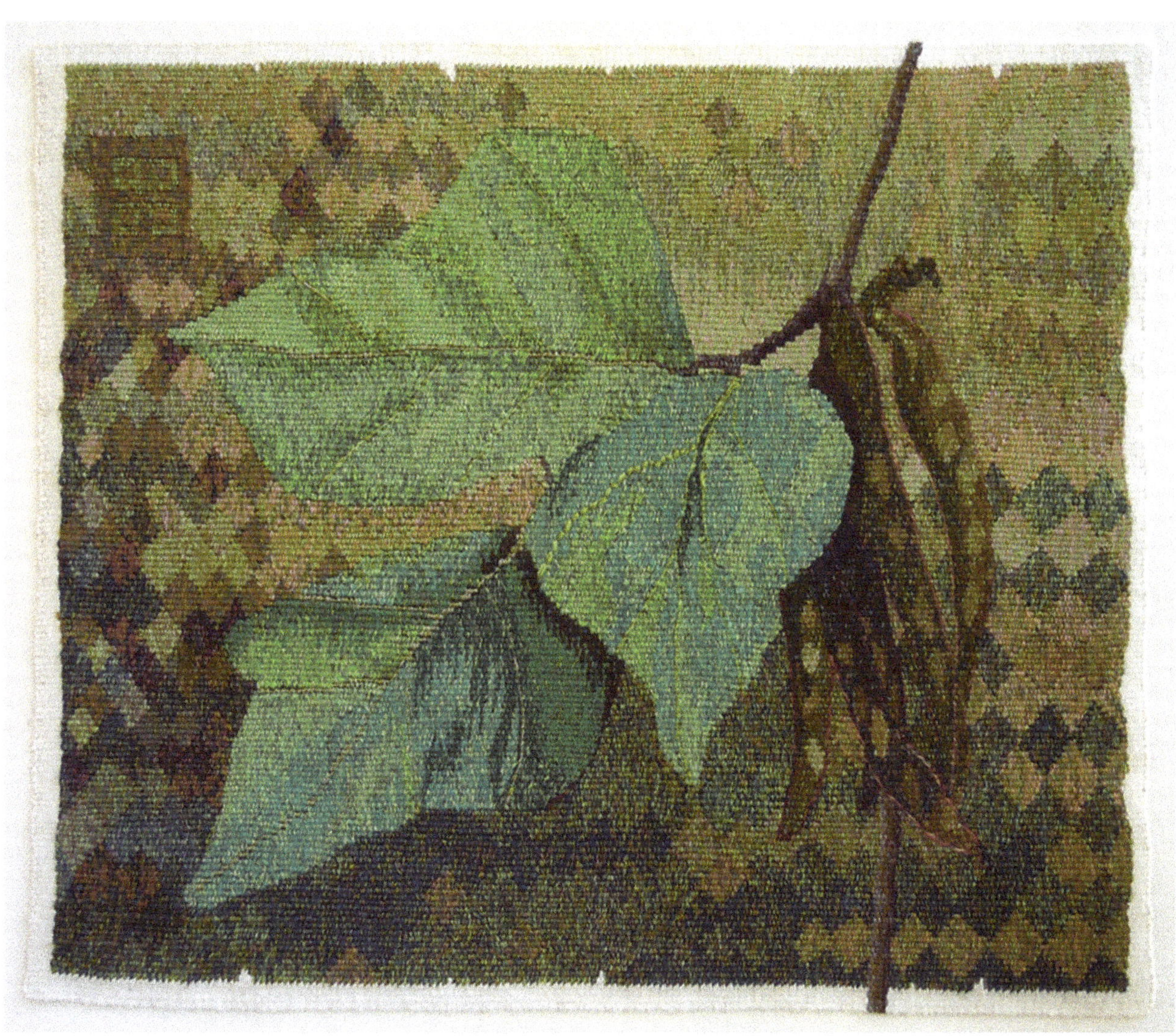

Figure 8.15
Kudzu: Bad Seed, 16 inches by 18 inches, 2010

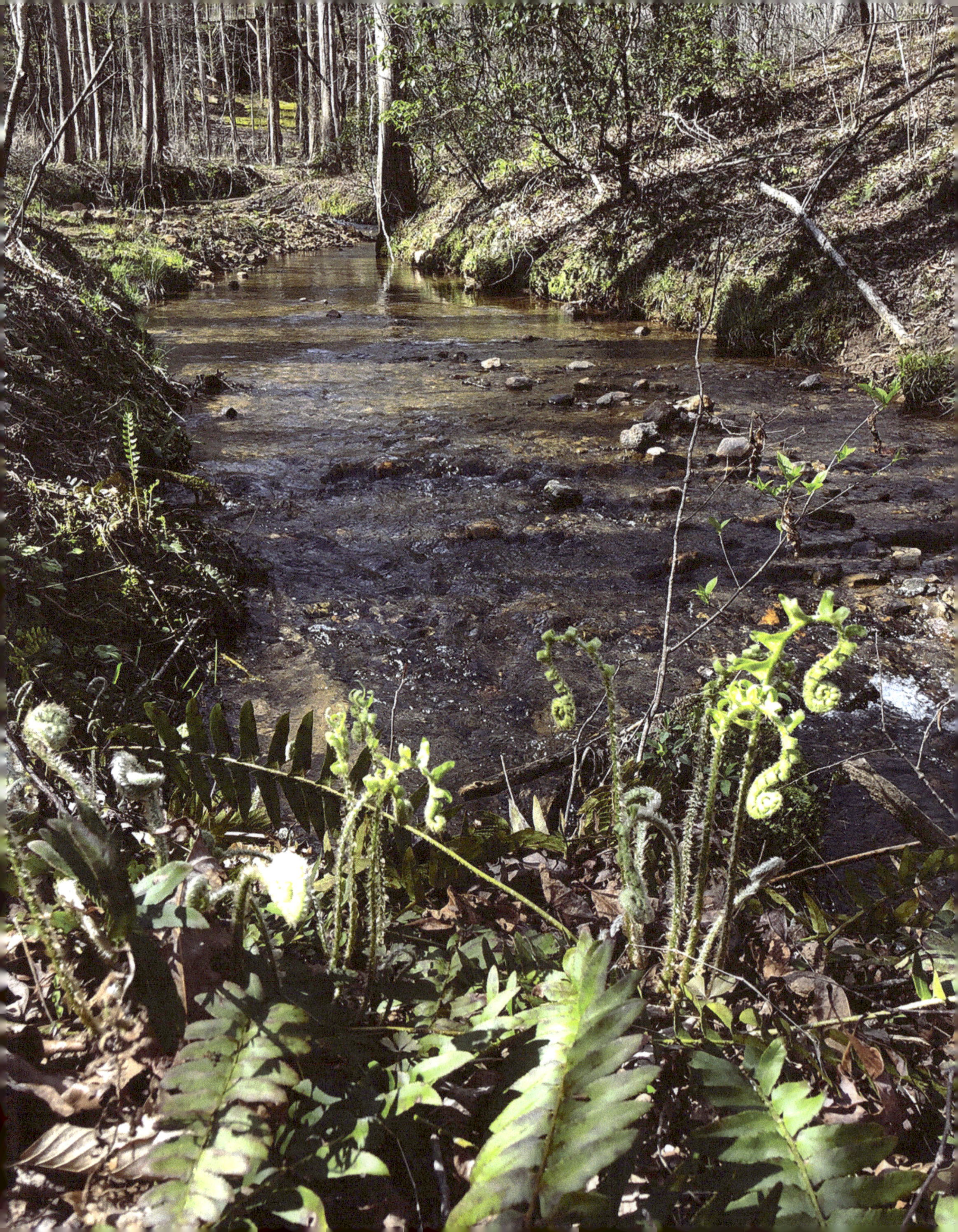

9
Spirals

In the springtime a few years ago, my husband and I were staying at our getaway in the woods. One morning, I decided to walk along the edge of the nearby creek, and on the way, there I noticed a tiny spiraling green form that had emerged from the leaf litter. When I stopped to take a closer look, I suddenly realized it was a fiddlehead, the young furled fern frond, coming up. As I looked around, I saw that there were hundreds of fiddleheads almost carpeting the forest floor as they pushed their way through the dead leaves from the past season.

Why hadn't I spotted those before? I've been out in the woods many times, but I'd never noticed the renewal of ferns as they emerged as fiddleheads. I was entranced and wanted to design a tapestry to record my "discovery" of this tiny miracle of life. Immediately, I started taking photos and soon was back in the woods with sketchbook and pencils.

Over the next weeks, I continued to visit the fiddleheads to see how they grew larger and unfolded. I made many visual studies and searched for information to identify the fern. Based on the appearance of the mature plant, it seemed to be *Polystichum acrostichoides* or Christmas fern.[1]

I read more about ferns and then about spirals. The differences between the Archimedean spiral and an equiangular or logarithmic spiral were described in Priya Hemenway's (b. 1982)

1 David B. Lellinger, *A Field Manual of the Ferns and Fern-Allies of the United States and Canada* (Washington, D.C.: Smithsonian Institution Press, 1985), 274.

Figure 9.1 (opposite)
View of the creek with fiddleheads along the bank

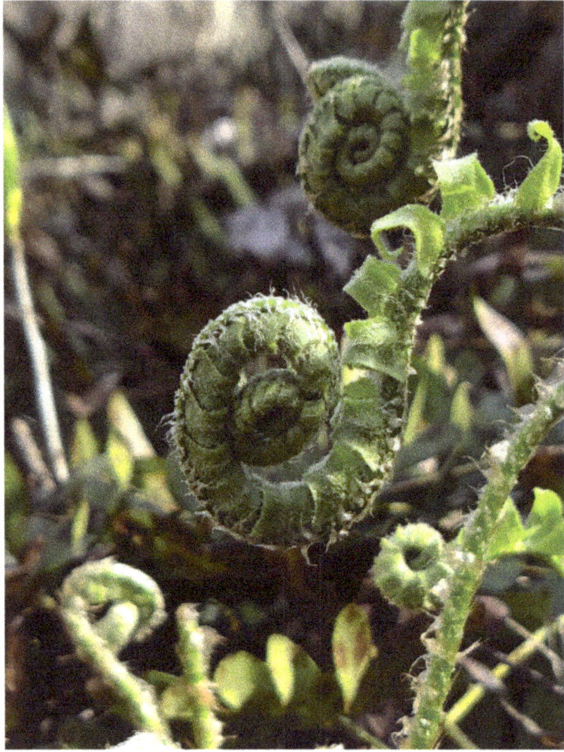

Figure 9.2
Fiddlehead, detail

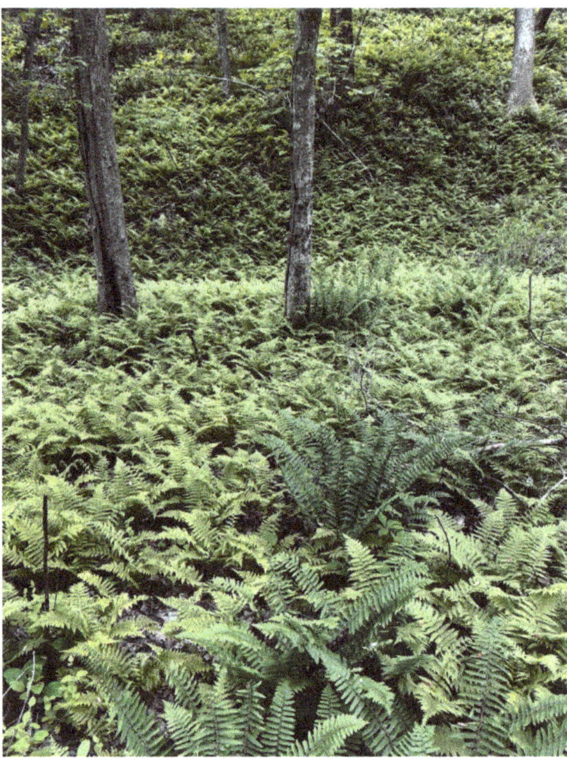

Figure 9.3
Mature ferns carpeting the forest floor beside the creek

book, *Divine Proportion: Phi, in Art, Nature, and Science* (2005). She noted that the Archimedean spiral is one in which the distances between the arms of the curve are constant. In the logarithmic spiral, the distances increase in geometric progression. The spirals of the fiddleheads are of the latter type, one also known as the "spira mirabilis" or the growth spiral.[2]

I discovered that "pteridomania," or fern fever, was a craze for ferns that swept through the British Empire and even into America in the mid-to-late 1800s. During that time, ferns were widely collected, and images of ferns in all stages of growth were popular motifs in decorative art.[3] I began to immerse myself in a visual exploration of fiddleheads as I made many studies before my tapestry design was finally completed. It seems I must have also had a touch of fern fever during my time of fascination with fiddleheads.

It was many months before I finally

2 Priya Hemenway, *Divine Proportion: (Phi) In Art, Nature, and Science* (New York: Sterling Publishing Co., 2005), 127–132.

3 Sarah Whittingham, *Fern Fever: The Story of Pteridomania* (London: Frances Lincoln Limited, 2012), 35. In America it was described as "fern mania."

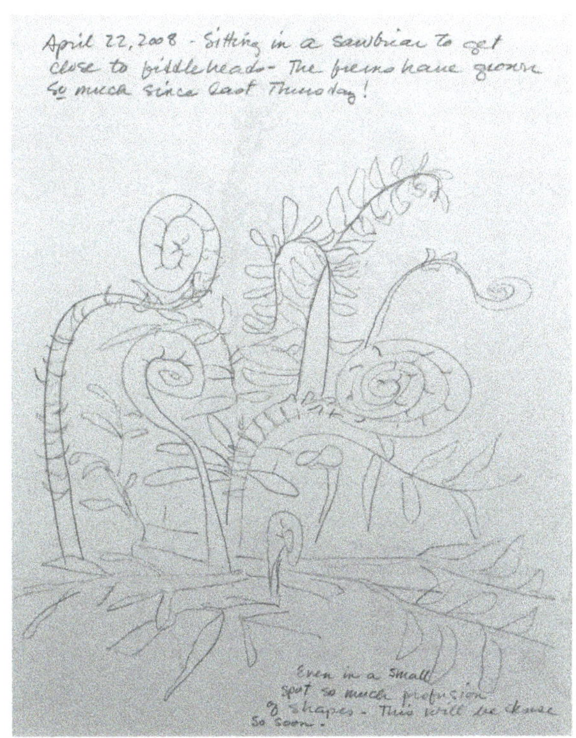

Figure 9.4
Fiddlehead sketches made soon after making the discovery of this emergence of new life. (photo by Christopher Dant)

decided upon a design for a tapestry based on the fiddleheads. Little did I know as I began the tapestry that my fascination with the tiny spiraling form discovered on that springtime walk would be one that would fuel my design ideas for five tapestries made in the next several years.

Spring Profusion, woven in 2008, was the first of those that came from my fiddlehead obsession. The title encapsulated my feelings about coming upon that first fiddlehead and suddenly becoming aware of all the others surrounding it. The fiddlehead studies also resulted in the tapestries *Once Upon a Time, Gray Dawn, Fiddleheads Return,* and *The Greening.*

Once Upon a Time began with the session of very quick gesture drawings I mentioned earlier, the ones done with soft vine charcoal and a timer set for sixty seconds along with fiddlehead photos as reference. Those quick drawings were scanned and printed in several copies so I could make variations of value changes from black through grays using a pencil, a tool that wouldn't smudge like the charcoal.

I selected one from the group of reworked drawings to design a tapestry using only black, white, and tones of gray yarns. Before I left the studio on the first day of working

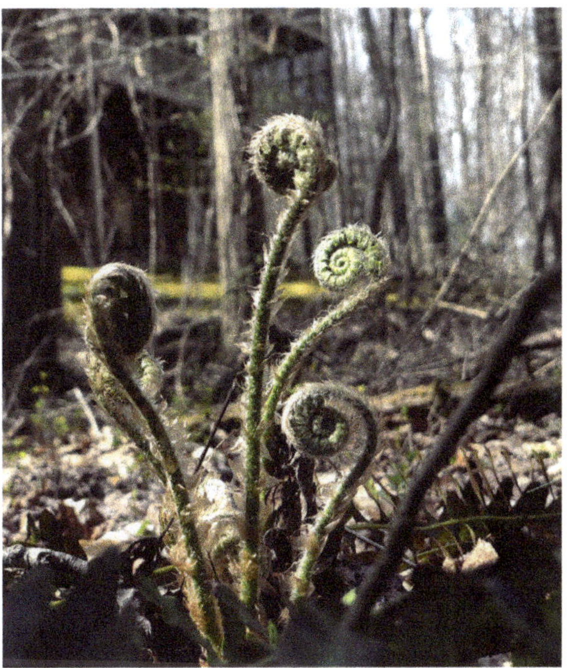

Figure 9.5
Fiddleheads and the creek house in the background

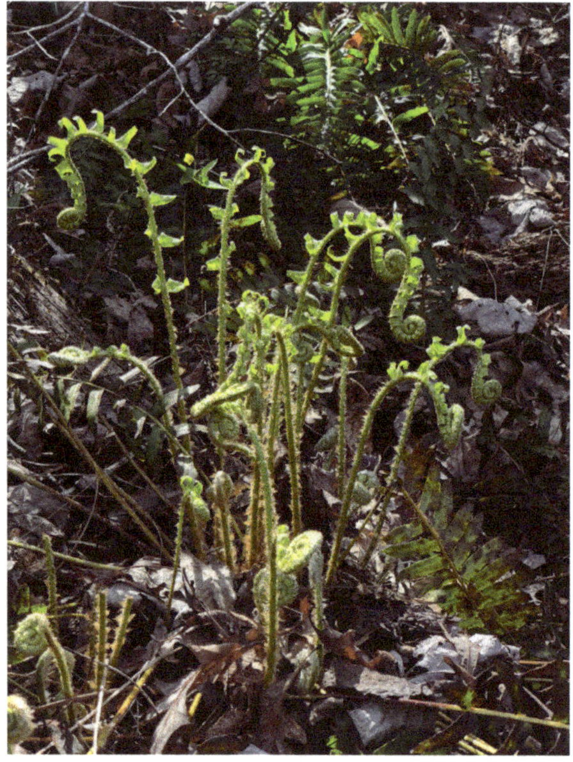

Figure 9.6
More fiddleheads—it's hard to stop photographing them.

on the new tapestry, I happened to notice the irregular contour of the top edge. The upper portion of weaving was flowing and organic, as were the shapes within the cartoon. Taking those few moments to look and think about what had happened at the loom that day motivated me to try something I'd considered before but had never gotten around to doing. Why not mark each day's weaving progress in an obvious way as a small reminder of a bit of time, contained forever within the tapestry?

To carry out the idea, the next day I placed a single pick of red-orange weft yarn across the top of the previously-woven area. Then I continued weaving. On each day afterwards, before the next session of weaving, I placed a pick of the red-orange yarn across the contour at the top of the woven web.

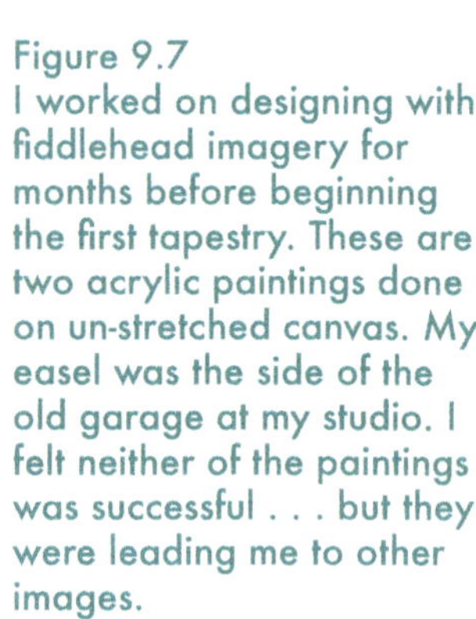

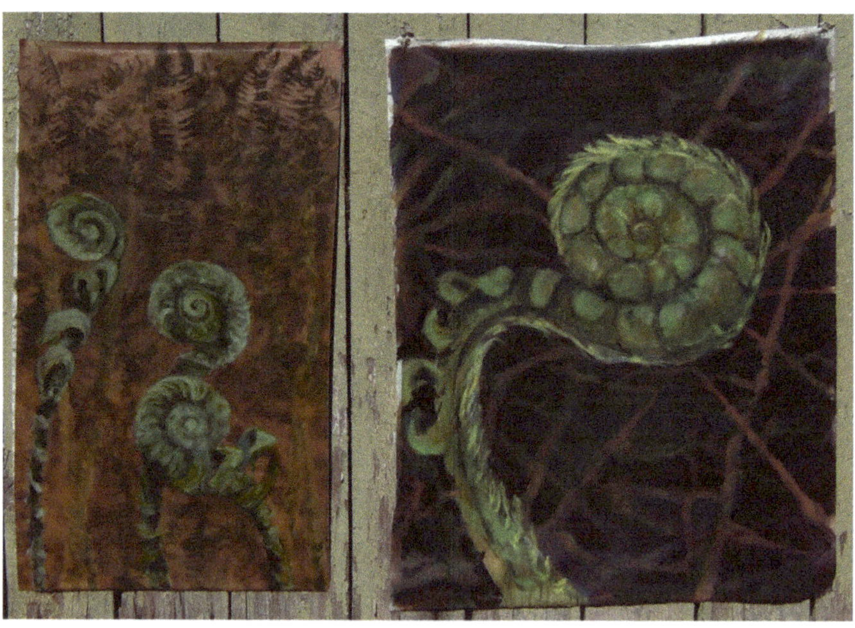

Figure 9.7
I worked on designing with fiddlehead imagery for months before beginning the first tapestry. These are two acrylic paintings done on un-stretched canvas. My easel was the side of the old garage at my studio. I felt neither of the paintings was successful . . . but they were leading me to other images.

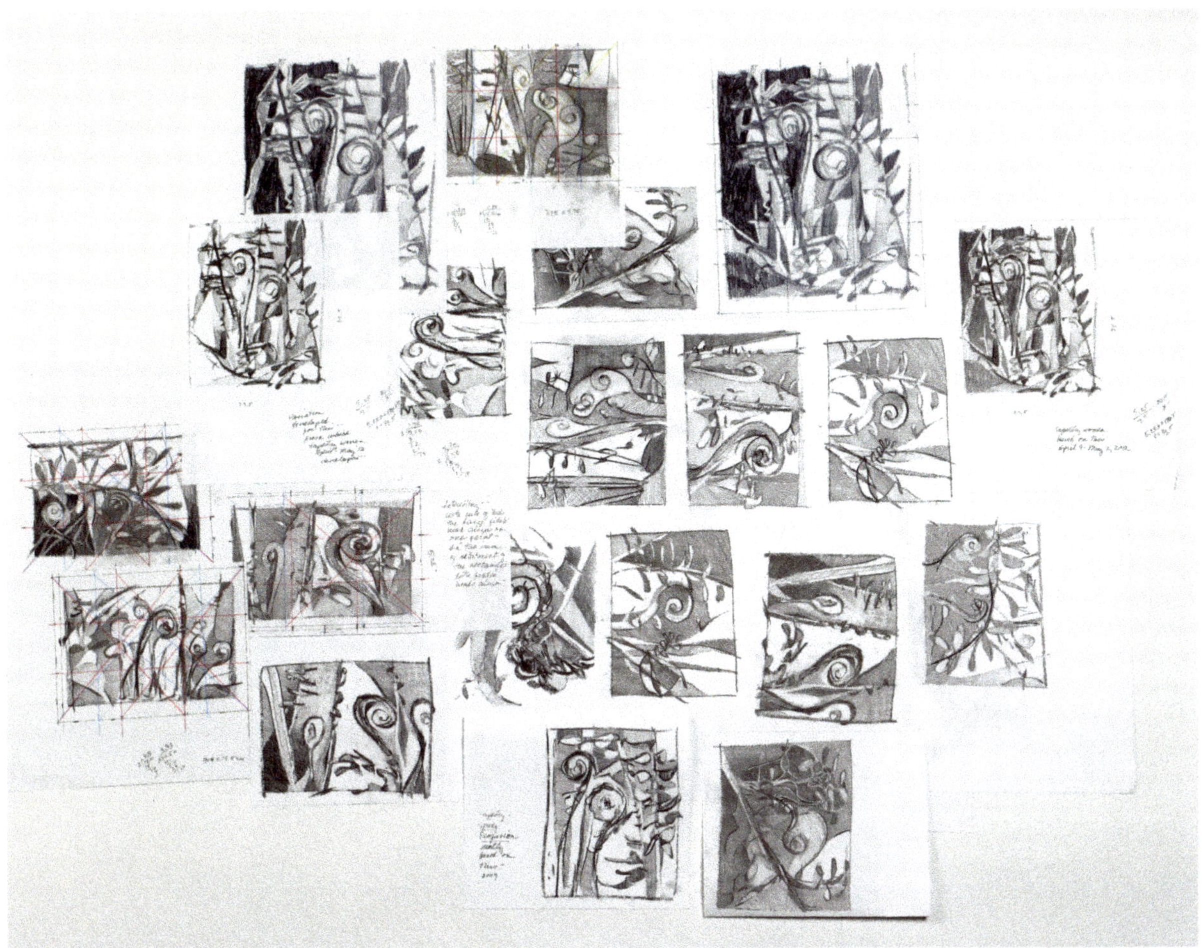

Figure 9.8
Value studies done from scans made of earlier gesture drawings. Those were shown in Figure 5.7. (photo by Christopher Dant)

In the finished piece, the thin red-orange lines run irregularly across the width of the tapestry at intervals of a few inches apart. Those lines remain as constant reminders of a thought I'd had, once upon a time, to try something different and to finally do it.

The tapestry *Gray Dawn* was also woven in an achromatic palette and was planned for a 2012 themed exhibit, organized by the Southern Highland Craft Guild, called *Black & White 3*. I was still captivated by the visual possibilities of the spiraling fiddleheads and decided to continue exploring the theme. For the new design, I chose a few of my photographs to work from as the basis for a 42-inch square painting. Spirals of fiddleheads, as well as vines and leaves in tones of gray and deep black, filled the work.

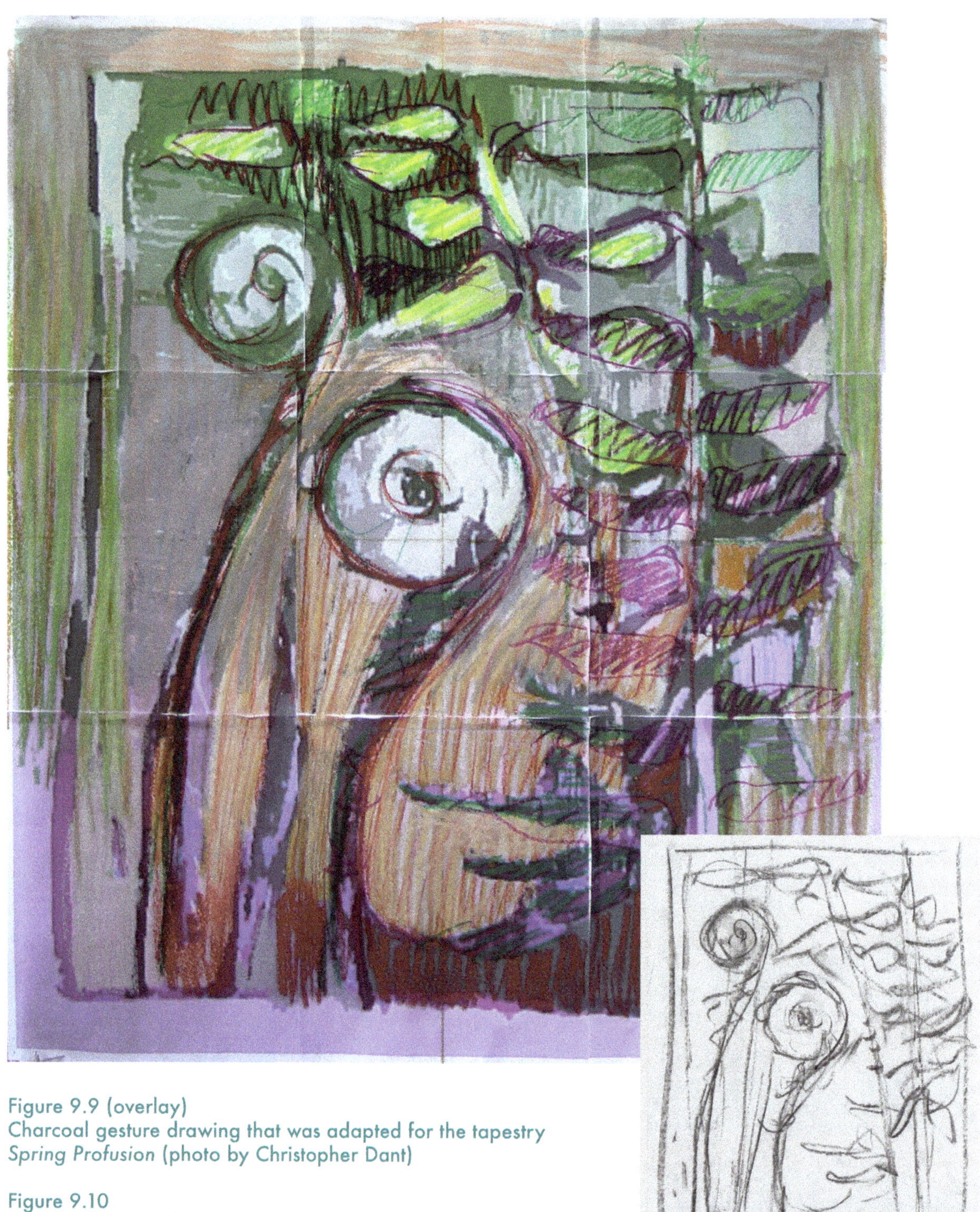

Figure 9.9 (overlay)
Charcoal gesture drawing that was adapted for the tapestry *Spring Profusion* (photo by Christopher Dant)

Figure 9.10
Cartoon from which *Spring Profusion* was woven (photo by Christopher Dant)

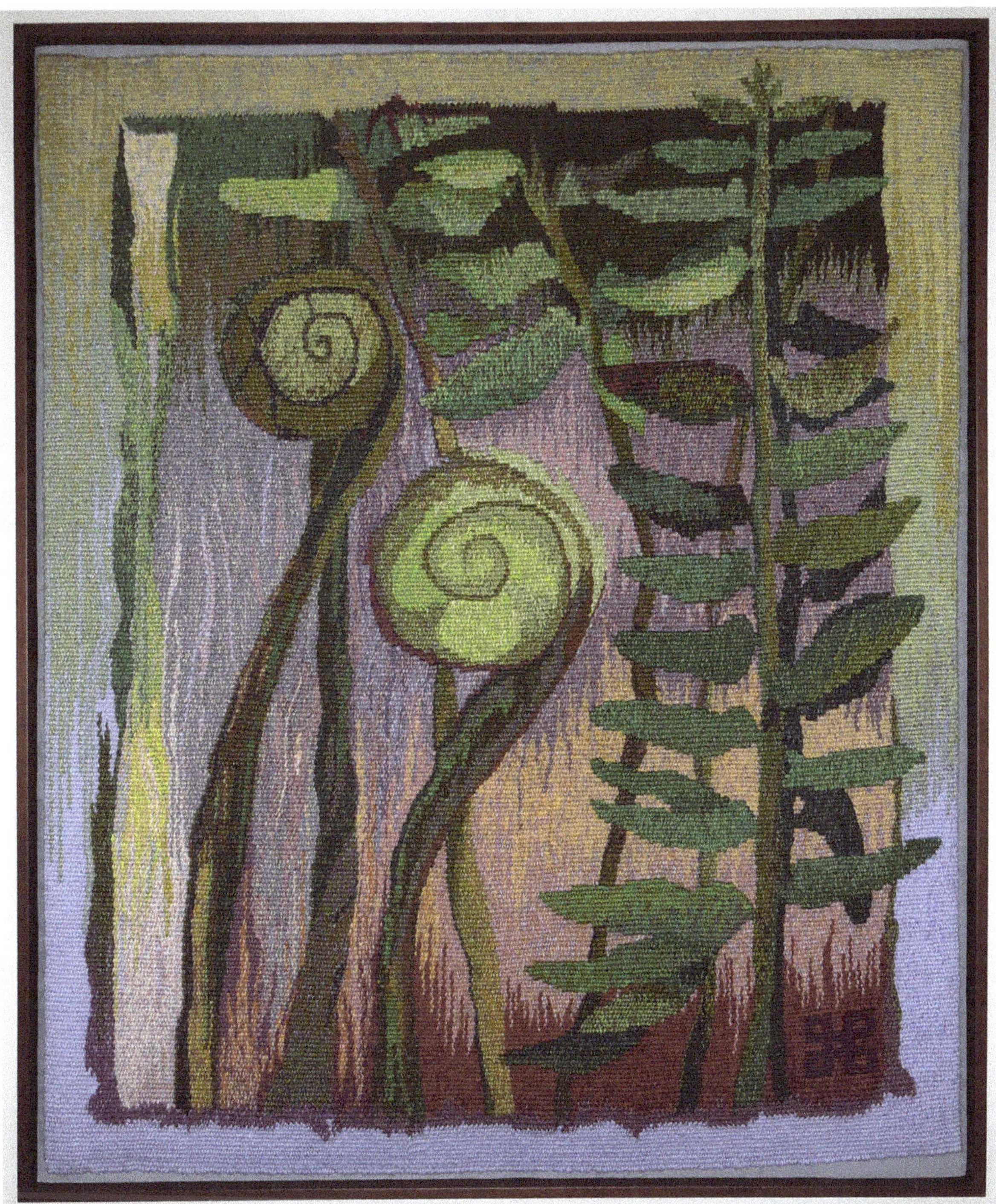

Figure 9.11
Spring Profusion, 31 inches by 25 inches, 2008

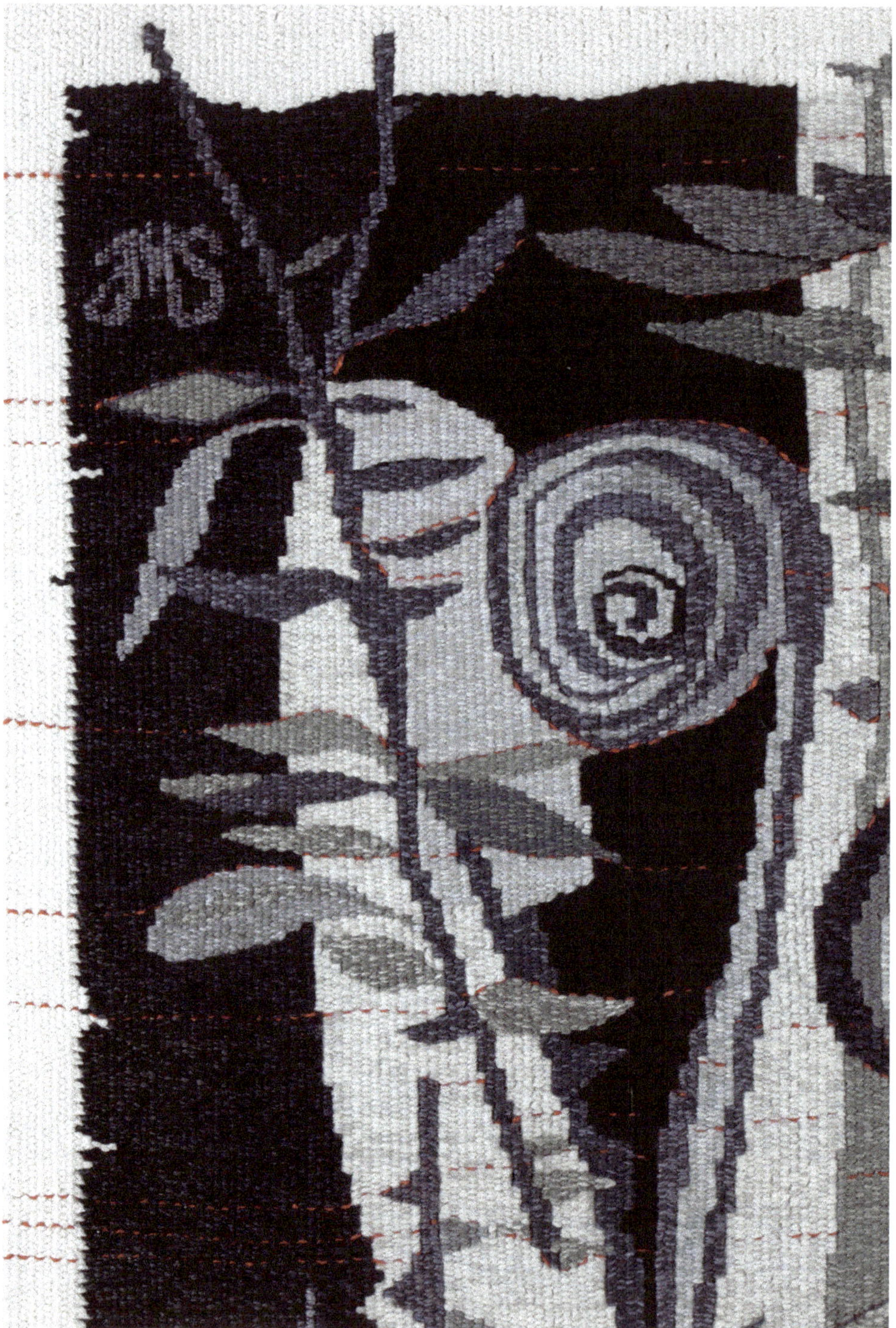

Figure 9.12
Once Upon a Time, detail (photo by Tim Barnwell)

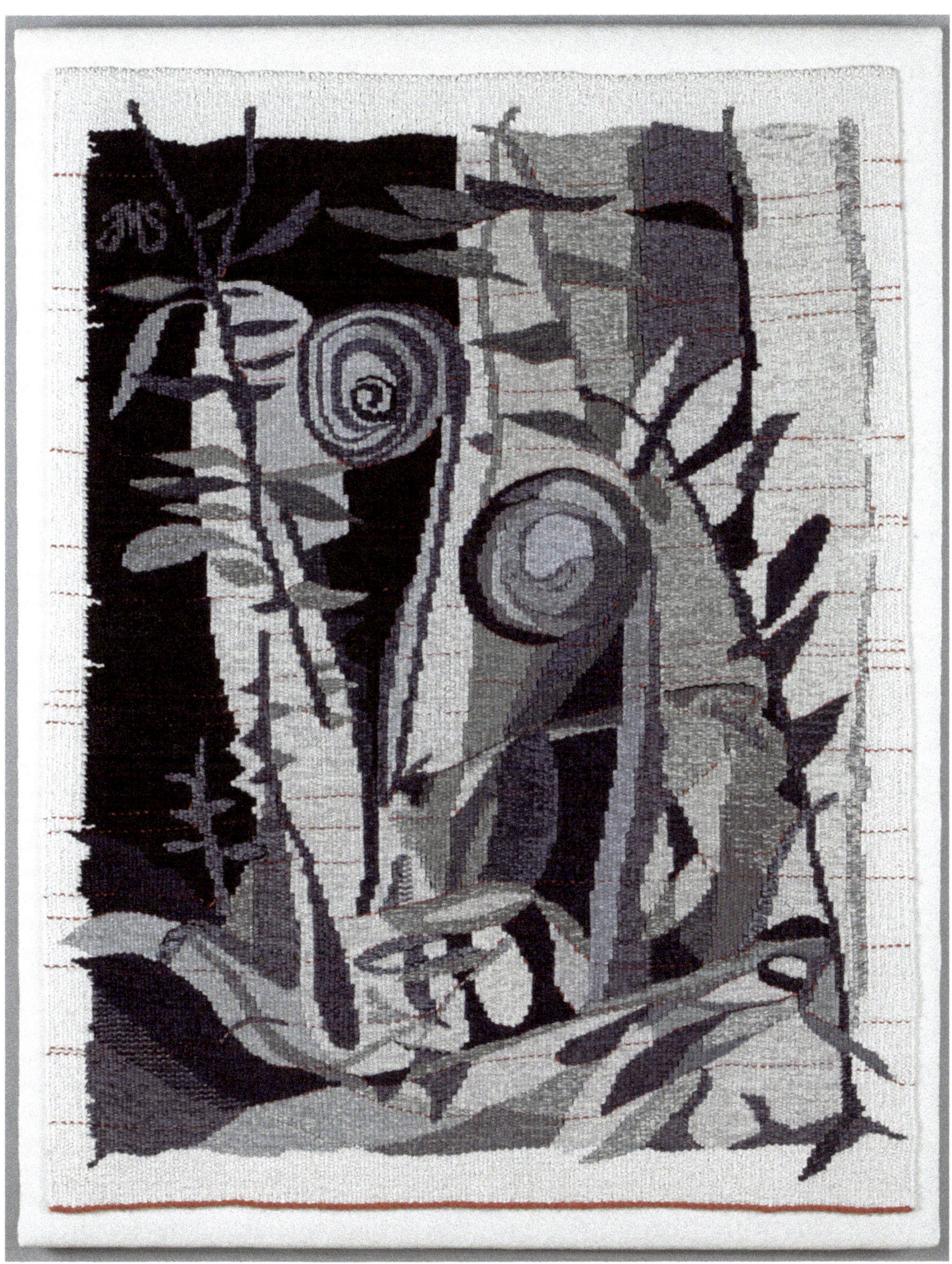

Figure 9.13
Once Upon a Time, 32 inches by 24 inches, 2012 (photo by Tim Barnwell)

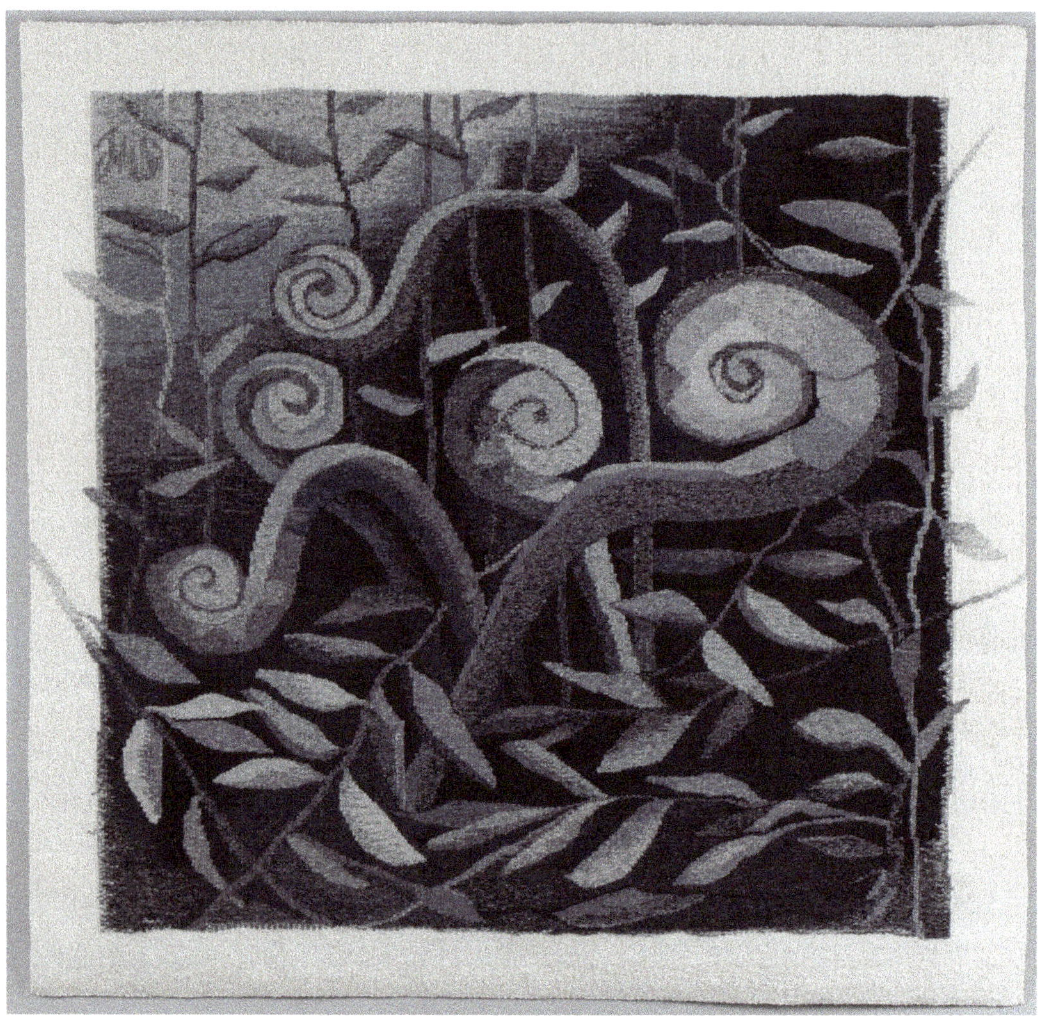

Figure 9.14
Gray Dawn, 42 inches by 42 inches, 2012 (photo by Tim Barnwell)

In the background, the upper left side was lighter in value—almost like the glow in the sky just at daybreak.

As I wove, the fact that I was rendering the vital yellow-greens of the emerging fiddleheads in a color scheme devoid of color seemed paradoxical. In the painting, not only were the ferns and other foliage gray but so also was the sky. The glow at the upper left became even more evocative as I thought about the reality that our world might indeed someday face mornings of only gray dawns if the pollution of our atmosphere continues. That feeling remained with me as I wove and the title *Gray Dawn* came from that.

Fiddleheads Return was a small study for a larger piece I was designing for a commission. After working out the basics of the composition on paper using graphite and paint, I selected a small portion of the design to weave as a sample to explore the colors of yarn to use.

Pleased with results of the small study, I finalized the larger design, made the cartoon, set up the loom, and prepared to weave. Then I got the news that the client was declining the piece. At first, I was disappointed. After all, I'd spent several months of research on the commission, including planning the larger cartoon and then weaving the smaller study. But in the end I felt strongly enough about the image to weave the tapestry, whether it would be sold to someone or not.

The composition was sixty inches wide and only sixteen inches high and had been designed to fit the area in which the potential client wanted to use the tapestry. The proportion of the layout wasn't something I'd used before. It was a new way of thinking about the design space and, as it turns out, I've since used a wide and narrow format for several other tapestries.

As with *Spring Profusion* and *Gray Dawn,* titles sometimes come from thoughts that emerge while a tapestry is being woven. That was the case with the last tapestry of the fiddlehead series. I called it *The Greening* because the forest floor does indeed experience an overall "greening" as the fiddleheads turn into ferns and all the other plants fully leaf out in spring and summer.

The several years I spent engrossed with the fiddlehead study gave me a greater appreciation for one more small and fleeting aspect of the cycle of life. Through my research to learn more about fiddleheads and ferns, I discovered much about spirals and growth patterns in nature, and I continue to find more examples of "spira mirabilis" almost daily. The unfurling spirals of the tiny fiddleheads beautifully represent the renewal of life—and are one more reminder to me to be grateful for a small place on this fragile earth.

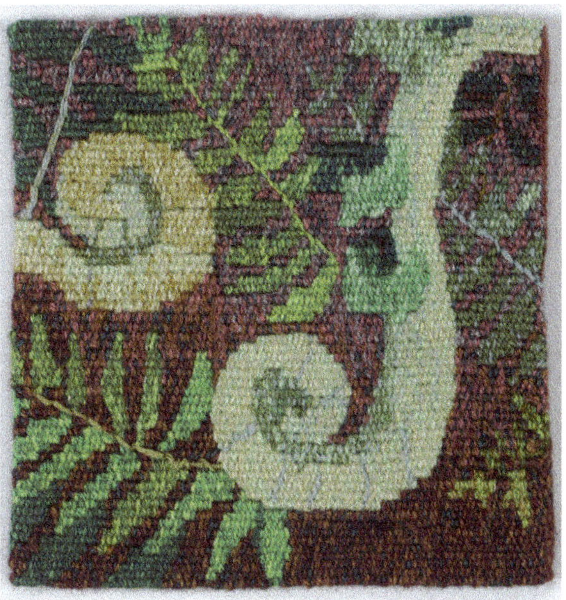

Figure 9.15
Fiddleheads Return, 8 inches by 8 inches, 2013 (photo by Tim Barnwell)

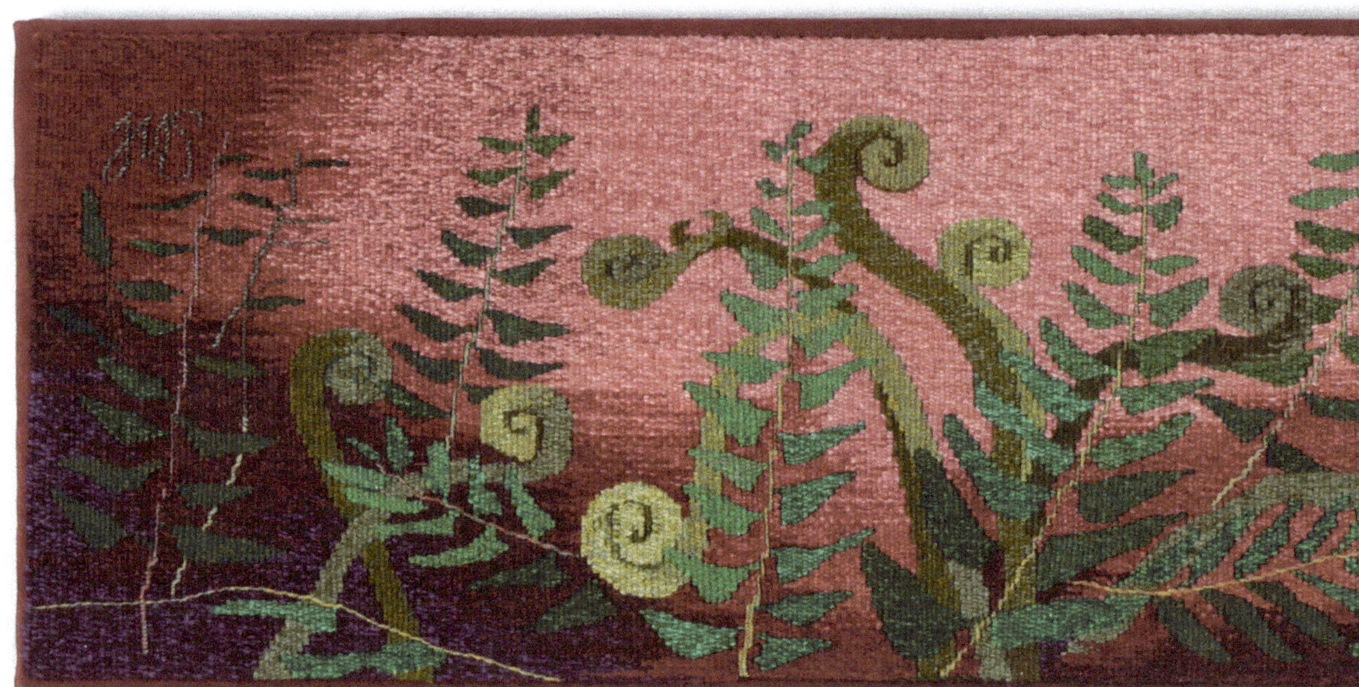

Figure 9.16
The Greening, 16 inches by 60 inches, 2013 (photo by Tim Barnwell)

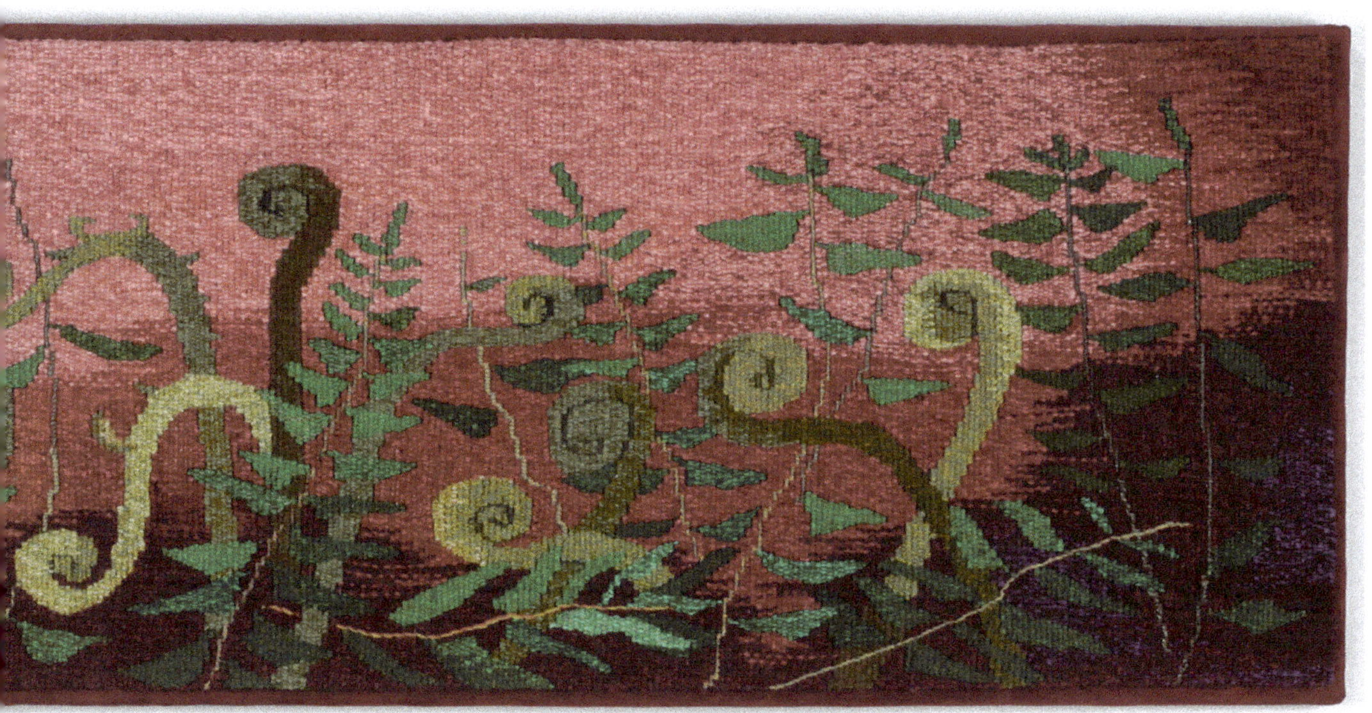

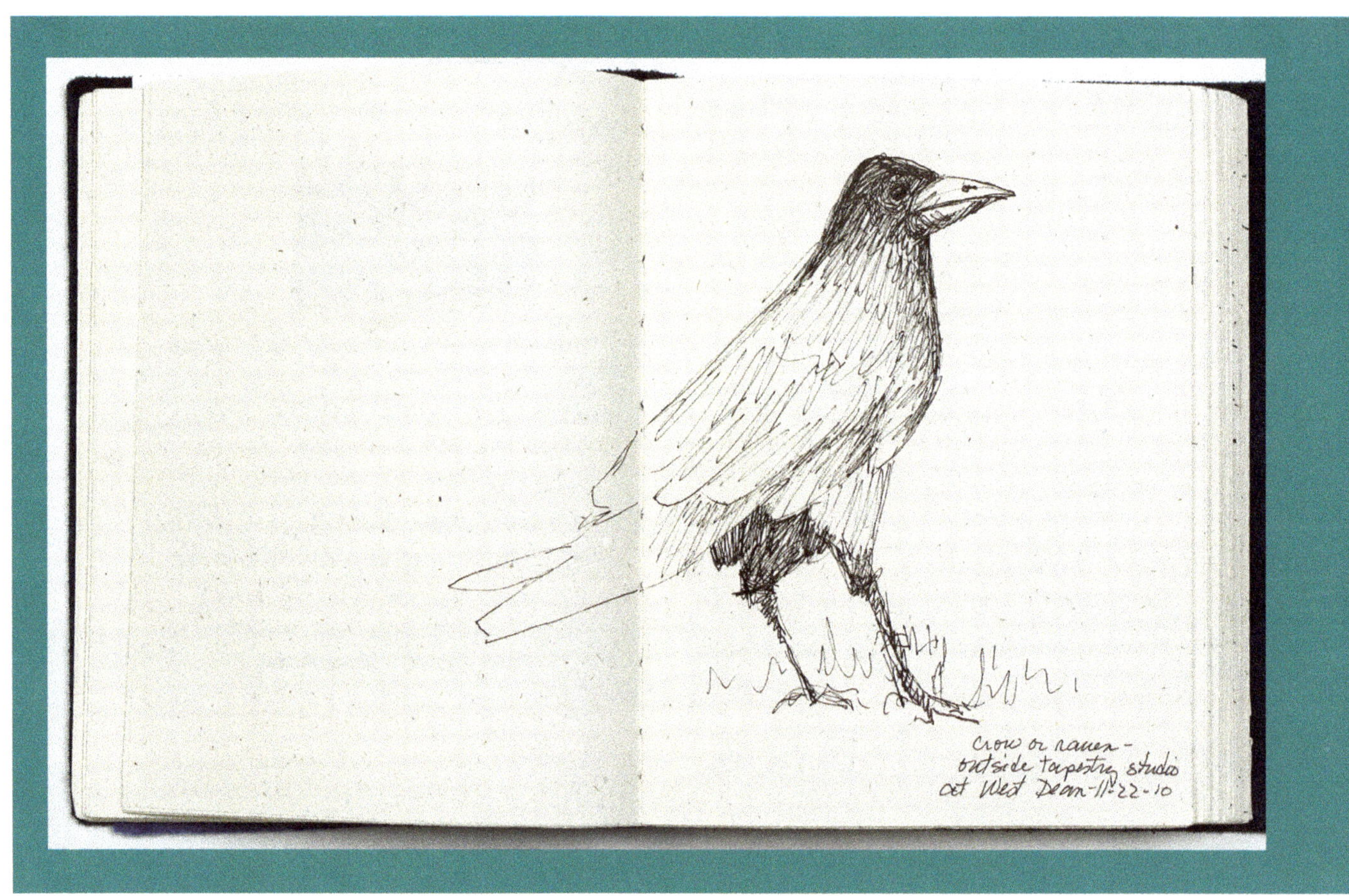

Figure 10.1
Crow or raven, sketch made when I was studying at West Dean College in England, 2010. (photo by Christopher Dant)

10

Feathers

I once heard that birds are descendants of dinosaurs. For some reason, that thought captivated me. Each news report of another finding in the fossil record showing a link between those ancient ancestors and the birds that are among us today is thrilling to me. I love to think of the crows that are in the yard right now as distant cousins to a velociraptor.

Crows especially fascinate me. I watch them stalk through the grass, bodies moving back and forth with a husky rhythm as they pick up walnuts and pecans. But it seems that as soon as I begin to watch them from my window, they up and fly away. Do they know I'm watching? If they do, how do they sense my attention? I make no movement other than to glance up, and then—off they go! Do they have extrasensory perception to alert them to my notice?

One afternoon, I heard the caws of many crows in the pecan tree next to the house. I'd been trying to see if I could sketch some of the birds when they would be occupied with their nut harvesting. I rushed to the window with pencil and sketchpad and quickly sat down, and as soon as I was ready to draw, off they flew. I sat there, waiting for them to return. Of course, they didn't.

Finally, I began to notice that there were many other smaller birds in the branches busily pecking at insects in the bark. That particular lesson from the crows perhaps was to be patient. Wait for the unexpected.

I often think of feathers as "bird petals" because they remind me of the petals of flowers. Of course, I know that analogy is odd. But I use it anyway, at least in my mind. Flower petals

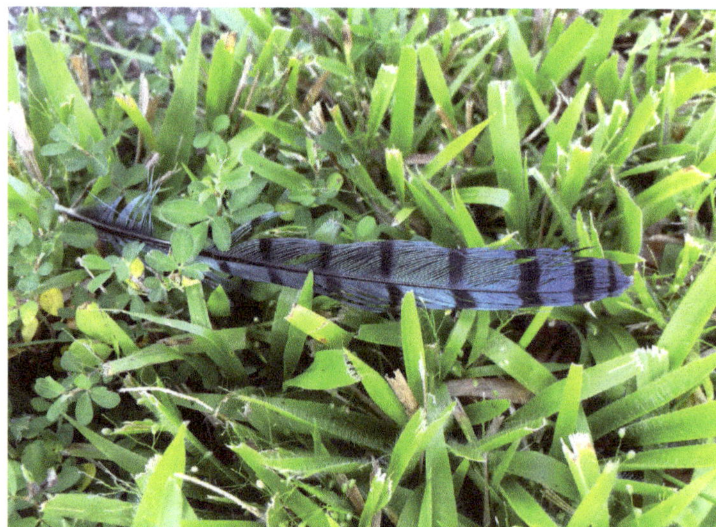

Figure 10.2
Blue jay feather in the front yard

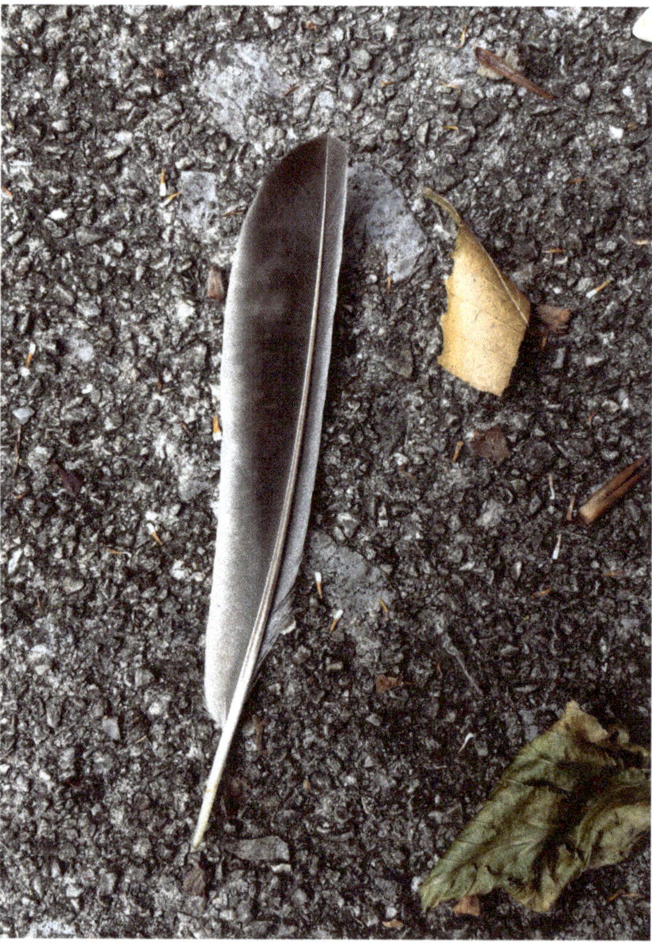

Figure 10.3
Feather on the sidewalk at Arrowmont School of Crafts, Gatlinburg, TN

fall off, and so do the feathers of birds. When I find a feather as I'm out walking, I consider it a gift. I usually photograph them where they're found. I've made many sketches of feathers over the years. Feathers have also been the subjects of several tapestries.

One of the feather tapestries began this way: a few years ago, I started making marks on a large piece of paper without my having any subject in mind. I began by drawing with a soft graphite stick and using big, sweeping arm movements, back and forth, up and down, all across the paper. I drew quickly and freely.

After a few minutes, I stepped back and noticed that the random marks seemed to suggest overlapping feathers. I realized this could be developed into something other than haphazard scribbles so began to explore the idea by using feathers as reference. I switched from graphite to acrylic paint and made lots of changes as I refined the image, covering over some of the marks and building on others. The composition soon began to resemble overlapping feathers that seemed to be floating or falling. After working on the painting for few days, I decided to use it for a tapestry design.

At the start, I had no idea where those few scribbled strokes might lead. Afterwards, traces of the original drawing could be seen in the background, an unintended palimpsest as evidence of the process. For the tapestry, my initial thought was to focus on the eight feather shapes that were dominant in the composition. The faint marks still slightly evident throughout the background of the painting now seemed to be important to the concept. And so I decided to incorporate them in the image.

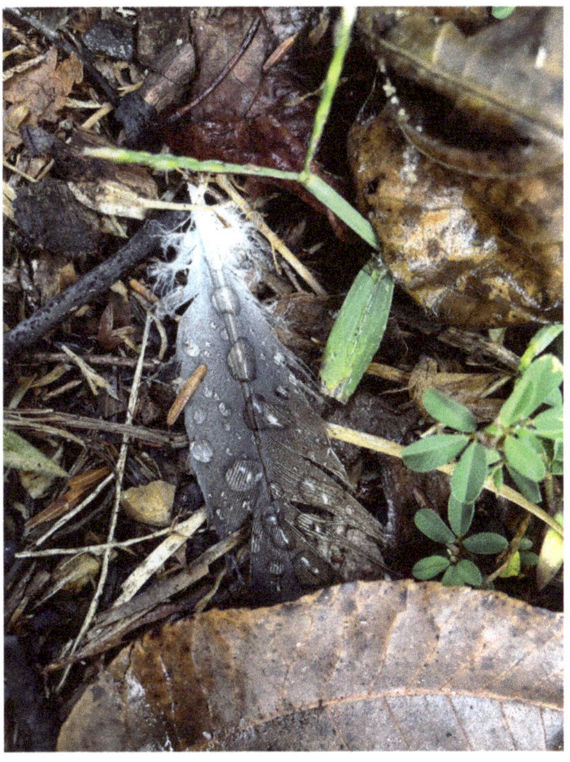

Figure 10.4
Feather and raindrops, found while walking one morning

In the tapestry, those marks were done with a technique called "soumak." This is a method of wrapping a supplemental yarn around warp threads during the course of the weaving to give a linear surface effect similar to a stitched line. I used the soumak

Figure 10.5
Feather and brick sidewalk, downtown Dahlonega.

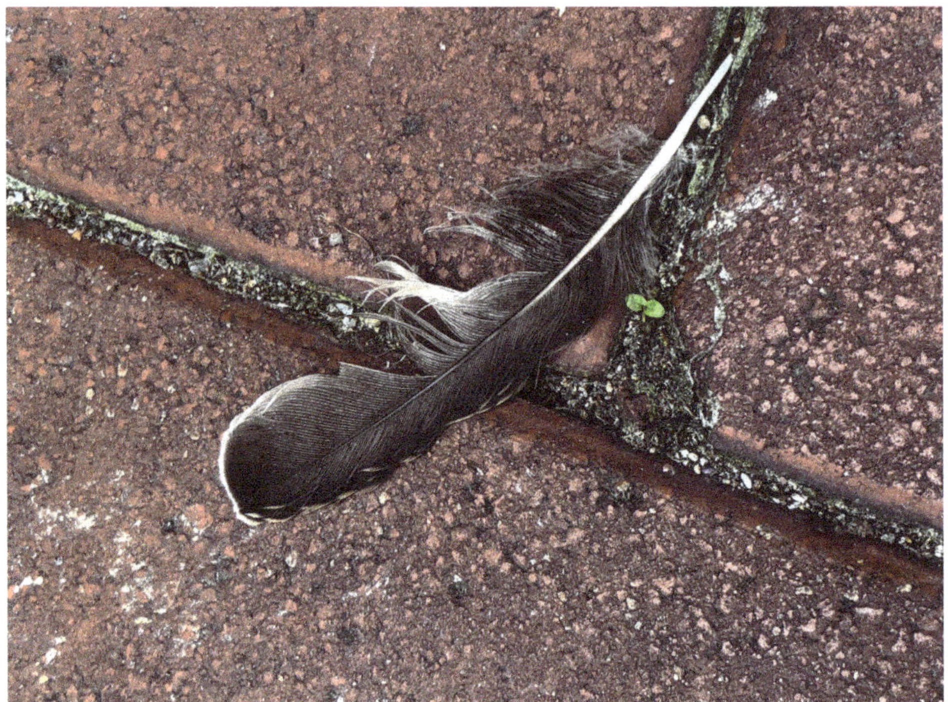

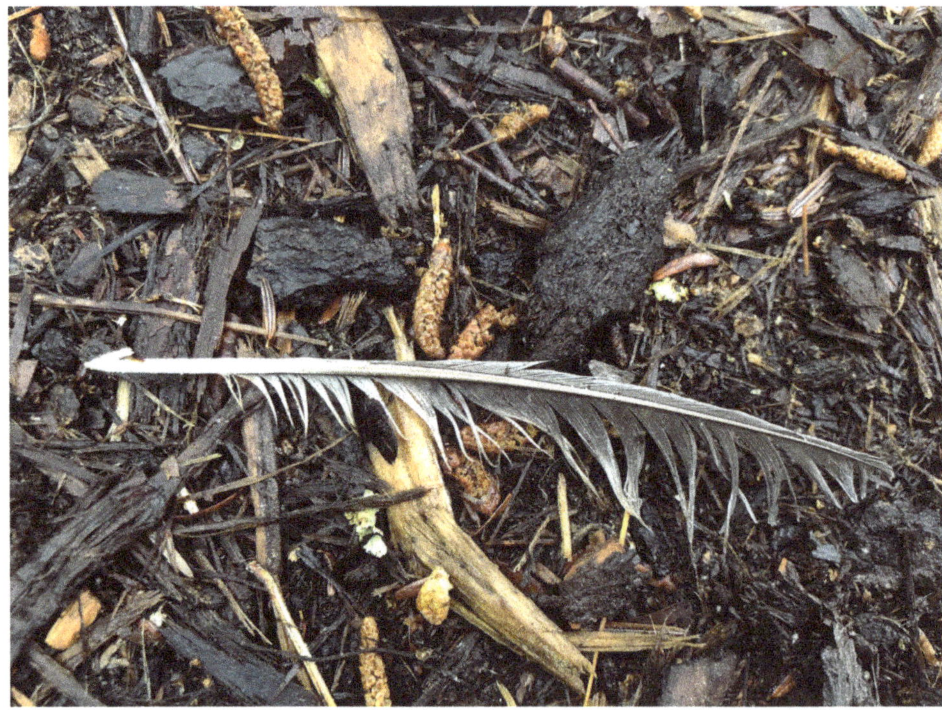

Figure 10.6
Feather found in the back burn area off Patterson Gap Road, near the Hambidge Center, Rabun County, GA.

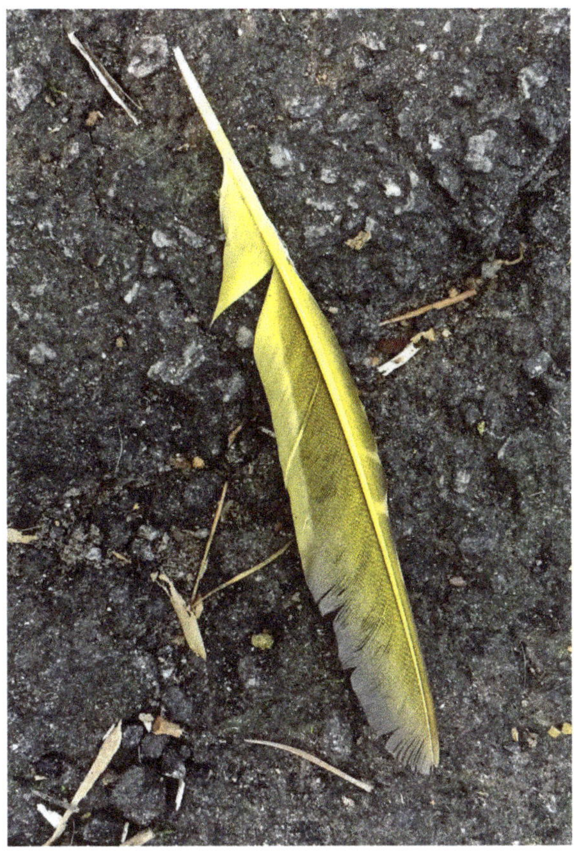

Figure 10.7
Northern Flicker feather

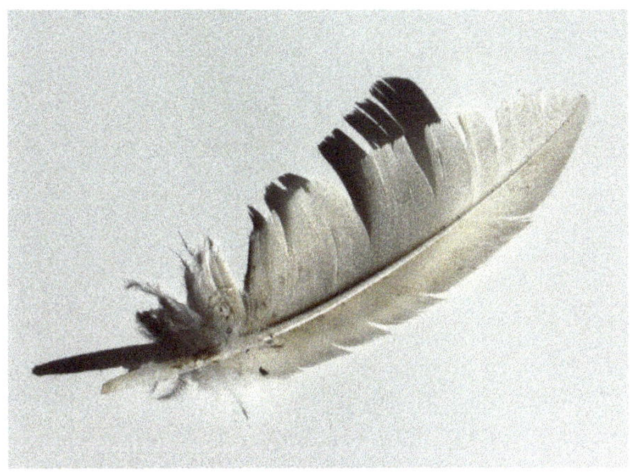

Figure 10.8
Turkey feather from my friends' birds.

threads to float across the surface of the background in sweeping diagonal directions, to be caught every few centimeters around a warp end. Those lines enhanced the concept of lightness and floating of the tapestry I called *Flight*.

Soon after completing *Flight*, I happened to be at the LES Center in an artist residency. On two consecutive days, I found feathers of a pileated woodpecker when I was walking in the woods. I felt those gifts from the bird were calling for attention, so I made paintings based on the feathers. Soon afterwards, I found yet more feathers, this time on a street in Asheville, North Carolina. I photographed them where they lay and later developed a composite image of four feathers as a design for my next tapestry.

I'd explored the linear effects of soumak on the surface of the tapestry when doing *Flight*, and I decided to use those qualities in the next piece to create thin detail lines within the woven feathers. There would also be shapes suggestive of shadows underneath the feathers to give them visual weight. I made the cartoon, put a warp on the loom, and began the tapestry.

One day when I was several inches into the weaving, just about halfway through the second of the four feathers, one of those moments came that sometimes happens—a moment when the design seems to take/suggest/demand a new direction. That

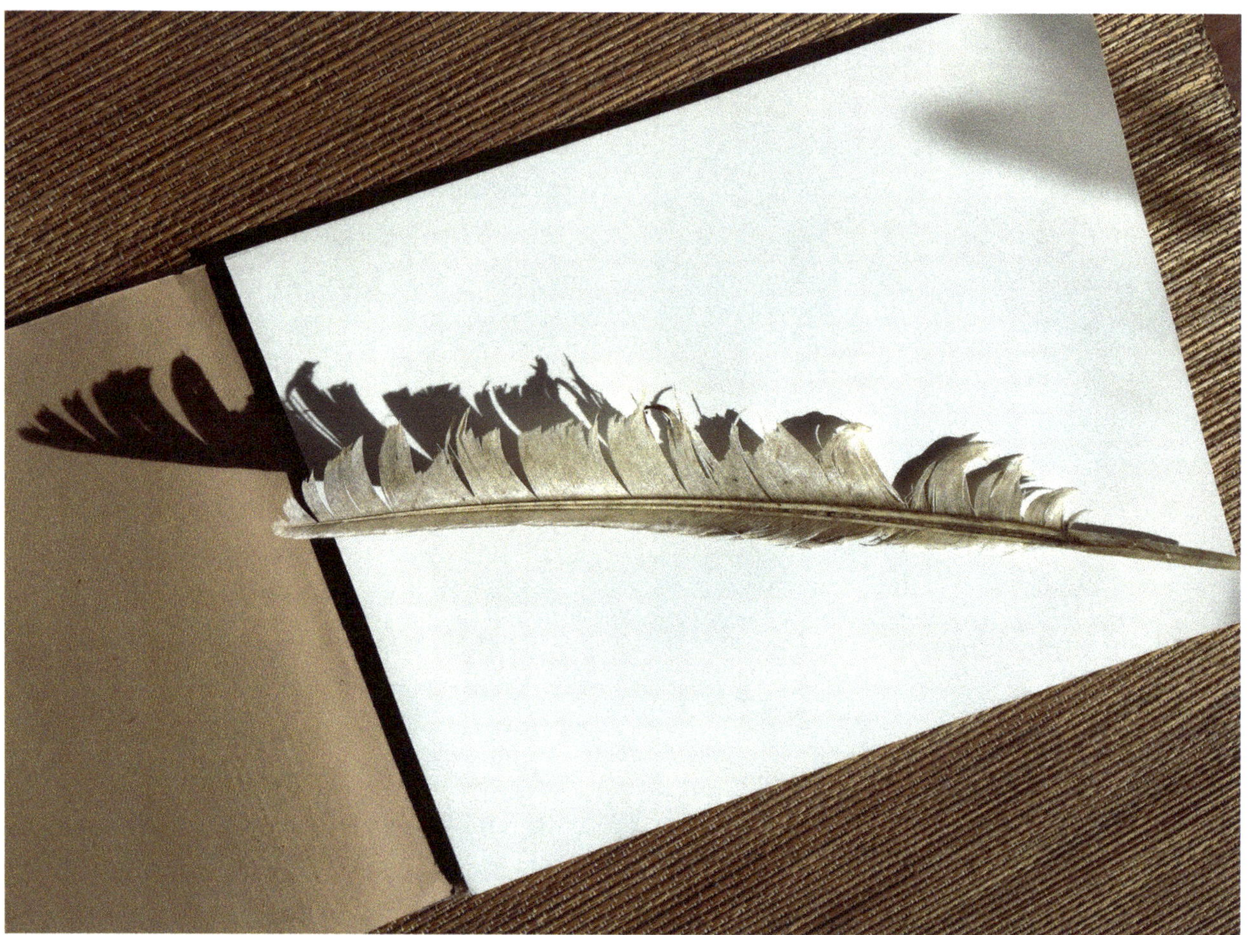

Figure 10.9
Turkey feather and sketchpad. The shadows make distinctive shapes in the strong afternoon light.

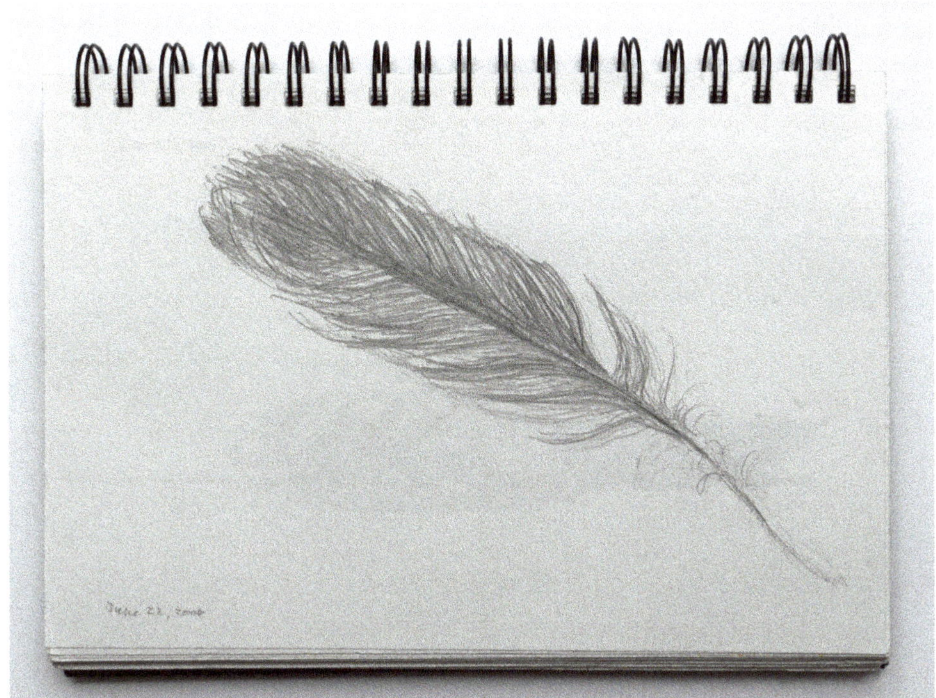

Figure 10.10
Feather sketch, 2008 (photo by Christopher Dant)

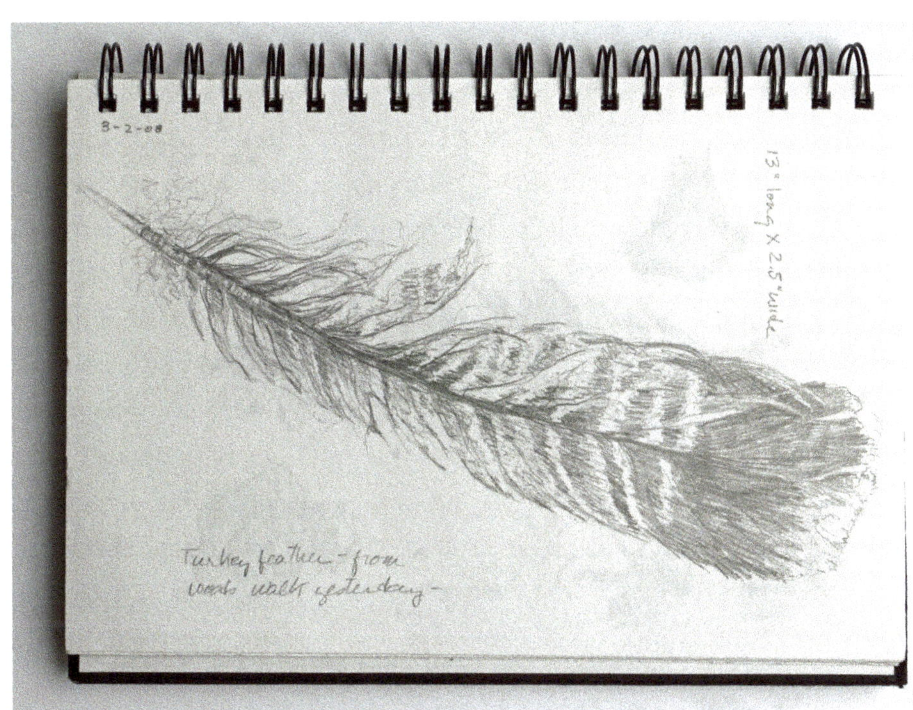

Figure 10.11
Sketch of a wild turkey feather found in the woods at friends' property near Sapphire, NC (photo by Christopher Dant)

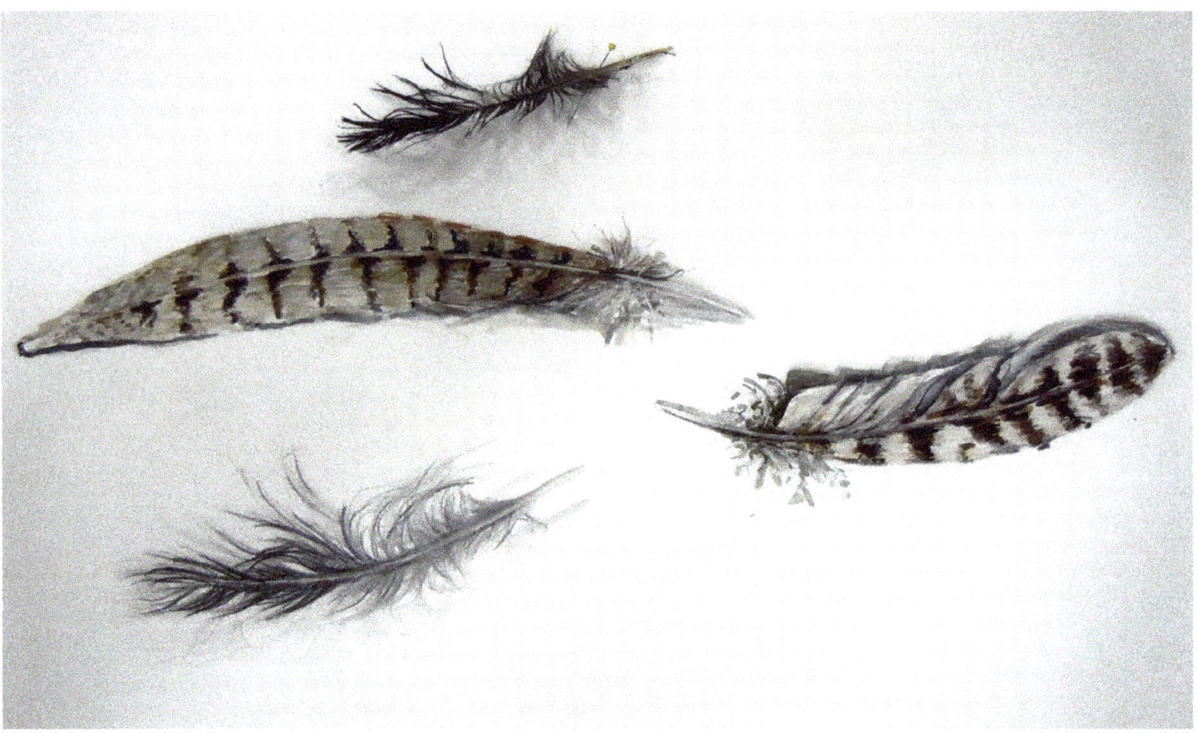

Figure 10.12
Feather and three feather paintings made while at West Dean College.

afternoon as I was leaving the studio, I happened to see the effect of the cartoon outlines behind the warp threads—perhaps the light from the window in back of the loom was just right at that particular moment. The lines from the cartoon visually merged with the solid areas that were already woven and suggested a "what if?" moment—what if I began to change from the colors of the background and feathers into a neutral single color for the background. And what if the remaining feathers of the design were done with soumak lines only? And what if the soumak lines became fainter in value of color and thinner than the background threads? And what if the final feather of the four were placed just slightly higher and farther away from the other three?

Would I take the chance to modify the image? It was only weaving after all, and if I didn't like it, I could unweave it, couldn't I? When I returned to the studio the next day, I began to answer those questions as I made drastic changes to my initial plans. When it was done, the resulting tapestry was not only visually stronger but also had much more meaning than originally envisioned because I was willing to see beyond the

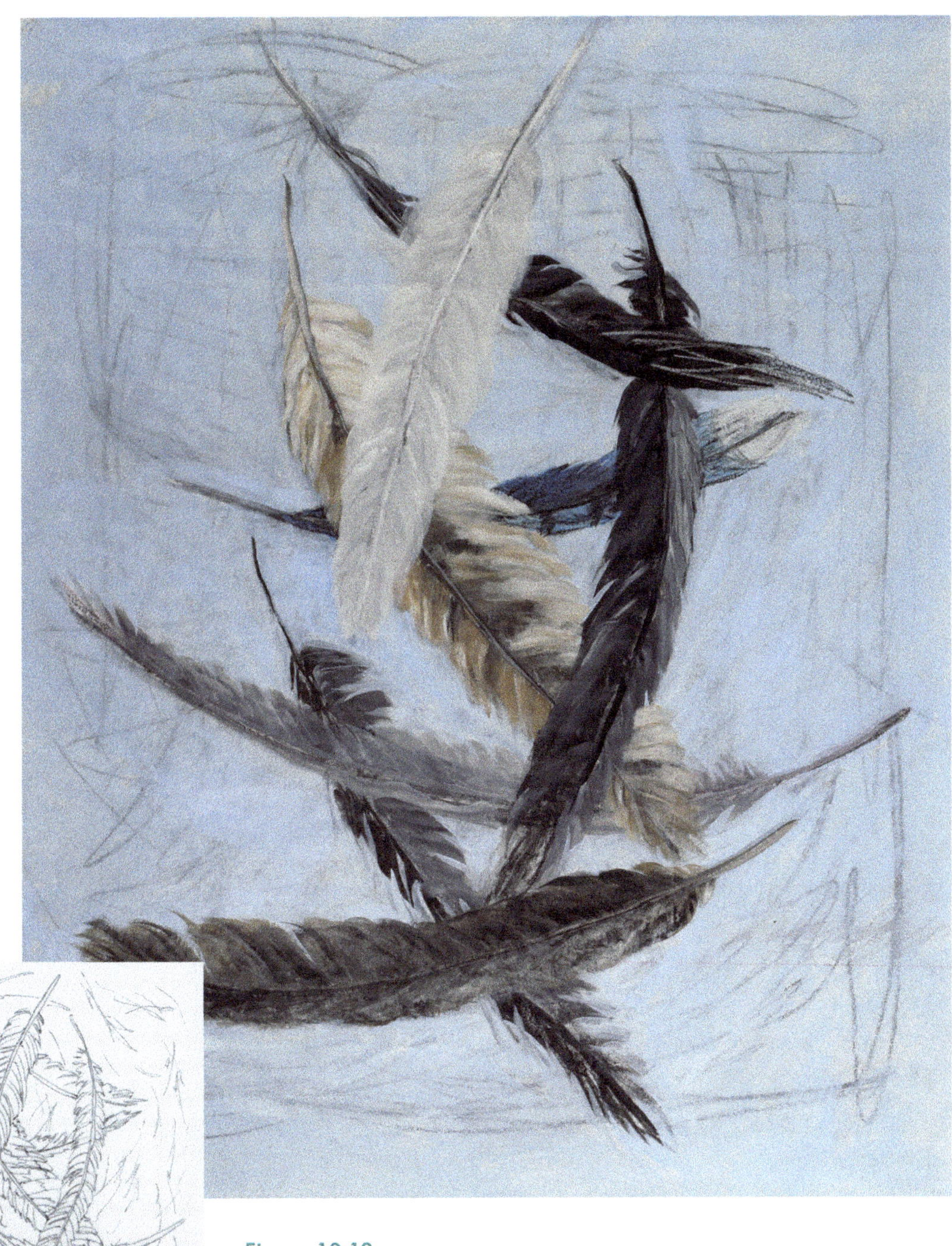

Figure 10.13
The painting that became the source of the cartoon for the tapestry *Flight* (photo by Christopher Dant)

Figure 10.14 (overlay)
Flight, the small working drawing that was enlarged for the cartoon (photo by Christopher Dant)

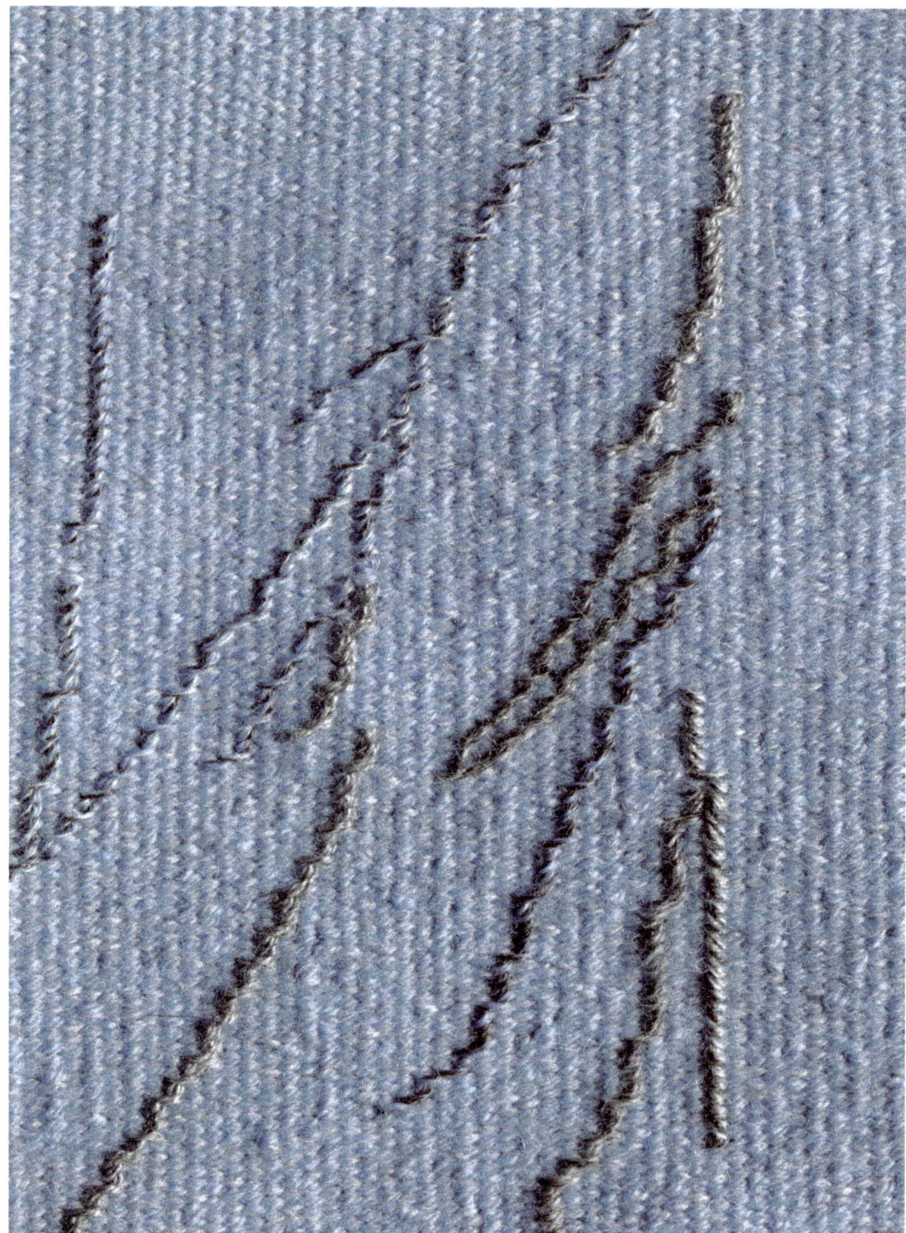

Figure 10.15
Detail of the soumak lines floating across the surface of the background in *Flight* (photo by Tim Barnwell)

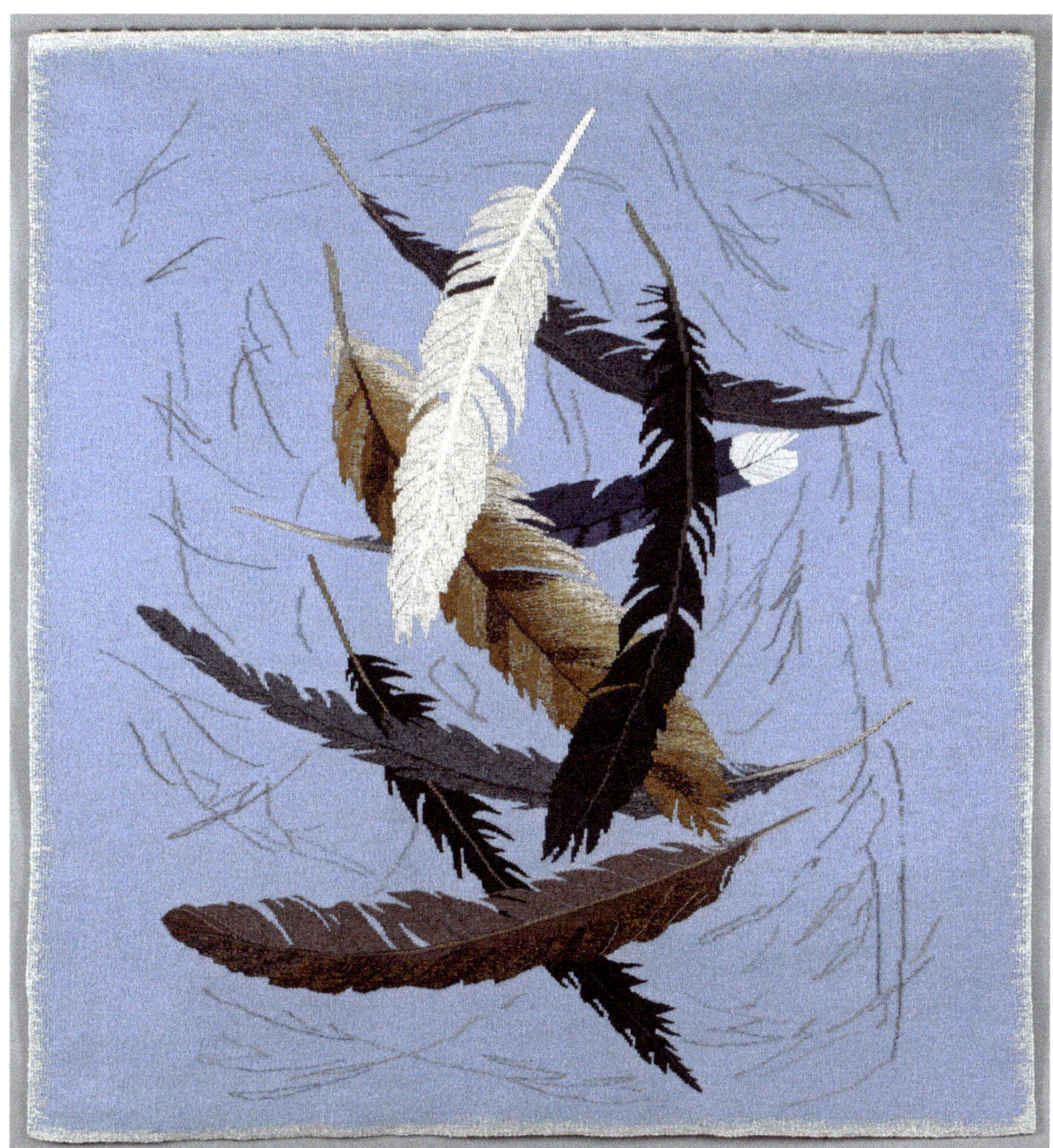

Figure 10.16
Flight, 62 inches by 56 inches, 2013 (photo by Tim Barnwell)

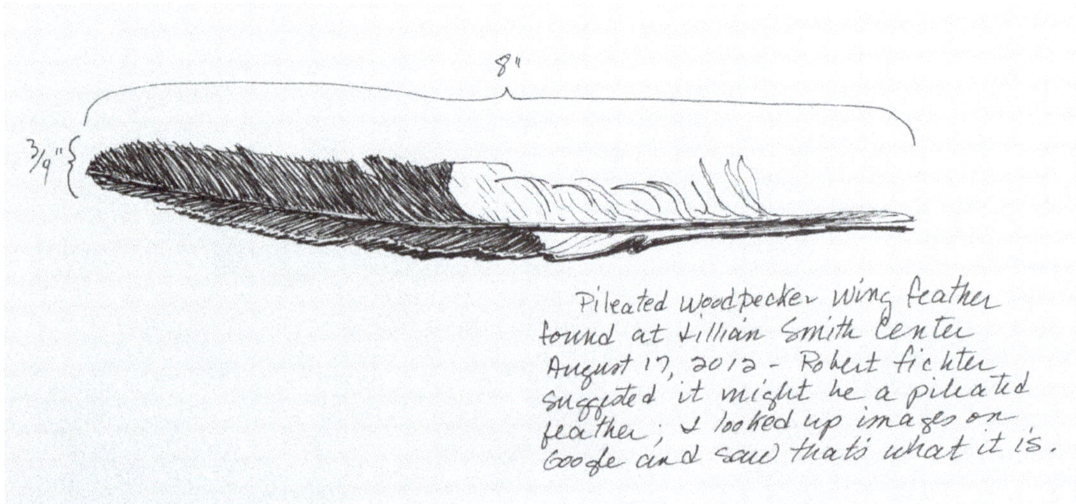

Figure 10.17
Ink drawing of a pileated woodpecker feather, found while at an artist residency at LES Center, 2012 (photo by Christopher Dant)

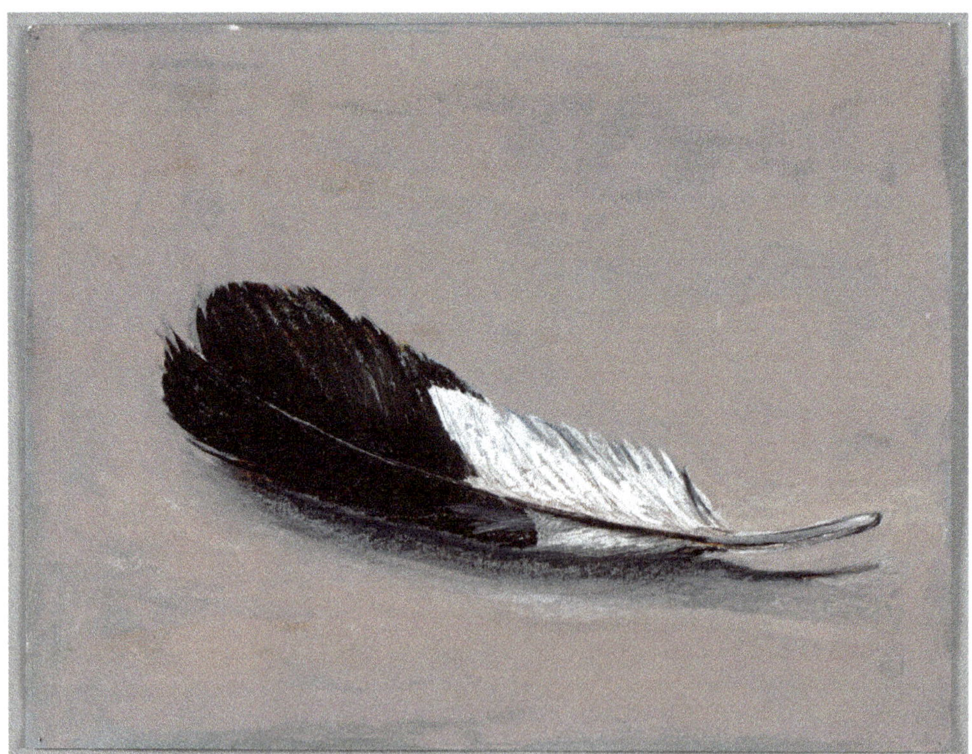

Figure 10.18
Graphite and acrylic painting of pileated woodpecker feather, 2012 (photo by Tim Barnwell)

Figure 10.19
Lone Feather, 7 inches by 3 inches, 2012. Soumak lines were used to "draw" onto the surface as the tapestry was being woven. (Photo by Tim Barnwell)

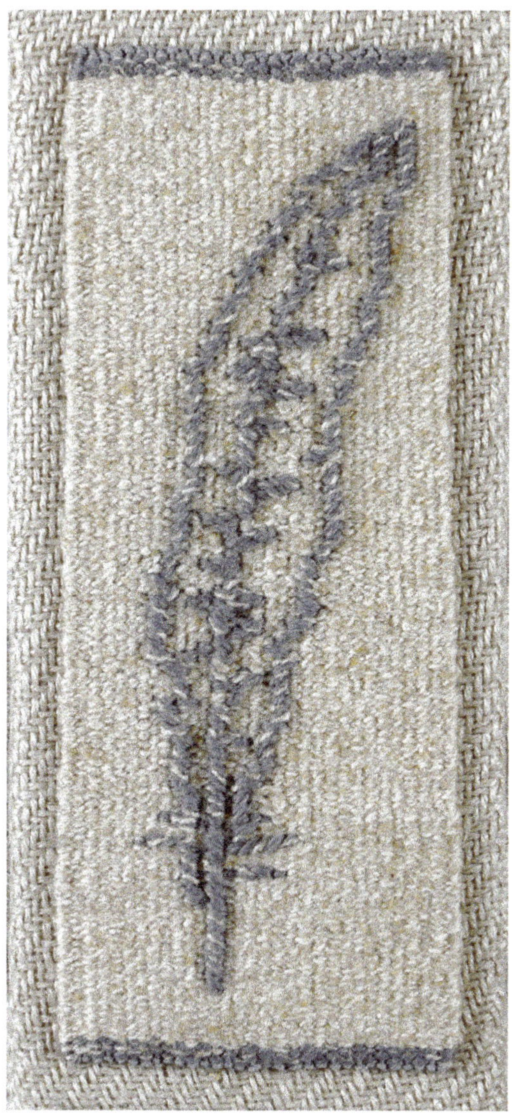

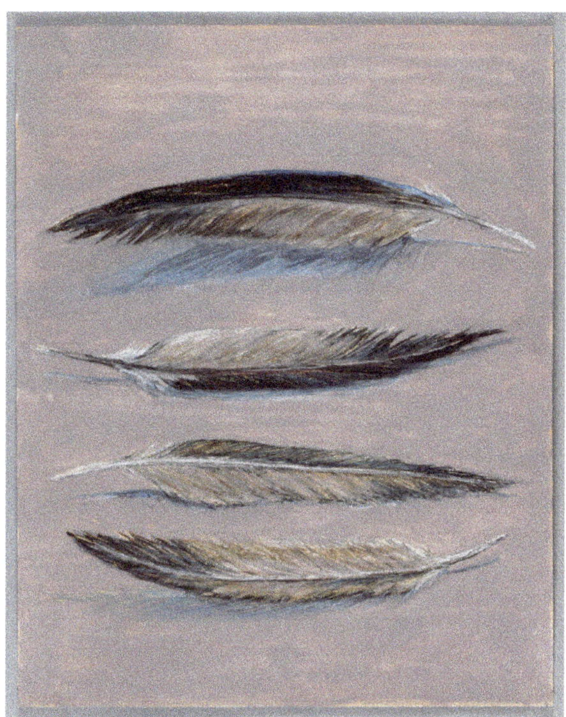

Figure 10.20
Graphite and acrylic painting of four found feathers, 2012 (photo by Tim Barnwell)

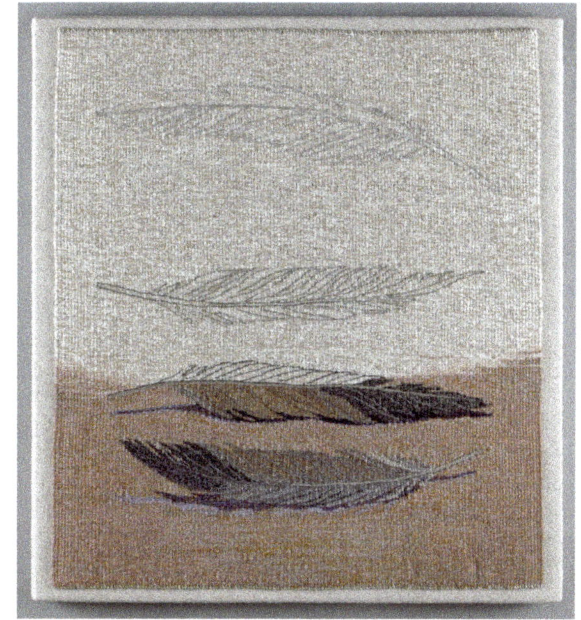

Figure 10.21
In Spirit, 26 inches by 23 inches, 2013. The image source for the tapestry was the painting of the four found feathers. It changed during the course of the weaving to become an image quite different than the original design. (Photo by Tim Barnwell)

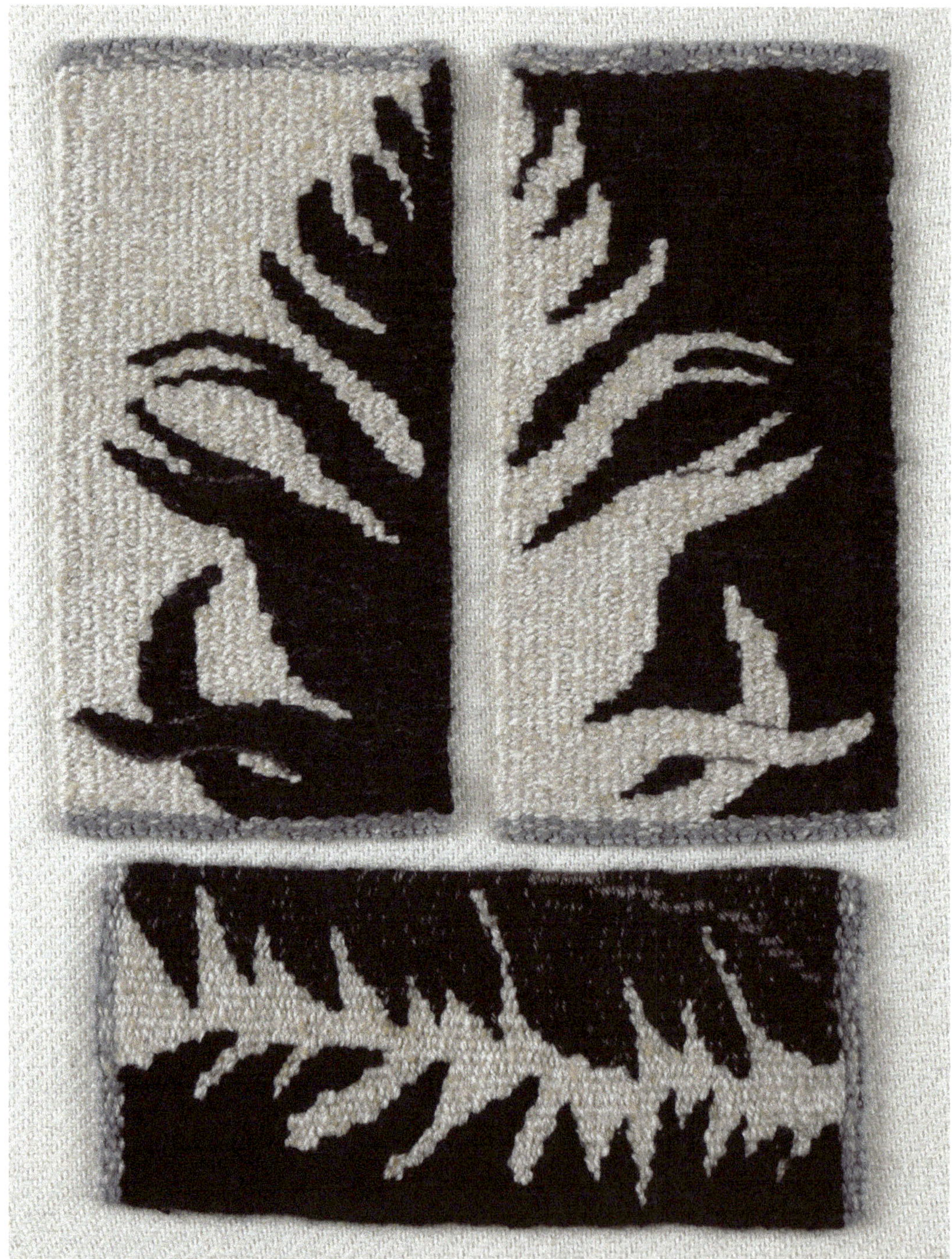

Figure 10.22
Echo Feather, 9 inches by 6 inches, 2012. The tapestry is made up of three components in a positive/negative design. (Photo by Tim Barnwell)

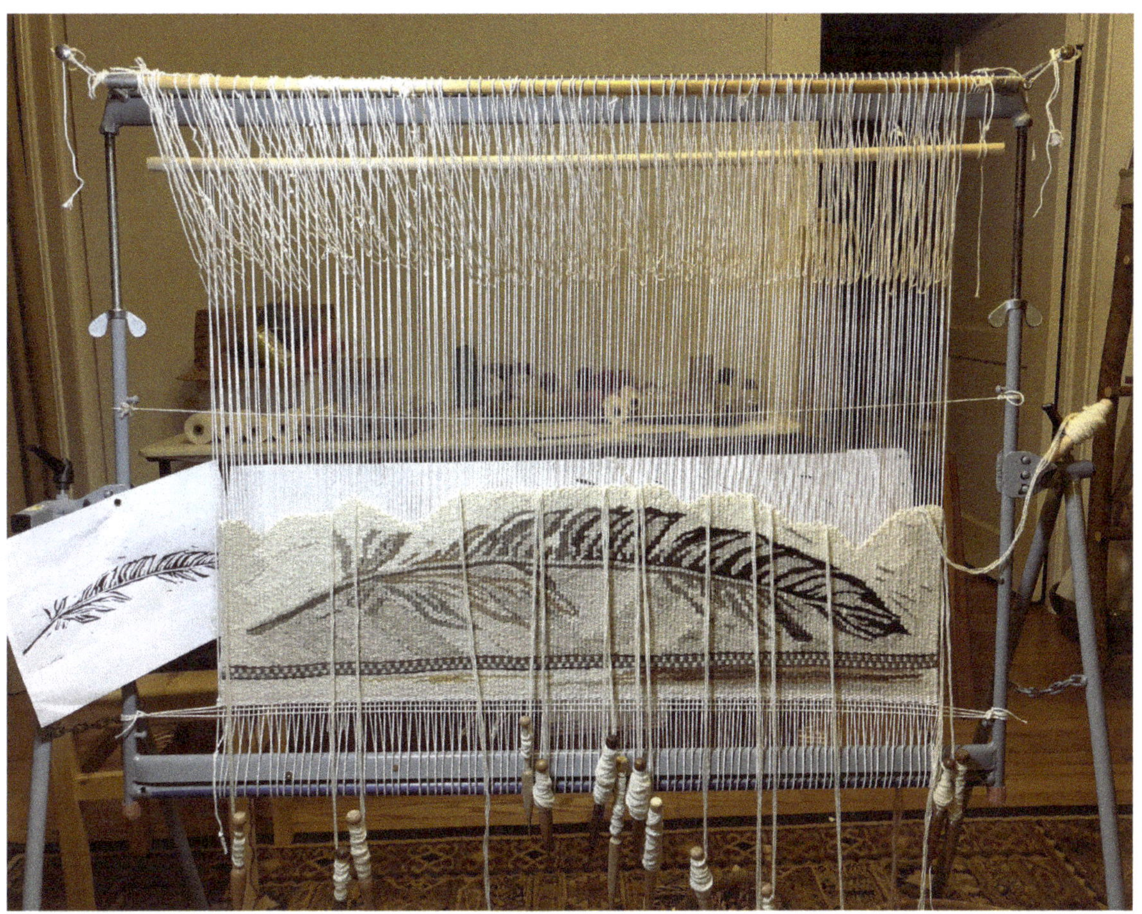

Figure 10.23
Weaving the tapestry *Hope is the Thing With Feathers* in 2018. The design was based on a linoleum block print I'd made a few years earlier; one of the prints is hanging at the left of the loom as reference as I weave. Black walnut natural dyes were used for the darker colors of the wool weft.

planned design, listen to the questions that the new observation asked, and answer them with woven actions. I don't know where questions like those come from, but I do know that I don't always respond to them by altering my design. Perhaps my tapestries would be much better if I would.

Making those changes to the planned design caused the image to move from a literal representation of four feathers into something more evocative. The woven feathers within the tapestry had changed from being substantial to more suggestive of evanescence. The tapestry was called *In Spirit*.

I've explored the visual qualities of feathers in four other tapestries. In one, I used the line-making quality of soumak to

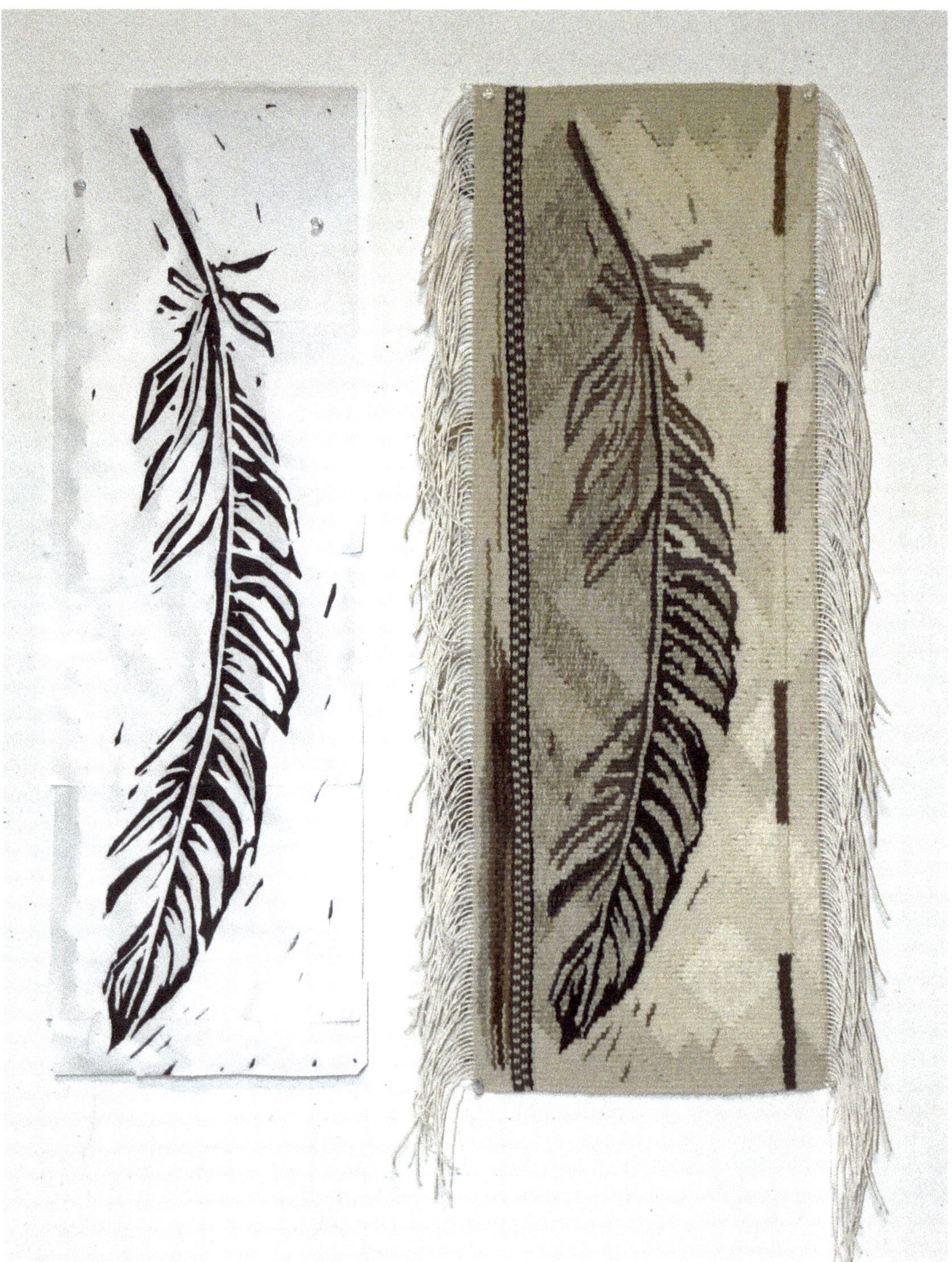

Figure 10.24
Completed tapestry cut from the loom with the cartoon used hanging at the left.

"draw" a single feather upon the surface of the woven background. In another, subtle effects from thin lines of soumak were used to outline the shapes and add details within them. In a third tapestry, I explored the dark and light of simplified feather shapes, symmetrically balancing positive and negative contrasting images in the composition, almost in a yin and yang effect.

One of the feather-image tapestries was designed by adapting a linoleum block print I'd made in which there were only a few bold graphic lines. It was an interesting transition to move from observing a found feather, making first a preliminary drawing then a printed image, and finally to creating a cartoon and weaving a tapestry. Words from an Emily Dickinson poem became the title: *Hope is the Thing with Feathers.*[1]

Maybe I'll return to weaving feathers in the future. In the meantime, I continue to listen to bird songs in the woods, watch the crows stalk around the yard, look for the next news report linking birds with the world's past creatures, and find fallen feathers to draw—beautiful gifts from the birds.

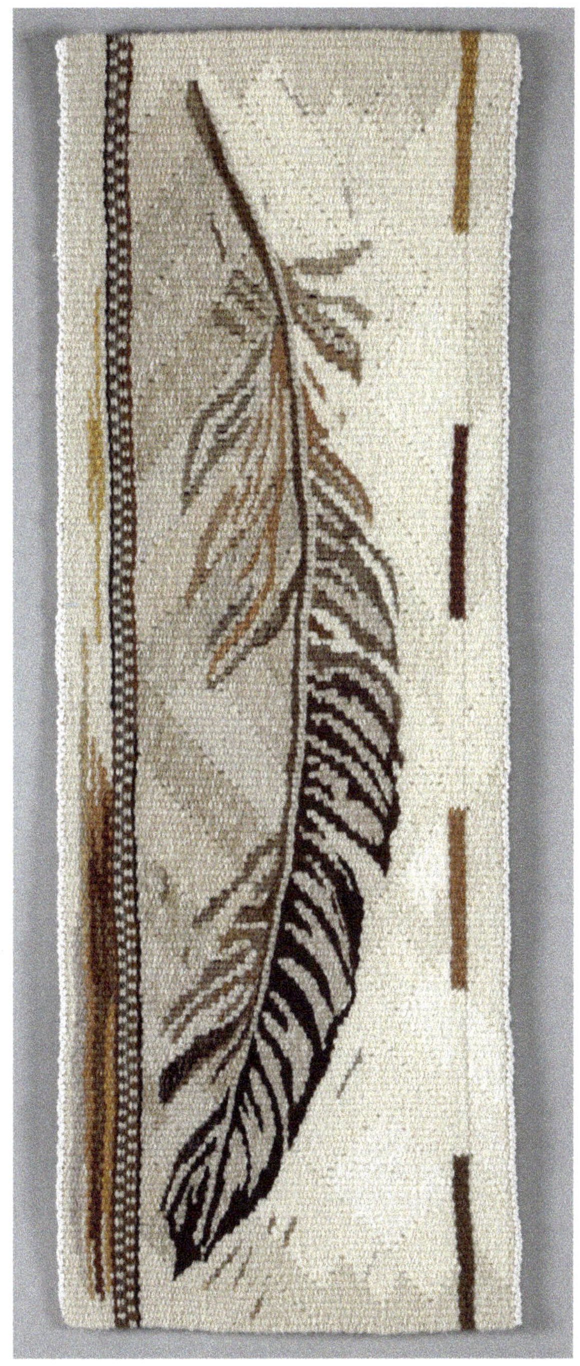

Figure 10.25
Hope is the Thing With Feathers, 32 inches by 12 inches, 2018 (photo by Tim Barnwell)

1 *The Collected Poems of Emily Dickinson,* "XXXII" (New York: Fall River Press, 1993), 19.

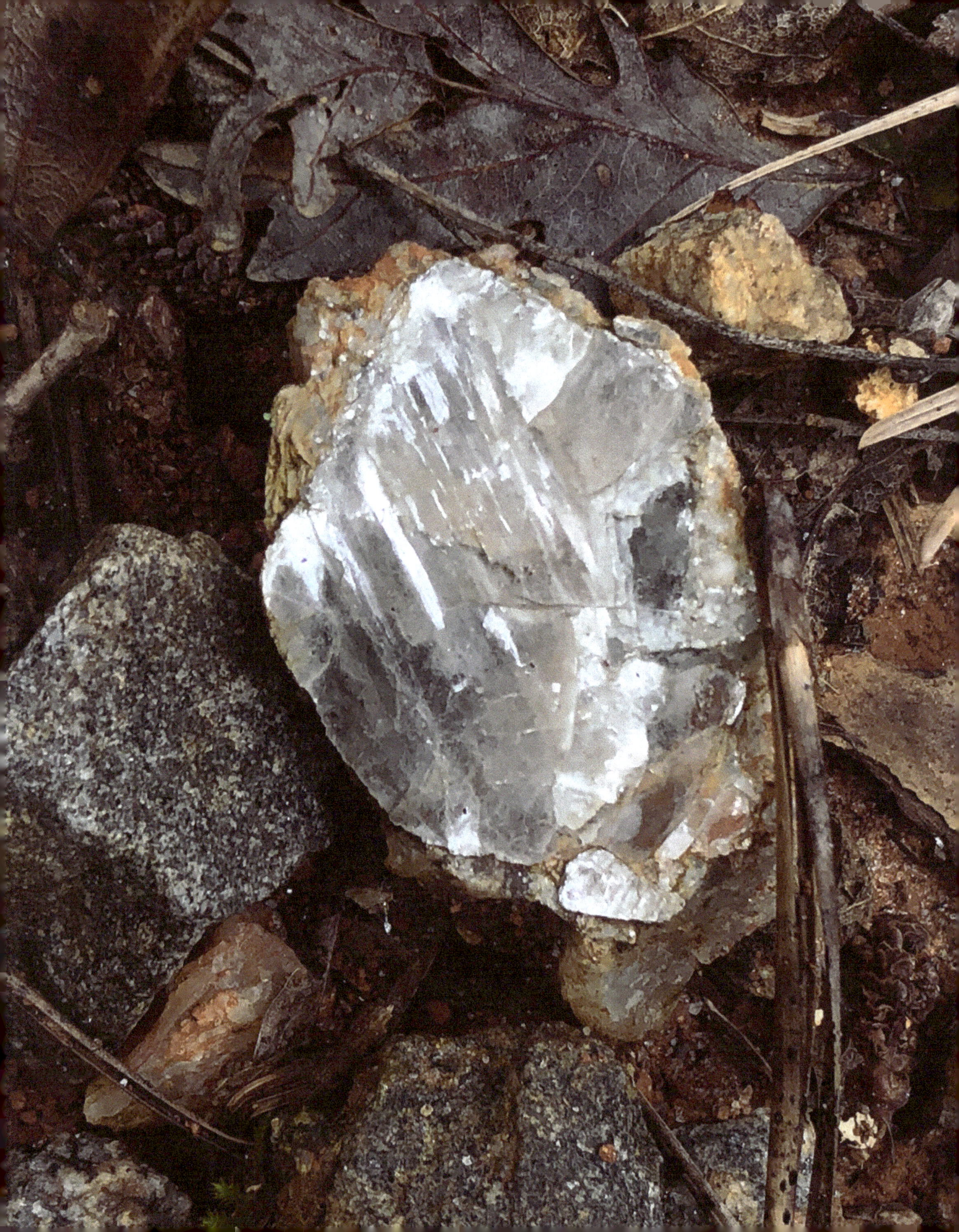

11

Stones

Stones speak to me. Not in words but in images. I'm not sure when I first began to notice stones, but I remember as a child that I would collect pieces of mica and quartz when I was searching for arrowheads around my home. Later, I spent a summer as a counselor at a camp for girls in Rabun County, Georgia. When out exploring, we would often find small pieces of amethyst and garnet embedded in quartz in the nearby road banks. As I collected stones, I noticed the textures and colors and loved to see the distinct shadows made by the edges of stones when strong sunlight struck one side.

I grew up seeing the icicles that formed in winter on the rock faces beside the roads in the mountains of North Georgia. I also stumbled on stones many times and skinned my knees when falling in gravel. Growing up, I also faced the sad occasions of a pet's death. After the burial at the edge of the woods, my sister and I would solemnly place a little rock on top of the small grave as a headstone.

In my first years as an art instructor at NGC, I would occasionally accompany my colleague and his students on painting excursions to a small waterfall at a nearby creek. As we tried to represent the water tumbling over the rocks, Bob gave this advice: "Don't paint the water, paint the rocks."

Bob's perceptive observation has stayed with me for years whenever I've looked at all rocks, not only those where there are waterfalls. I recalled my earlier thoughts about how shadows

Figure 11.1 (opposite)
Mica

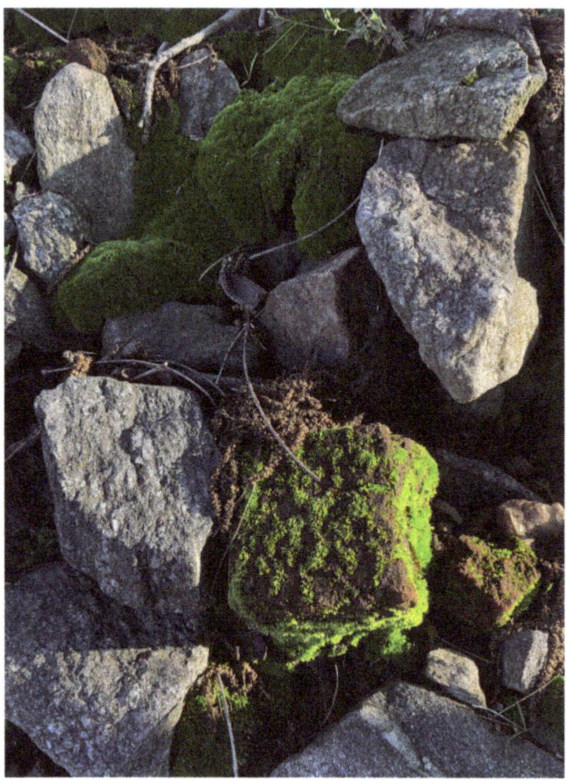

Figure 11.2
Stones, light and shadow

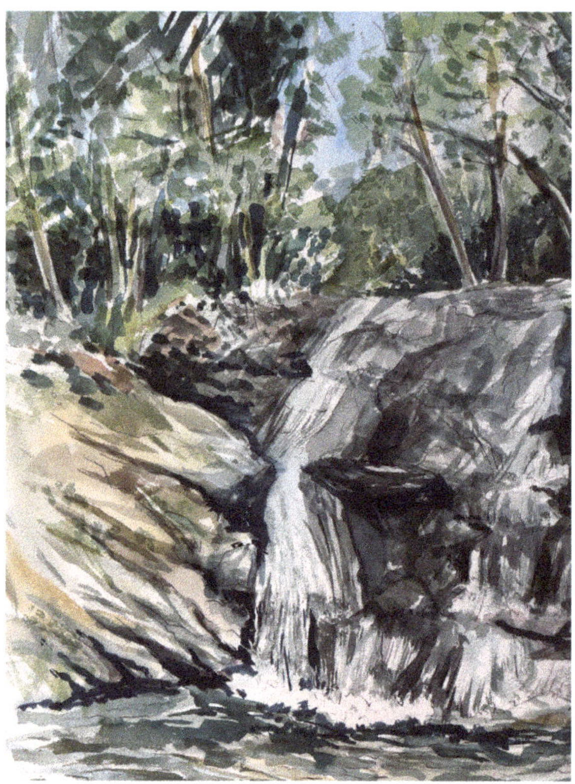

Figure 11.3
Cane Creek Falls, watercolor painting, 20 inches by 14 inches, 1988

are cast by stones as I tried to render their essence by looking at the light and shadow that I saw. Since then, I've painted rocks and waterfalls many times, but I've only woven a single tapestry from those studies, one that I titled *Rocks and Water* to acknowledge the wisdom of Bob's comments.

I was drawn to other stones as a subject for visual study when I had my first artist residency at the LES Center in 2010. There is a beautiful stone chimney at the Center, the only remains from a structure that was destroyed by fire. The chimney is now a memorial site as Lillian Smith is buried beside it. A large stone lays across her grave, and atop it is a bronze marker with a quotation from one of her books: "Death can kill a man, that is all it can do to him. It cannot end his life, because of memory. . . ."[1]

I always begin my days at the Center with a walk and start out at the chimney to read the words on the marker. I've made many photographs of the chimney, both the

1 Lillian E. Smith, *The Journey* (New York: Norton, 1965), 201.

Figure 11.4
Lillian E. Smith Center, stone chimney

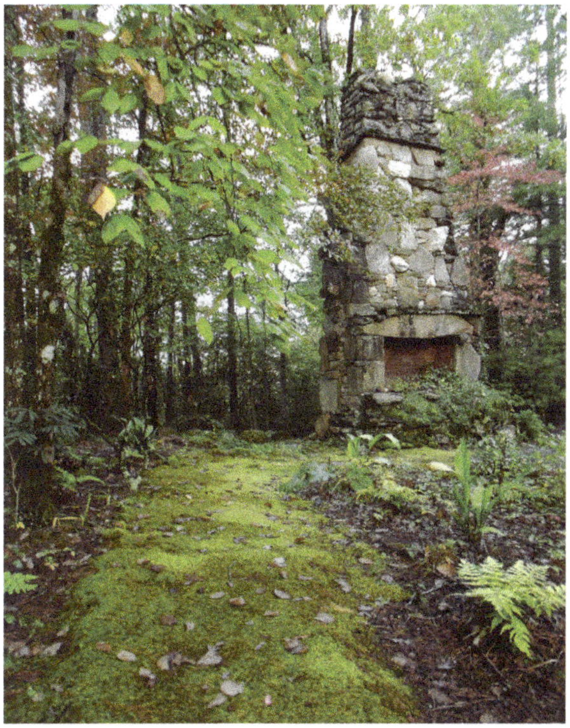

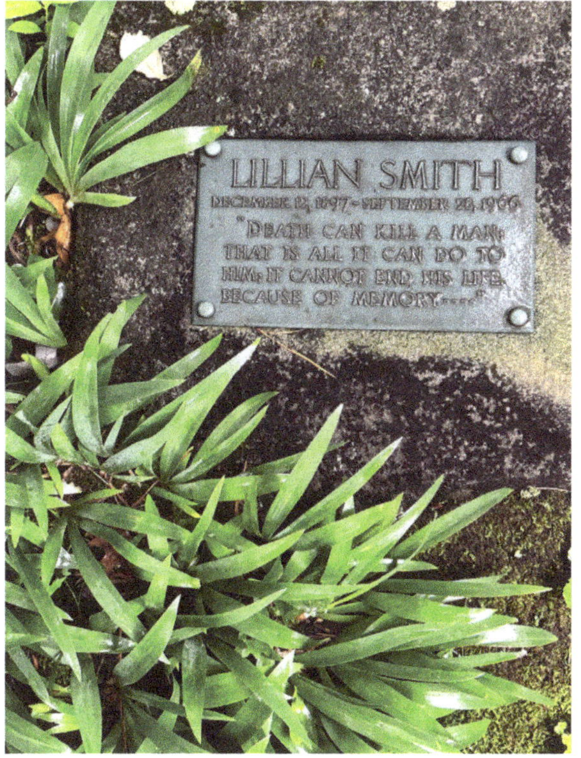

Figure 11.5
Lillian Smith's grave marker

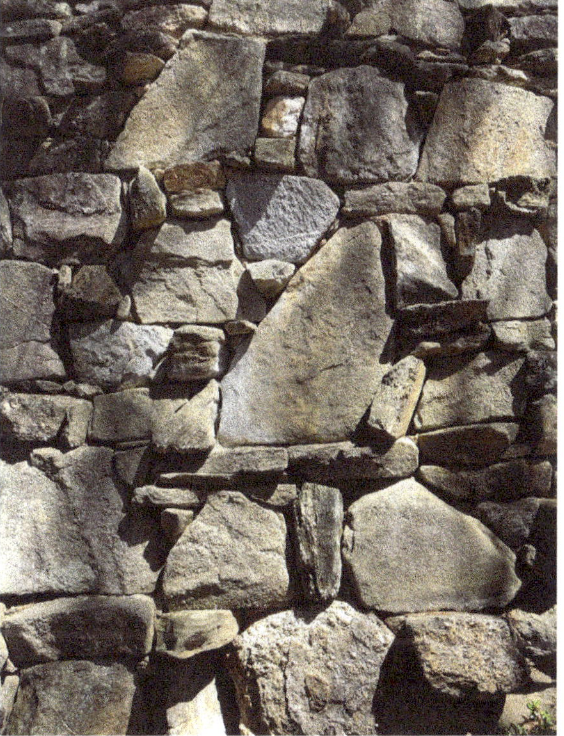

Figure 11.6
Detail of chimney stones

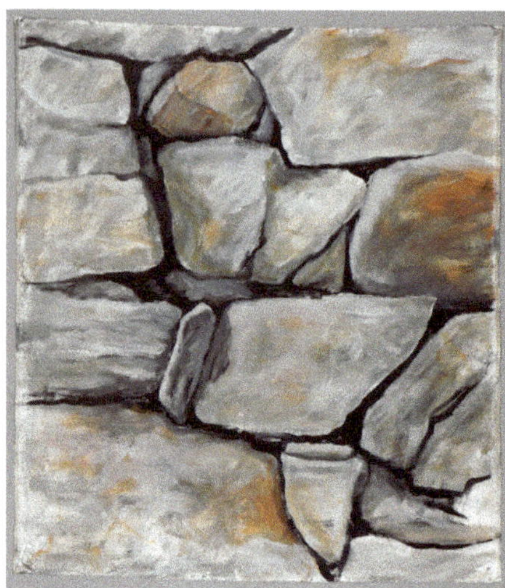

Figure 11.7
Acrylic and earth pigment painting based on a detail of the chimney

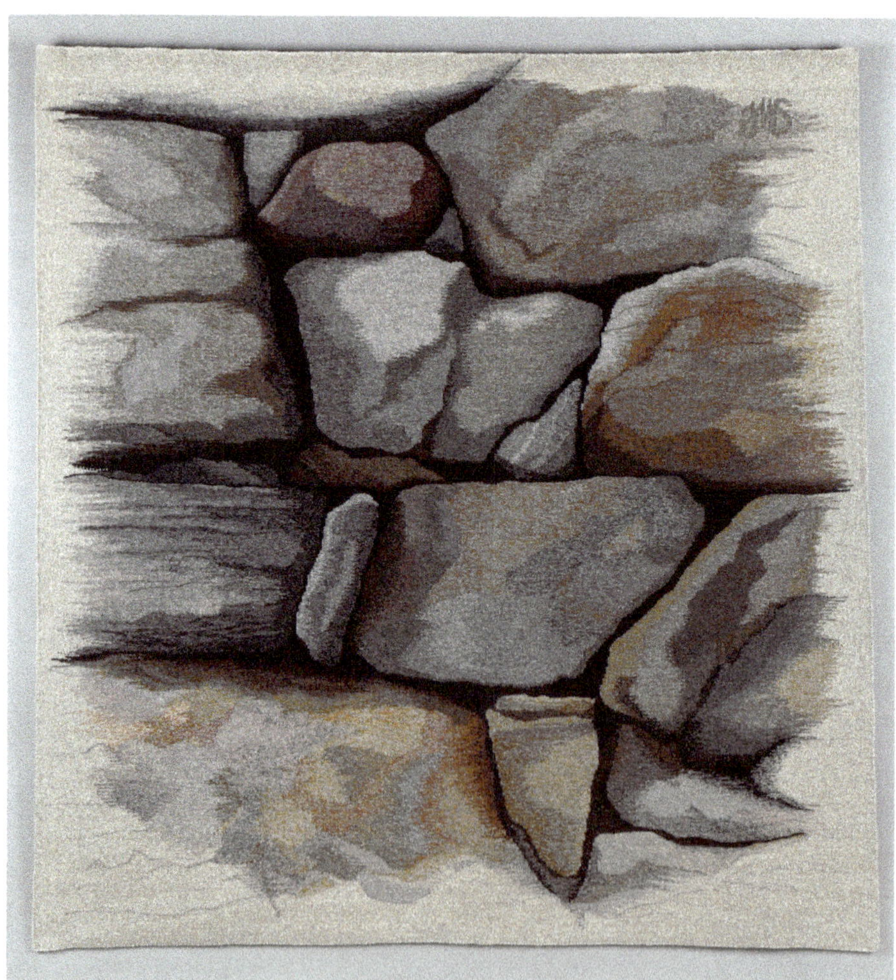

Figure 11.8
Because of Memory, tapestry, 60 inches by 54 inches, 2014 (photo by Tim Barnwell)

whole of it and details. Finally in 2014, I felt compelled to use the chimney's stones as the subject for paintings and hoped a tapestry would grow from one of those.

As I worked on the paintings, the quote on the grave marker kept running through my mind like a mantra, especially the ending phrase: "because of memory…" After returning home I designed a tapestry based upon one of the paintings. The tapestry is called *Because of Memory*, not simply as a reminder of the inspiring moments I've had at the Center but more because I believe that memory is held in stones as well as in human minds. The memory of ages and forces shows in the stones and is more permanent than the memories of humans can ever be.

I've also made countless photographs of stones in other places. In 2016 when I was a resident at the Hambidge Center, I photographed details of the stones and bricks found in buildings on the property.

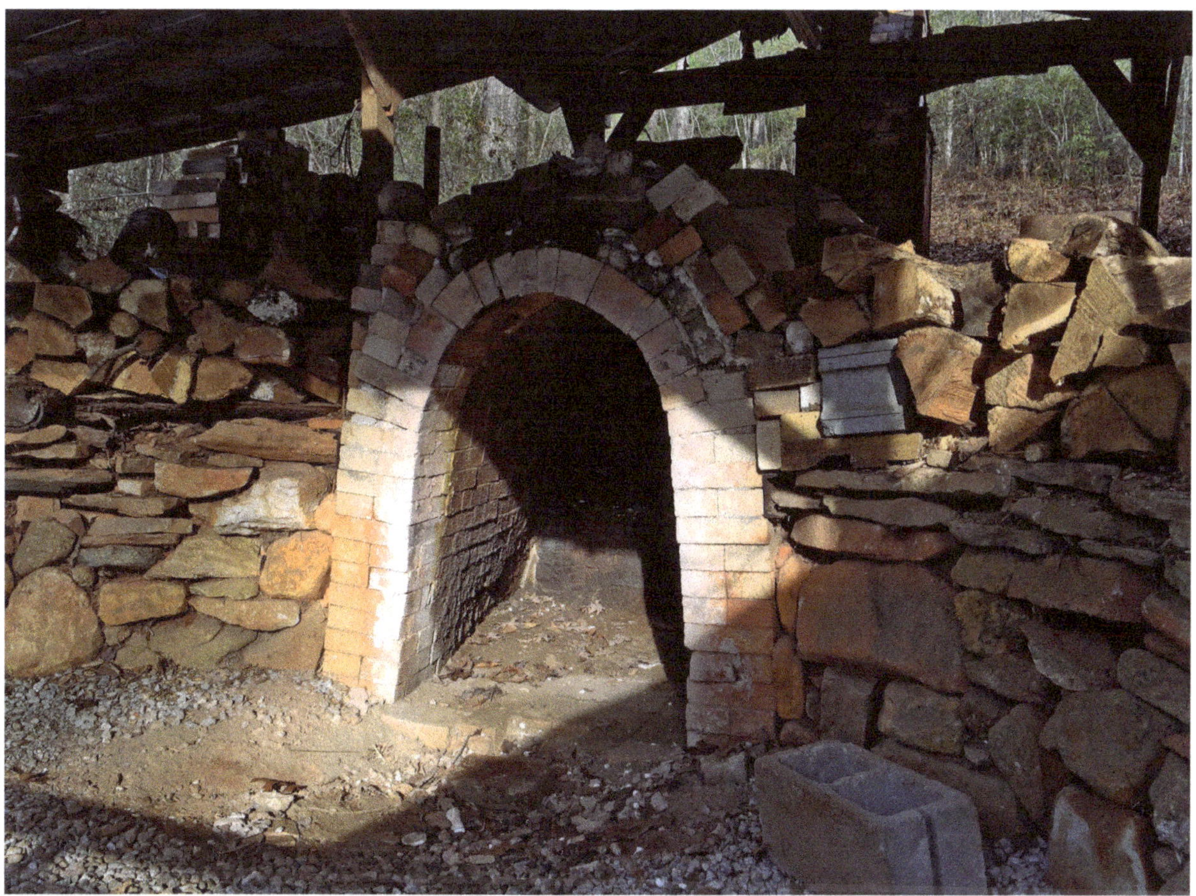

Figure 11.9
Anagama pottery kiln at the Hambidge Center, Rabun Gap, GA

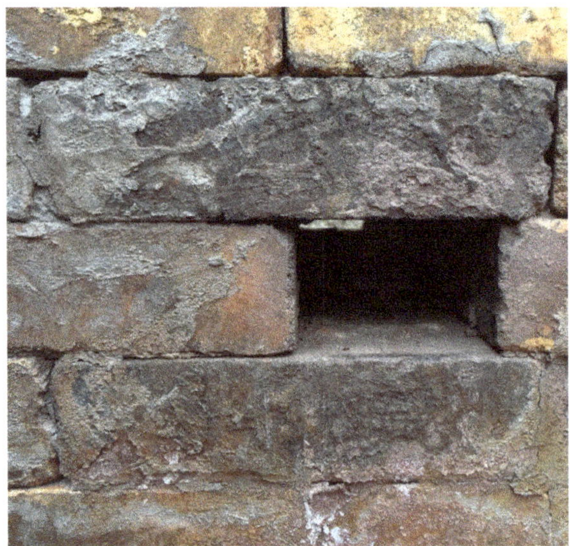

Figure 11.10
Detail from the chimney of the Anagama kiln

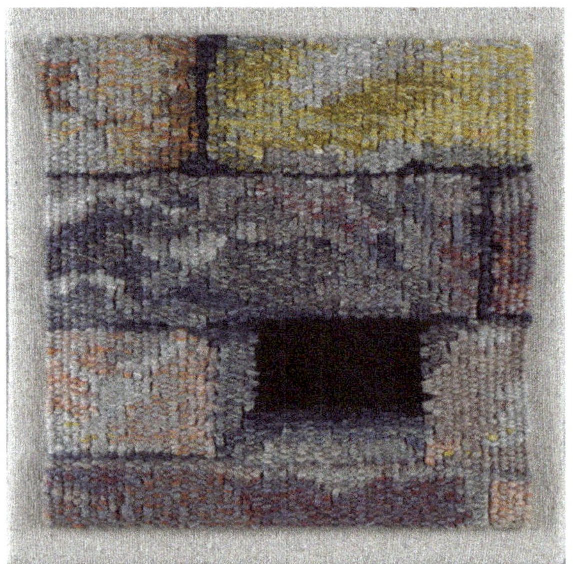

Figure 11.11
Hambidge Kiln Bricks, tapestry, 6 inches by 6 inches, 2015 (photo by Tim Barnwell)

From those, I chose three to weave as small tapestries.

One of the photos was a detail of the anagama kiln, a large outdoor pottery-firing oven built on the grounds of the Hambidge Center. The bricks of the kiln were beautiful reds, oranges, yellows, ochers, and umbers. Perhaps much of the color variety came from the effect of the heat of the kiln firings. As I moved around the structure making photographs, I noticed a dark rectangular void on one side of the chimney where one of the bricks had been removed. The dark hollow of the opening gave a stark contrast to the many colors of the surrounding bricks. That empty space as much as the bricks themselves called me to weave it, and the resulting small tapestry I titled *Hambidge—Kiln Bricks*.

The rock springhouse on the property became the subject of another tapestry. I've loved the springhouse from the moment I saw it on my first visit to the Center in the early 1990s. The stones are warm ochers and iron oxide colors, and they contrast with the dark and light greens of the mosses that grow on them. In the tapestry, I wanted to capture the warm and cool contrast of those stones and moss, as well as make the surface of the tapestry reflect some of the texture differences between them. *Hambidge—Springhouse Stones* was the resulting tapestry.

A third small tapestry was designed from a photo of the foundation stones at Mary Hambidge's former home. The stones were roughly rectangular in shape. At one spot, I noticed a thin crack running through the mortar from bottom to top of the foundation. The fracture moved in an irregular zigzagged path upward. Both the horizontality of the stones and the contrasting diagonal movements of the fracturing line were visually interesting. The tapestry I wove from that image was *Hambidge House—Foundation Stones.*

One day at home as I was taking a morning walk, I noticed the shadows cast by some gravel that had washed over the sidewalk in a recent rain. I began to think how the cast shadow would change with the sun's position throughout the day. I considered drawing an outline of the shadow shape at different times of the day, sort of like a very rudimentary sundial.

I've now done that several times by placing a small stone on a piece of white drawing paper where it will be in sunshine most of the day. Each hour, I draw the outline of the new shadow position and note the time. Maybe a tapestry will develop from this curious activity some day. If not, one way or another, I know I'll return to stones for inspiration.

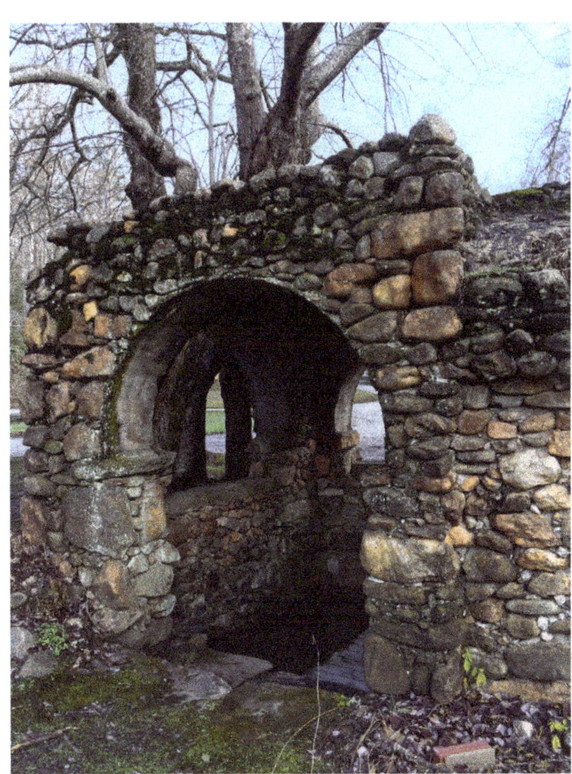

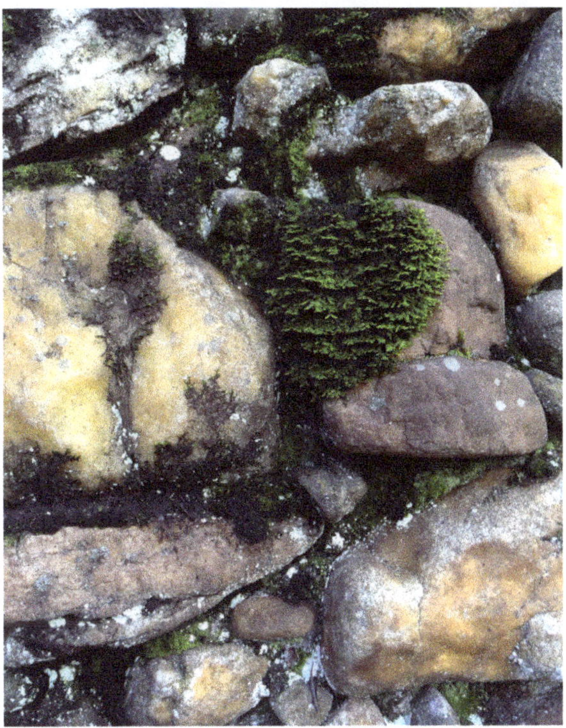

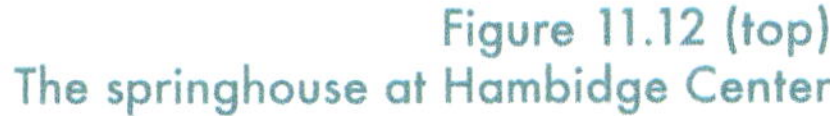

Figure 11.12 (top)
The springhouse at Hambidge Center

Figure 11.13 (bottom)
Detail of stones and moss at the springhouse

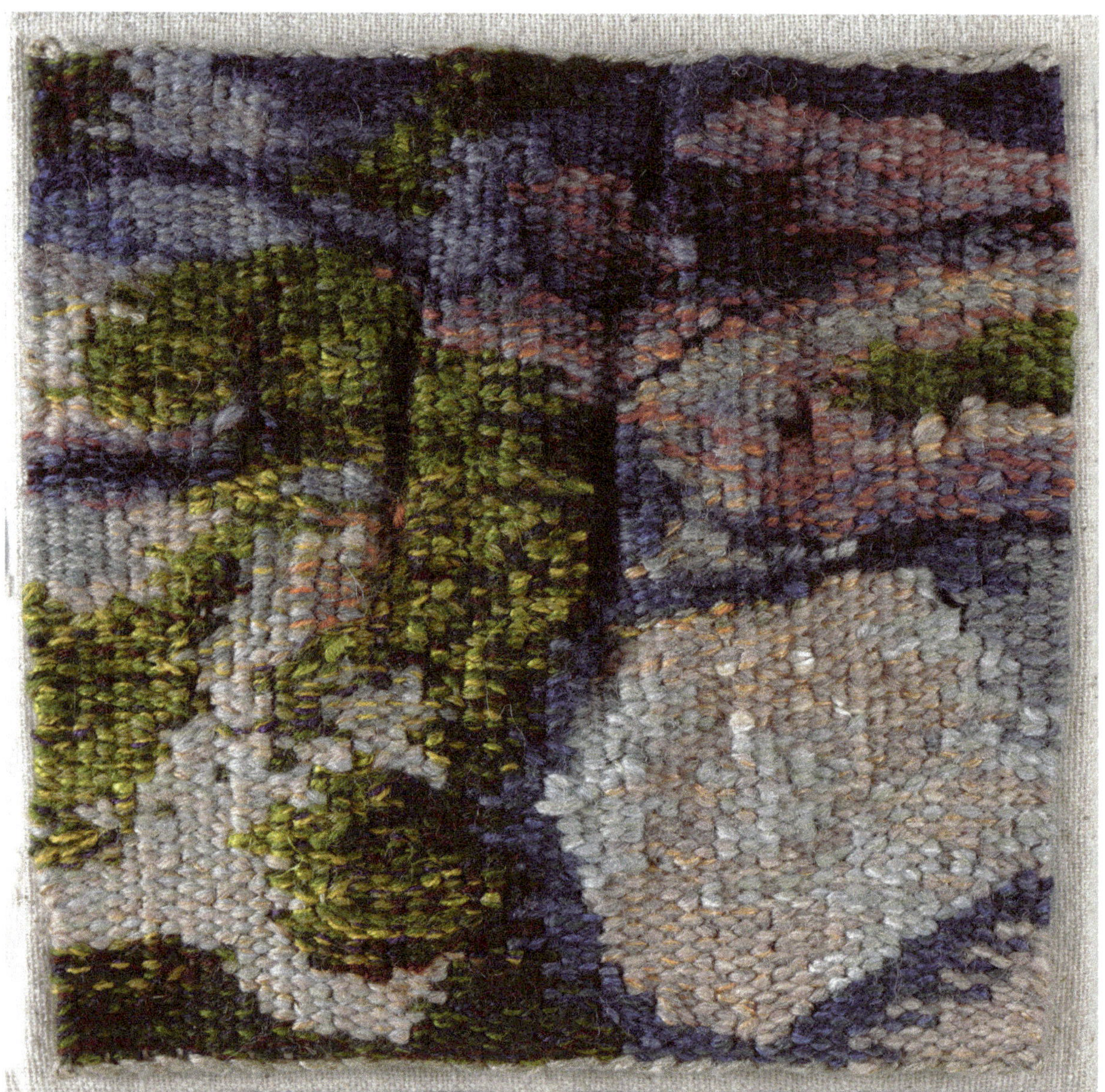

Figure 11.14
Hambidge–Springhouse Stones, tapestry, 6 inches by 6 inches, 2015 (photo by Tim Barnwell)

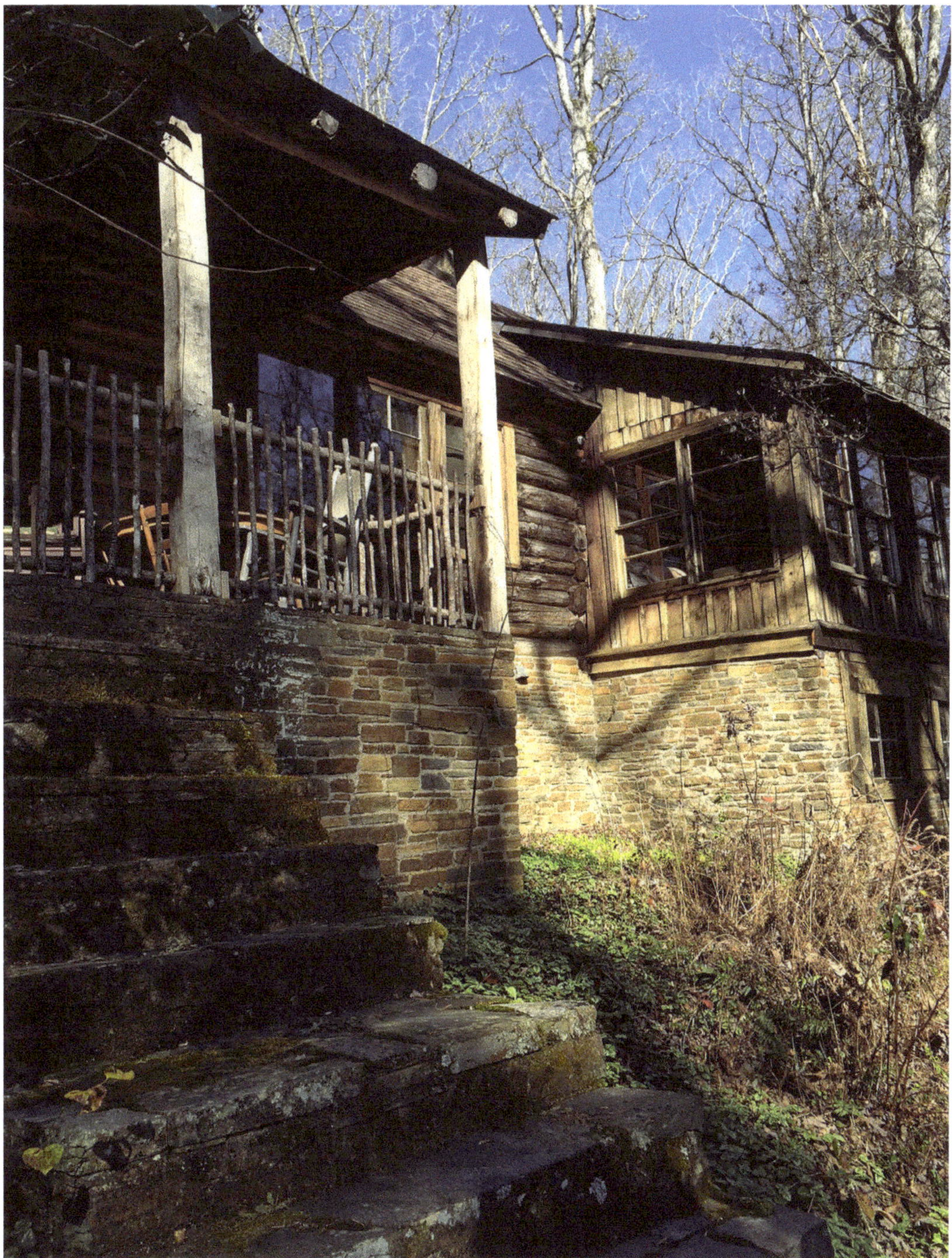

Figure 11.15
Mary Hambidge House at the Hambidge Center

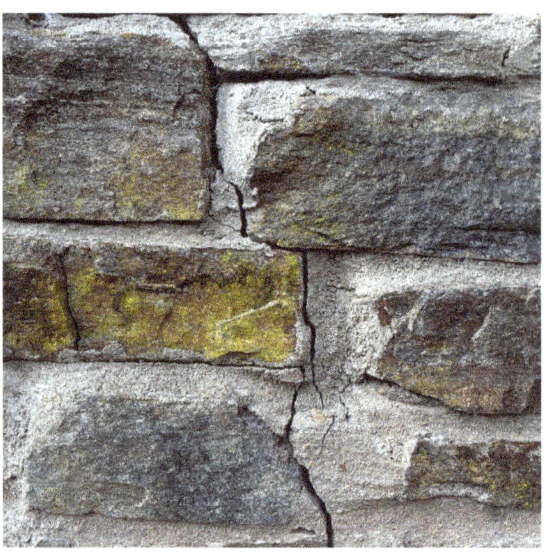

Figure 11.16
Detail of the foundation stones at the Mary Hambidge House

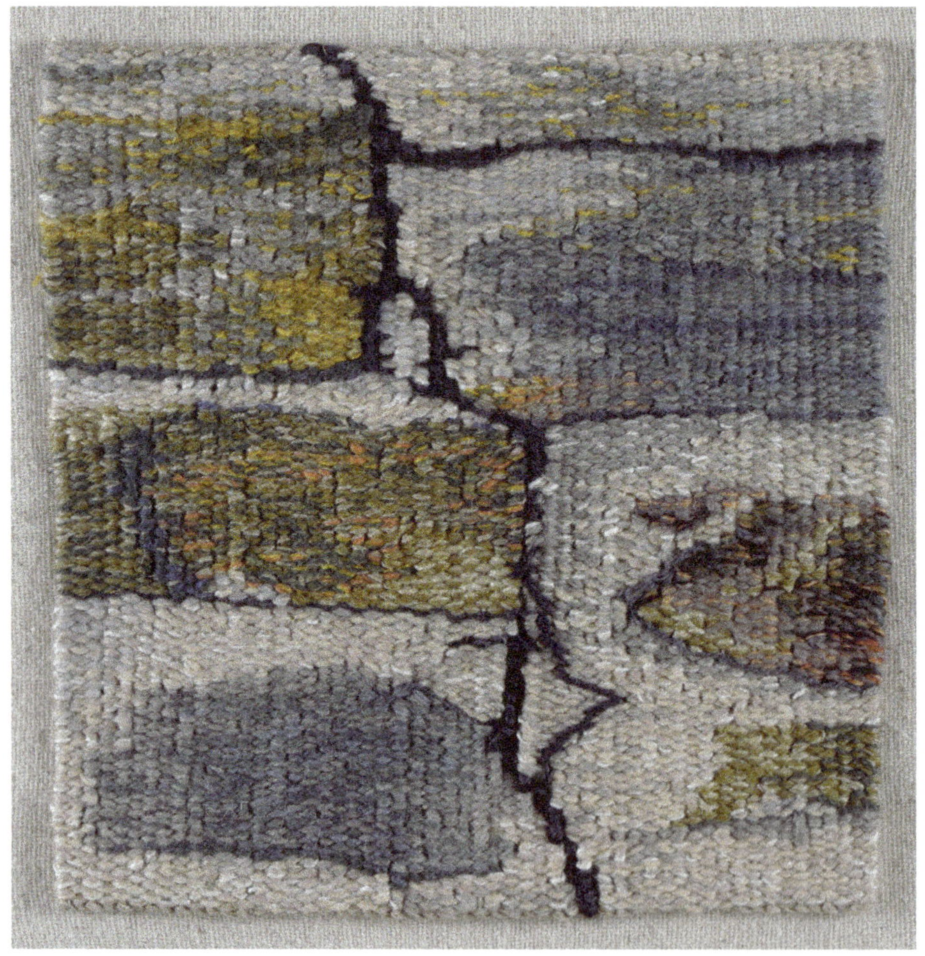

Figure 11.17
Hambidge House—Foundation Stones, tapestry, 6 inches by 6 inches, 2015 (photo by Tim Barnwell)

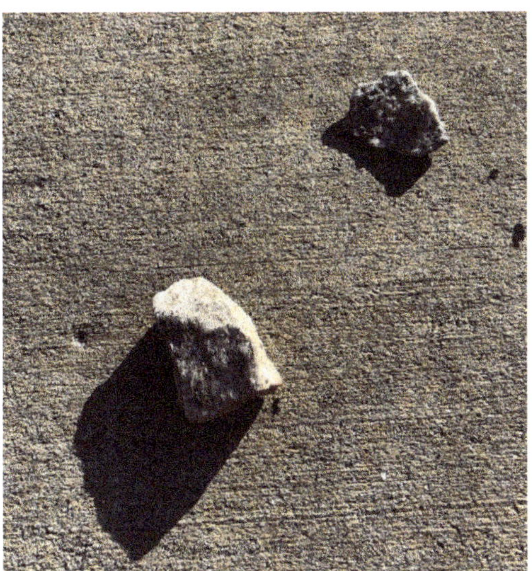

Figure 11.18
Gravel and shadow on the asphalt. Seeing shadows like these caused me to wonder about drawing the outline of the shadow shapes cast by a simple stone each hour throughout a day.

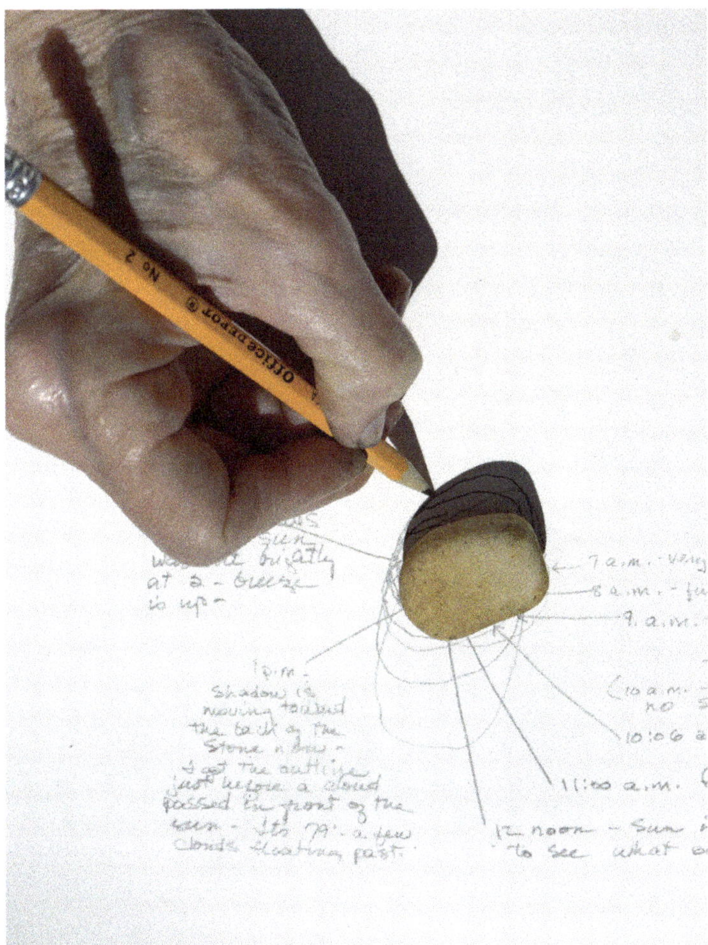

Figure 11.19
Drawing the shadows to experiment with the idea—a rudimentary sundial.

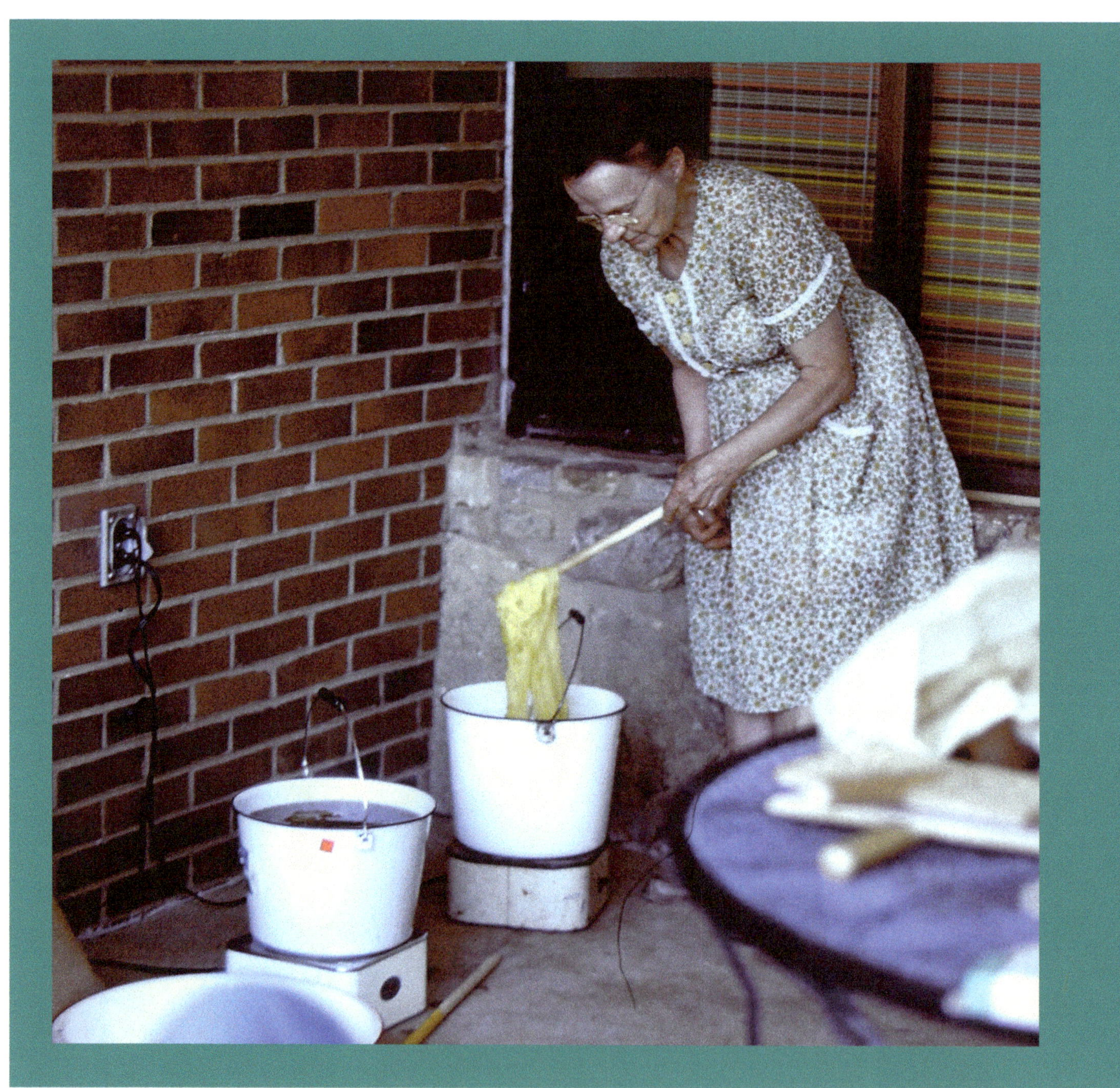

Figure 12.1
Mary Frances Davidson demonstrating natural dyeing at a festival at North Georgia College in 1974.

12

Black Walnuts and Red Earth

What goes around comes around. Decades after my first experiences with natural dyeing for yarn and using earth pigments for painting I found myself working with both once more.

I was introduced to natural dyeing in a 1974 workshop with Mary Frances Davidson (b. 1905–d. 2002) soon after I had become an instructor at NGC. Her book, *The Dye Pot* (1974), was one of the few about natural dyeing available at the time.[1] Bob knew Mary Frances and asked her to be one of several craftspeople invited to the college to lead workshops during a three-day festival the department held for campus and community that year.

Mary Frances was a dynamo—a tiny, red-haired woman with a gigantic personality and huge knowledge of natural dyeing that came from her many years of experience. She sent a list of plants that we should collect before the workshop. When she arrived, she directed us to chop the plants, immerse them in water, then heat the water to nearly boiling to extract the dye. She brought indigo and cochineal because those were dye materials that we wouldn't find as we searched the fields for plants.

Mary Frances led us through the basics of preparing wool yarn by a process called mordanting. Mordants are mineral salts used with natural dyes to increase the colorfastness. She stressed that the mordants would let the dye "bite" into the wool to make a chemical bond between the fibers and the dyestuff. Next, we immersed the yarn skeins into the pots of dye we were brewing; right away, the wool was transformed. Yellows appeared as we dyed

1 Mary Frances Davidson, *The Dye Pot* (Gatlinburg, TN: printed by the author, 1974).

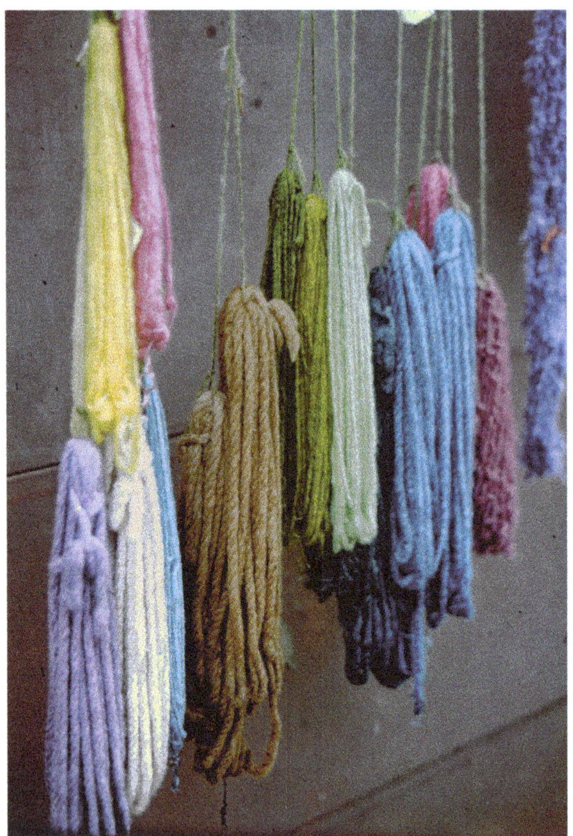

Figure 12.2
These were some of the dyed skeins of yarn from Miss Davidson's workshop.

with marigolds. And the cochineal, made up of the dried and crushed bodies of the cochineal insect, astonished us with the brilliant reds that came out of the dye pot. A vat of indigo gave us blue and then green when we dipped in some of the yellow yarns. And purples followed as we overdyed some of the skeins of red with the indigo.

After those few intense days with Mary Frances, I was hooked on natural dyeing. For several years, I continued to use the process in my work as well as with several of my classes at the college. The students and I loved the colors of the yarns, and we enjoyed finding and trying different plants for dyes. But I gradually dropped natural dyeing from my curriculum planning as the need to focus on other things took over. Likewise, I stopped dyeing yarns for my own weaving when I moved in other directions.

Even earlier than my introduction to natural dye was my first encounter with earth pigments as a painting medium. Bob was also responsible for that experience. In the art education course at NGC, he taught about art techniques that could be used in public school classrooms. Among those was an activity he called "earth pigment painting."

One day as class ended, Bob asked us to bring in several small bags of different colors of soil for our next class session. That afternoon, a couple of friends and I drove around the county searching for interesting finds along the roadsides.

With those finds, Bob showed us how to sift the dirt to remove sticks and stones by using window screen wire stapled to a wood frame. After shaking it through the screens a couple of times, we mixed in diluted Elmer's glue until the dirt reached a consistency suitable for painting. Because we only sifted the earth with coarse window screen wire and didn't grind it more finely with a mortar and pestle, the resulting paint was quite gritty.

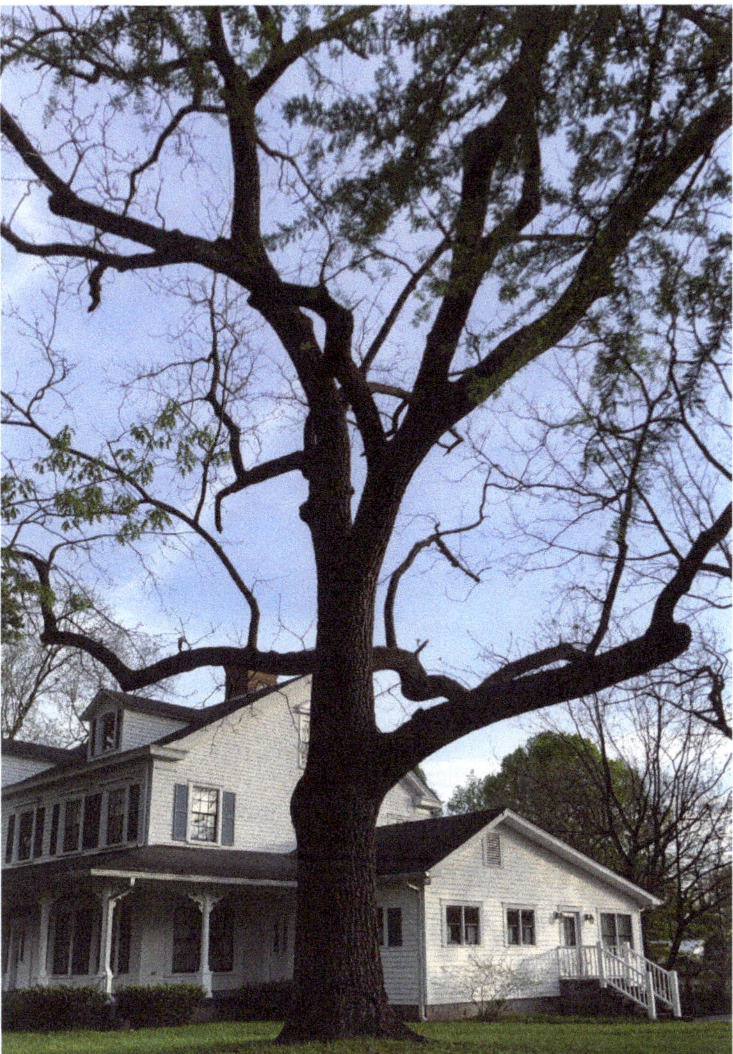

Figure 12.3
Black walnut tree in our front yard, Dahlonega, GA

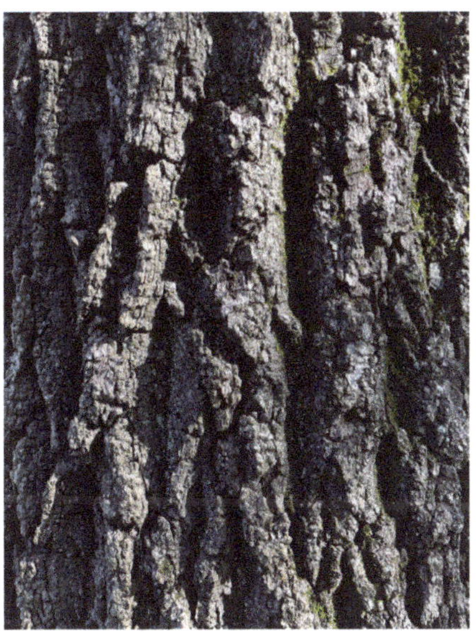

Figure 12.4
Bark of the black walnut tree is deeply furrowed

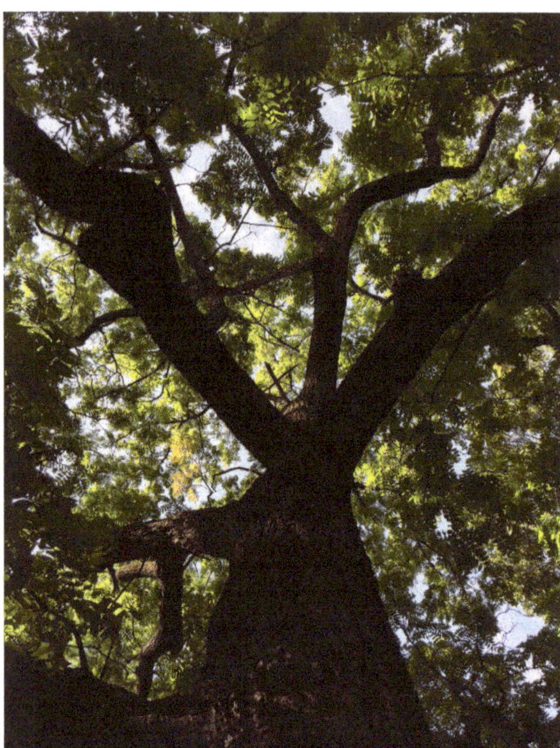

Figure 12.5
The limbs expand out in meandering ways

Figure 12.6
The leaves in the fall are intense golden hue

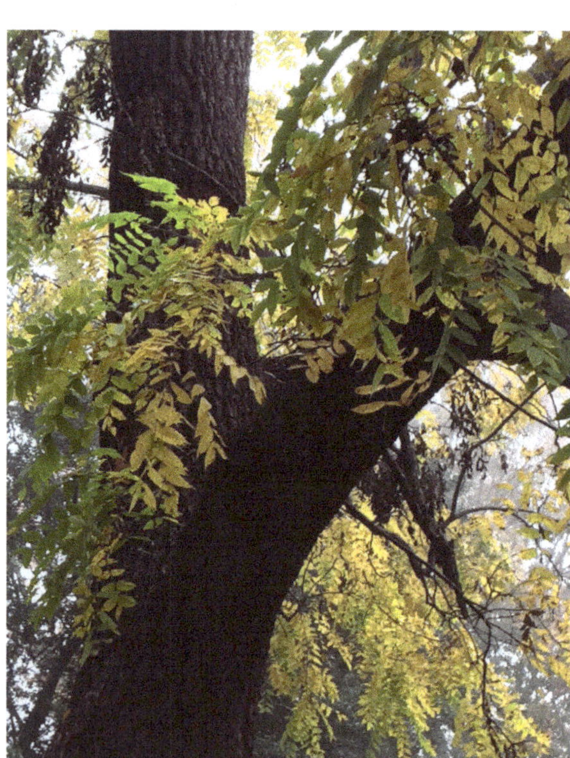

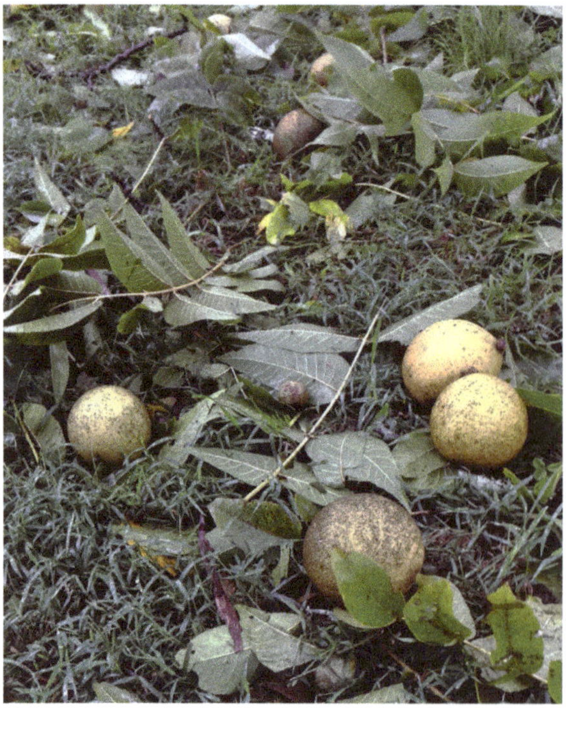

Figure 12.7
Black walnuts drop from the tree in the fall of the year, covering the yard and the driveway.

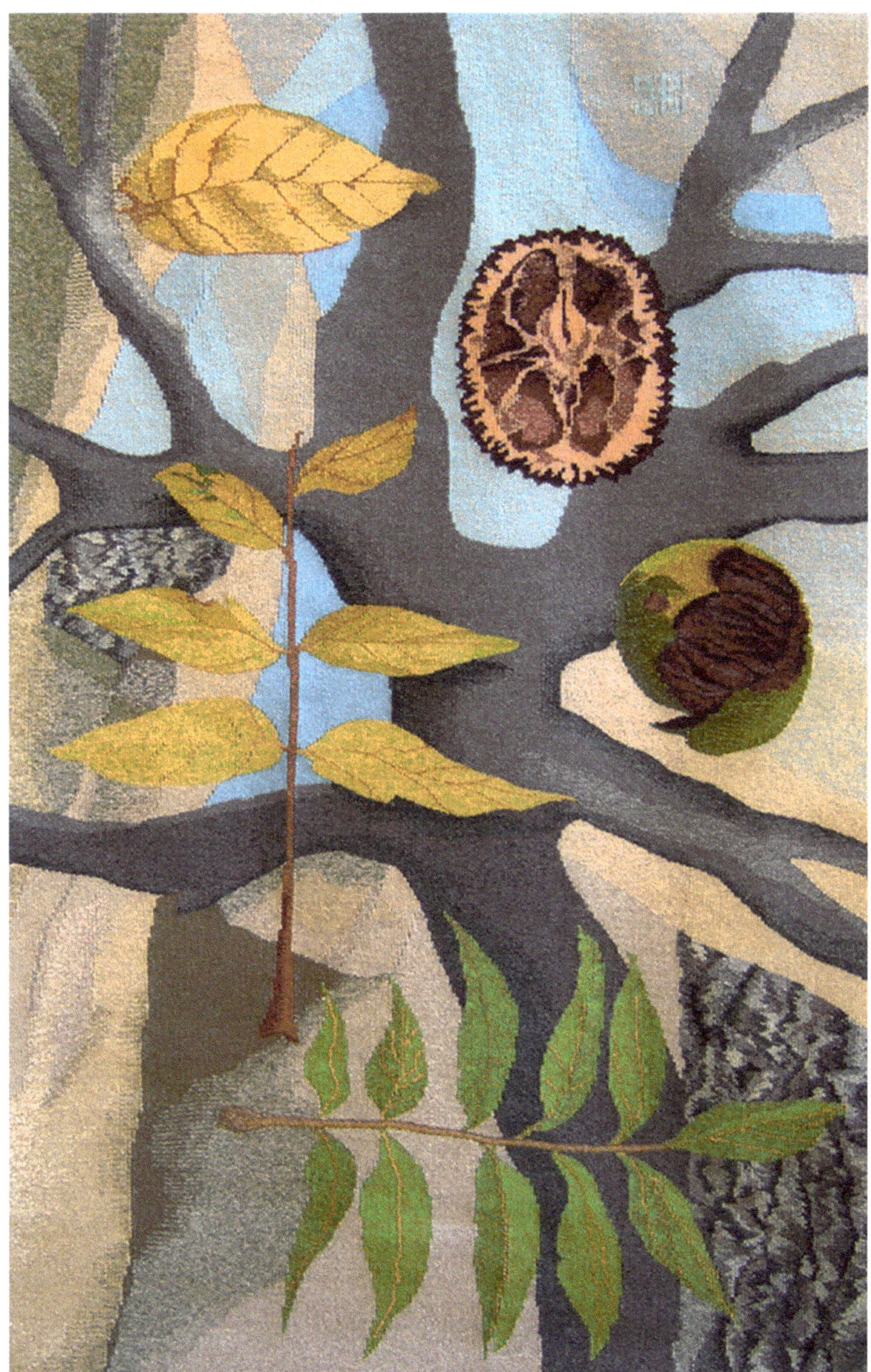

Figure 12.8
To the Essence of Every Nature, tapestry, 54 inches by 34 inches, 2007 (photo by Randy Crump)

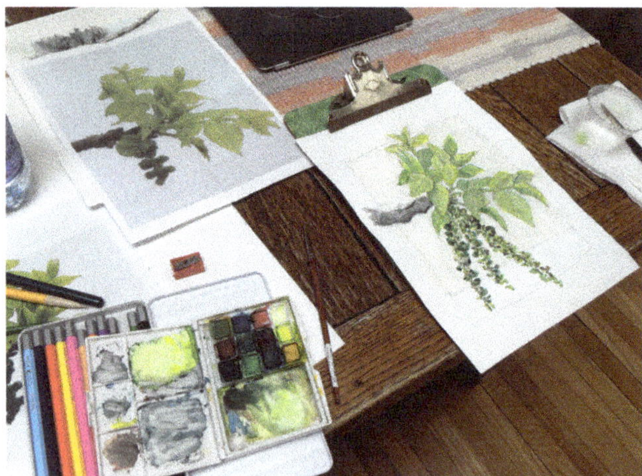

Figure 12.9
Watercolor painting of black walnut catkins and leaves, in preparation for a tapestry cartoon of a section of a larger painting.

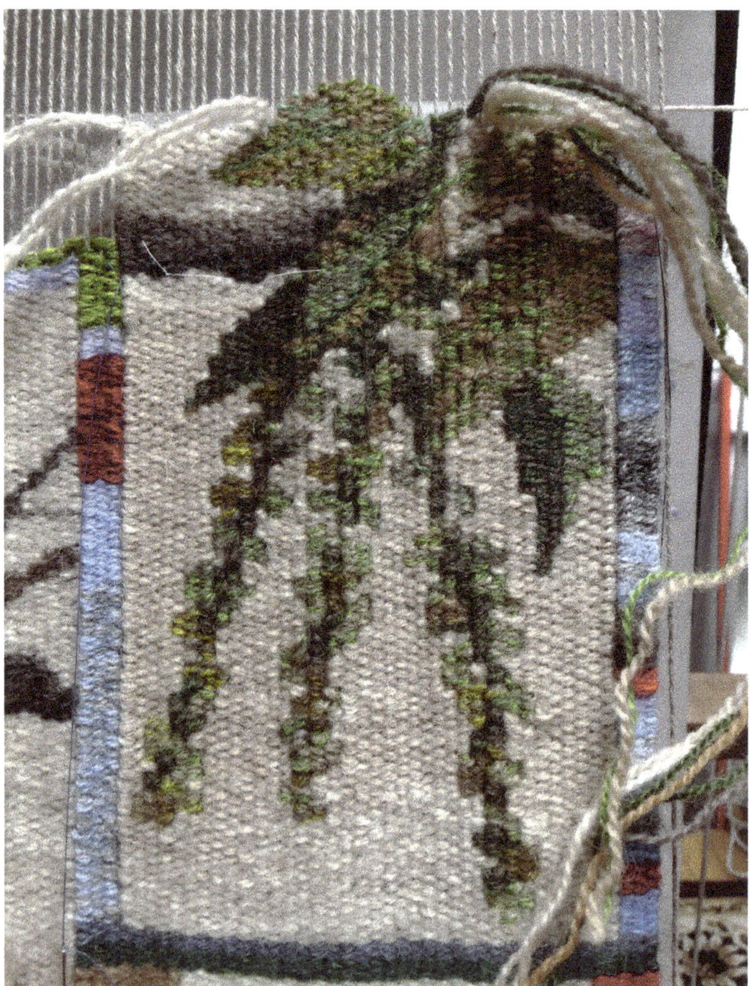

Figure 12.10
The catkins being woven into the tapestry.

Nevertheless, it was thrilling to see our papers fill with the red of Georgia clay and the many other colors we'd found under our feet on our excursions.

When I began teaching, I used the same simple method for earth pigment painting in both high school and after-school children's art classes. Students of all ages had a great time collecting the dirt and then shaking it through a simple screen sieve to make their paint. But after a few years, just as with natural dyeing, I stopped using earth pigment painting as other things took priority in my teaching.

I fondly recalled those earlier experiences when, in 2016, I once more began to explore both natural dyes for yarn and earth pigments for painting. As it happened, it was the large black walnut tree in our front yard that led to my renewed interest in these methods.

The tree has been a favorite of my husband and mine for many years. It's the largest of several trees on the property, and its trunk is much larger than my arms' span. A tree age calculator based on circumference showed that the black walnut was probably at least 160 years old. In that case, the tree would have been well established when our house was built in 1871.

Its bark is dark gray and deeply furrowed. Its limbs branch out crookedly from the massive main trunk. In spring, its catkins and young leaves are bright yellow green; in the summer, its compound leaves are abundant and deeper green; and in the fall, its foliage turns to golden yellow. The nuts begin to fall in October and continue through November. A thick, bright green hull covers the hard shell holding the nutmeat.

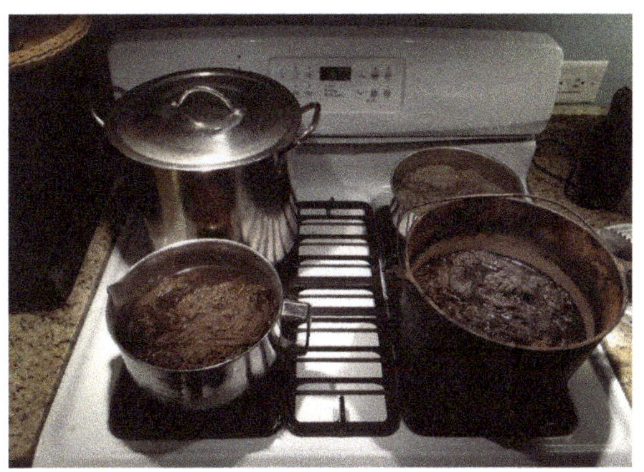

Figure 12.11
Dyeing wool yarn with black walnuts

Squirrels make homes in the tree's top and scurry around the ground, finding the walnuts and gnawing off the outer hull with their sharp teeth to get to the nut inside. The crows also harvest the nuts when the hulls begin to break off after they've lain on the ground for a few weeks, making raucous comments all the while. I've even seen a crow drop a nut into the street from the phone line outside, dropping it over and over until the nut cracked. The black walnuts make quite a thud when falling on the skylights in the kitchen and are ankle twisters to walk

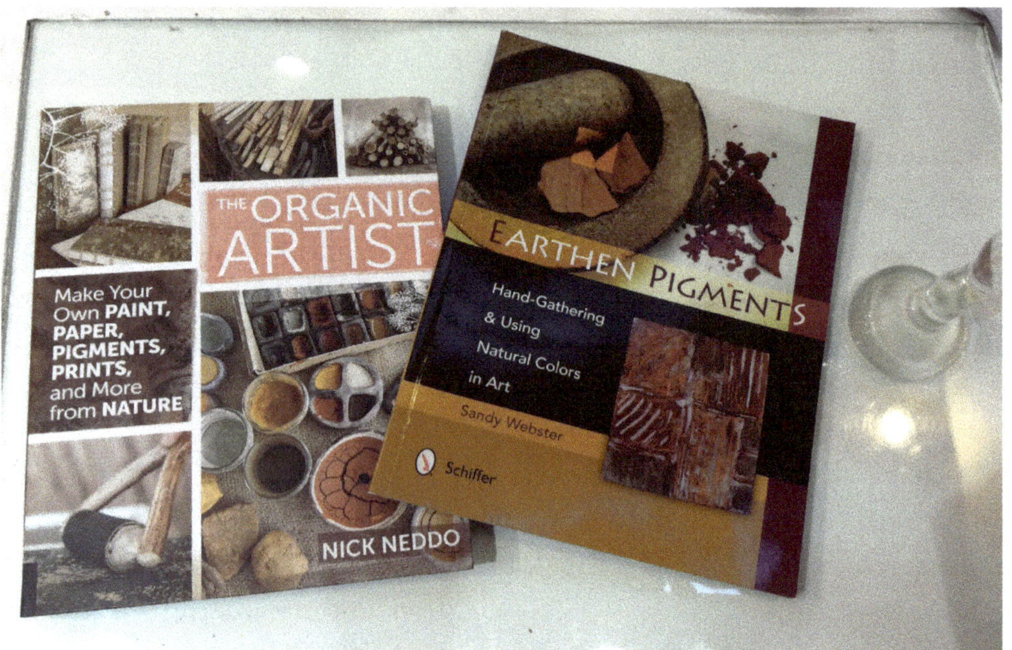

Figure 12.12
Sandy Webster and Nick Neddo's books about using natural materials for art making.

among if you're not careful. Each fall the cement of the driveway is again stained a deep brownish gray with the mashed hulls as the cars drive over them.

I've photographed the tree often since we've lived here, and it was the basis for the tapestry *To the Essence of Every Nature*, completed in 2007. In that composition, a large simplified tree trunk spread from bottom to top, with limbs branching off to left and right. Superimposed over those were woven enlarged details of the bark, leaves, and nuts at different seasons.

As 2016 began, I wanted to use the black walnut tree as a tapestry subject once more and to further represent the seasonal changes that happen over twelve months. So I devoted a year to making the tapestry—a visual diary of the passing of time.

Each month I made a small watercolor painting representing a different aspect of the tree. For instance, in January the painting was of a dried black walnut hull; a few months later, the catkins of spring were featured. A detail of tree bark was the subject for one of the paintings, and an overall view of trunk and several limbs was shown in another. The monthly painted studies became the source of twelve small cartoons, each woven during a particular month as part of the ongoing tapestry. The tapestry that resulted is called *A Year of My Life—2016.*

I'd used the black walnuts to dye some of the yarn for this tapestry. As the year progressed, I became curious to know if they could be used to make drawing ink. In my quest for information about inks, I contacted two artists whose work I knew. One was Michael W. Hughey (b. 1945), a calligrapher who I thought may have created inks with natural materials. The other, Sandy Webster (b. 1947), is well known for using natural materials on fabric and paper. I wondered if Sandy also made inks. Possibly these two could point me in the right direction to investigate deriving ink from black walnuts.

Michael shared several references and sent a packet of black walnut ink crystals I could try. Sandy provided a page copied from Nick Neddo's (b. 1979) book *The Organic Artist* (2014) in which he described the process of making ink from not only black walnuts but also acorns and other raw ingredients. His book soon became part of my growing library on natural sources for art materials.[2] Thinking about inks from walnuts and reading Neddo's book reminded me of the rudimentary earth pigment paintings I'd done decades before.

I purchased Sandy's book, *Earthen Pigments* (2012); it provided excellent instructions of equipment and steps needed for preparing soil. She described how to sift the dirt through increasingly-finer mesh sieves and then grind it between a glass slab and muller, using water and a binding medium like gum arabic.[3] Both books were valuable as I began to more deeply explore earth pigments for painting and natural materials for inks and dyes.

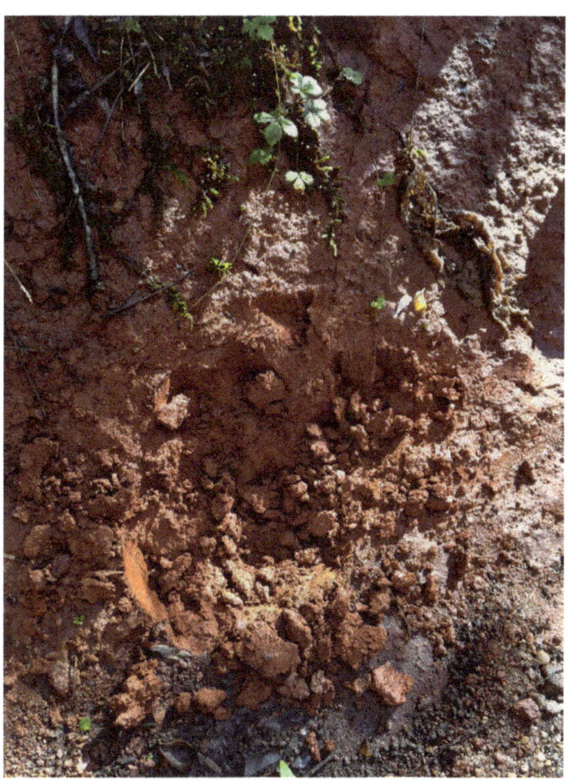

Figure 12.13
Digging earth pigments in Rabun County, GA

I collected many colors of dirt from around home, the Hambidge Center, and the LES Center. Armed with information from my readings, I refined the pigments more

2 Nick Neddo, *The Organic Artist* (Beverly, MA: Quarry Books, 2015).

3 Sandy Webster, *Earthen Pigments: Hand-Gathering and Using Natural Colors in Art* (Atglen, PA: Schiffer Publishing, 2012).

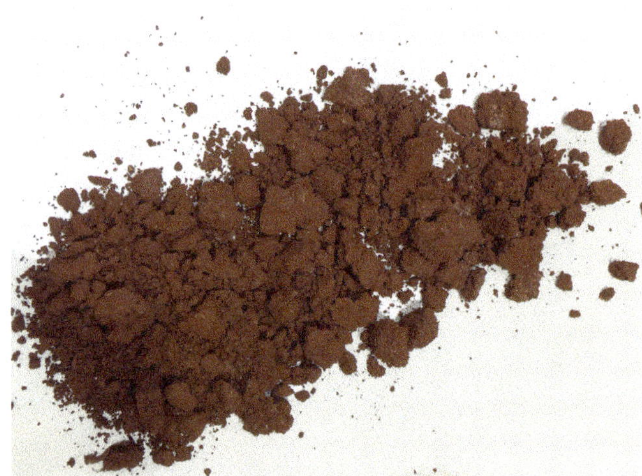

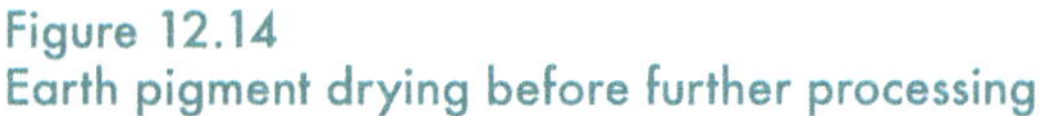

Figure 12.14
Earth pigment drying before further processing

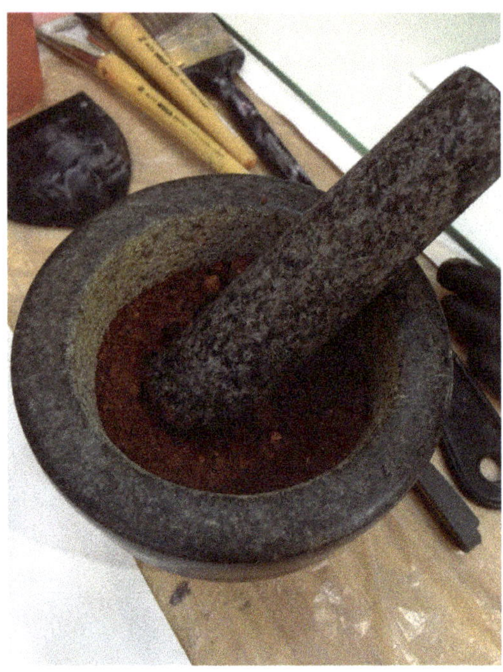

Figure 12.15
Grinding the pigment with mortar and pestle

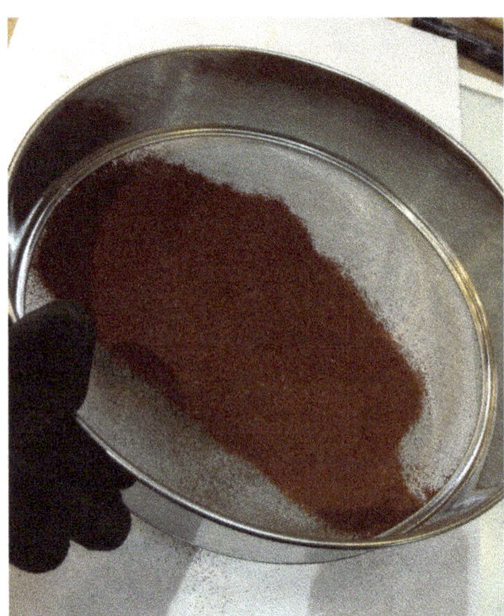

Figure 12.16
Sifting to refine the earth pigment into finer particles

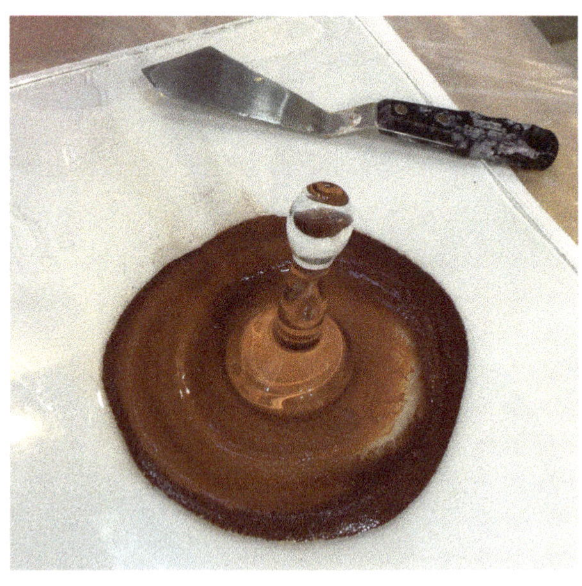

Figure 12.17
Using a muller and water to blend the earth pigment before combining with painting medium. In this case, gum arabic was used to make watercolor.

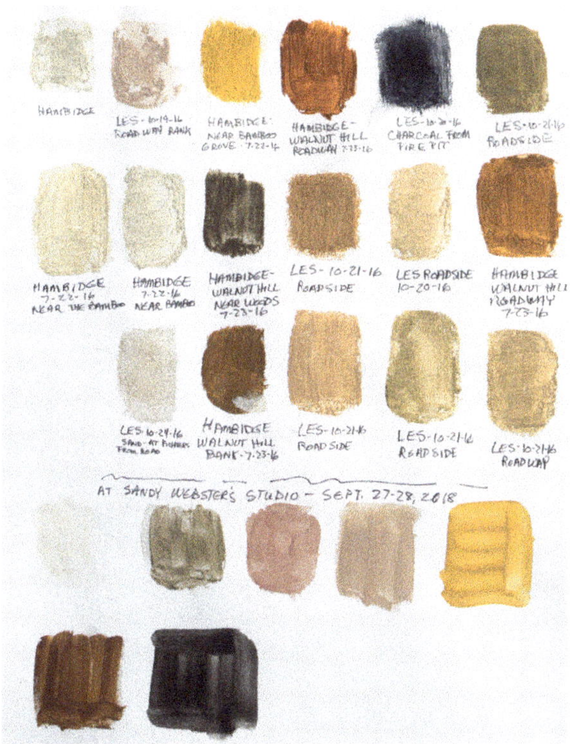

Figure 12.18
Samples of the earth pigment colors collected (photo by Christopher Dant)

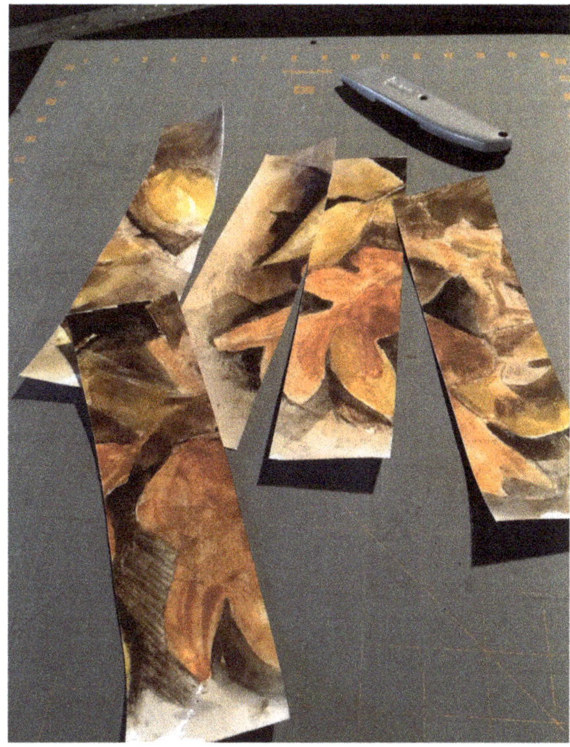

Figure 12.19
A small earth pigment painting that was cut into strips. A tapestry was designed based on one of the small pieces.

thoroughly than I'd done years before. I also continued to dye yarn and make ink from black walnuts. In the midst of this study, I discovered I could tone paper with the dye and that I could draw with dry black walnut twigs into the damp, dyed papers to give a subtle mark.

Throughout 2016, I made many drawings and paintings using both the walnut inks and the earth pigments. From those, I developed designs for several tapestries. One originated from a small strip cut from a larger earth pigment painting based on colors of leaf litter seen on the forest floor. Leaf litter, the decomposing remains of not only leaves but also sticks, lichens, and tree bark is an important organic part of the forest. It is a haven for tiny organisms that are important to the vitality of the surroundings.[4] The colors of the decaying matter are a wide range of warm, earthy hues very much like the pigments I used for the painting. I later

4 Kevin Lin, "Seasonal Science: What Lurks in the Leaf Litter?" *Scientific American: CityScience*, October 18, 2012. https://www.scientificamerican.com/article/bring-science-home-leaf-litter-biodiversity/

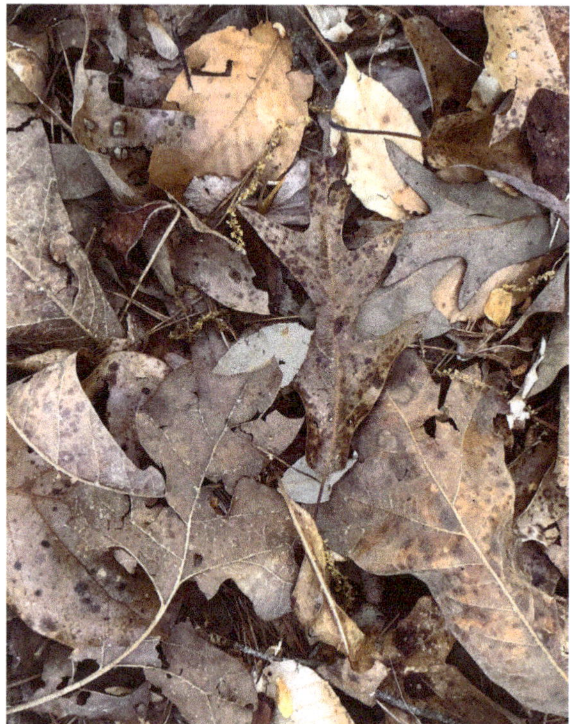

Figure 12.20
Leaf litter, a detail of a few square inches of the organic matter that carpets the forest floor.

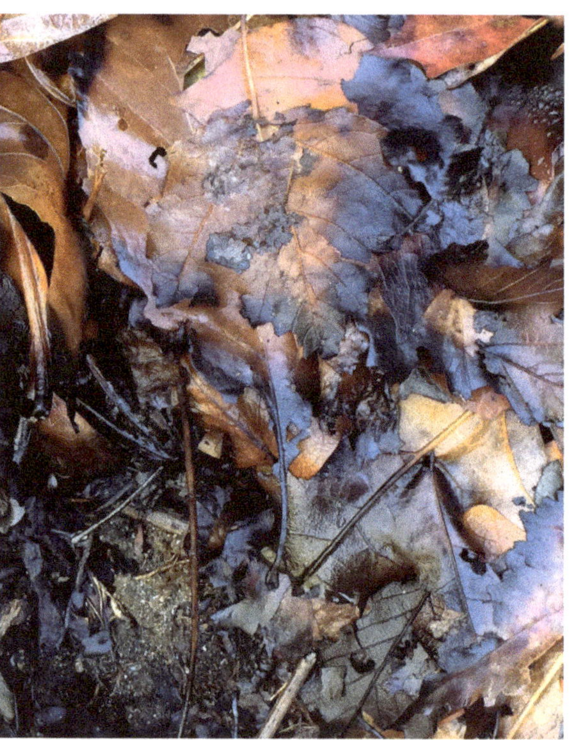

Figure 12.21
Detail of burned leaves

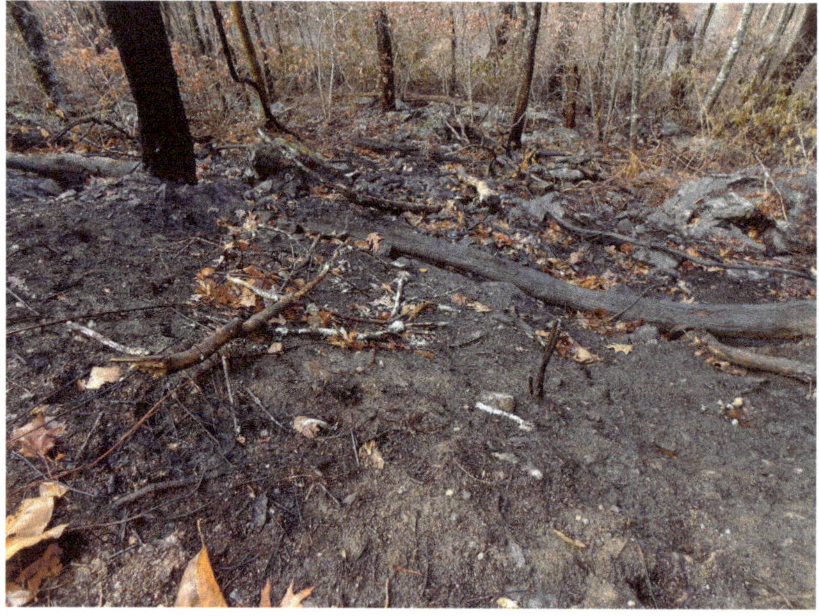

Figure 12.22
Area of control or "back burned" area of forest near the Hambidge Center, Rabun Gap, GA

enlarged the small strip into a cartoon for a sixty-inch high by thirty-inch wide tapestry.

Soon after I began weaving the tapestry, wildfires swept through the Southern Appalachian Mountains. I thought about how the layers of leaf litter in the forests had combined with prolonged drought of up to two months in some areas of the Southeast to turn thousands of acres of woods into tinderboxes.[5]

I knew then that the image I was weaving, designed to celebrate the beautiful colors of the leaf litter, was no longer relevant due to the devastation caused by the wildfires. Instead, the impact of the fires should become part of the tapestry. I felt that could only be done by making drastic changes in my plan, especially for the colors. But how to do that was a puzzle. I really needed to see some of the burned areas to help with those decisions.

The forests near the Hambidge Center had been in danger, so many acres were put into control or back burns as a preventative measure. I stayed several days at the Center to make photographs of burned landscape and to work on a series of images based on the fires. I also collected charred sticks to use as drawing tools along with earth pigment paints.[6]

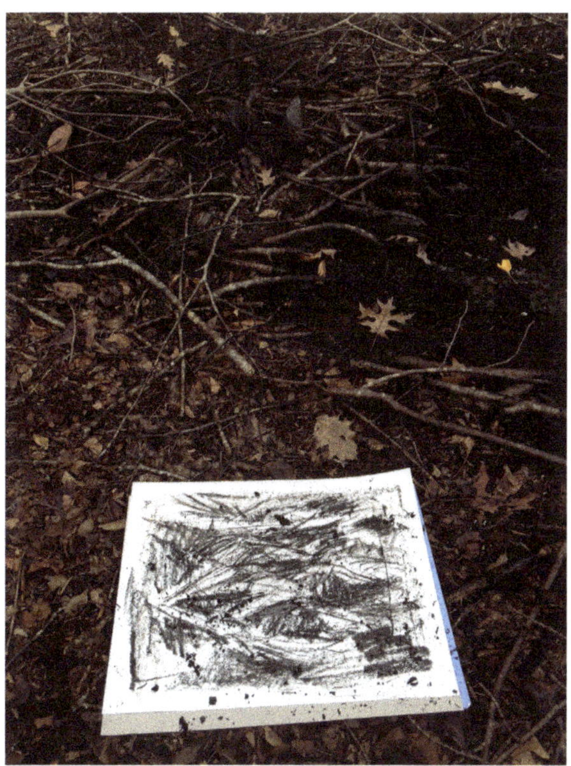

Figure 12.23
At one of the back burned sites I used some of the charred wood as drawing tools.

From those reflections and observations—thinking about the destruction, seeing burned areas, making photos and paintings—I redesigned the remaining part of the tapestry to include a large section to signify the charred forest. The tapestry that had started out with hues of dull reds and oranges representing leaf litter now incorporated grays of all tones—ashen, burned colors.

As the tapestry grew through the winter, my thoughts about it continued to change

5 NOAA (National Oceanic and Atmospheric Administration)—National Centers for Environmental Information, "Drought—November 2016." https://www.ncdc.noaa.gov/sotc/drought/201611#det-seus

6 Tommye McClure Scanlin, "Hambidge Days." December 27, 2016. http://tapestry13.blogspot.com/2016/12/hambidge-days.html

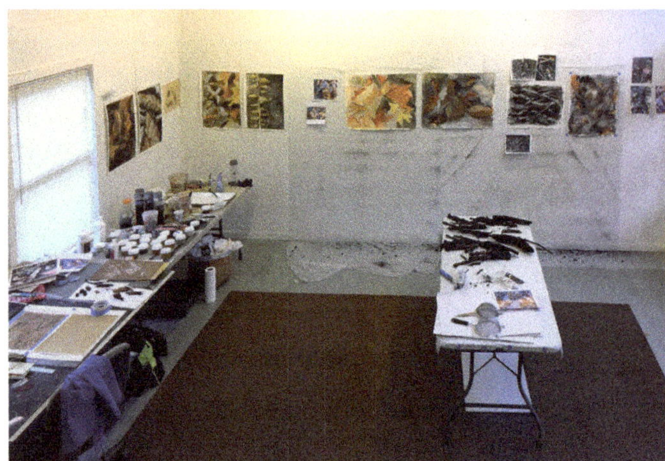

Figure 12.24
Interior view at Fisher Studio at Hambidge Center. Earth pigment and charcoal from the back burned areas were used for a series of paintings based on the wild fire devastation.

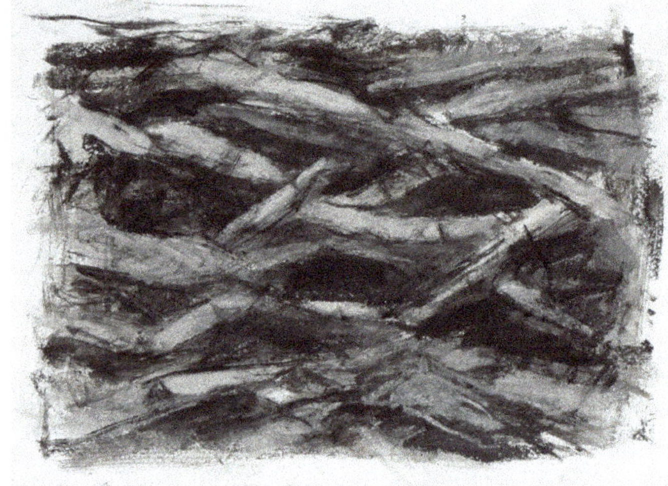

Figure 12.25
Burned Sticks, charcoal drawing, 32 inches by 24 inches, 2016 (photo by Tim Barnwell)

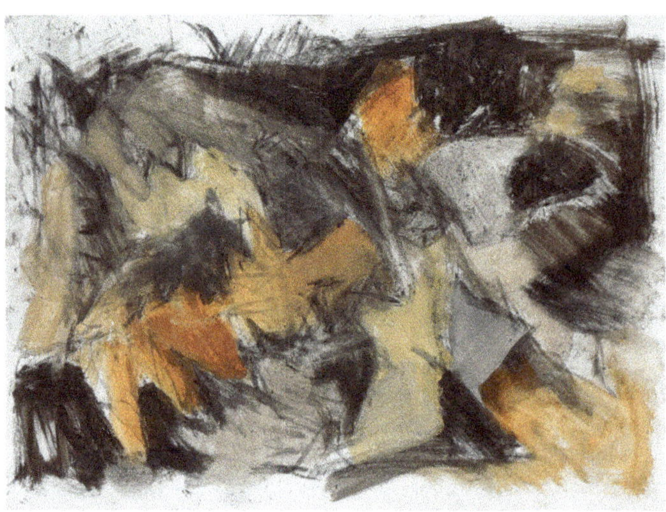

Figure 12.26
Leaf Burn, earth pigment and charcoal, 32 inches by 24 inches (photo by Tim Barnwell)

as I realized spring was soon returning. Even though the forest had been extensively burned, there wasn't total devastation. New growth would emerge. Over several months as the tapestry built up, I considered the events of the year, especially the contrasts of loss and renewal. In the last few inches, I acknowledged the new life to come by incorporating small areas of green yarn in the midst of the ashen colors. When the tapestry was finished, it seemed appropriate to call it *Phoenix*.

The exploration of earth pigment painting continued when, in late 2018, I had a private tutorial with Sandy Webster at her studio in Brasstown, North Carolina. She led me to ways of preparing the earth colors more exacting than my previous attempts and guided me to sources for finer mesh sieves than I'd located on my own. Many small studies of leaves, twigs, and stones have now been done with earth

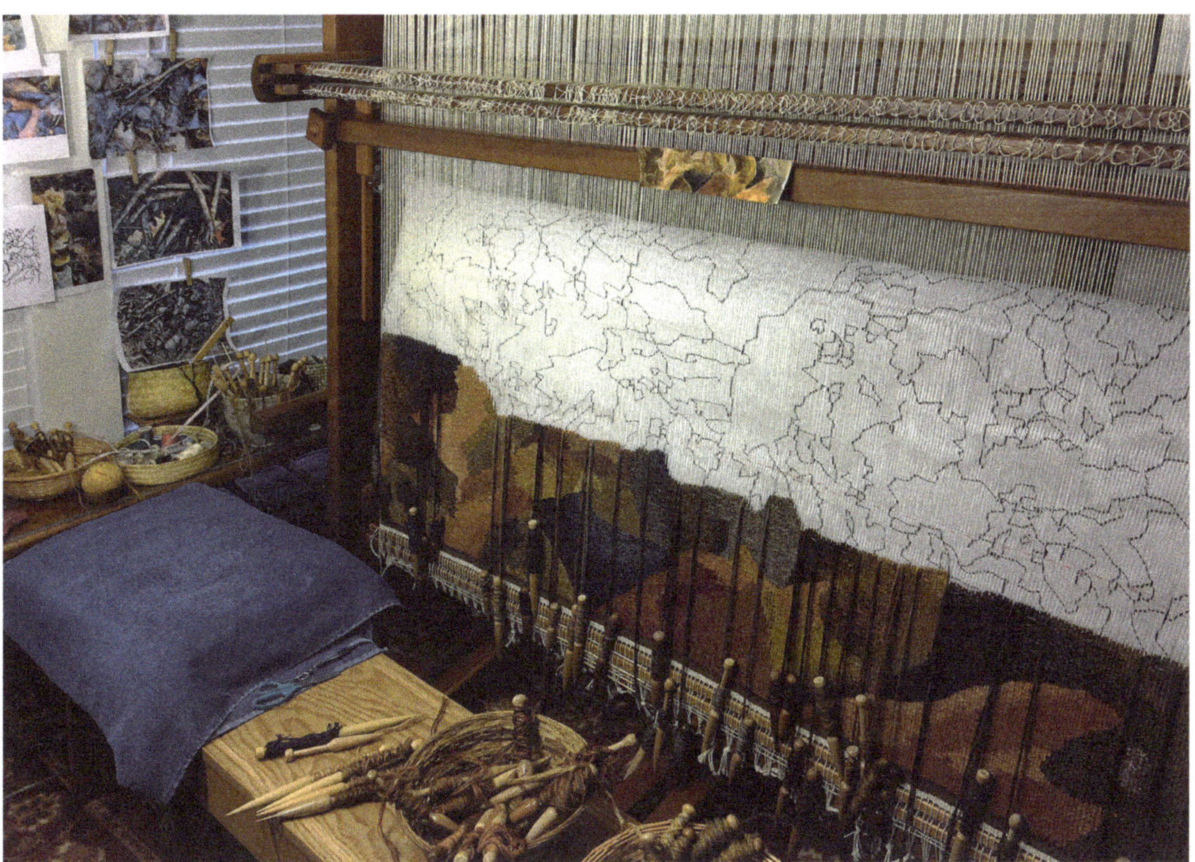

Figure 12.27
Weaving the tapestry that was designed from the small earth pigment painted strip. The design changed after seeing and working from the back burned areas.

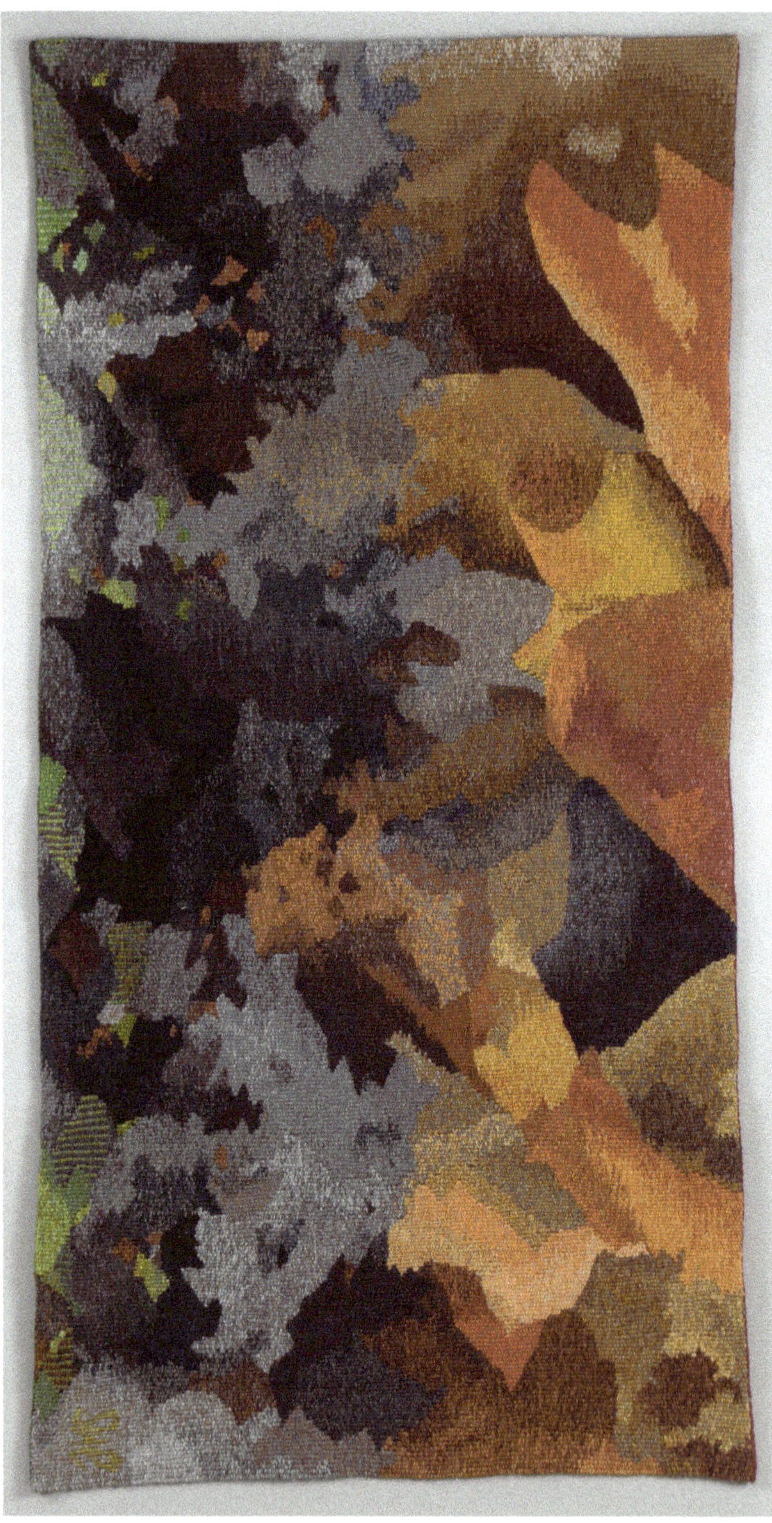

Figure 12.28
Phoenix, tapestry, 60 inches by 32 inches, 2017 (photo by Tim Barnwell)

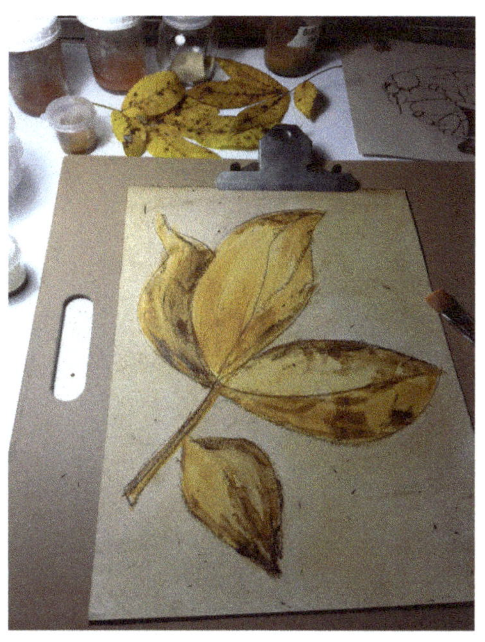

Figure 12.29
Painting hickory leaf using earth pigment paints at a residency at Lillian Smith Center, 2017

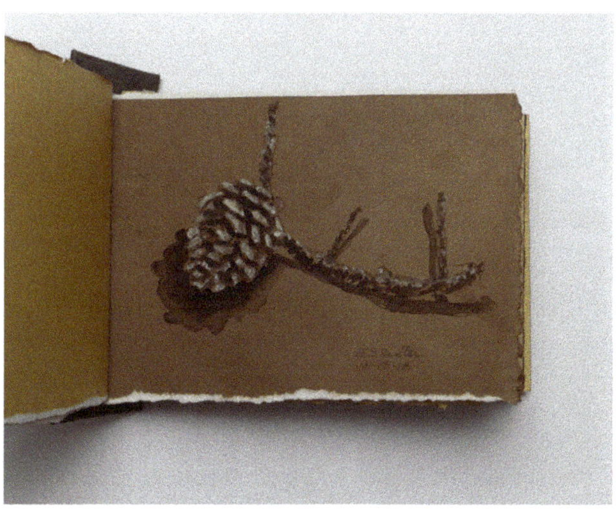

Figure 12.30
Pine cone painting, earth pigment on paper toned with natural dye (photo by Christopher Dant)

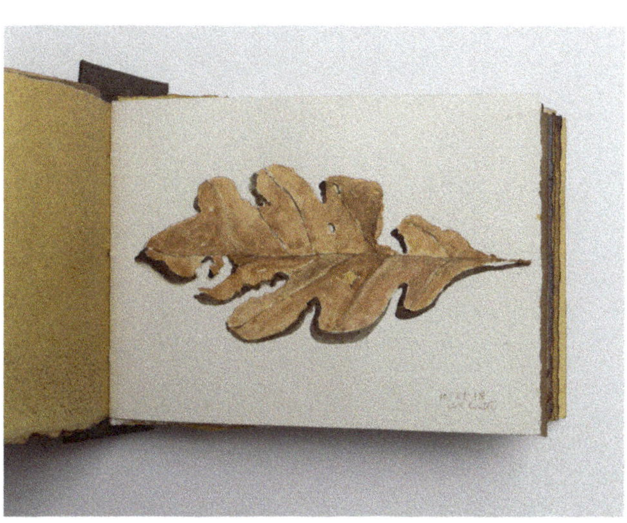

Figure 12.31
Oak leaf painting, earth pigment (photo by Christopher Dant)

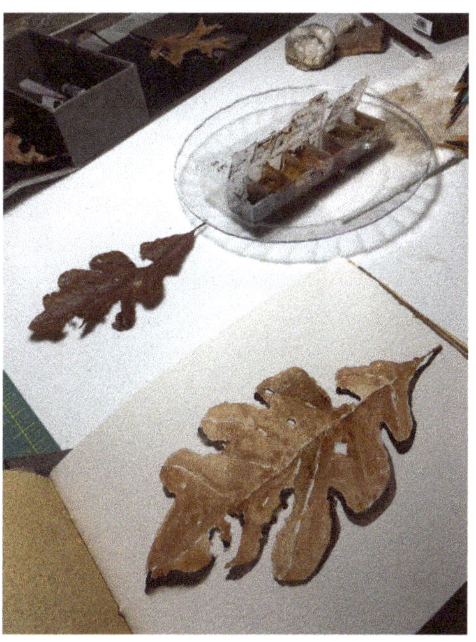

Figure 12.32
Sketchbook with oak leaf model and the earth pigment painting based upon it. This, and many others, were done at the Lillian Smith Center during a residency in October, 2018.

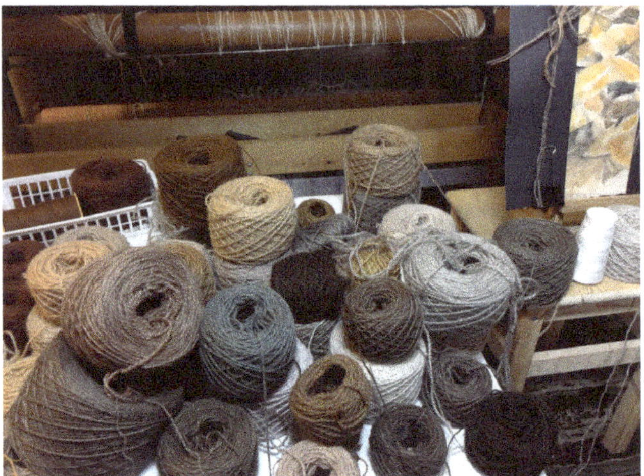

Figure 12.33
Yarns dyed with black walnut and henna

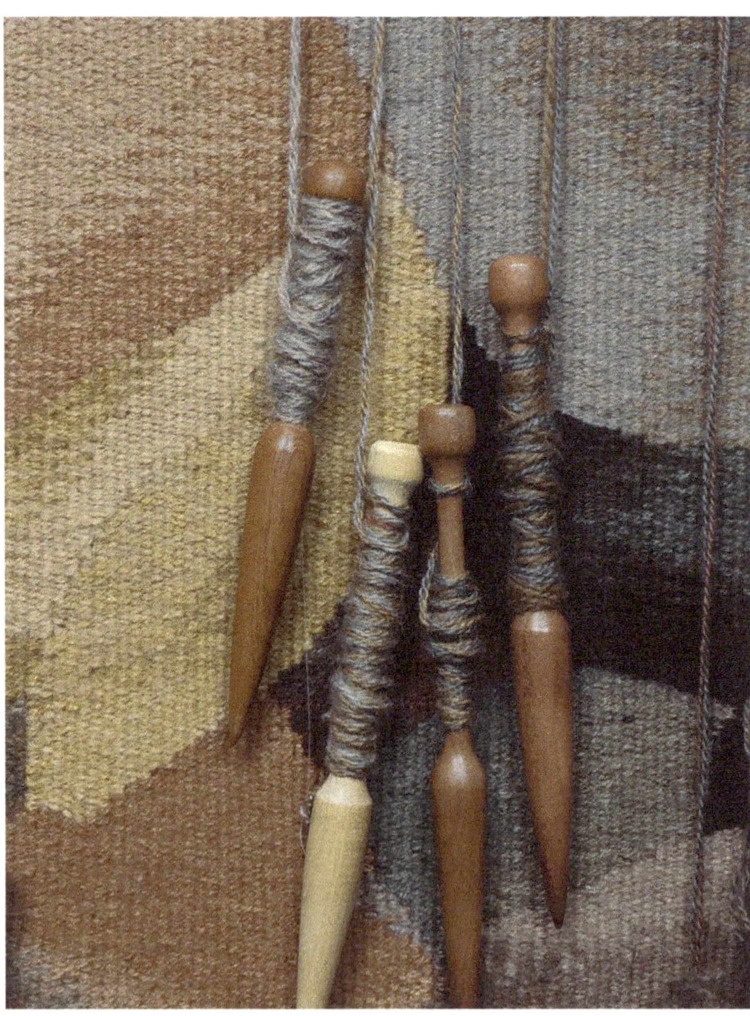

Figure 12.34
Bobbins filled with the natural dyed yarns in use with a tapestry

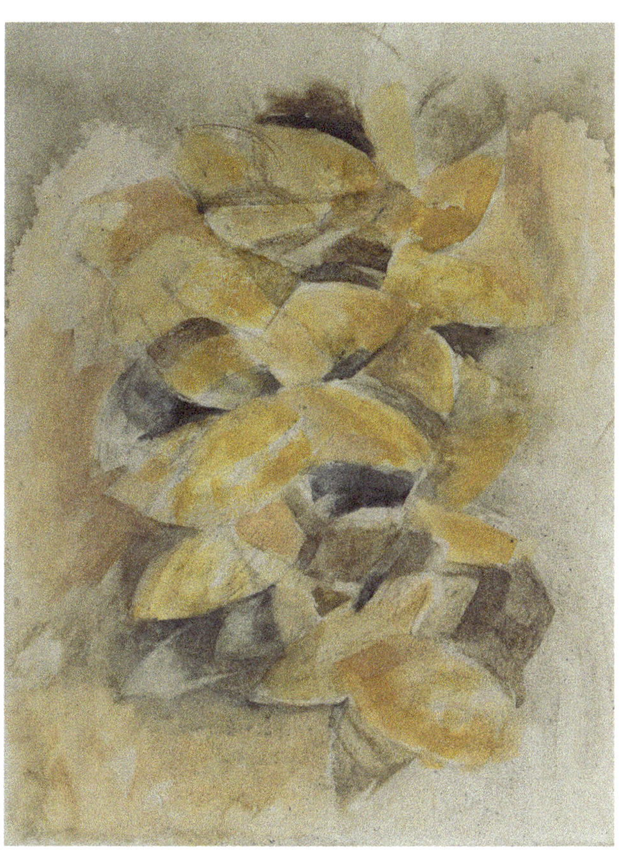

Figure 12.35
Earth pigment painting, a section of which was used as the basis of the tapestry *Earth Echoes*.

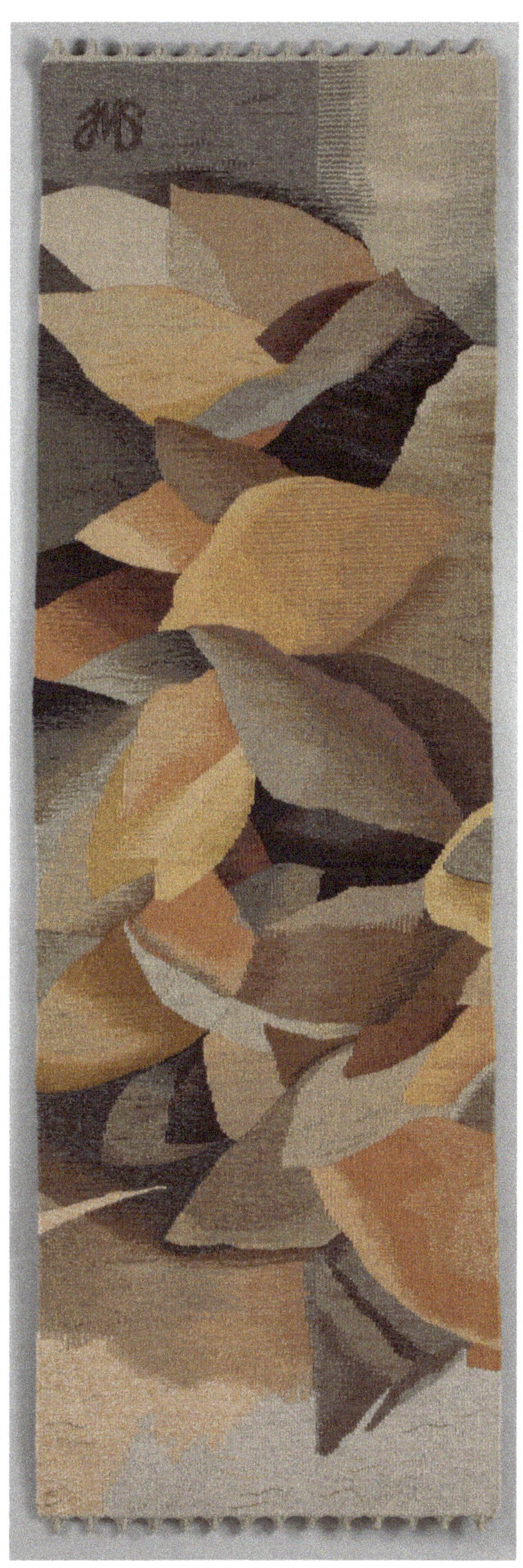

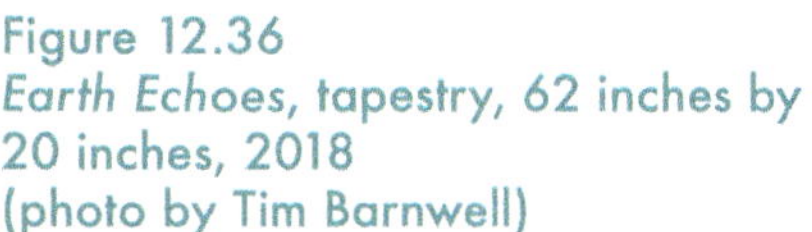

Figure 12.36
Earth Echoes, tapestry, 62 inches by 20 inches, 2018
(photo by Tim Barnwell)

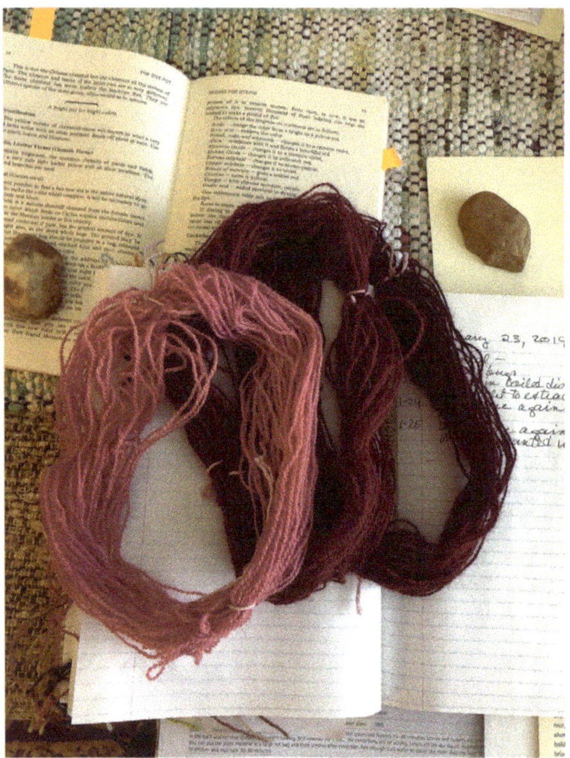

Figure 12.37
Yarns dyed with cochineal

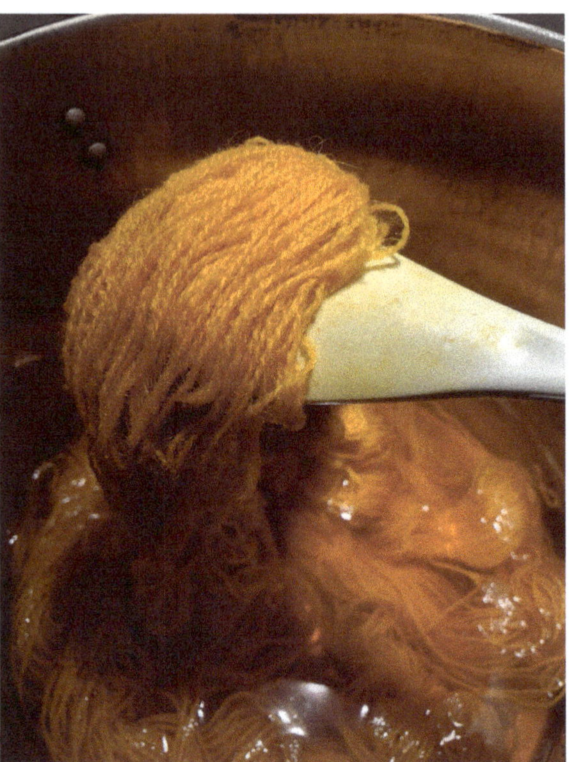

Figure 12.38
Dyeing with Osage orange

pigment watercolors I made while with Sandy.

Natural dyeing can be a painstaking craft, with careful measuring and record keeping for the dye materials and the chemical assistants. Or it can be done in a more casual way, as I'd practiced by dumping skeins of yarn into a pot along with a pile of black walnut hulls. A few plants are able to produce a good dye without additional mordant. With my informal approach, I was glad that one of those plants was the black walnut. The black walnut contains a direct dye in the active compound *juglone* found primarily in the outer husk.[7]

I continued to dye with black walnuts throughout the year and found that all parts of the tree—from the hulls to leaves to even the bark—gave various shades of brown and gray.

When I wanted to expand the palette of dye colors, still hoping to find other things to use without the pre-mordanting step, I sought advice from natural dye expert, Catharine Ellis (b. 1951). She mentioned

7 Catharine Ellis, "Black Walnut Season." September 11, 2016. https://blog.ellistextiles.com/2016/09/11/black-walnut-season/

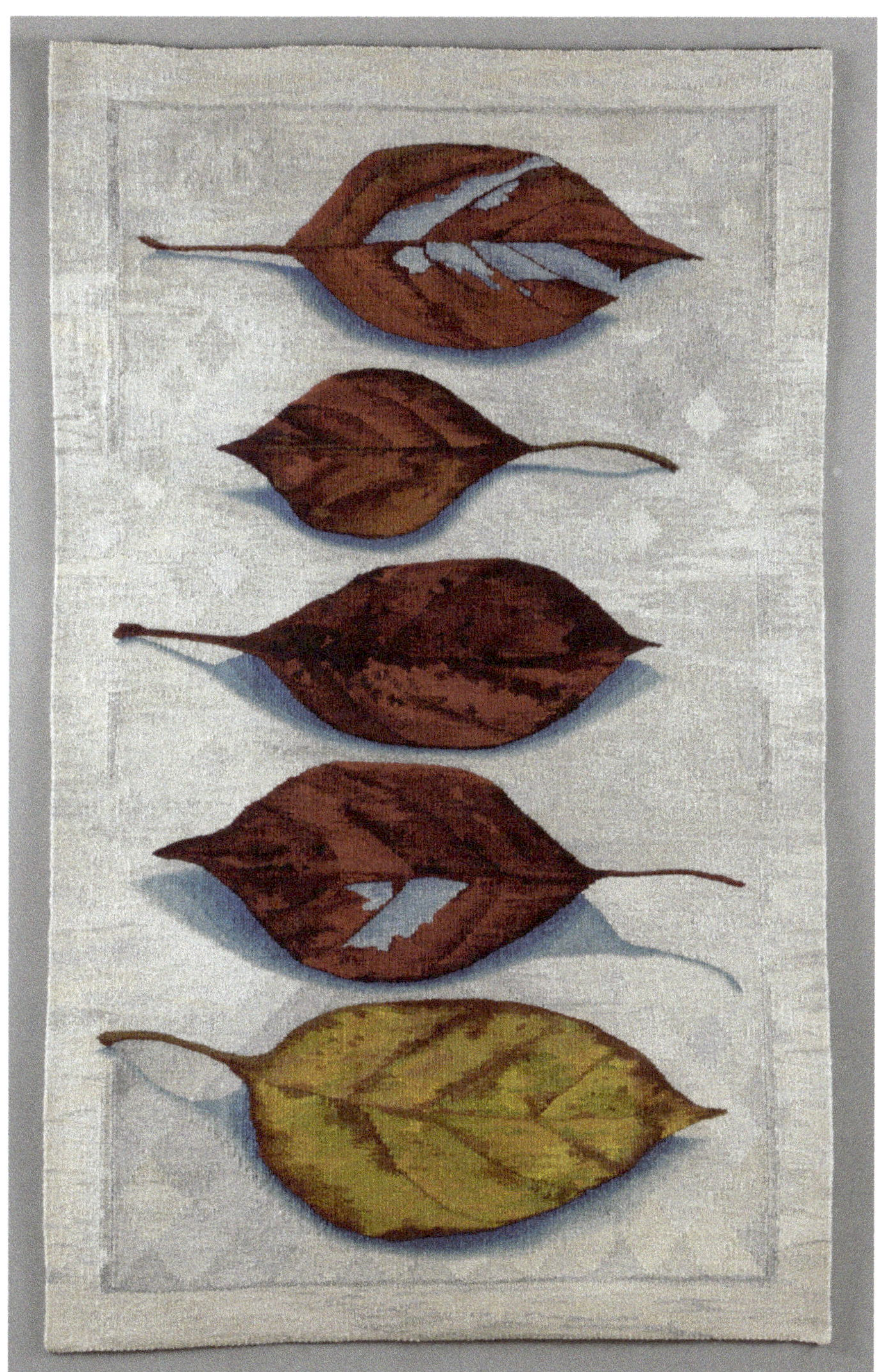

Figure 12.39
Five Leaves for Miss Lillian, tapestry, 60 inches by 32 inches, 2018 (photo by Tim Barnwell)

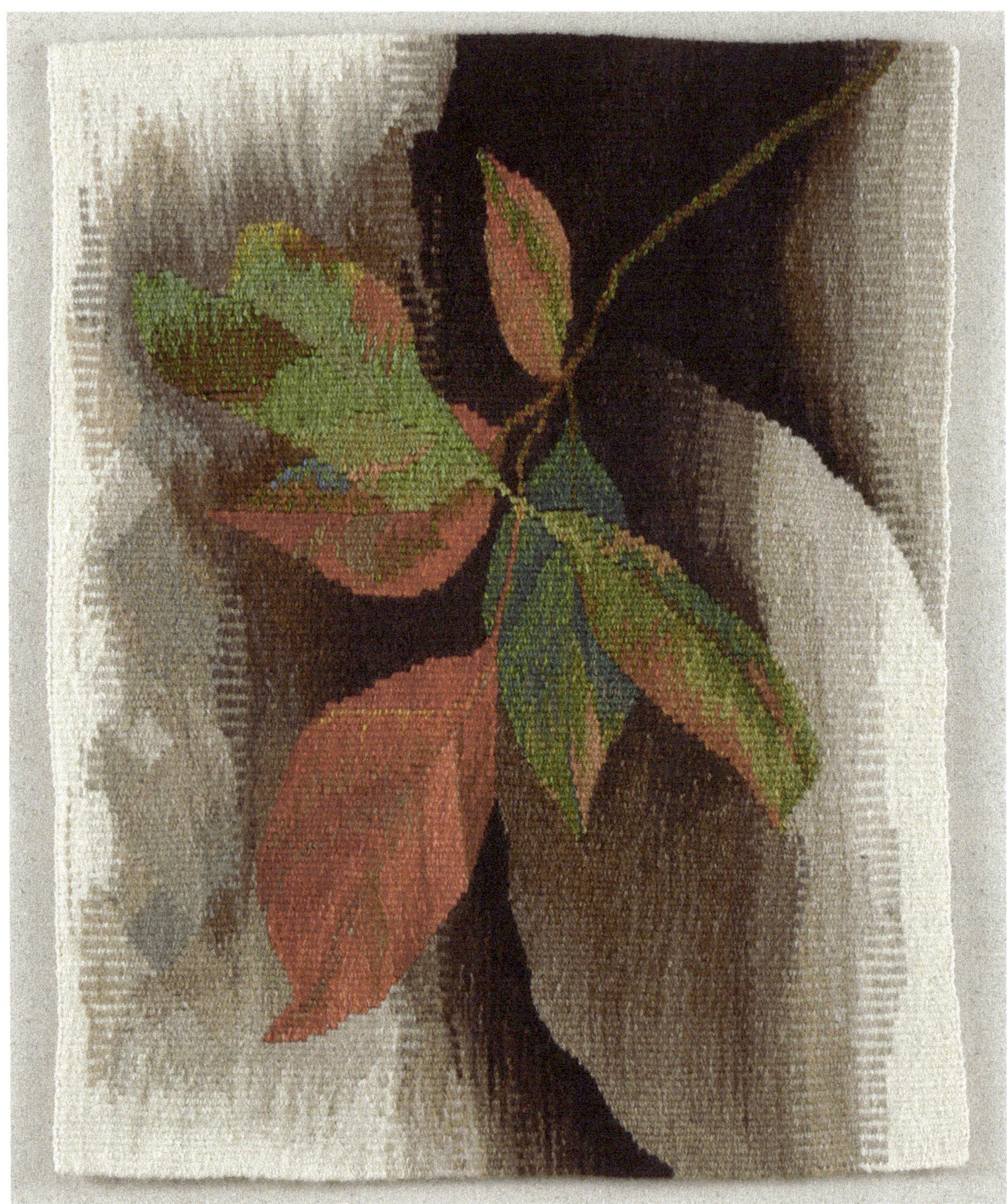

Figure 12.40
Fall Returns, 12 inches by 18 inches. Natural dyes of black walnut are joined by reds from madder and greens made by top dyeing Osage orange yellow with indigo. (Photo by Tim Barnwell)

henna as another option. Henna comes from the dried and ground leaves of the shrub *Lawsonia inermis* and is often used to dye hair and to make temporary tattoos. Dyeing wool yarn with it gave beautiful muted oranges of several tones and, when combined with the variety of browns and grays from the black walnut, the yarn colors resembled the earth pigment paintings I was making.

The paintings and natural dyeing experiences of 2016 and 2017 resulted in several tapestries in addition to *A Year of My Life—2016* and *Phoenix*. One was a long, narrow piece I called *Earth Echoes* in which both black walnut and henna-dyed yarns were used. The image for the tapestry came from a section of a painting made with earth pigments on paper stained with dye from cooked and strained acorns. I wove a few other smaller tapestries using those yarns from designs derived from other earth pigment paintings.

Later, I expanded the color range for the yarns by taking time to do the mordanting step prior to dyeing. Madder and cochineal yielded red from warm to cool tones. Osage orange, marigolds, and zinnias were used for a variety of yellows. An indigo vat gave blues, greens, and purples as needed. I gained additional valuable information about natural dyeing in a 2019 workshop with Catharine Ellis. Natural dyes in the wider color palette were used in the tapestries *Five Leaves for Miss Lillian*; *Fall Returns*; *A Year of My Life—2018*; *A Year of My Life—2019*; and *Eight Leaves*.

Perhaps I won't dye all of the yarns to use for tapestry, nor will I exclusively paint with earth pigments in the future. Nevertheless, these explorations were rewarding. Delving into ideas and images of the natural world by using materials derived from nature makes tangible some of the pleasure I feel in the surroundings of the forests and fields where I choose to live.

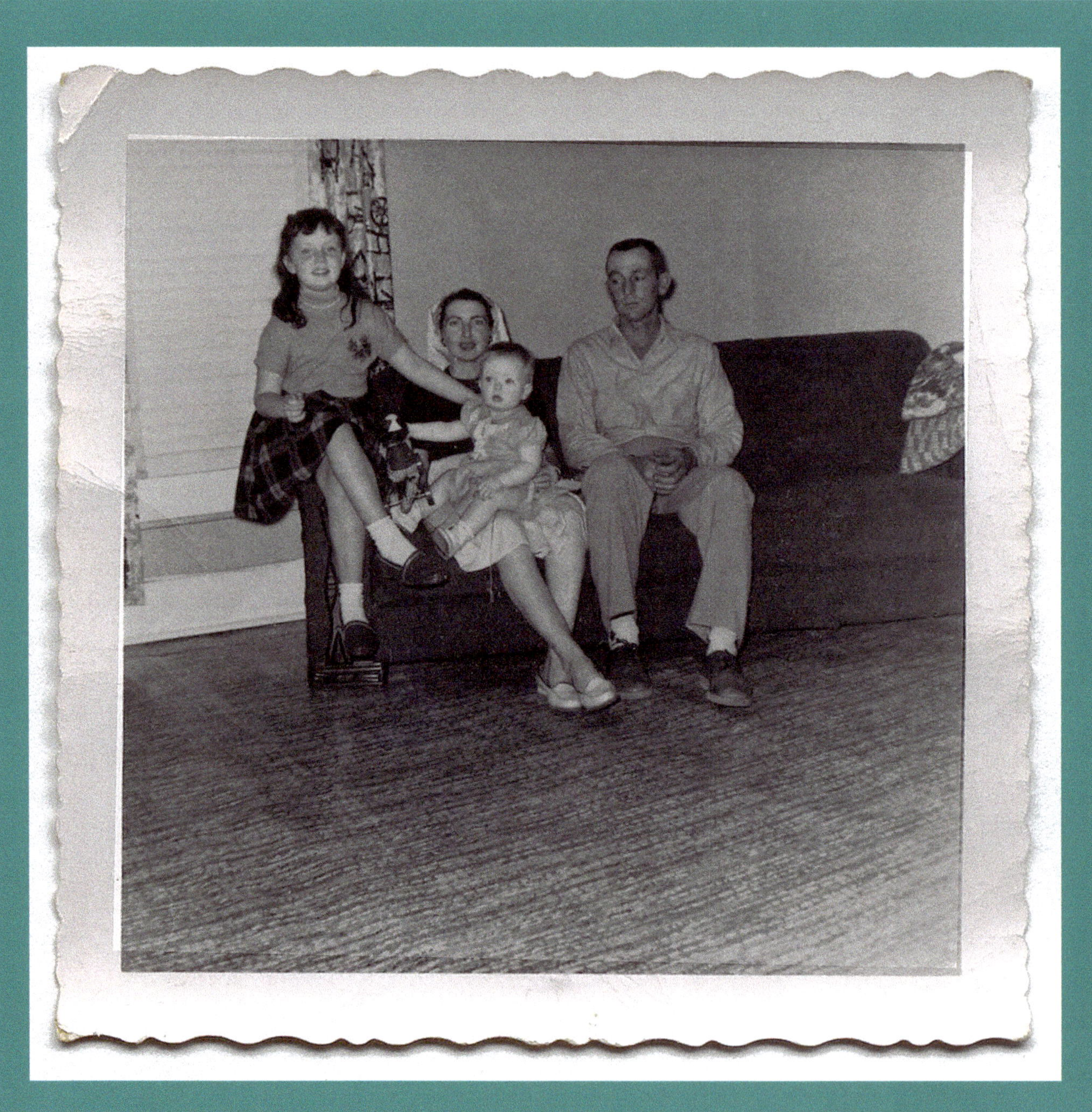

Figure 13.1
Family photograph of me, my parents, and my younger sister. This was taken about 1956, a few years before my father died.

13

Coping with Reality

It was December 16, 1959. I was twelve years old and in the 7th grade. That morning I was in the school library checking out a book when the principal came to get me. He said he needed to take me home. That hadn't happened before, but I didn't ask why. I just gathered up my things, put on my coat, and got in his car to drive the mile to my house. On the way, he said, "It's terrible, terrible!" then asked if I wanted him to tell me what was wrong. I said I didn't want to know.

He pulled the car into the driveway at my grandparents' house instead of across the road where we lived. There were lots of people standing around, and, when I got out of the car, Mother came up to me. "Daddy's dead," she said and then broke down crying. They later told me I threw my books in the air. But I don't remember that. In fact, I don't remember much from the next week except terrible grief in our house, but I do remember reading incessantly. Now I realize I was trying to stop thinking about the reality of what was happening to our family. Trying to find a child's way of coping.

Reading to escape reality has always been a fallback coping strategy for me since that first tragedy I faced as a child. In college, I learned through the study of art history that making artwork in response to tragedy and emotional crises could also be powerfully cathartic. Encouraged by that understanding, I found that art making has helped me deal with distressing situations several times over the years. The first was the trauma of being robbed at gunpoint as a young adult.

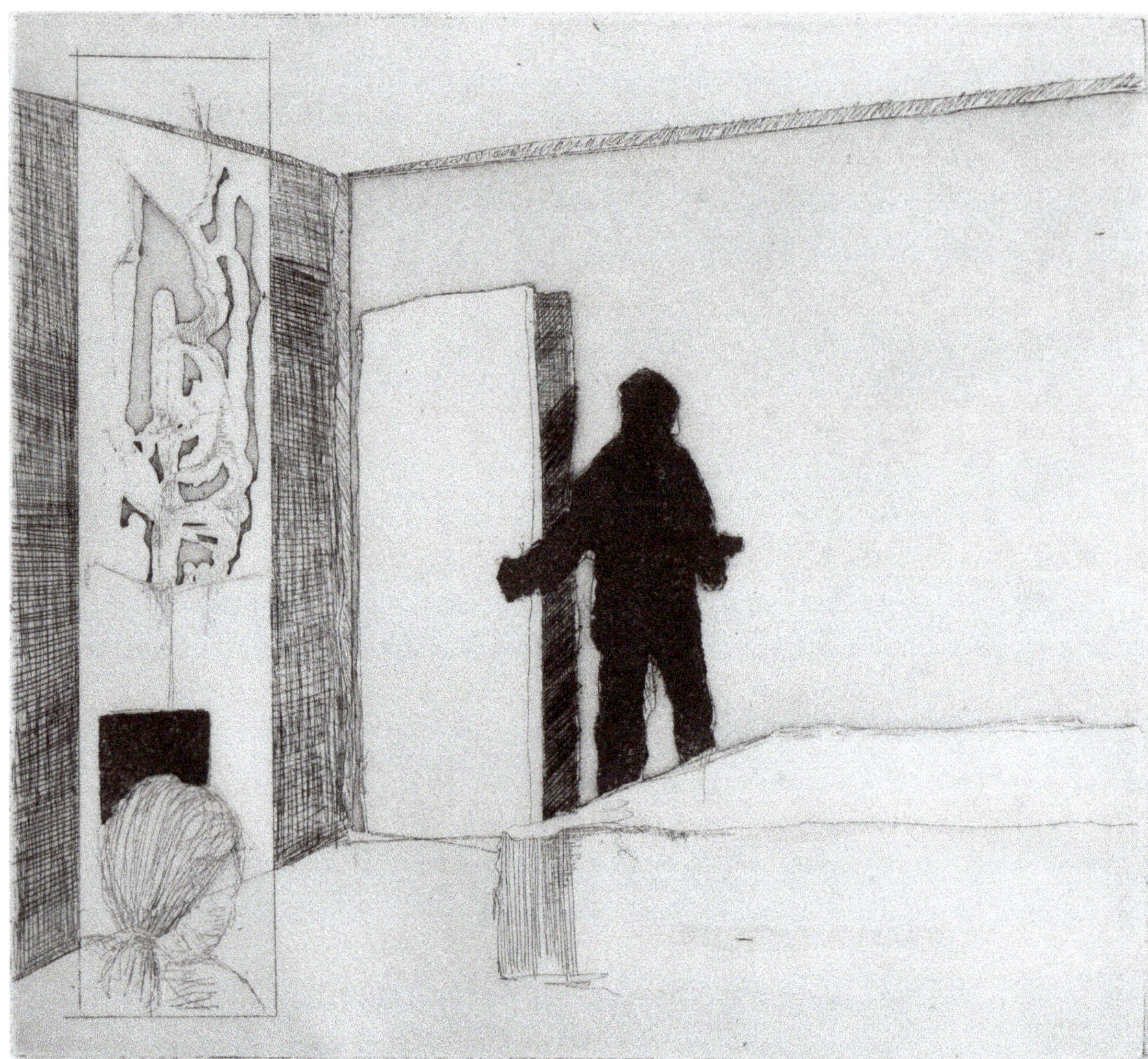

Figure 13.2
Etching in response to robbery at gunpoint, made about 1975 (photo by Christopher Dant)

In December of 1972, a few of us who were involved with a craft cooperative in Northeast Georgia traveled to Washington, D.C. for a small exhibit and sale. This was one of many cooperatives in the U.S. started in the late 1960s by Volunteers in Service to America (VISTA). VISTA sponsored the event in D.C. to showcase this aspect of the work being undertaken by the program. At the time, I was working at the Tallulah Falls craft shop on some weekends while teaching at NGC during the week.

Two of us were staying in adjacent rooms at a hotel near DuPont Circle. On the second evening, the man who'd driven the van-load of crafts from Georgia came to my room so we could discuss plans for the next day. When he walked in, I saw that he didn't completely close the door behind him. I simply thought, "Oh, he's leaving in a minute; no need to get up and shut it."

Just then, a young man holding a pistol pushed open the door and stepped into the room. Yelling at us and waving the pistol around, he demanded our money. I was terrified, but I was also angry. How dare he do this—I knew the instant he came through the door I would die and that filled me with fear. My anger came from the fact I would die near Christmas, just as my father had thirteen years before. What followed were minutes of terror before the intruder rushed out with all the money we had between us, the craft cooperative's funds for the trip, plus cash from the sales. Fortunately for us his, motive was a quick robbery and not murders.

Although I wasn't physically hurt in the incident, I suffered emotionally from the robbery for years afterwards. The sight of the man coming into the room stayed with me. My mind replayed the scene with the guy, dressed in a black pea coat and holding a shiny handgun, pushing open the door and stepping in. The starkness of the image was firmly burned into my mind, and I couldn't seem to shake it.

The next year, the memory of that dreadful night became the subject of an etching made in a printmaking course. I hoped by turning the mental image into a tangible one I could find relief from the constant anxiety I felt. Maybe I could finally stop turning this episode over and over in my mind.

In the etching, the gunman stood in a doorway holding a pistol. In a separate section of the composition, there was a figure watching this happen. Above the watcher's head were vague shapes. Did they represent fears? Probably, and of course I was surely the watcher.

The etching was my first attempt to use images to mitigate distressful emotions and feelings of anxiety.

A few years later, visual expression again became a source of solace after learning of the death of a relative. I was at a fiber conference in Chicago in the summer of 1988 when I telephoned my mother to see how things were at home. She told me that my cousin had just died. He and I were a month apart in age and had been close friends throughout our childhood and teens. After graduating from high school in 1965, he enlisted in the Marines and was soon sent to Vietnam. Not too many months later, he was wounded and his good friend was killed in a grenade blast.

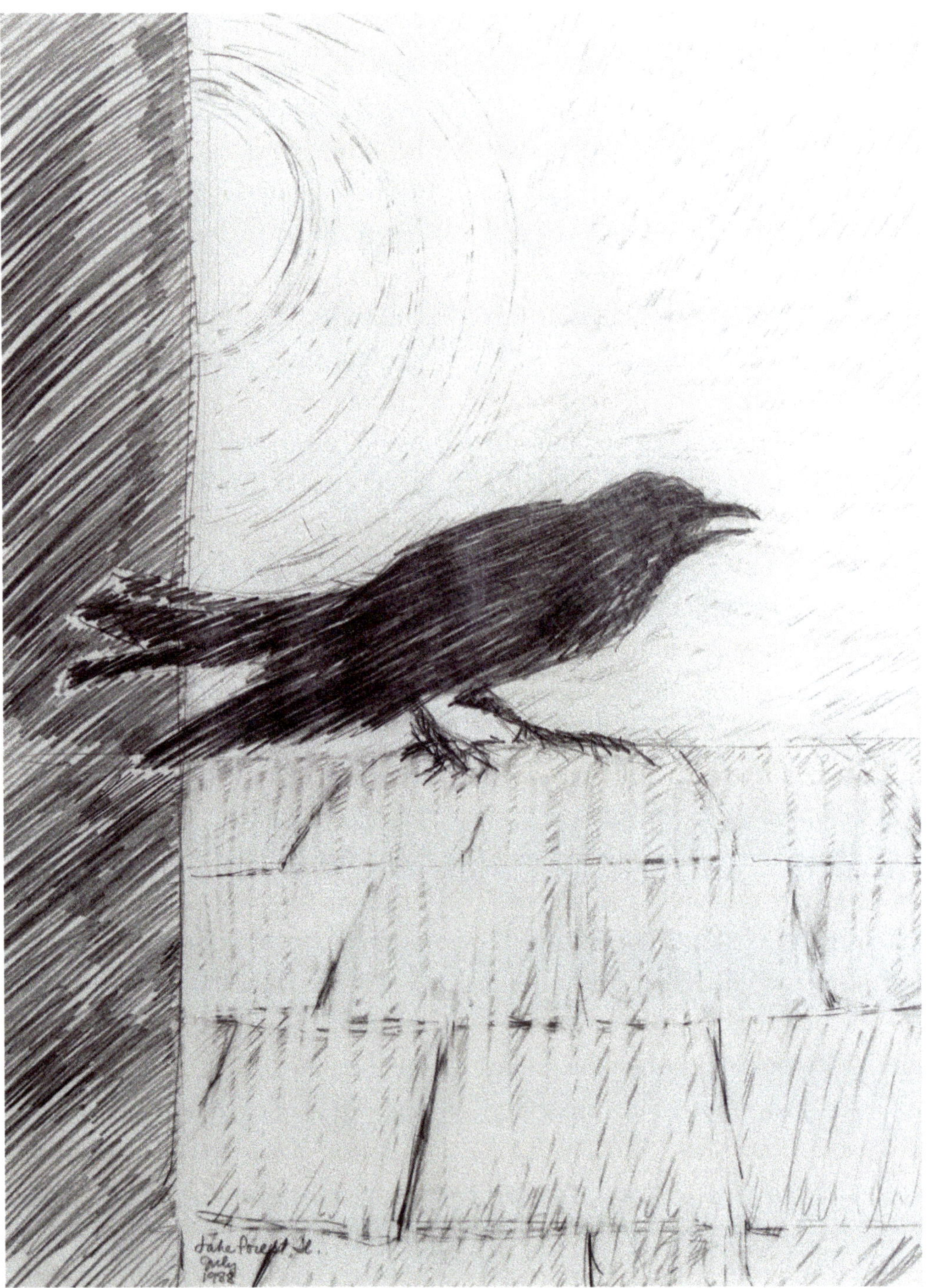

Figure 13.3
Crow drawing made in 1988 after learning of my cousin's death (photo by Christopher Dant)

After returning home, my cousin, a gentle spirit by nature, suffered emotionally as well as physically from his wounds. While his body healed as much as possible, he continued to struggle with what he'd seen and done while in Southeast Asia. He later told me only a little of the horrific events he lived through while he was there and about the depth of despair he felt. He tried hard to have a normal life once he was home. He married, and, in the next few years, the couple had two children. But the trauma he'd experienced in Vietnam was too great for him. Their marriage suffered as he fought in vain to ease his physical and emotional pain with alcohol and drugs. He and his wife divorced. Gradually he became ill. In his early 40s, he passed away.

After I heard he'd died, I walked back to the dorm where I was staying for the conference, my eyes filled with tears. As I approached the building, there was a single crow on the roof, silhouetted in the sun, and it was cawing, cawing, cawing. It seemed the crow was also crying for him. I made a drawing in my sketchbook that day of the crow and the sun behind it, not knowing then how significant crows would later become for me as a visual symbol in emotionally-stressful times.

The robbery I'd experienced in 1972 and the 1988 death of my cousin were distressing. Both times I'd used image making afterwards as a way to come to grips with my feelings. It seems that I'm anxiety prone at the best of times, but, by the mid-1990s, several events resulted in panic attacks and depression. In those emotionally-troubled times, in addition to seeing a counselor, I made many images and wrote about my feelings. In those, I felt compelled to use crow images in symbolic ways.

In addition to the images on paper in which I expressed my generalized anxieties, two tapestries I wove in the 1990s were developed in response to troubled times. Both of the tapestries included lines from poems I'd written and crow images as symbols for anguish and as omens of change.

But See the Dark Shine is a tapestry in which I revisited the image from the robbery. In the woven version, the robber appeared as a flat, dark human form standing in an open doorway, pistol in hand. The figure stood on the silhouette of a large, flying crow. In the tapestry, diagonal lines flew out of the pistol he held. Bold X marks were all over the composition, including over the figures of man and crow, signs of "crossing out" the event from my mind. I wove the words: "But see the dark shine with the gloss of crow wings" along the right side of the tapestry.

Crow—Dark Angel showed fragmented crow-like shapes in the central part of the composition surrounded by the words I'd written earlier in a poem: "Crow—Dark

Angel/ When you are present you dominate my sight/ When you go I begin to see the others."

I spent many unsettled days and nights during the years I coped with fear and anxiety. Looking back to some of the journal entries, poems, drawings, and tapestries I made then, it is evident how desperate I often felt. It seems that expressing my emotions in both written and visual ways possibly saved my life.

Art making also became a way to contend with emotions when my brother-in-law died. My sister's husband was just two months shy of his fifty-eighth birthday when he passed away in late winter of 1999. In the mid-1990s, he was diagnosed with Non-Hodgkin Lymphoma and told he had perhaps four years to live. He went through many evaluations and treatments from the time of the diagnosis until his death, most likely from the effects of his exposure to the herbicide called Agent Orange when he was in Vietnam.

My brother-in-law had been a U.S. Army Ranger and had served three tours in Southeast Asia where he was frequently in the field as an advisor with South Vietnamese troops. He was one of the many thousands who came into contact with herbicides being used by the U.S. military in defoliation efforts to strip vegetation as a way to deprive the North Vietnamese and Viet Cong of ground cover and to destroy crops.[1]

Agent Orange was only one of several herbicides used in Vietnam, each having a color name. The names came from the particular color marked on the storage barrels to identify the different chemicals. The herbicide that was known as Agent Orange had been developed and used in the U.S. for several decades in agriculture, although in much less concentration.[2]

Millions of gallons of herbicides were used in Vietnam, and millions of words have been written about the effects of the chemicals on the land and its people and on those who served in the military there. As I began to read about Agent Orange after my brother-in-law's death, in addition to deep sorrow, I felt so much confusion: What was the truth in all of those words I was reading? What was false? How could I ever know?

---

1 According to information from House Resolution 2634: Victims of Agent Orange Relief Act of 2011 (7-25-11; referred to subcommittee)

> *(1) From 1961 to 1971, approximately 19,000,000 gallons of 15 different herbicides, including 13,000,000 gallons of Agent Orange, were sprayed over the southern region of Vietnam. Many of such herbicides, including Agent Orange, were based with the toxic contaminant, known as dioxin.*

2 Referring to the use of the herbicide in Vietnam, "Since Agent Orange was being used to strip the land of all vegetation and not just to control weeds, doses 5 to 10 times higher than what was used for American Agriculture was sprayed. About 13 million gallons of Agent Orange were supplied by several companies to the US military." http://www.ffrd.org/Voices/History.htm

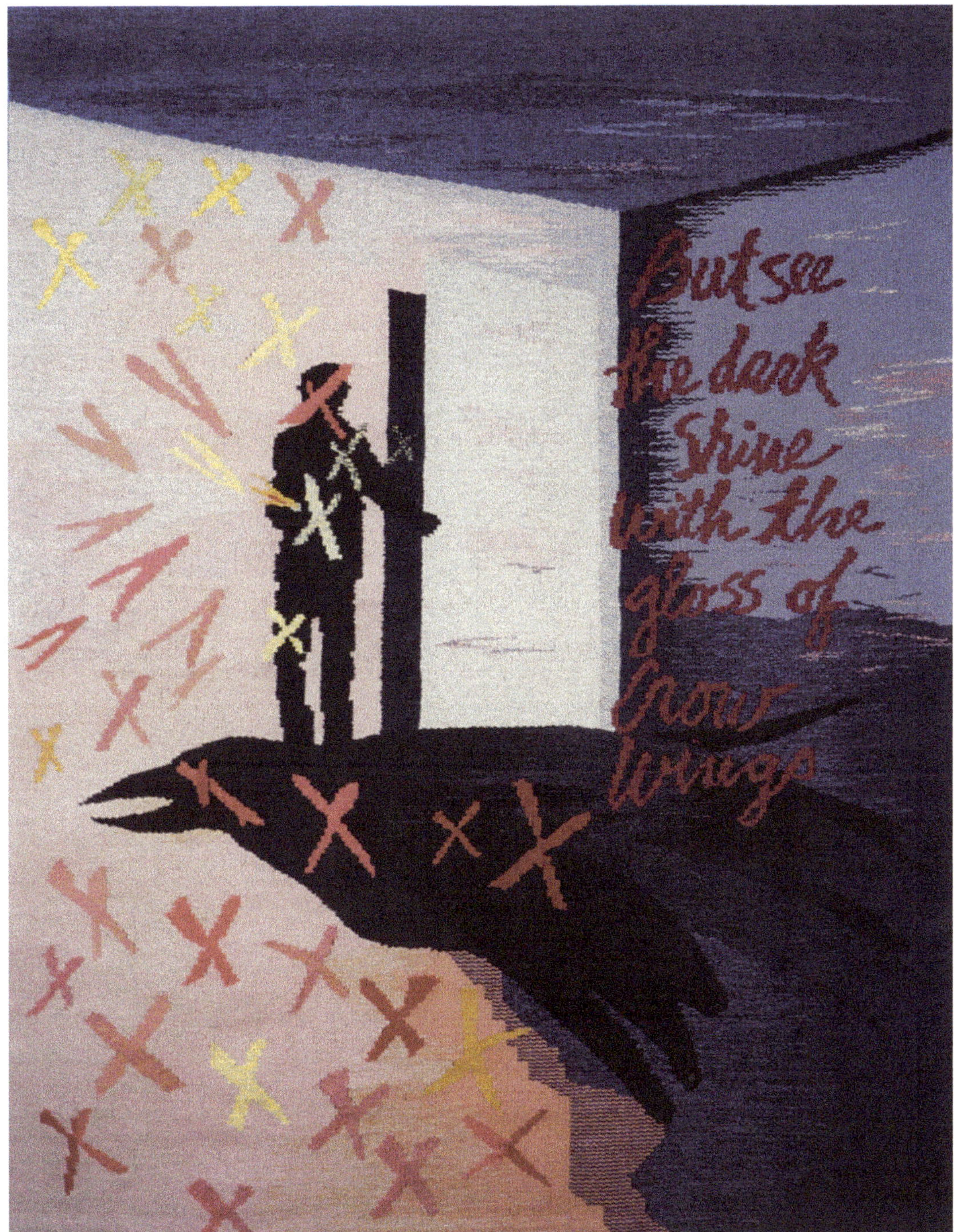

Figure 13.4
But See the Dark Shine..., tapestry, approximately 62 inches by 48 inches, 1994 (photo by Michael Woods)

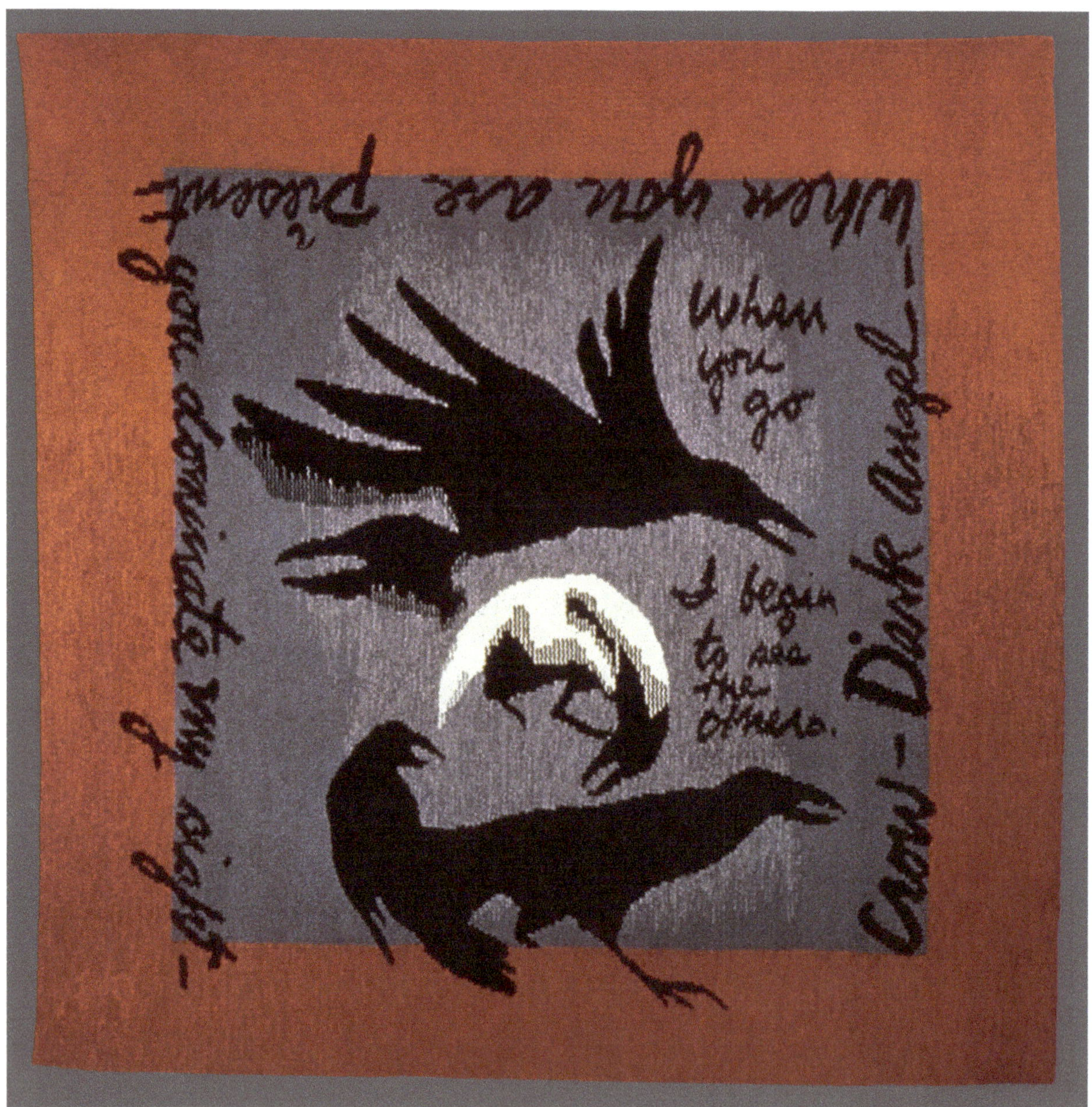

Figure 13.5
Crow–Dark Angel, tapestry, 60 inches by 60 inches, approximately, 1994 (photo by Michael Woods)

Figure 13.6
Part of the collection of images and text about the use and effects of Agent Orange during the Vietnam conflict. (Photo by Christopher Dant)

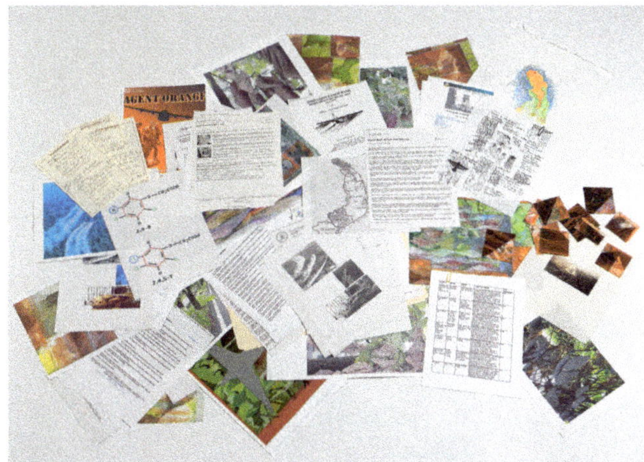

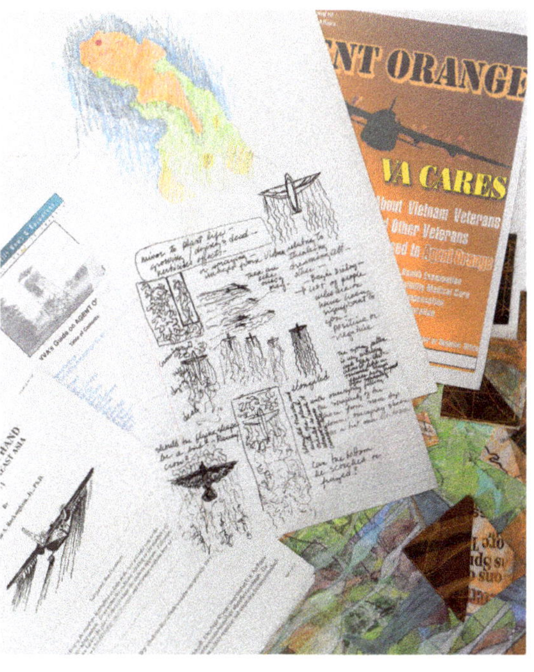

Figure 13.7
Detail of some of the items (photo by Christopher Dant)

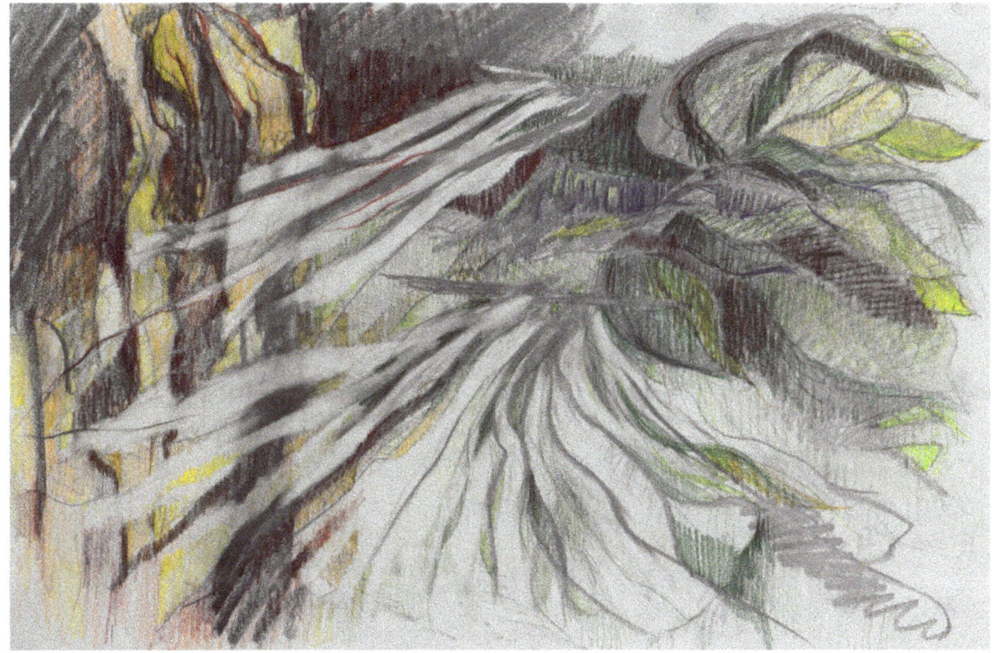

Figure 13.8
Agent Orange: drawing based on spraying of chemicals from airplanes over the vegetation. (Photo by Christopher Dant)

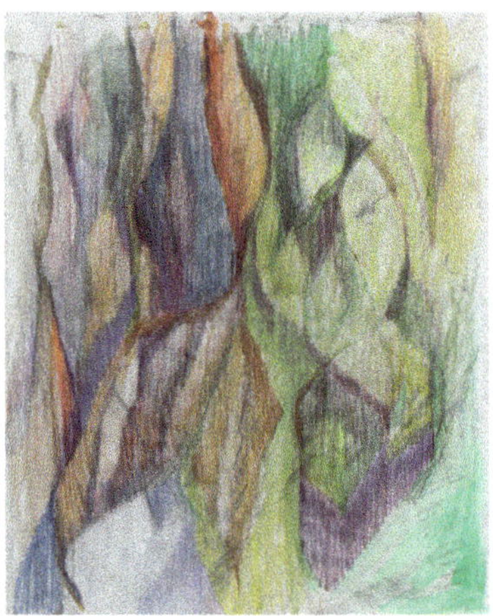

Figure 13.9
Agent Orange: drawing of foliage, alive and dying. (Photo by Christopher Dant)

Figure 13.10
Agent Orange: drawing of foliage, alive and dying, second version. (Photo by Christopher Dant)

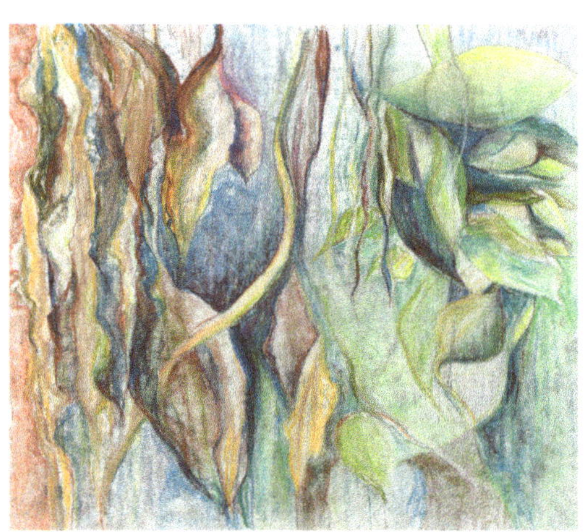

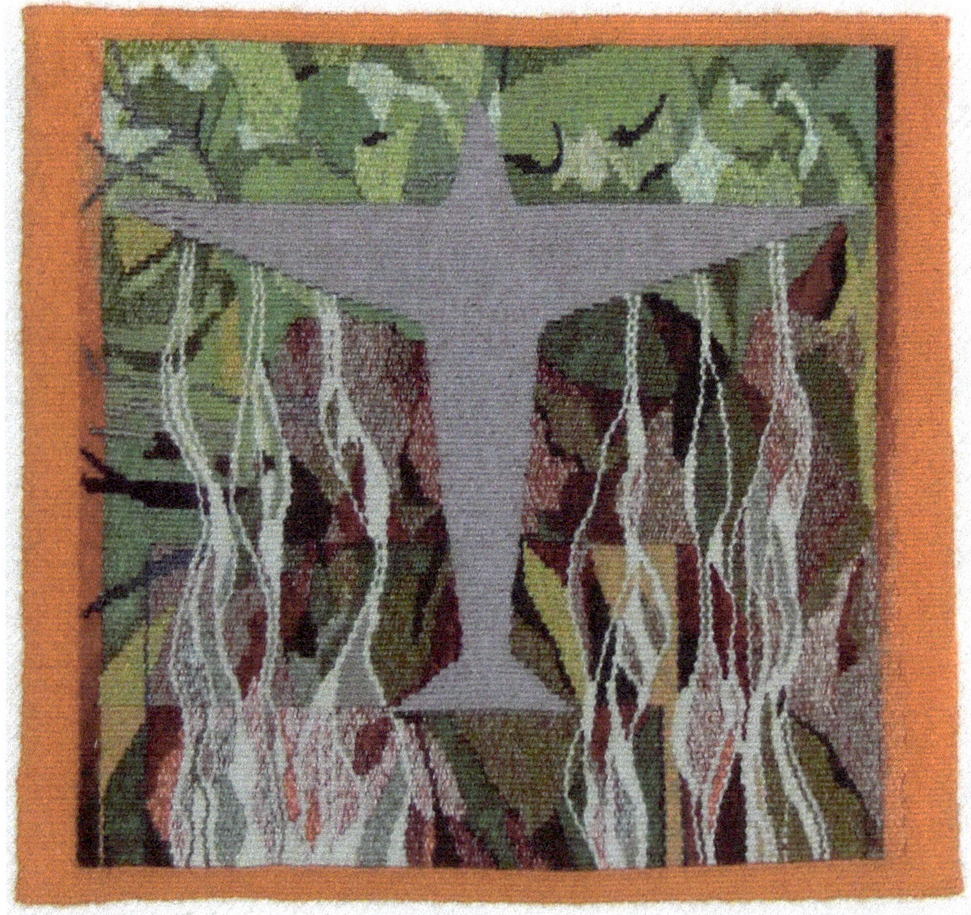

Figure 13.11
One Million Hectares, tapestry, 14 inches by 14 inches, 2004

Words became part of the artworks that resulted and were often hidden or partly hidden within the works to signify what I felt to be the futility of ever understanding why decisions were made to use this chemical warfare method.

As words turned out to be important to what I wanted to convey, so also did the color orange. Rather than associations of cheerfulness that the warm color might seem to suggest, for me orange became a symbol of decline and death. In the art works, I often paired orange hues with blues and greens. In this way, orange and my association of it with decay contrasted with the vitality of blue and green colors. The first tapestry of several I wove while exploring how best to express my concerns and sadness was called *One Million Hectares.* When I read that over one million hectares of land had been sprayed with the herbicides, I was astounded. According to one report, nearly ten percent of the land area of South Vietnam was sprayed at least once. [3]

Fragmentation was another concept I felt represented the multiplicity of opinions surrounding the Vietnam War, the use of herbicides, and the consequences for the land, civilians, and military.

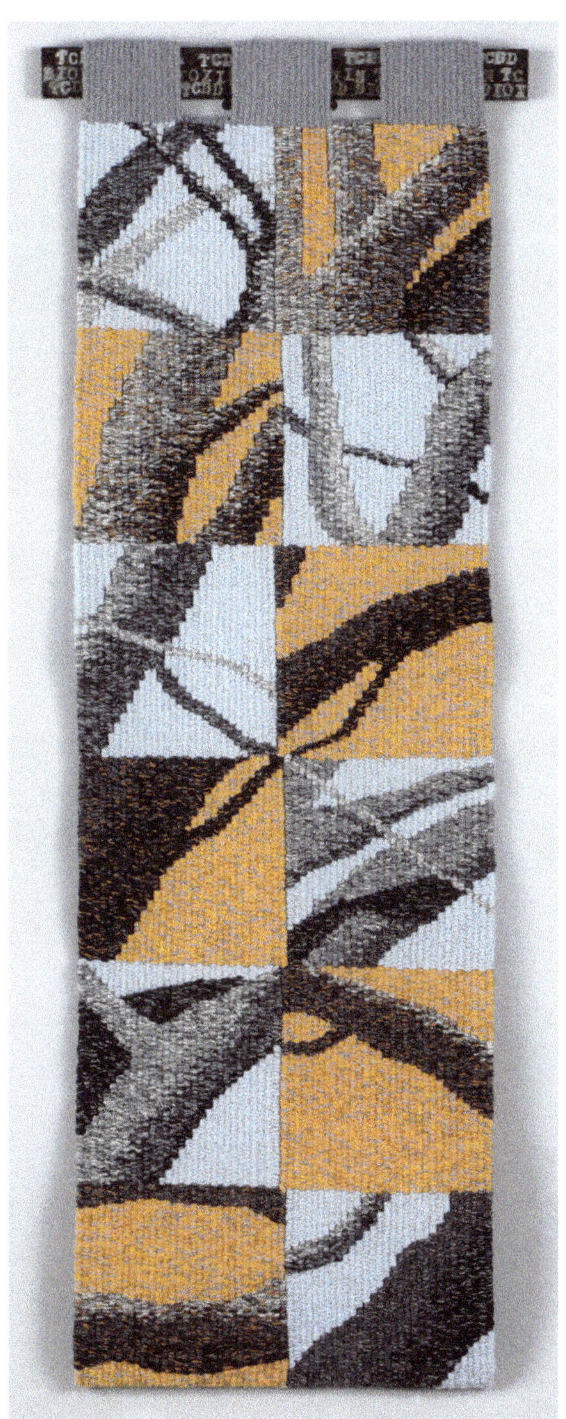

Figure 13.12
Legacy of Operation Ranch Hand: Tree Fragments, tapestry, 40 inches by 12 inches, 2005 (photo by Tim Barnwell)

---

3 Institute of Medicine (US) Committee to Review the Health Effects in Vietnam Veterans of Exposure to Herbicides. (Washington, D.C.: National Academies Press,1994). https://www.ncbi.nlm.nih.gov/books/NBK236347/#ddd00073

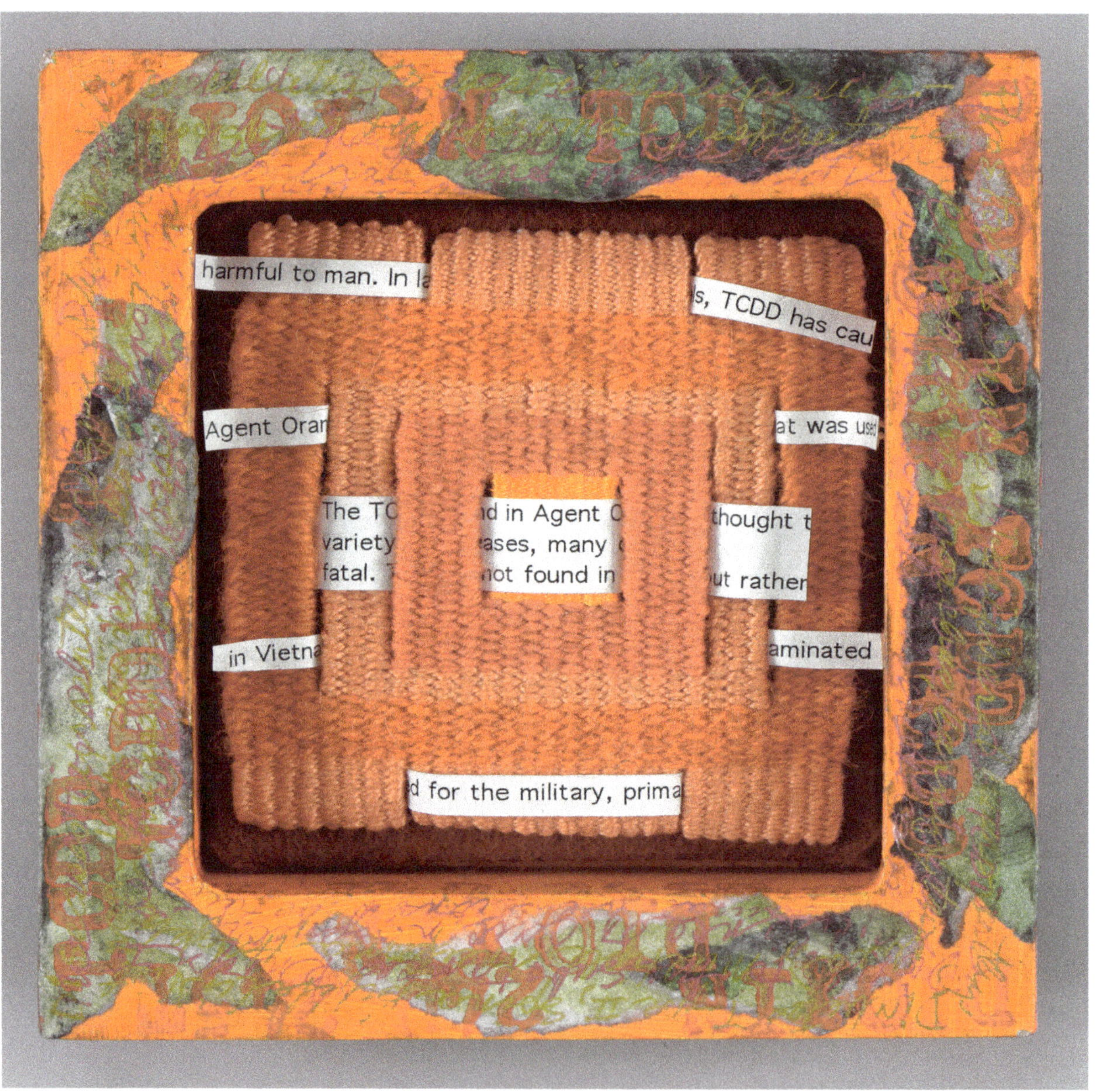

Figure 13.13
Harmful to Man, mixed media including tapestry, painting, and collage, 6 inches by 6 inches by 1 inch, 2005 (photo by Tim Barnwell)

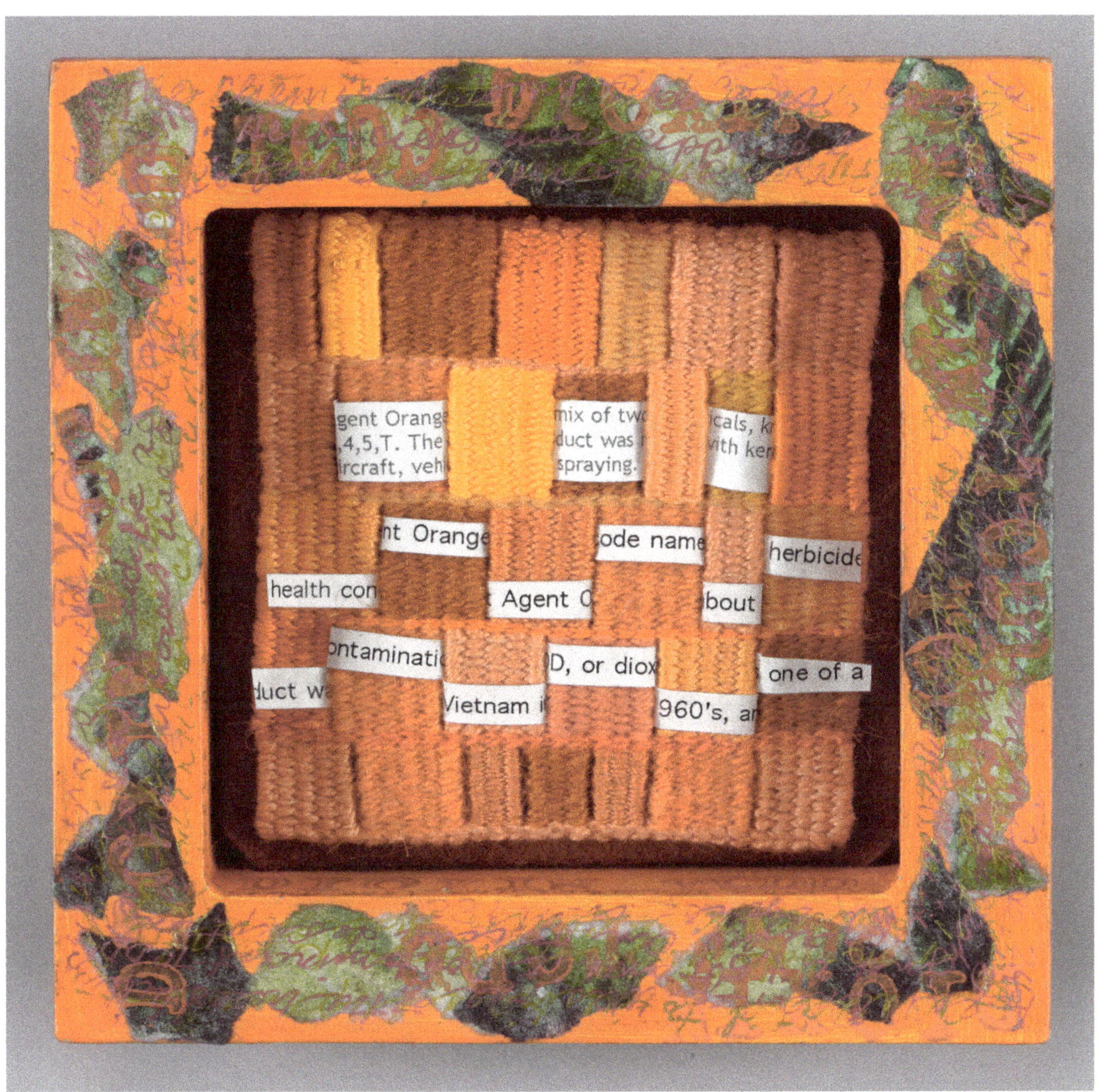

Figure 13.14
Health Concerns, mixed media including tapestry, painting, and collage, 6 inches by 6 inches by 1 inch, 2005 (photo by Tim Barnwell)

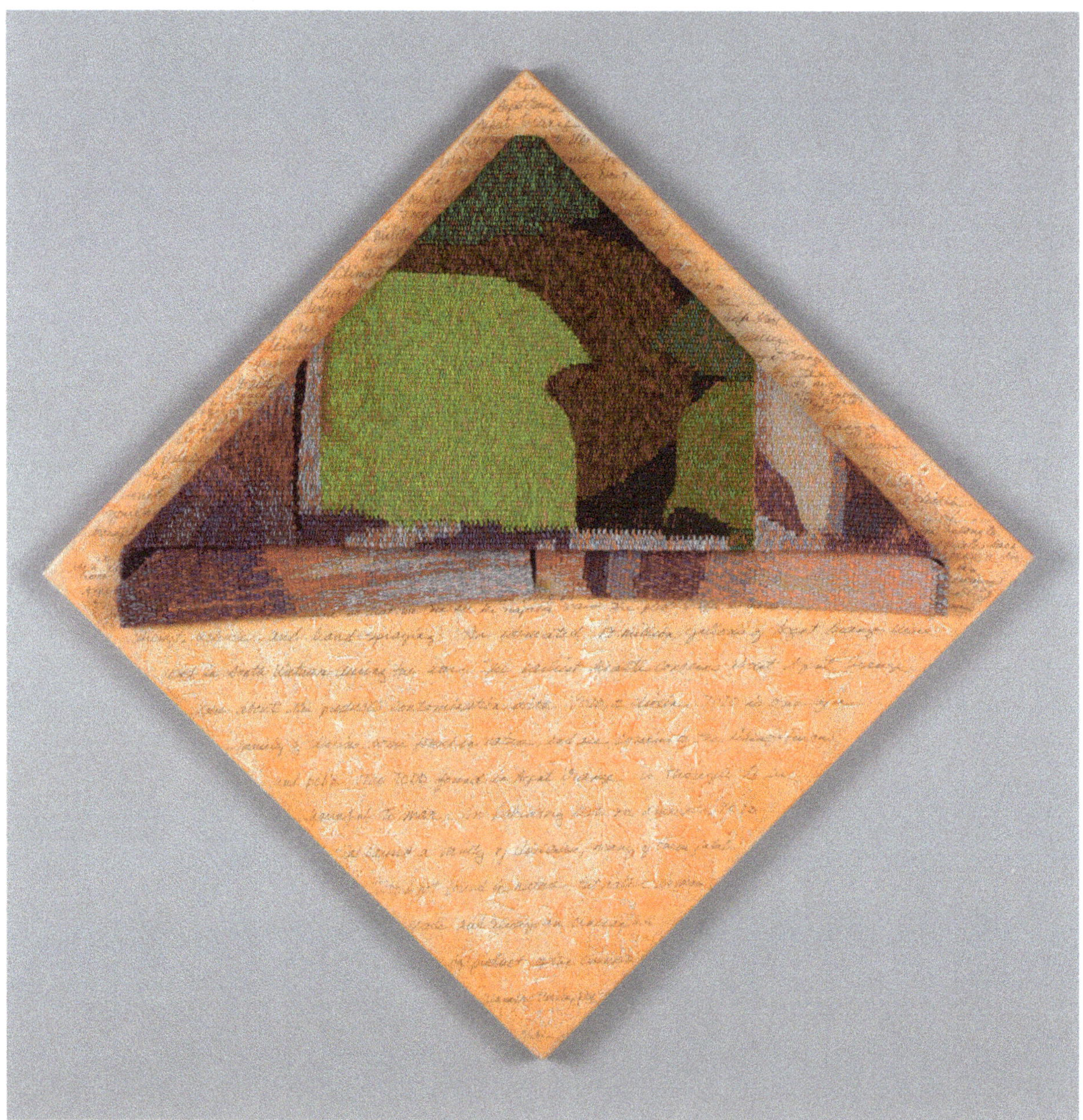

Figure 13.15
Legacy: Folded, mixed media including tapestry, artist canvas, acrylic paint, 24 inches by 24 inches, 2006 (photo by Tim Barnwell)

Thus, some of my works in this effort showed only parts of the image.

I made artworks about Agent Orange for almost a decade. I reworked several of those as my thoughts changed and I tried to clarify aspects of my feelings. The Agent Orange artworks were part of the ways I sought to resolve my emotions of sadness, loss, confusion, and anger as I considered the results of human use of chemicals to manipulate nature.

The loss to our family with the death of my sister's husband was tragic. The consequences of this particular warfare method also affected thousands, maybe millions, of other families. The last tapestry I did in this study was in honor of my brother-in-law, but it was also for all. It was a small tapestry with a simple design of an empty chair and doorway to symbolize those losses. It was called *Final Passage.*

After spending years immersed in thoughts of the magnitude of herbicide use in Vietnam, my thoughts turned to how often human actions have effects that are potentially harmful to all life, even when the aims seemed otherwise.

In particular, I began to think about the impact of invasive plant species, including the accidental introduction of the blight that devastated the American chestnut trees on the North American Continent in the early twentieth century. Another accidentally-introduced pest, the Hemlock Wooly Adelgid (HWA) is now decimating the Eastern Hemlocks of the U.S. It seems that the popularity of Japanese gardens, designed for the Gilded Age mansion gardens of the early twentieth century, may have led to the introduction of the HWA in North America. These gardens often included Hemlock species from Asia, and these non-native trees may have brought with them the HWA—for which there was no natural predator on this

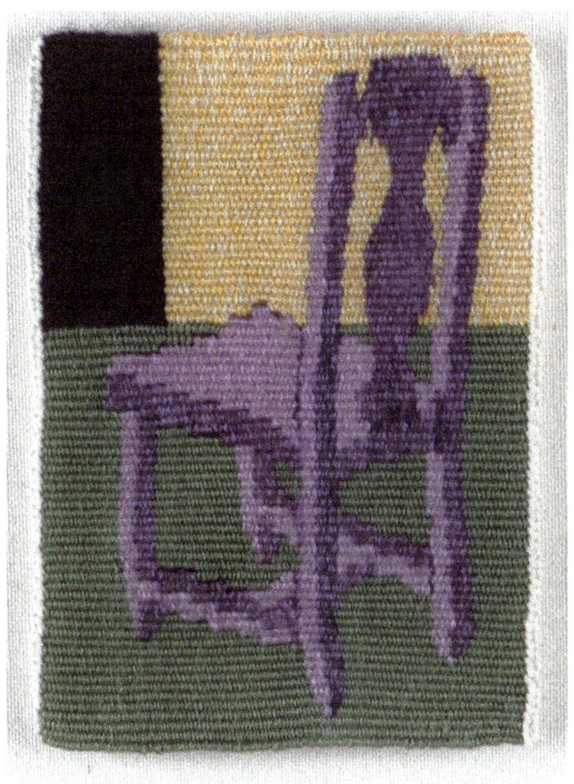

Figure 13.16
Final Passage, tapestry, 7 inches by 5 inches, 2006

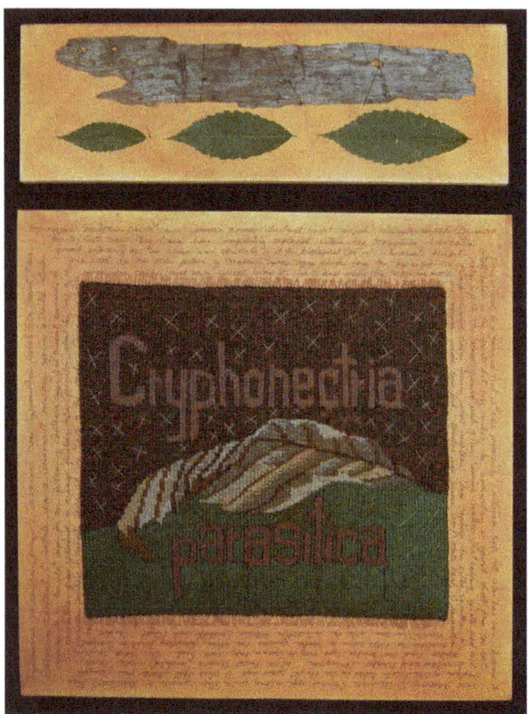

Figure 13.17
Cryphonectria parasitica (Chestnut Blight), mixed media including tapestry, artist canvas, paint, stitching, American chestnut wood and leaves, 2006

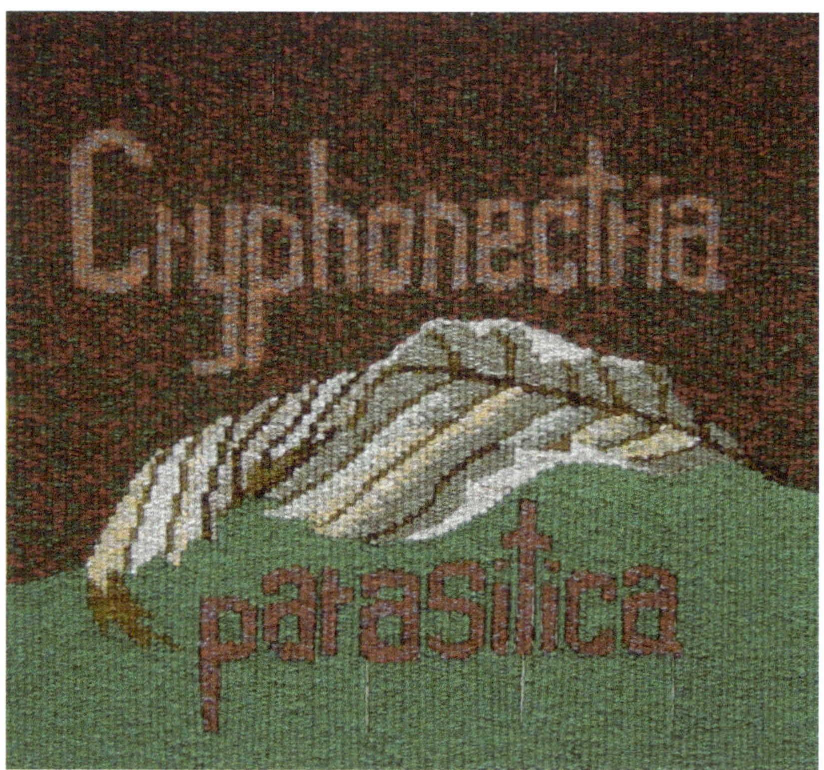

Figure 13.18
Cryphonectria parasitica detail

continent.[4] Now, decades later, the pest is rampant in Hemlock trees throughout the Eastern U.S.

Anxiety and stressful events provoke questions for most people, and I can certainly say that is so for me. Perhaps for an artist, searching for visual answers provides ways of coping with feelings, if not directly resolving the reality of the problems. I simply know that the art works I've made in stressful times have helped me process feelings of anxiety and dread. They have given me constructive ways to move through grief.

4 Patrick Horan, "How Was HWA Introduced? The Gilded Age Garden Hypothesis, How, When & Where was Hemlock Woolly Adelgid Introduced to the Eastern US?" http://savinghemlocks.org/gilded-age-garden-hypothesis/

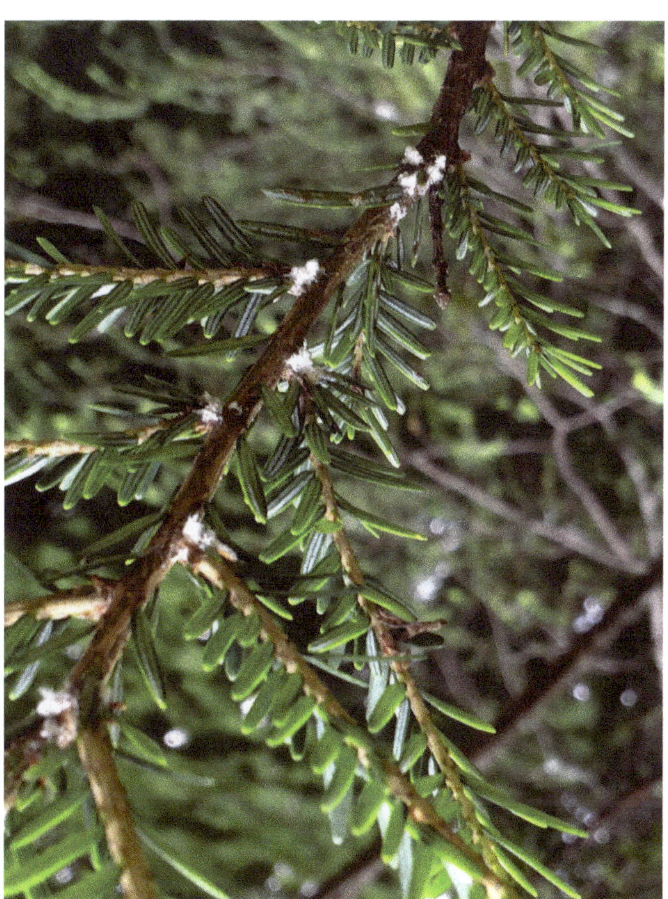

Figure 13.19
Hemlock Wooly Adelgid (HWA) seen on Eastern hemlock foliage

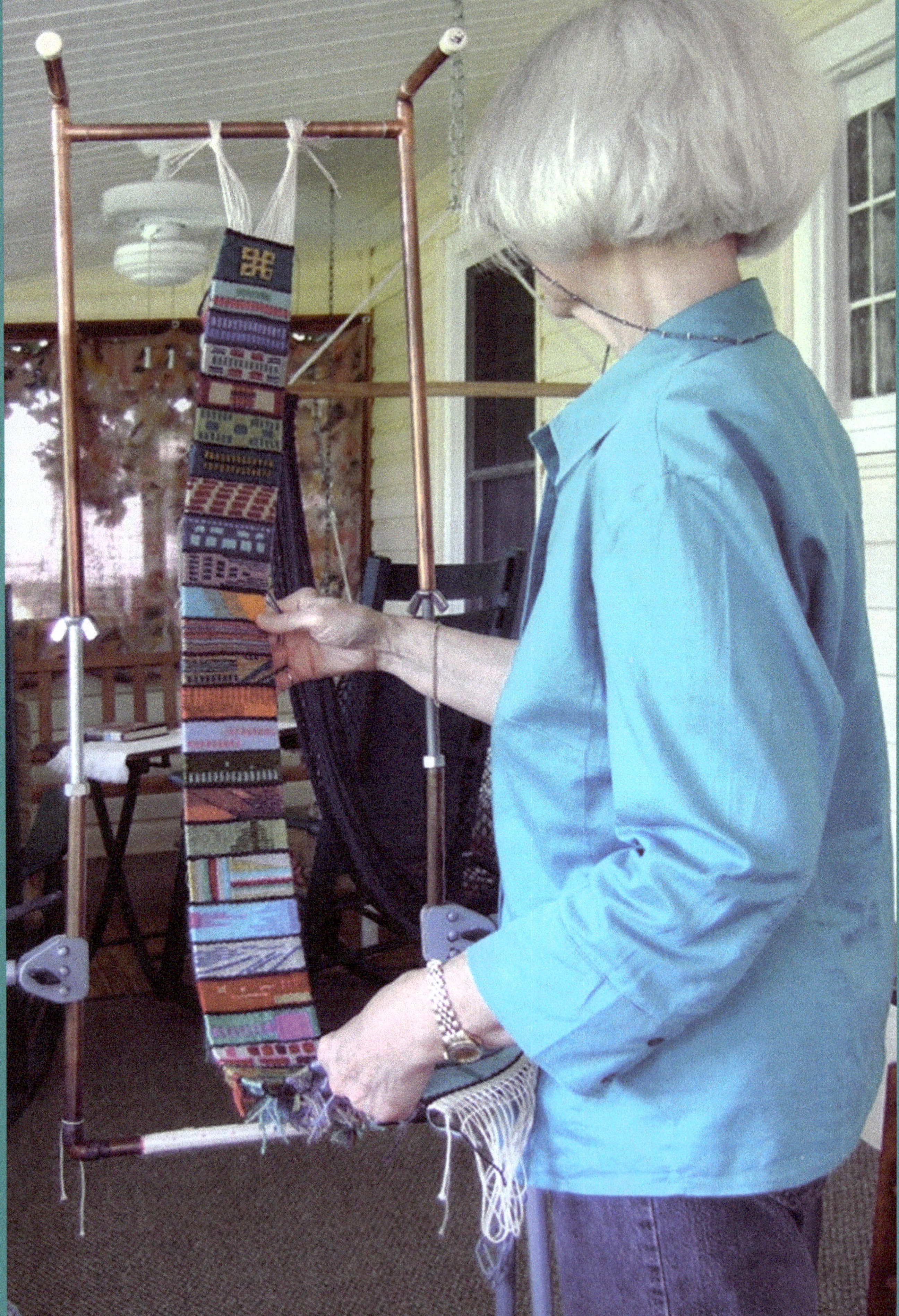

14
Threads of Time

Diaries, journals, daybooks, blogs—all are used to record passing time. I've been an intermittent journal writer and blogger for years. And as a tapestry weaver, I'm acutely aware of the passage of time because it takes so long for a tapestry to grow to completion at the loom. Every trip of the weft through the warp threads represents several seconds, and it takes many thousands of those weft trips to complete the tapestry.

Things happen as a tapestry grows. The days bring different weather conditions and seasonal changes. There are sad times and joyful ones as the narrative of one's life fills with the parts and pieces from which it is made.

For many years, I've thought about the concept of time and how important it is in the making of tapestry. Would there be a way to visually represent the daily passing of time with tapestry? The idea nagged at me. In 2008, I finally decided to make a small tapestry in which each day's small increment would be determined as it was woven. That experiment was the beginning of what I came to call my tapestry diaries.

I chose to work small because I wanted to spend no more than thirty minutes each day with the project, since my other studio activities had priority. The first of May was approaching; that seemed a good time to begin. There were a few trips planned during the month, so a frame loom was set up with a four-inch wide warp. The loom had a warp long enough to devote about an inch-and-a-half in height across the width for each day of the month. In

Figure 14.1 (opposite)
The first tapestry diary is being taken off the loom. This was done throughout the month of May 2008.

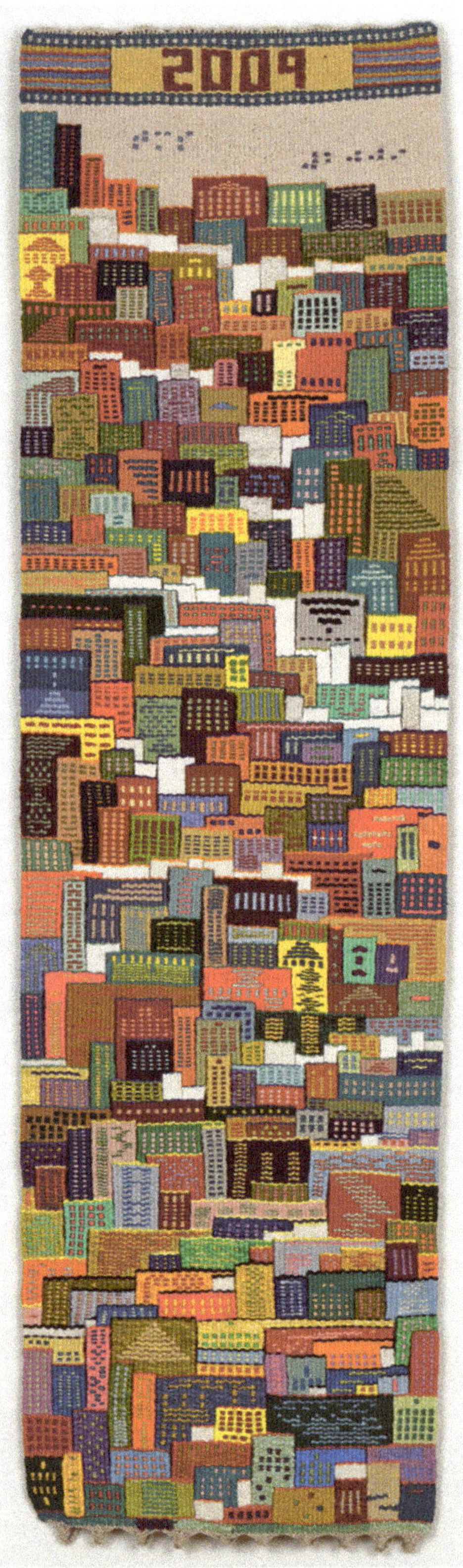

this way, I could take the little tapestry-in-process with me when I traveled. Would I have the discipline to carry out the project for the whole month? Maybe.

Each day's part was to be unique. I also wanted the month-long effort to be visually related rather than an apparently-random assembly of colors. Establishing a few "rules" seemed to be the way to go.

The first rule was easy to make: use only remnants of wefts from past tapestries. There were plenty of those in the studio. I also decided to weave an indication of the date in a simple way, such as with "pick and pick" (where each trip, or pick, of the weft across the width alternates between two different colors, resulting in parallel vertical bars). Another way was by using narrow horizontal bands equal in number to a day's date. A thin line of black yarn at the top of each day's weaving served as a separating mark between days.

Although the tapestry was small, I still found it demanding to do. Occasionally, making the time and having a clear enough mindset to devote to weaving even an inch or so high across the narrow width was a chore. But eventually, May 31 arrived, with a narrow little tapestry resulting from the month-long task. I was pleased with it.

Figure 14.2
Tapestry Diary for 2009, 43 inches by 12 inches. This was the first full year of weaving a small bit each day. The white rectangles throughout represent days I was away from home and not able to weave on the piece. (photo by Tim Barnwell)

Would I have the discipline to do this daily process for a whole year, I wondered? I decided to give it a go.

On January 1, 2009, the yearlong attempt at daily weaving began. I had no definite plan for the size, because the tapestry would be growing day by day in parts of uneven sizes. To make sure there would be enough length for the year, I decided to use a tapestry loom with a warp beam onto which I wound a seventy-two-inch long warp. Surely that would last for the year of weaving an inch or so each day. The width of the tapestry would be twelve inches.

In addition to those parameters, I followed a few other simple plans in weaving the tapestry. Once again, as with the one-month experiment, I would use only remnants from past tapestries. I would denote the days of each month with a small woven line of a different color across the top. For instance, January had a red-orange line, followed by February with black at the top.

The increased width of the tapestry allowed for several days to be woven side by side. I used rectangles and squares of different heights for the days and wove across the width, ten days at a time. Soon I realized there would be occasions, such as travel obligations, when I couldn't weave on the tapestry. My solution was to weave simple white shapes for the missed days before making the new entry for the next day.

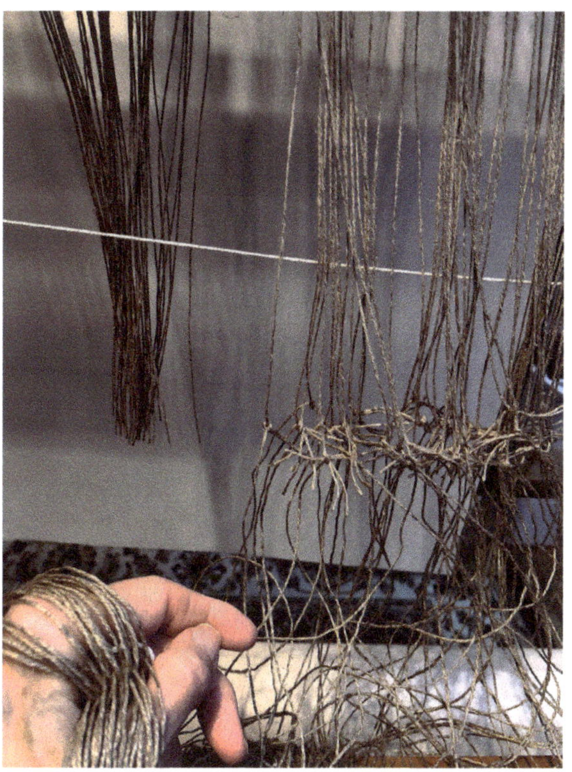

Figure 14.3
Tying the warp threads of the new year's length onto the ends remaining from the previous year's tapestry diary.

The tapestry grew daily, and it was over forty-inches long when completed on December 31, 2009. When unrolled, the tapestry showed my days as woven, one by one, throughout the months and served as evidence for the yearlong effort of my self-assigned task. I had indeed made weaving a small amount of tapestry a daily practice over the past 365 days, and I wanted to continue.

I tied a new length of warp onto the ends from the previous year and wound them

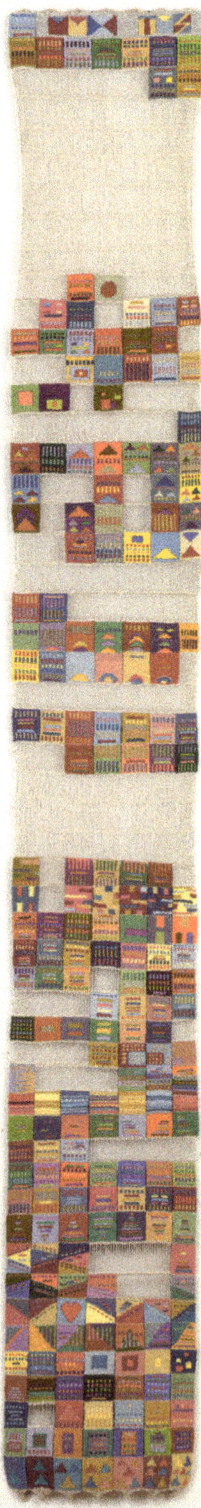

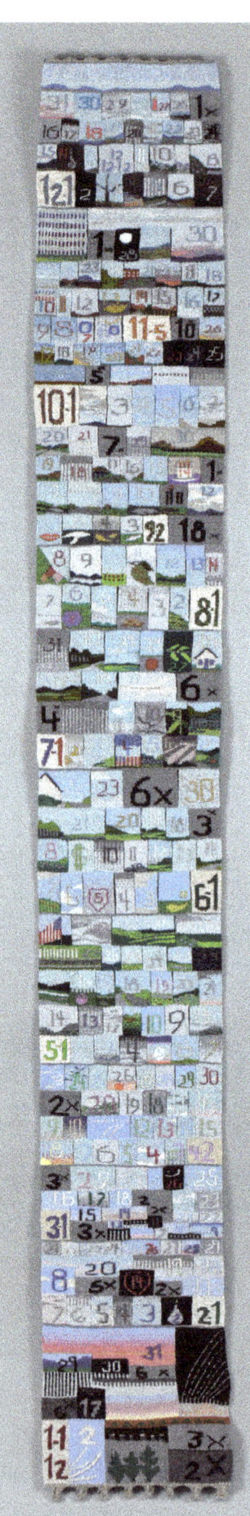

on the loom to prepare for the next year's weaving. Doing this was a practical matter of using the same width and number of warp threads as before to save time with the loom set up, but I also felt the ties symbolically linked one year to the next.

Throughout 2010, I had scheduled several teaching engagements and conferences; additionally, for six weeks, I would be in England at West Dean College. I wanted to show those times distinctly in the piece and felt that leaving empty warp threads amidst the woven areas to complete when at home would be the answer. That plan presented a technical challenge because subsequent areas of weaving had to be supported in some way.

My solution to this problem was to account for the missing days by weaving thin strips of stiff paper into the warps when I returned home. I used a simple knotting method, called half hitch, to secure the empty warps at the bottom and top of the strips. The half hitches also kept the wefts below and above the empty days in place when I removed the paper at year's end. The unwoven warp threads throughout the

Figure 14.4 (left)
Tapestry Diary for 2010, 95 inches by 12 inches. Empty warps represent the time I was gone. (Photo by Tim Barnwell)

Figure 14.5 (right)
Tapestry Diary for 2012, 89 inches by 12 inches. In this yearlong tapestry I used simple pictographs for some events. (Photo by Tim Barnwell)

tapestry were clear reminders of the many activities and travels of 2010.

In 2011, several scheduled obligations would call me away again. Instead of making a long, continuous warp on the loom at home, I decided to set up a small frame loom with a new warp each month. That way, I could take the tapestry diary loom along with me to allow my keeping up the daily practice. Each month was of a different size and design plan, but still the daily weaving was the primary focus.

In January, I used soumak in several ways; in May, I wove Arabic and Roman numerals as date indicators; for June, July, August, and September, I cast a die each day to make a random choice from simple shapes—square, rectangle, or triangle—and six colors. At year's end, I mounted the twelve small tapestry diaries onto fabric-covered boards.

The twelve separate tapestries allowed me to weave each day because I could easily take the loom with me wherever I traveled. Because they were somewhat unrelated, they didn't suit my wish to have a visual record of each day of the year as a unified whole. Maybe using the same size and plan for the months might have given greater coherence to the design and indicated the daily relationship. However, I realized the visual impact of a whole year of daily additions in one tapestry was preferable. Thus, I set up

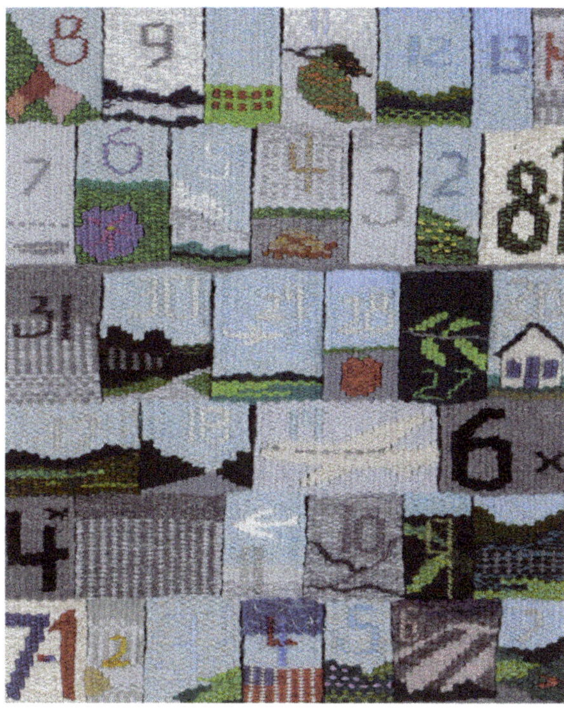

Figure 14.6
Detail for parts of July and August 2012 showing individual days in the tapestry diary. There are three airplanes represented, for instance. Those were for trips taken by me and also by my sister. The Fourth of July is shown with a stylized flag of red, white, and blue. (Photo by Tim Barnwell)

the 2012 tapestry diary once more using the larger loom.

As with all of the previous tapestry diaries, I made a few changes to the rules for the year. One modification was how I indicated my times away from home. Upon returning, I wove an Arabic number followed by an X for the missing days. For instance, 8 X meant I was gone for eight days.

In this way, I noted most of the dates with a numeral, usually using soumak

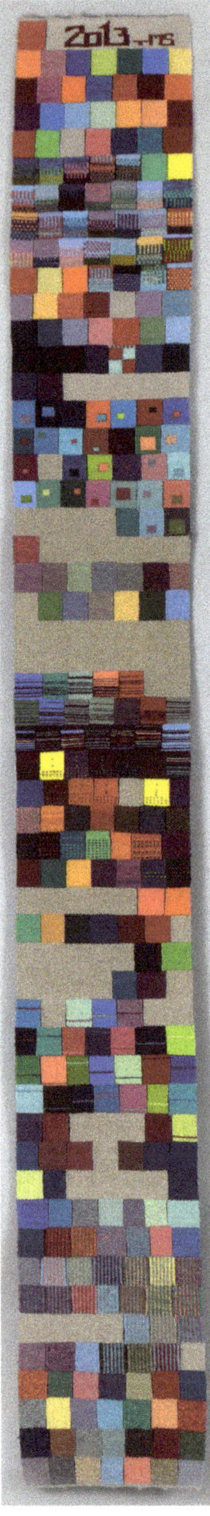

Figure 14.7 (left) Tapestry Diary for 2013, 90 inches by 12 inches. For this year I wove areas of linen to represent away times. The colors were from hand dyed wools. (Photo by Tim Barnwell)

Figure 14.8 (below) Tapestry diary for 2014, 42 inches by 12 inches. Away times were shown as alternating shapes of black or white. The days for each month were woven in a slightly different method; for instance, diagonal shapes were used for a month, followed by the next month of square shapes for the days. (Photo by Tim Barnwell)

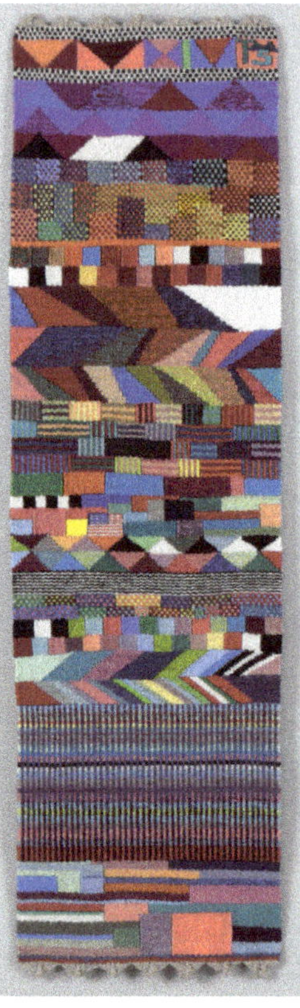

technique. For 2012, the weather, time of day, and season played a significant role in color choice. I also used simplified pictorial representations during the year. For instance, after finding a feather on a morning walk, a simplified feather shape became that day's entry. Occasionally, I symbolized significant events with a pictograph, as when I recorded the date a friend's husband passed away with a teardrop shape. Although it happened in 2001, I chose to represent September 11 of 2012 with two vertical gray bars topped with red to represent the planes striking the Twin Towers.

In 2013, I selected wefts from a past series of dye mixtures I'd been hoarding for years. There were over one hundred colors in the dye samples but only a few yards of each color; those small amounts were still enough to weave an inch or so to represent individual days.

The overall design concept for the year was a simple format of squares with slight daily variations within each. This served well to let the dyed colors play the major role. I filled days away from home with solid linen wefts in size equal to the dimensions of the days that were missed. Those parts of the tapestry distinctly showed at a glance when I'd been gone—as did the empty warp threads of 2010 and the white spaces in 2009—and emphasized the importance of the daily color.

When 2014 arrived, a lot of the hand-dyed yarns remained, so I once more used those as the wefts. The plan for the year was to use a different "weaverly" way of making simple shapes. For instance, the perpendicular relationship of warp and weft lends itself to shapes being woven side by side in a vertical separation, or along a diagonal slant. Those are weaverly solutions to creating shapes. I wove black or white alternately to signify any days away from home.

For six years I'd found simple ways to weave the passing of days in the tapestry diaries. In 2015, I decided to add a pictorial approach along with individual days. Because sense of place is important to me, I selected four different views of plants found on our property to represent the months of the year. Those images were determined as each month arrived and were surrounded by the weaving of the days.

In January of that year, there were the fallen oak leaves in our yard, followed by pecans in February, the time when the last of our pecan tree's bounty is usually being cracked and stored. The weavings for March were of twigs that fell during a brief ice storm. April held views of daffodils. In May, the buds of the Gingko tree became full-fledged leaves during the month of weaving.

June was for the "wedding roses," wild roses like the ones we'd picked for our wedding day from the yard where we lived at the time. The rest of 2015 was filled with representations of the monthly changes seen in our surroundings. I truly enjoyed selecting and designing the images as the weeks of the year went by. Working in this way also very much satisfied the "picture maker" in me.

Because incorporating the pictorial within the simplicity of the blocks of the days had been pleasing, I decided to do again in 2016, with a modification that there would be twelve larger areas to represent

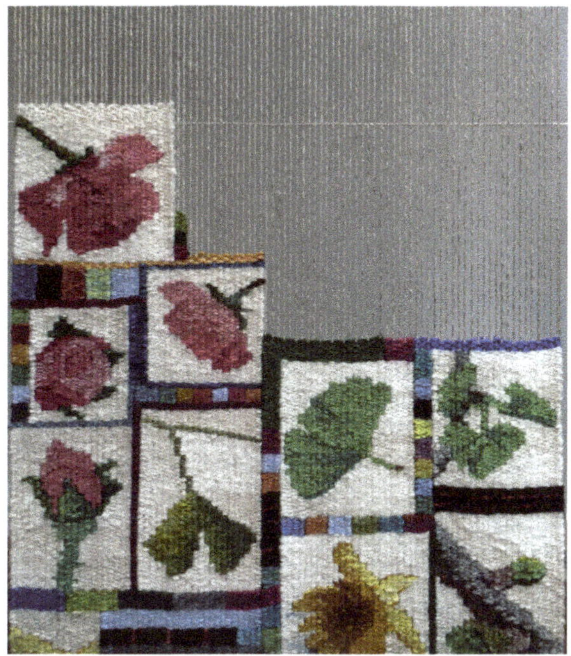

Figure 14.9
During 2015 I began to use a more pictorial approach. There were four views of something growing at or found on our property during each month. For instance, the detail shows roses for June and gingko leaves for May.

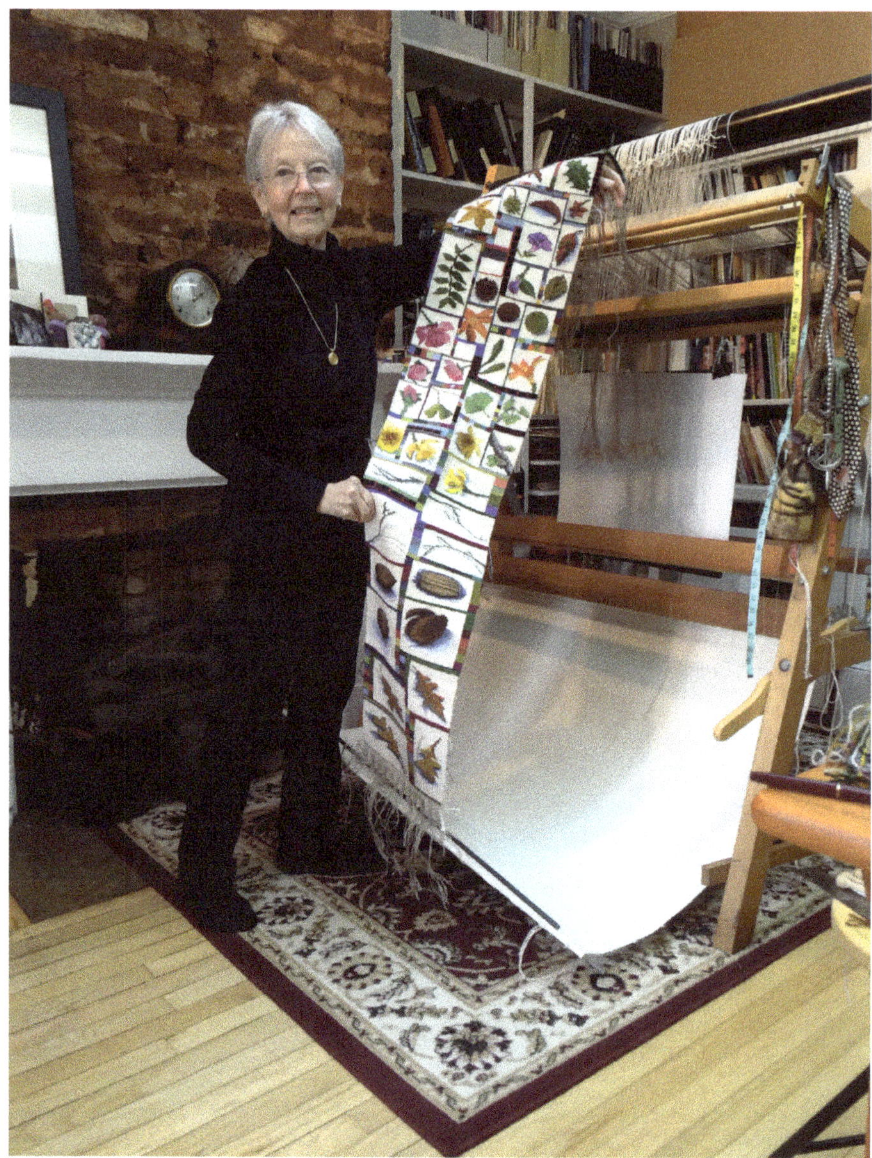

Figure 14.10
Cutting off the 2015 Tapestry Diary on December 31. (Photo by Thomas Scanlin)

each month. I would surround those with the smaller parts that would be woven each day.

The seasonal changes of the black walnut tree on the property became the theme for each month. At the first of the month, I made a small painting of a detail relevant for the changes happening in the growth process of the tree at the time. I did that part of the weaving over the month. Adding to the theme for the year, I used black walnuts from the tree to dye some of the wefts.

The year of 2017 was full of commitments, including co-teaching a class during Spring Concentration, an eight-week session at Penland School of Craft in March and April. In October, I planned a two-week artist retreat. I prepared the warp on a large, yet portable frame loom that I could take along so I could keep up with the diary weaving when away.

The design idea for the year was to continue a monthly component surrounded by the individual days. I chose to use flowers that would be in bloom wherever I would be during each month. I based cartoons on photographs of flowering plants that I found on site. I took the flowers out of their natural color context, showing them as simplified images with a woven white background.

As 2018 approached, the phrase "Sticks and Stones may break my bones/ But words will never harm me" kept coming into my thoughts. It seemed to reflect the antagonistic mood of society then prevalent in the U.S. So I planned the tapestry diary to reflect that phrase by using a stick or a stone image for each month. Daily woven areas surrounded the larger month designs.

I selected subjects for each month's design from somewhere nearby as each month arrived, or from a collection of stones I have from past travels. Next, I placed the item onto a white background with a strong light directed from the side to give distinct shadows. I then made a painting to use as reference for the cartoon. The shadow shapes became as important in the composition as the images of stick or stone. I used natural dyes for the wefts throughout the tapestry.

For 2019, I returned to flowers as monthly subjects; instead of the white background of 2017, I included shapes and colors from the surrounds. I chose natural dyes in a variety of primary and secondary hues and cast a die to select the daily color to use: one meant red; two, yellow; three, blue; four, green; five, orange; and six, purple. The colorful woven day parts surrounding the more naturalistic colors of the flowers gave a lively effect to the tapestry.

In the years of doing the tapestry diary process, I've written about it at my blog and in a couple of magazine articles.[1] Other people have noticed the diaries and begun their own. In 2016 and 2017, several of us with similar daily woven practice mounted an exhibit called "Time Warp—and Weft," shown first in Topeka, Kansas, at NOTO Gallery and later in Athens, Georgia, at Lyndon House Arts Center.

I've spoken with many people about the concept of keeping a diary through tapestry weaving. In 2012, I taught a class

1 Tommye McClure Scanlin, "Time Warp and Weft: A Celebration of the Passage of Time Through Weaving," *Shuttle, Spindle & Dyepot*, Summer 2017, 36-40.

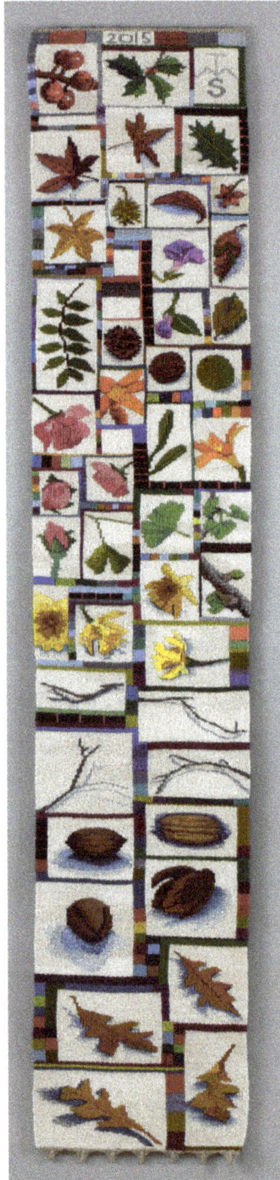

Figure 14.11
Tapestry Diary for 2015, 60 inches by 12 inches (photo by Tim Barnwell)

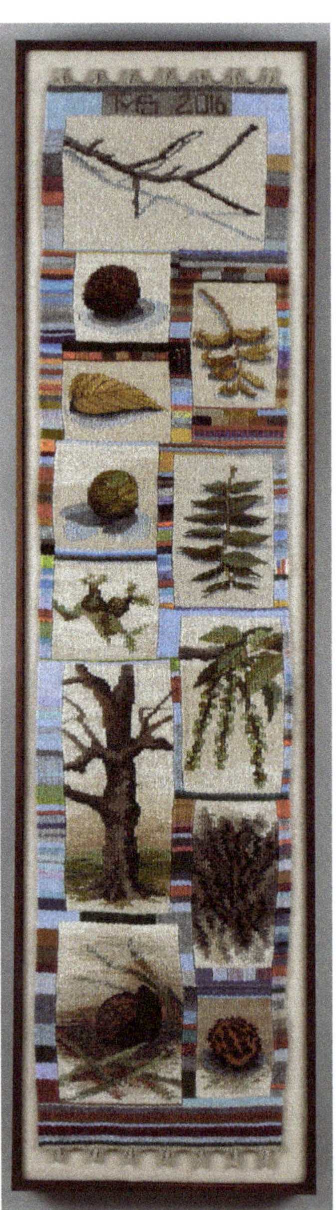

Figure 14.12
Tapestry Diary for 2016, 49 inches by 12 inches (photo by Tim Barnwell)

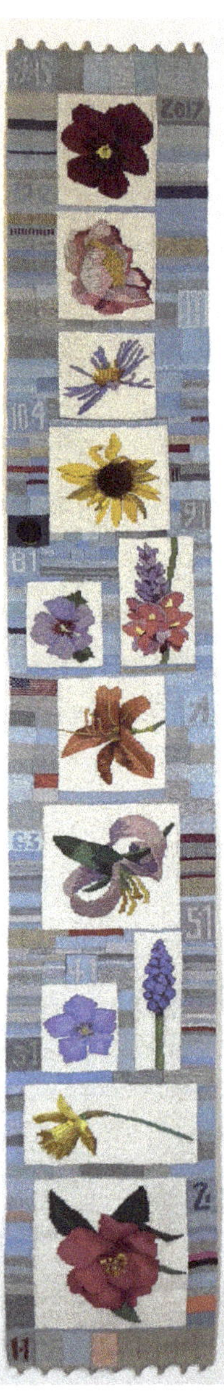

Figure 14.13
Tapestry Diary for 2017, 78 inches by 12 inches (photo by Tim Barnwell)

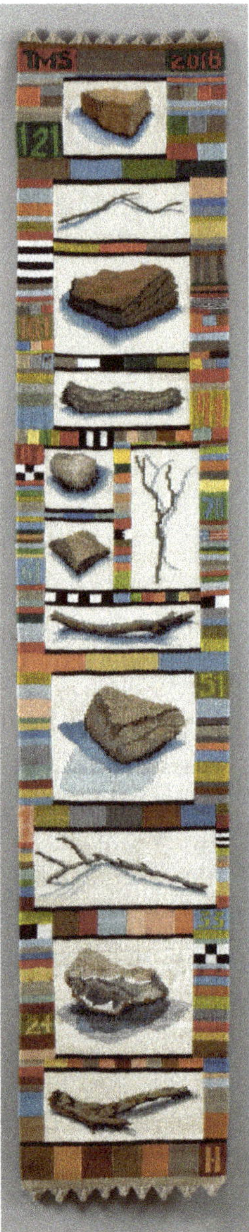

Figure 14.14
Tapestry Diary for 2018, 62 inches by 12 inches (photo by Tim Barnwell)

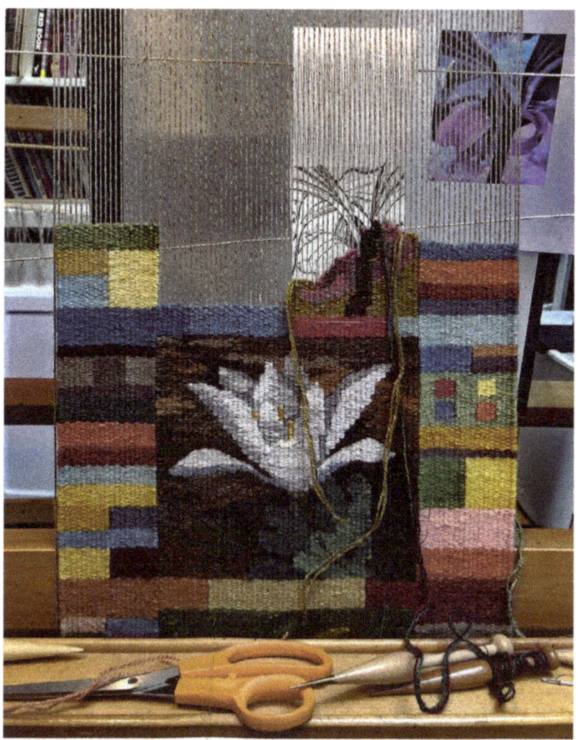

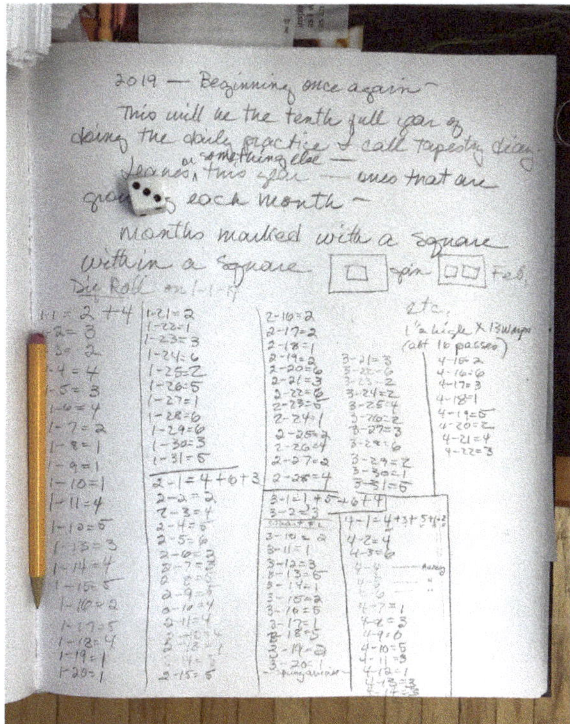

at Arrowmont School of Crafts called "Weaving the Days of Our Lives," in which I encouraged students to explore the concept of daily weaving as a way to study tapestry technique. In 2018, I taught a version of that class for the Weavers of Orlando in Winter Park, Florida.

The daily weaving practice continues to intrigue me. Having said that, I do have to admit that it is sometimes difficult to find time to weave even the small amount for the day. I also find it a bit of a quandary deciding how to use similar methods for the days yet make each distinct from the other. Even so, by sitting down at the loom each and every day to weave for a short time on the tapestry diary, I'm continuing a ritual of practice that enriches the discipline necessary to be a tapestry maker. The daily commitment to the ongoing tapestry diaries—as well as my engagement in looking at, thinking about, and designing from the world around me—is how I weave the threads of my life, one day at a time.

Figure 14.15 (above)
Tapestry Diary for 2019, in progress on April 22, 2019. Flowers growing seasonally are the subjects for each month. Natural dyes are being used for all weft colors. Day colors are being selected by a throw of a die.

Figure 14.16 (below)
Detail of recording the rolls of the die to select the colors of the days.

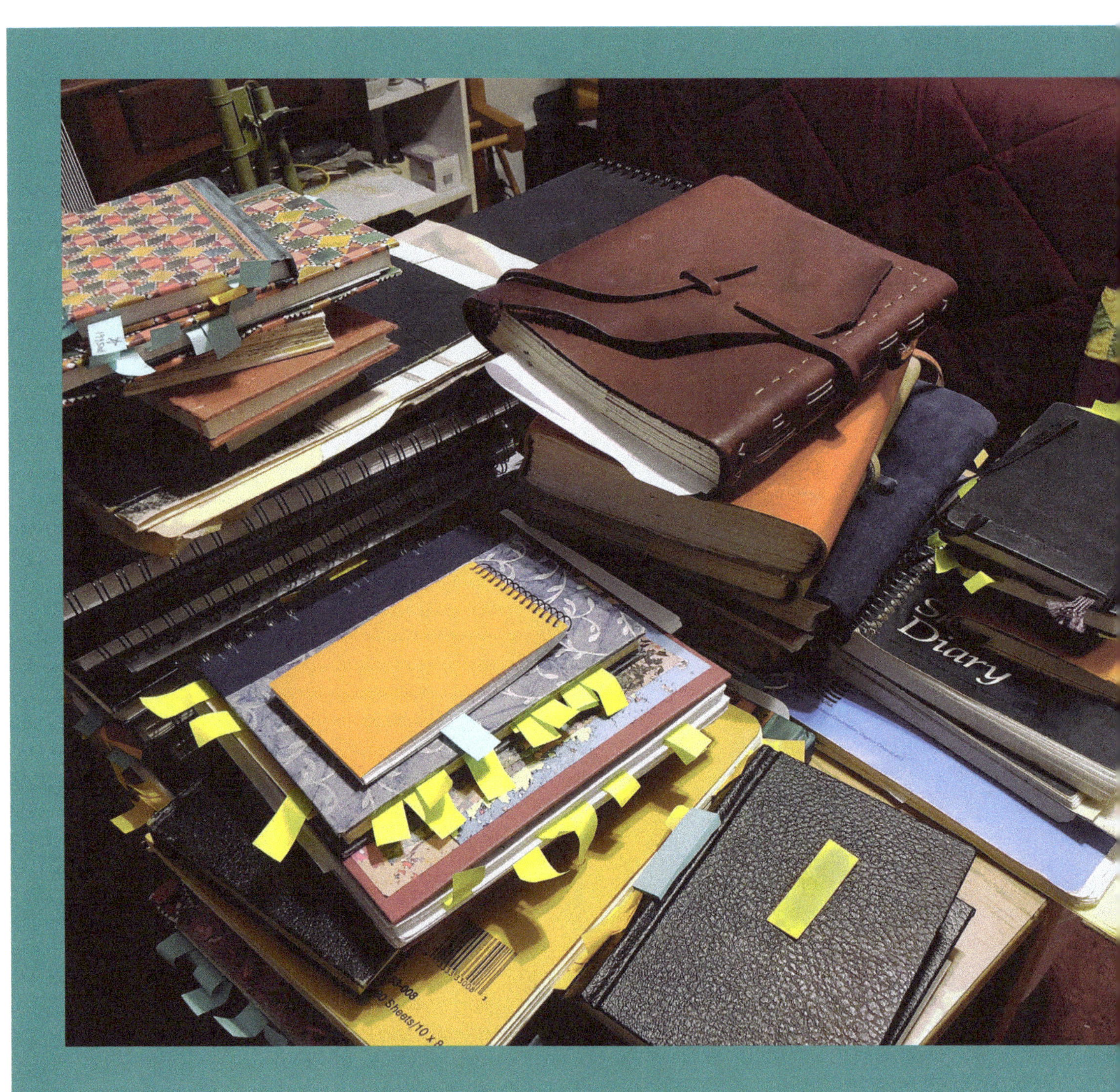

Figure 15.1
Sketchbooks and journals amassed over the past three decades.

15

Doubts and Decisions

July 1995—Absolutely drawing a blank on ideas—the well, never too full, is dry, it seems.

June 23, 1998—the same old dilemma—too many possibilities but not enough good ideas.

Sometime in 2005—This whole piece is growing and changing—almost daily—I don't know how it's going to end—the whole process is an unfolding of ideas.

January 4, 2008—do I have anything to say, anything in my work that would cause a viewer to think about something other than just the visual impression of the work—and do I even need to "say something?"

October 2008—Struggling as usual with concept and design. . . . I need to think differently, see differently, move images around in a way that's new for me—I'm locked into the same old struggle trying to force the idea into shape.

November 8, 2010—Do I have enough years of time . . . ? Don't get discouraged. I can only do what I can do—nothing more.

December 5, 2014—(other) visual artists' work always is a bit more something than mine—more conceptual? More intellectual? But I don't really think I should try to be doing anything other than what I am—and it's OK—I have to continue to remind myself that it's OK as it is—my work is what it is—nothing more—nothing less. . . .

December 30, 2015—Another blah day . . . I absolutely can't get motivated to weave—I'm stuck. Nothing excites me about what I'm working on either on the big loom or the frame loom . . . I am dead in the water with tapestry right now—why? I haven't been excited about an image to weave in awhile. Why? What's going on—or not going on—that seems more to the point. I don't know—don't know.

<u>*November 17, 2017, morning pages excerpt*</u>*—Is there any evidence of creative thought without tangible action? Does process of making, whether it's words written or weavings made, show evidence of creativity (sometimes) and so is the product of creative thought—does it become a creative act? To act creatively—is that possible or is the act only the motor response to the internal thought? If that's the case then there is no creative process. There is creativity and there is process. Creative thought may or may not lead to a process where a unique thing comes into being. Is this accurate? Anyway—all this wondering this morning to get to the point that I don't have any "creative" idea (yet) for any of the warps I'm putting on the looms—but I shouldn't worry about that—let the cycle continue—don't yet begin to feel frantic or frustrated. Do work toward the end goal of making tapestry. Every stage of the way is needed—get there by going there.*

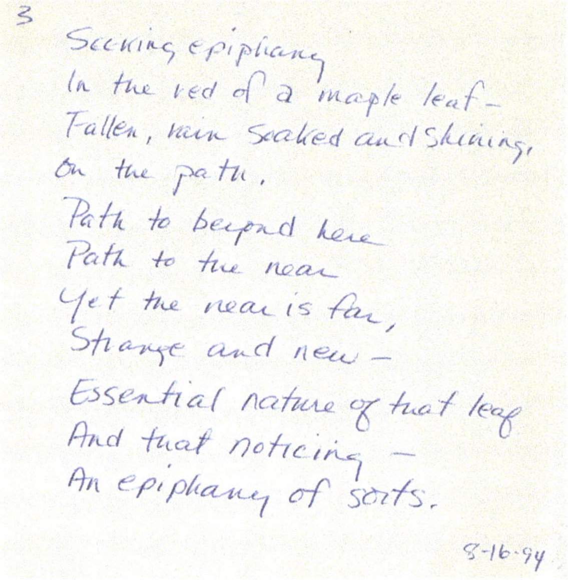

3
Seeking epiphany
In the red of a maple leaf—
Fallen, rain soaked and shining,
On the path.
Path to beyond here
Path to the near
Yet the near is far,
Strange and new—
Essential nature of that leaf
And that noticing—
An epiphany of sorts.

8-16-94

Figure 15.2
During my first artist residency at the Hambidge Center in 1994, I spent days walking in the woods, reading, and writing. This is one of the poems from the time.

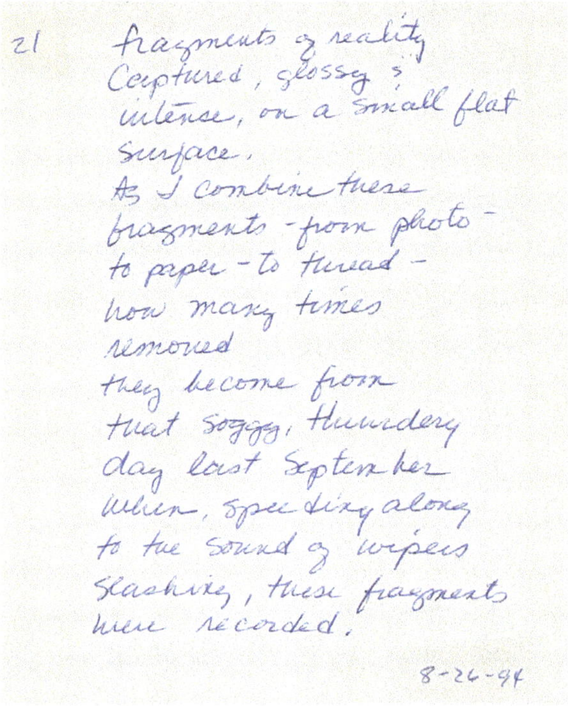

21 fragments of reality
Captured, glossy &
intense, on a small flat
surface.
As I combine these
fragments - from photo -
to paper - to thread -
how many times
removed
they become from
that soggy, thundery
day last September
when, speeding along
to the sound of wipers
slashing, these fragments
were recorded.

8-26-94

Figure 15.3
Written on August 26, 1994, the description was of a photograph I was using as reference for a painting. The image created was later used for a tapestry called *Rainstorm on the Road to Tallahassee*.

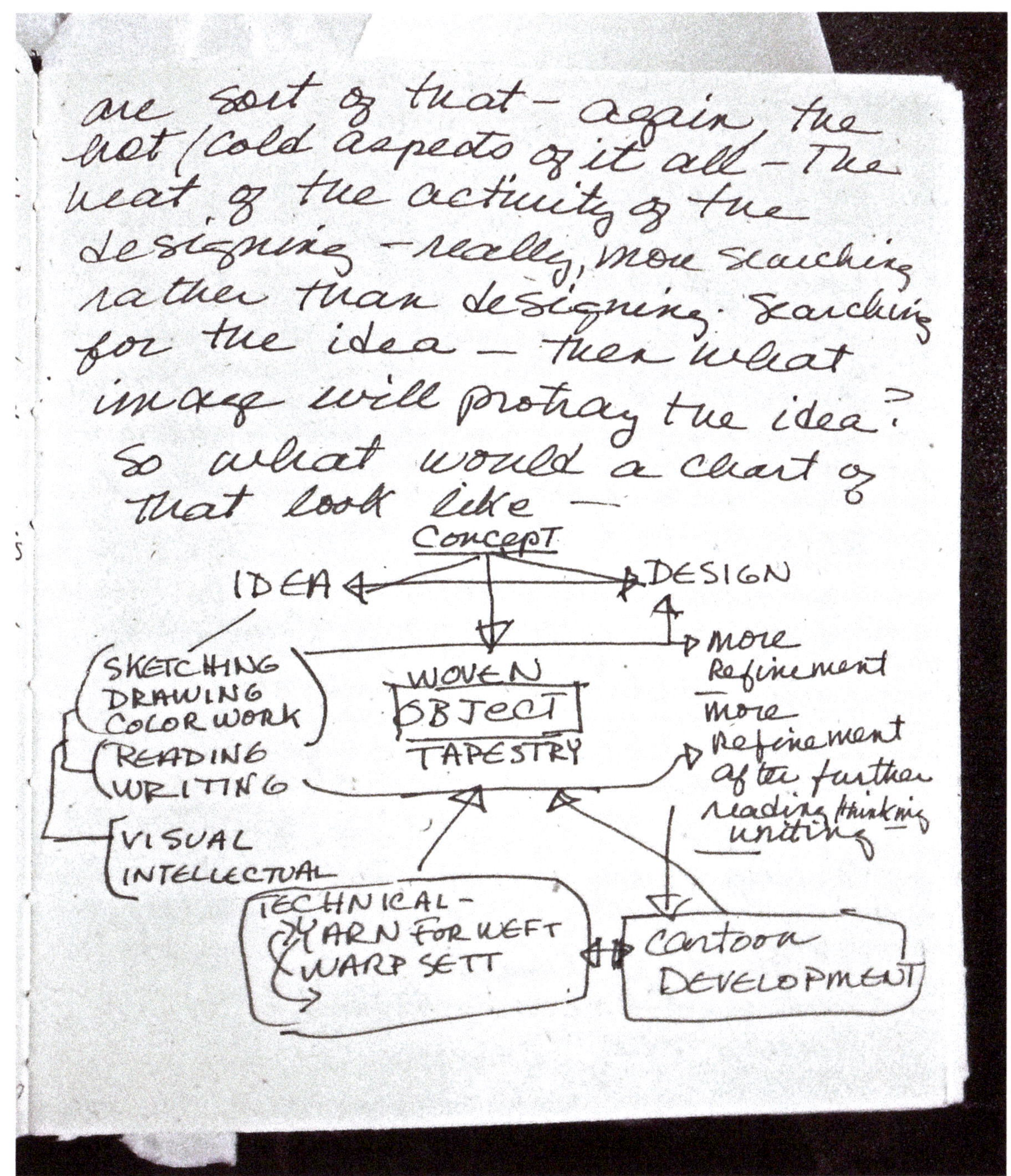

Figure 15.4
A journal page in which I drew a chart of the process for designing it seems I often use.

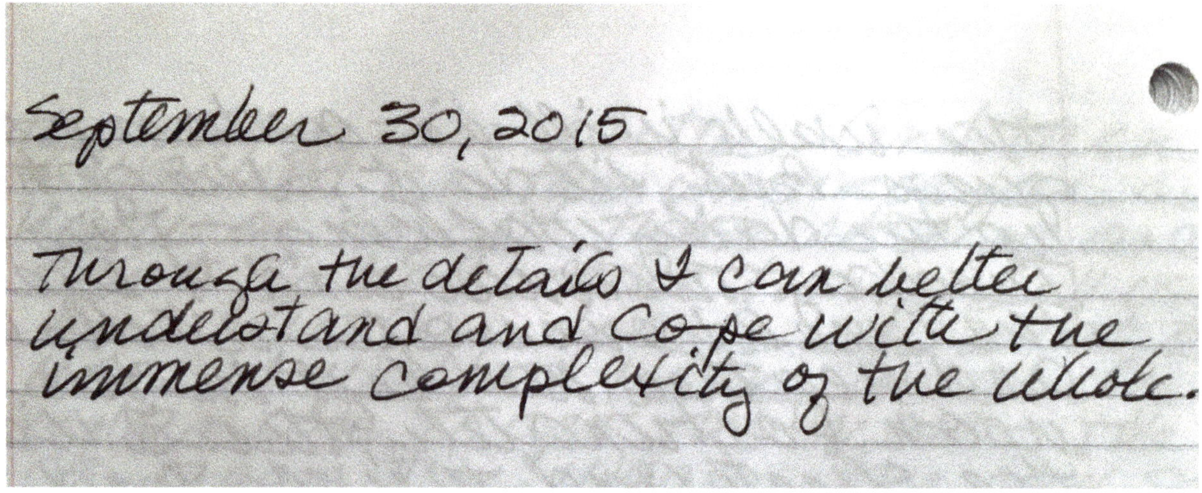

Figure 15.5
A brief entry into my morning pages journal. I don't reread the morning pages but sometimes photograph a snippet of what I write to remember later. This was one of those: "Through the details I can better understand and cope with the immense complexity of the whole."

In these few fragments of journal entries spanning two decades, one can read some of my struggles with self-doubt. Of course, not all of the journal writings over the years are about indecisions and uncertainties. I've also reflected on in-progress artwork and frequently made planning notes for upcoming teaching engagements, as well as writing comments to myself once those classes were underway. I've written poems and wondered about many things.

Looking back, I can see that much of what's in the journals has been concerning my decision-making process. Usually an affirmative statement, often about a breakthrough of concept or composition that I reached, followed an entry like those above. I realize now if I'd taken to heart all of the uncertainties noted in the journals, I would never have created anything.

Writing down the blocks I face seems to help. I've found that, by describing a design impasse in words, an understanding of what needs to be done to resolve a composition may happen. It seems that articulating in writing often helps to clarify concepts I struggle with, making the visual representations more fully developed.

I've sometimes also found an answer for a visual question comes when I leave it alone for a while. That might mean simply coming back the next day to see the work with fresh eyes. However, it may mean storing something in a sketchbook or in a portfolio for a longer time, maybe even for years before rediscovering the possibilities

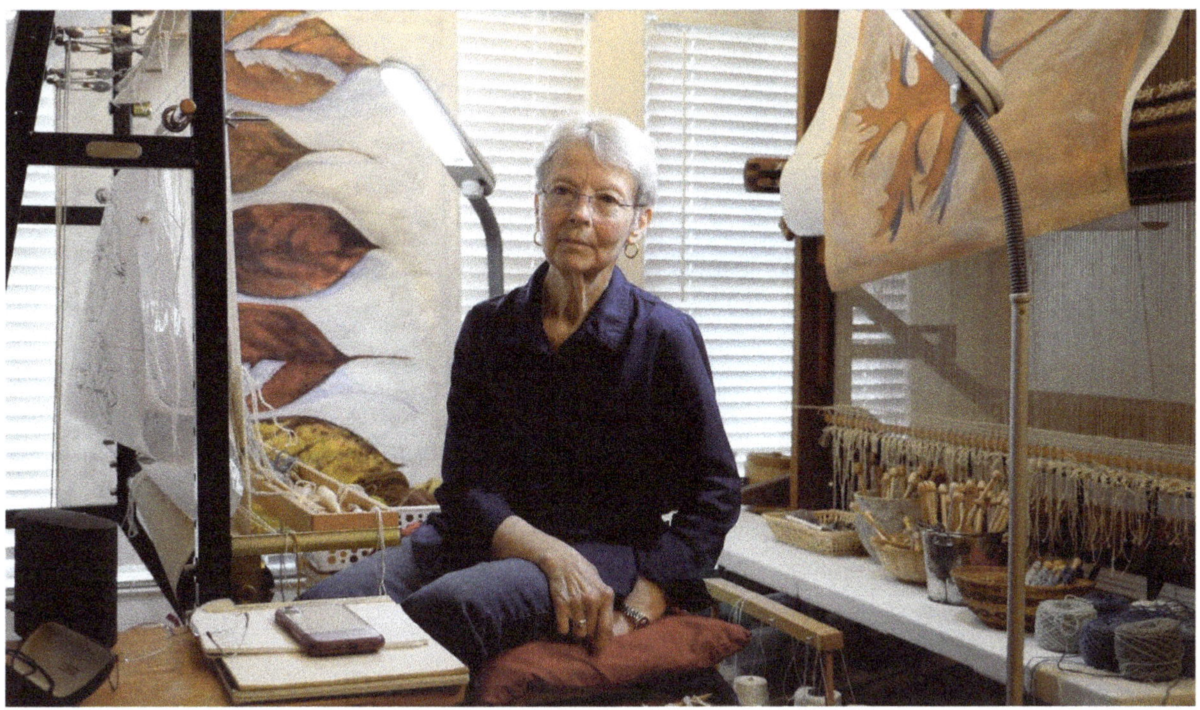

Figure 15.6
Photo of the author in 2018. Two looms are in the photo and a couple of paintings that are being used as the source for tapestries. (Photo by Hal Jacobs)

of the image.

I've finally recognized that the ebb and flow of creative energy I've felt through the years is exactly that—evidence of the *cycle* of growth and decline and growth once more. Even though I don't exactly welcome the down side, I now accept this cycle as one that offers both high and low points in my art-making abilities.

A few years ago, I wrote the following lines when I hadn't yet fully understood but sensed the significance of the flow of creative process:

The bright promise
of morning.
Light through
the leaves
breathes hope
again.
Dark is gone
but will return,
bringing
new
fears and imaginings.
Yet, to see this light
More clear
The dark is there.

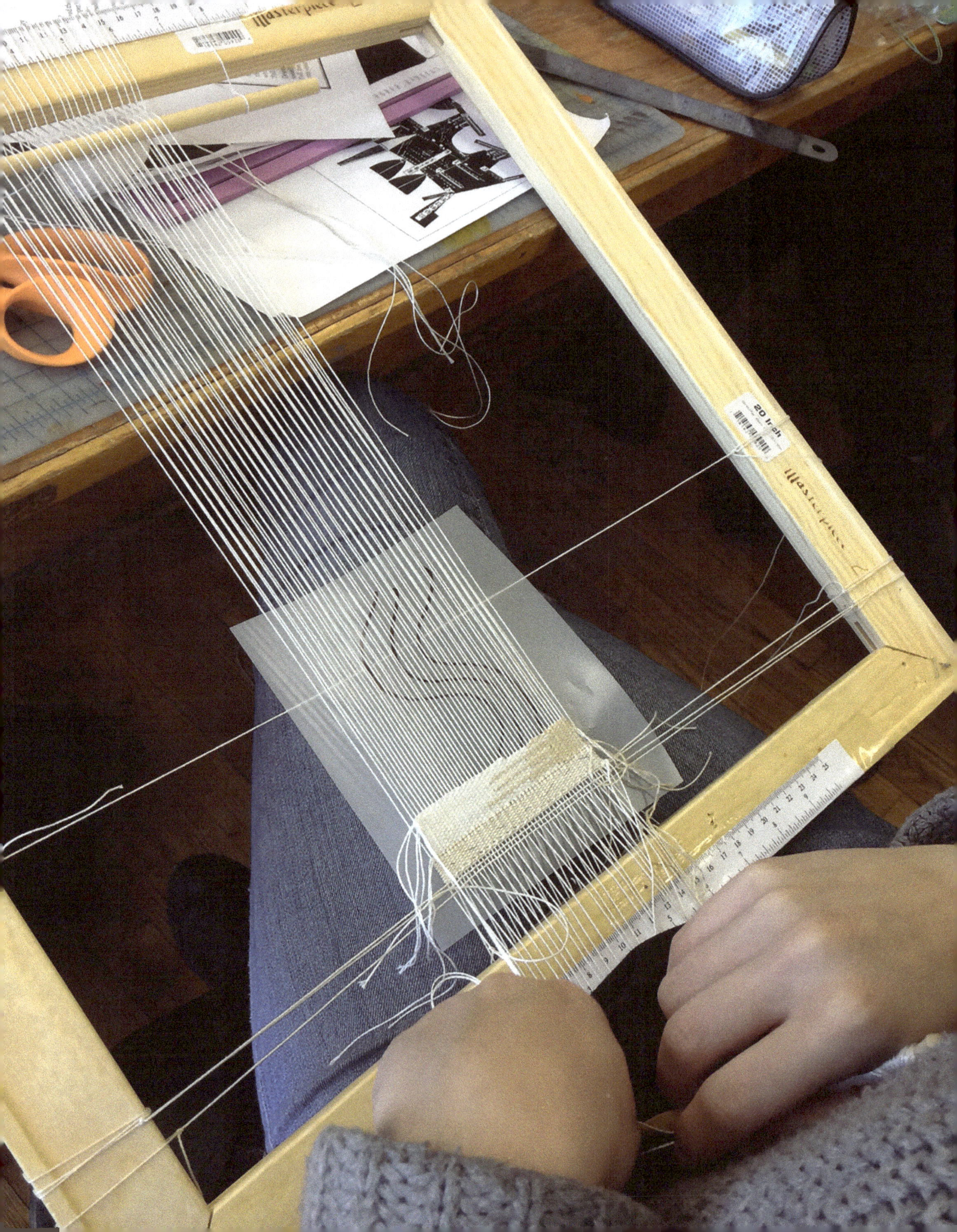

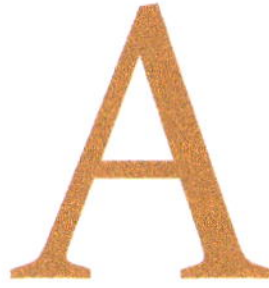

Tapestry Weaving Basics: A Primer

Weaving is a way to make cloth. So are knitting and crochet. But weaving is different because each of those other methods can be done with only two things: thread and the simple tools of knitting needles or a crochet hook. Weaving is a bit more complicated since it uses a few more items for making cloth. First, there are the threads to be used. One set of threads, called the warp, is evenly spread out on a loom and other threads, the weft, interweaves across the warp. Often a shuttle carries the weft.

Looms for weaving are of many kinds, sizes, and methods of operation. For instance, large, complex weaving machines in textile mills are daily producing thousands of yards of woven goods that are quite literally turned into the fabric of our lives. Handlooms are still very much in use by both professional handweavers and by hobbyists to create cloth at a slower pace. Looms used by hand weavers can be simple or quite complex, including computer driven looms, for instance. Or they may be very basic frame looms. Handweavers may choose from many techniques as they design and create handwoven fabric. (Fig. A.1)

The very simplest and most basic way that warp and weft threads can interweave with each other is in a method called "plain weave." To imagine this, think of two vertical, parallel lines. Then imagine two horizontal, parallel lines. Next, imagine the lower horizontal crossing over the first vertical line, then under the next. The second horizontal line does just the opposite so that each vertical line is now covered with one small part of each horizontal line. (Fig. A.2)

Figure A.1 (opposite)
A student frame loom being used for a learning exercise. This simple loom is made of artist stretcher strips.

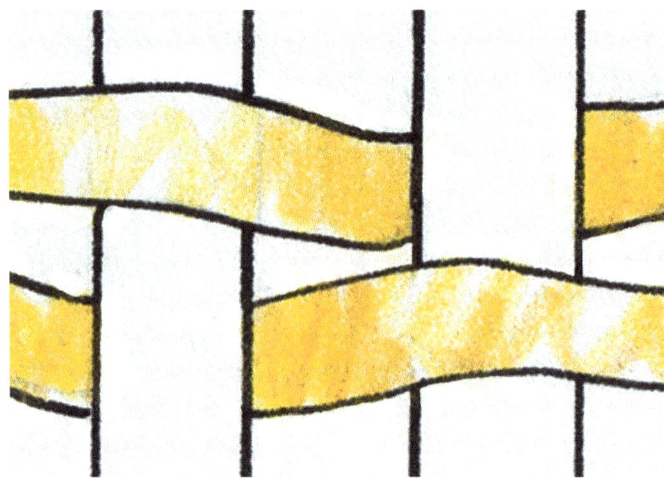

Figure A.2
The structure of plain weave: the two white warps are vertical and parallel to each other. They are crossed alternately with two horizontal wefts, shown in yellow.

Now, turn that mental image into many warp threads placed side by side. With plain weave, a weft thread will cross over and under, over and under . . . along a row to alternately cover every other warp in sequence. When the weft turns around and goes in the opposite direction for the next row, the alternate warps are covered. That's the essence of the plain weave structure: over one, under one, then alternating on the next row (or "pick") of weft. (Fig. A.3)

Cloth woven in plain weave may be of three types. For instance, if both the warp and the weft show up equally in the cloth, it's described as a balanced weave; both color and texture of the warp and weft plays a significant role in the appearance of balanced plain weave fabric. Or, if the warp threads are placed very closely together so the wefts are essentially hidden and only seen at the edges, it's called warp-faced; the beauty of this cloth comes from

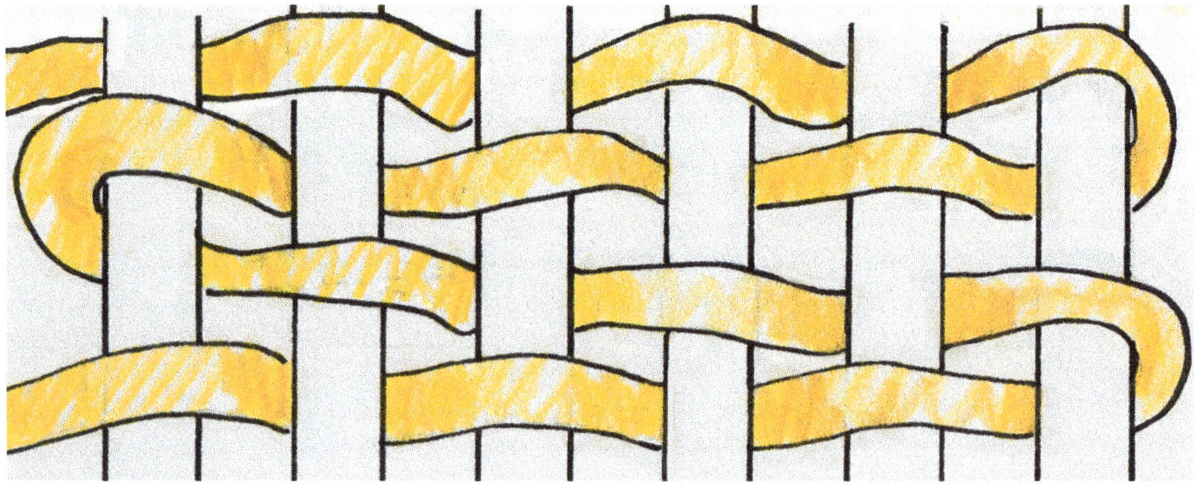

Figure A.3
Six warps are shown and four rows or picks of weft. In tapestry, these weft picks are packed down to completely cover and hide the warp threads.

the selection of the warp colors as the loom is set up. And, lastly, when the warp is totally hidden beneath the weft, the cloth is described as weft-faced. Some rug techniques as well as tapestry are among the weft-faced weaves. With tapestry weaving, the weft threads rarely go from edge to edge of the cloth; rather, they are used in an array of shapes to create the design. In this way, the plain weave structure of tapestry becomes anything but plain. Of all the many methods of weaving, perhaps tapestry weaving is the one over which the weaver has the most control, and certainly it's one of the slowest.

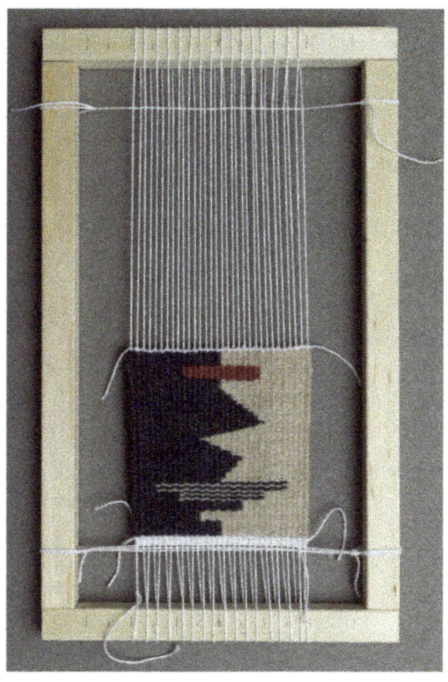

Figure A.4
A sample of basic techniques woven on a simple frame loom as described. Notice that the white warps are hidden by the colors of the weft. (Photo by Christopher Dant)

Although the plain weave of tapestry seems like it should be easy, it is anything but that. There are many subtleties to weaving tapestry that may take years to master. Things like setting up the warp so that it's evenly and firmly tensioned on a loom; making sure the weft is covering the warps consistently as each shape is woven—pulled not too tightly nor left too loosely; being sure the warp threads are regularly spaced throughout and ensuring the edges of the tapestry stay firm and straight. Adding to the technical considerations of the weaving process itself is the design to be woven. The tapestry weaver decides on what to weave and then how to best interpret it in the constraints of tapestry. For instance, when looking at the image, does the warp spacing allow for the smallest of the shapes of the design to easily be woven? If not, how will you simplify it?

Maybe you'll want to give tapestry a try. If you do, I hope these simple instructions will give you a taste for what might come if you really want to delve into the process. I'll describe a few basics of setting up a small frame loom. At the end, I mention resources where you may find much more about tapestry.

Here's a basic list to get you started with a tapestry sampler similar to the one shown:

1. Frame loom—A good size for a frame would be about twelve inches wide by eighteen inches high. This could be a frame made from artist stretcher strips, a needlepoint frame, or even an empty picture frame. A bit of disadvantage of this sort of loom is that

there isn't a way to change the warp tension once it's on the loom; however, for small pieces, that shouldn't be a problem.

2. Cotton thread for warp. You want something strong and smooth as the warp. A beginning suggestion is #3 size crochet cotton found at most hobby stores.

3. Thread or yarn for weft. Almost anything will work for this. If you have yarn you've used for other purposes like knitting, crochet, or embroidery you may want to begin with that. In fact, embroidery floss comes in many colors and is easily found at hobby stores.

4. A few large-eye plastic needles. These are optional, but you might find them helpful.

5. Scissors

6. A ruler, masking tape, and marking pen

7. Kitchen fork to use as a yarn beater—optional but you might want to try it.

Loom Preparation—Warping Steps:

1. Mark the loom along the top and the bottom with inch and half-inch marks. You can use a strip of masking tape placed along both edges of the frame if you don't want to mark on the loom. I'd suggest making about a four-inch wide warp for a first sample.

2. Crochet cotton, #3 size, can be used for the warp at eight threads in each inch. Because the warp will be wound around the loom as it is set up, you will put four threads over the top and bottom of the frame within each inch mark. These will be brought together before beginning to give the eight thread-per-inch total.
    - Begin by tying the warp thread on one side of the loom at the bottom, to the left or right of the center of the width. For instance, if you're putting on a four-inch wide warp, start by tying on the warp thread two inches from the center.
    - Take the warp thread to the top of the frame and go around to the back, then down to the bottom. Go back up to the top and around again.

- Continue to warp around and around the frame, putting four turns within each inch, until you reach two inches past the middle on the opposite side. Now you should have warp threads evenly balanced to four inches of width on the frame.
- Tie the last warp end to the bottom of the frame. (Fig. A.5)

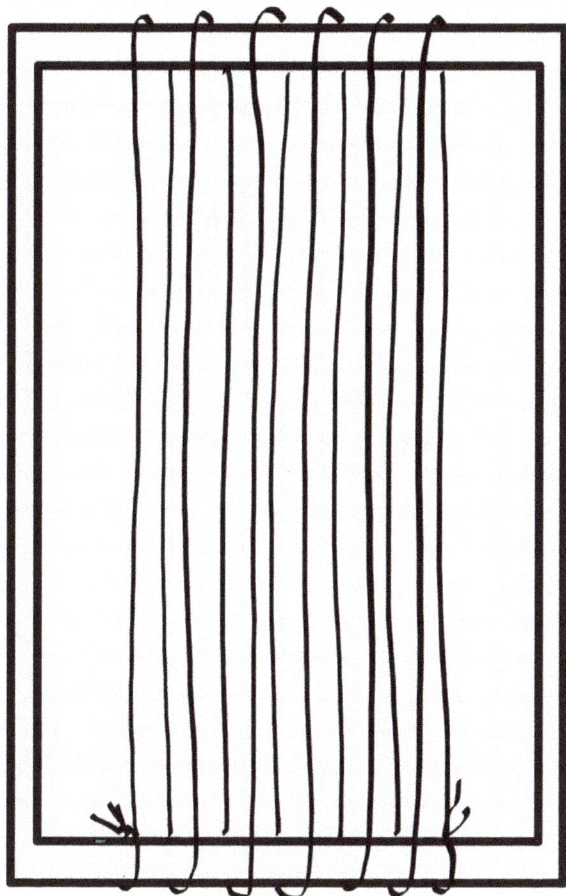

Figure A.5
Diagram of the warp placed on the loom. Keep in mind that the line diagrams do not show the closeness the warp threads will actually have on the loom.

3. When the warp threads are in place, the back and front threads will be brought together to give the total number needed within each inch—eight threads in this case. For a four-inch wide warp, you'll have a total of thirty-two threads when the back and front threads are pulled together. As you bring the back and the front threads together in this step, you'll also be making a firm base upon which to begin weaving. To do this, you will weave three rows using the same cotton as used for the warp. (Fig. A.6)

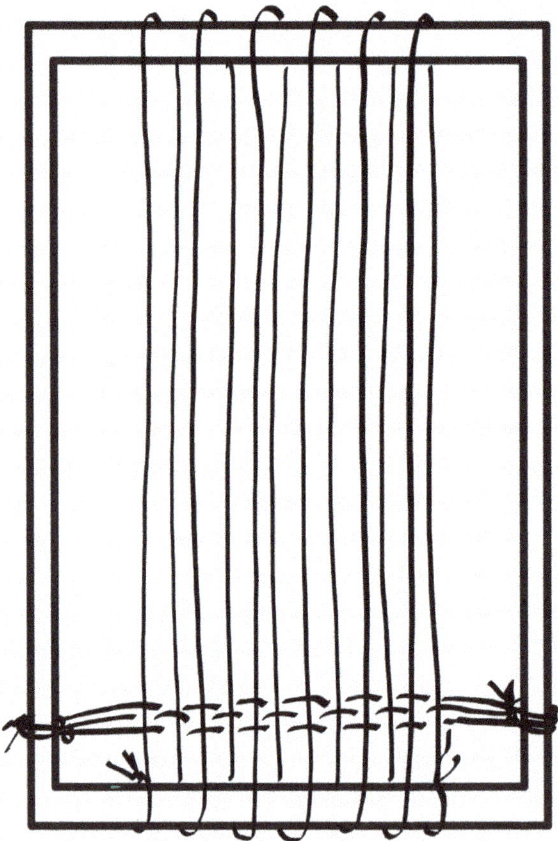

Figure A.6
The second step after putting on the warp would be to interweave three picks near the bottom of the loom. These are foundation threads to give a firm base to begin the weaving upon. They should be pulled tightly from one side of the frame to the other and tied to the frame and each other.

- Measure a length of the thread about four times the width of the frame.
- Tie one end to either the right or left side of the frame and near the bottom edge.
- Put the thread onto a needle and interweave over and under all the way across the width. The needle will go under the threads at the back and over the threads at the front. You'll find it easiest to interweave a few inches above where you want the thread to wind up because there will be a bit more space you can work into.
- Once in place, pull the thread very firmly and as straight across and level as you can. Tie it around the frame at the opposite side; be sure to hold the tension as you tie so the weft doesn't become loose.
- Weave back in the opposite path to the first side of the frame. That means if you went over a warp on the first row, go under the same warp on this return row. Again, you'll find it easiest to do if you work a few inches above where the row will be placed once woven. These two rows or picks of weft are the essence of the plain weave. Be sure to pull this second pick firmly and tightly and then tie to the side of the loom, catching the first pick into this tie.
- Weave a third pick back to the opposite side. Remember, if the previous weft went under a warp, this time it will go over the same warp. Each of the three picks of weft should be on alternate paths across. Pull firmly and tie to the frame with all three picks tied together.
- These three picks tightly woven across from side to side and tied to the frame will give a good firm base upon which to begin weaving. They will be taken out and discarded once the little tapestry is cut from the loom.
- To flatten out the warp, it will be helpful to put in *one* pick across the top in the same way as the first pick at the bottom. Tie one end near the top of the frame and pick up the threads that are down as you weave across. Pull firmly and tie off at the opposite side. (Fig. A.7)

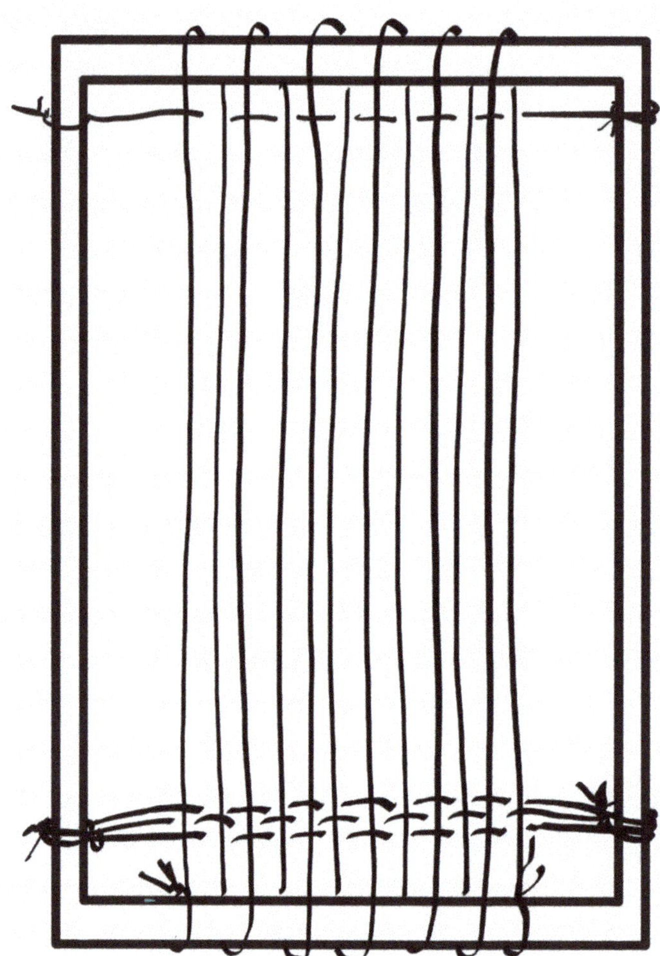

Figure A.7
At the top of the loom you may want to interweave a pick of weft, pulling it tightly and tying it onto the frame. This will help you see which of the warps you need to weave into since it will help to flatten out the plane of the entire warp.

Prepare for Weaving—Space the Warp Evenly:

Weave in about a half-inch of plain weave with the same thread as used for the warp. This will give you a chance to check the spacing of the warp to make sure it's evenly spread out to the eight threads per inch. This is called a header and will be unraveled once the tapestry is off the loom. (Fig. A.8) You can use the tip of the needle to push or pull the warps into position a bit even with the header in place.

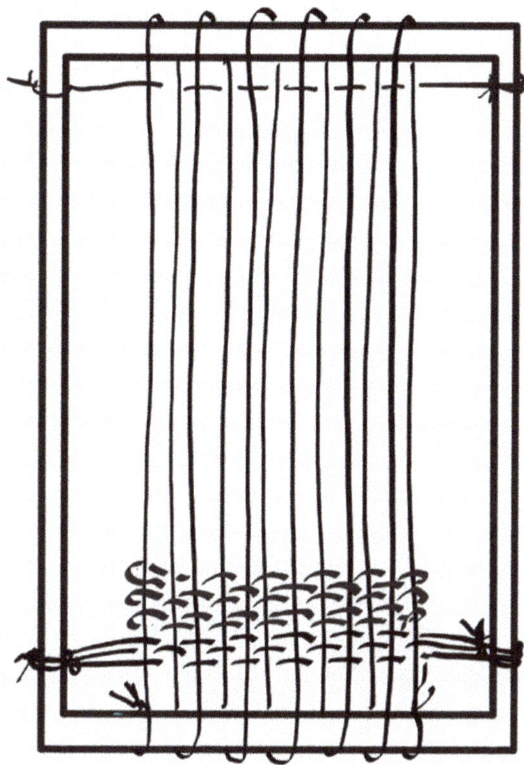

Figure A.8
A header is woven at the bottom and on top of the foundation threads. This is typically of the same thread as you've used for the warp. This time the weft will go only to edge of the warp threads (not to the frame's sides). The weft also should be bubbled so that it will cover the warps.

Starting the Weaving:

1. For this first tapestry, begin with two colors. It's helpful to see the difference if the colors of weft are contrasting in dark and light. And it's also good to use two weft yarns that are of the same type or size for each color. I'll describe how to introduce a third color later.

2. The size of the weft should be approximately the same as the space between two warp threads. If you're using a knitting yarn, one strand of it may be the right size. If you are using five-strand embroidery floss as weft, you may have to use a combination of two or more of the five-strand floss to equal the size of the space between the warps.

3. Begin with one of the colors at either the right or left side.
    - Secure the tail of the weft as shown in the diagram. You'll be weaving at the front of the tapestry, and this will put the starting tail at the back. (Fig. A.9)
    - Weave over and under across the threads, being sure to alternate in the correct up-down order. Go to the center of the width of the warp and stop.
    - Bring the weft out of the row and let it wait until the second color is entered.

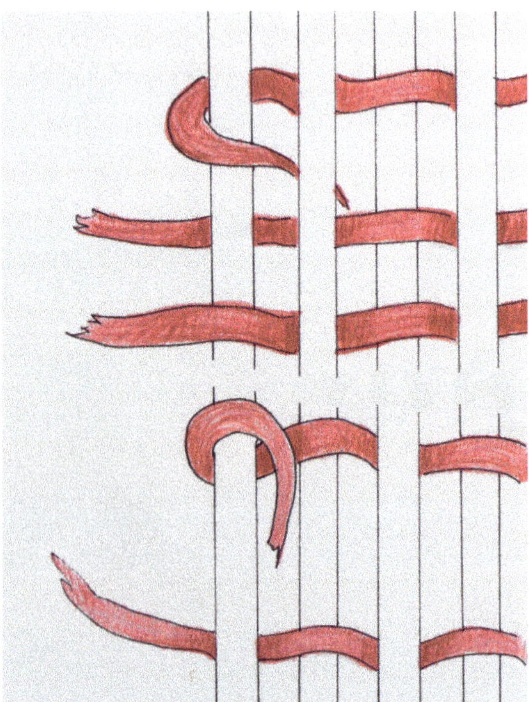

Figure A.9
The tails of the wefts will be taken to the back of the weaving. Hitch it over the warp and tuck away. Notice that there will be two ways this will be done, depending upon the position of the weft at the starting point.

4. Begin with the second color at the opposite side of the loom.
   - Secure its tail to the back, as shown in the diagram. Notice that the weft will act one of two ways when being taken to the back, depending upon whether it's on top of the warp or under the warp as you're tucking it away. *This will happen throughout the tapestry every time you add new weft yarn.*
   - Bring the second weft color to the center to the point where the first color has stopped. (Fig. A.10)

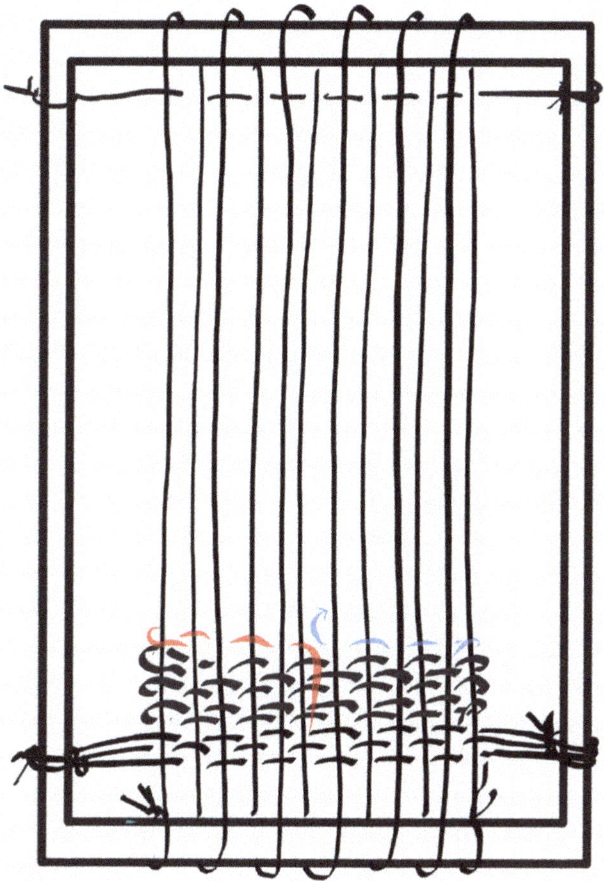

Figure A.10
Diagram of the loom with the first two colors entered so that they will travel opposite each other along the same row. This is called "meet and separate" and is important to building shapes individually in the tapestry.

5. As you weave, give the weft enough slack so that it will completely cover the warp threads when you pack it down. The easiest way to do this is to make a series of arcs or "bubbles" of the weft as you place it through the threads. Weave through for about an inch, make a bubble of weft and then pack it down, either with the tip of the needle, with your fingernail, or with the fork. (Fig. A.11)

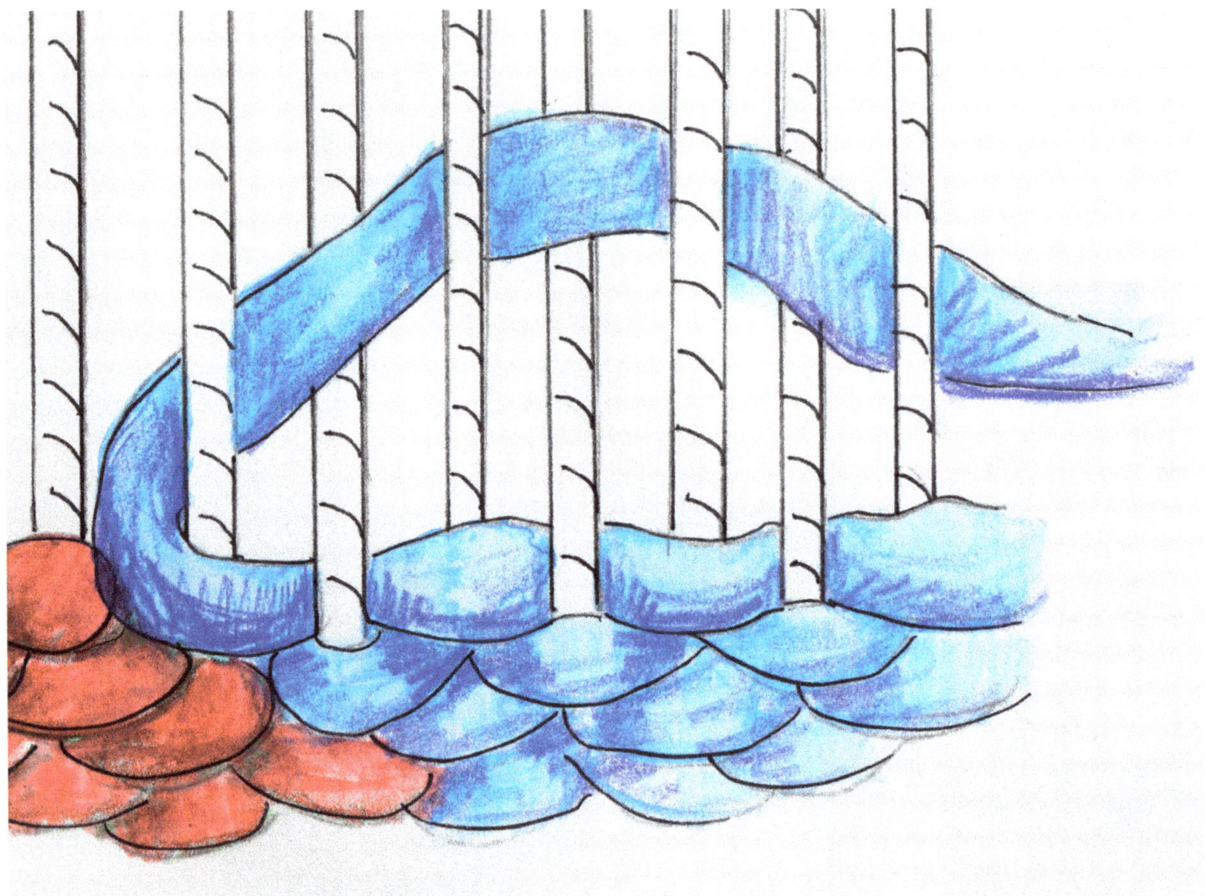

Figure A.11
Illustration of the amount of "bubble" you'll need to allow for the weft as it enters the warps.

6. When the second color meets the point where the first color has stopped at the middle, it's time to turn around and weave back in the opposite direction with each color. *Remember that two picks over alternate warps make up the structure of plain weave. These are called a "pass."*

Meet and Separate:

The fundamental nature of a tapestry is that the design is created as the weaving is made. Shapes within the design may be woven independently and then other shapes filled in at the sides and on top of those. Shapes must be built in decreasing ways when doing this because there must be support under new areas that are woven. You may also weave from side to side, filling in the design by changing the weft colors as you go across. Both methods are right. Try each way and see which feels most comfortable for you.

When the wefts are set up to travel in *opposite* directions along the same row or pick, the method is called "meet and separate." (Fig. A.12) By having the wefts interact in this way, it is possible for a color to overlap on top of a previously-woven pick without doubling up the yarn when making shapes. While this isn't terrible, if it happens over and over, you'll soon find it hard to completely cover the warp because of the double thickness of the weft in places.

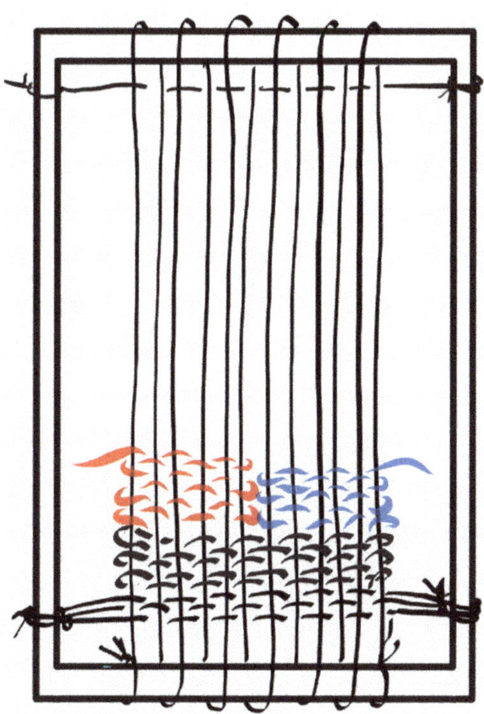

Figure A.12
Diagram of the meet and separate areas of two colors with both sides woven with the same number of picks, making them level. Remember, this is a simple line drawing and does not represent how the wefts will actually be covering the warp threads to hide them.

Remember the basic rule for meet and separate technique is that adjacent wefts go in opposite directions within the same pick. By doing this, the wefts will be in the correct sequence of plain weave as each area is woven.

Let's look closely at two wefts and how they will appear as they meet and then separate at the turn. You'll notice that each weft will cover the two adjacent warps—where the wefts turn to complete the pass—differently. This is described as being a "high" turn or a "low" turn. High means that the weft goes over the top of the warp as it turns on the next pick. A low turn will have the weft going under the warp when it turns around. (Fig. A.13)

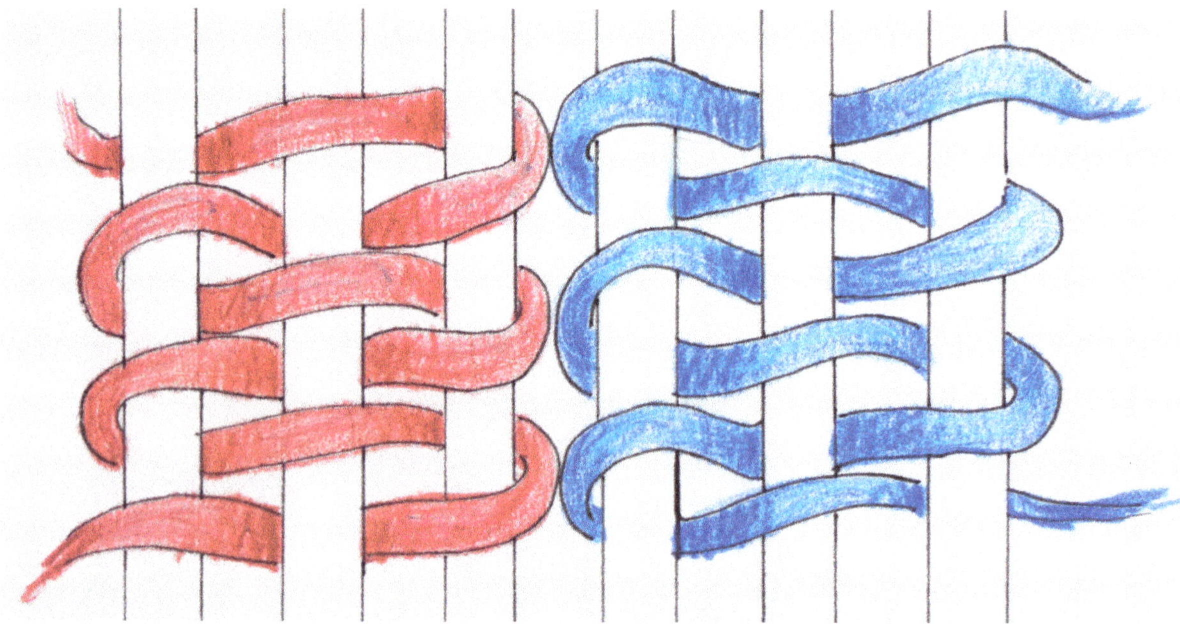

Figure A.13
Detail of how the two wefts will interact when they are set up to meet and separate correctly. Imagine that the red and the blue were one thread and continued along a row from one side to the other. See how each warp will be alternately covered as the weft goes across?

Being able to recognize the high and low turns is one of the keys to being able to use the meet and separate method successfully. And, remember, once two colors are set up to work correctly in this configuration, that's great! However, keep in mind that once a third color/shape is introduced, it will throw things off—but that's to be expected. I'll mention a way to correct the situation later. Soon you'll recognize how to keep the wefts in an order to allow you to build shapes without overlapping extra wefts where they aren't needed.

If you continue to use the same two adjacent warps as the turn-around points, you'll soon see a vertical opening between the two colors. This is called a "slit." It may not be desirable to keep the slit as-is in the long run, and there are ways to stitch it closed afterwards or even as you weave. However, on small pieces, vertical slits don't cause much problem with the structural integrity of the tapestry. On larger tapestries, stitching usually joins slits.

Horizontal Lines Called "Hatching:"

With two colors set up to meet and separate in the same row correctly, it's possible to create a pattern of horizontal lines between the two. This is called "hatching" and may be used to give an appearance of a third tone, even though only two colors are being used. It might be helpful to think of the colors as A and B at this point (in this example, color A is red and color B is blue). (Fig. A.14)

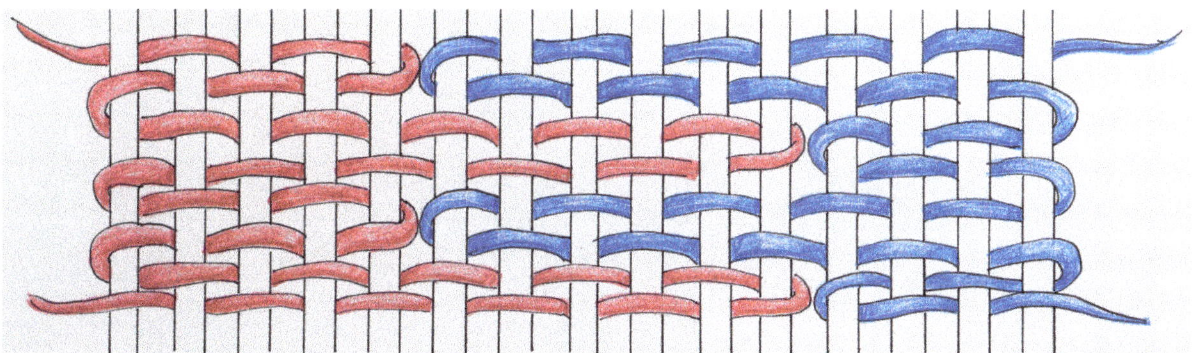

Figure A.14
Hatching is based on using meet and separate. First, one color makes a long pass and then a short pass. Those picks are next followed by the second color that will meet and separate at each of those turn points.

- To begin, color A moves over and returns, making a long pass.
- Next, color A makes a shorter pass.
- You now have two passes in place (or four picks) to start the hatching.
- The color B will now meet and separate with each of the two passes of color A: first pass of color B will meet the long pass of the color A, followed by the second pass of the color B meeting the short pass of the color A.
- If you keep the return points at the same place, thin horizontal lines of each color will build up between solid areas of the two colors.
- You may want to experiment with where the turning points for the passes will be made. This may be done in a regular way or more randomly. (Fig. A.15)

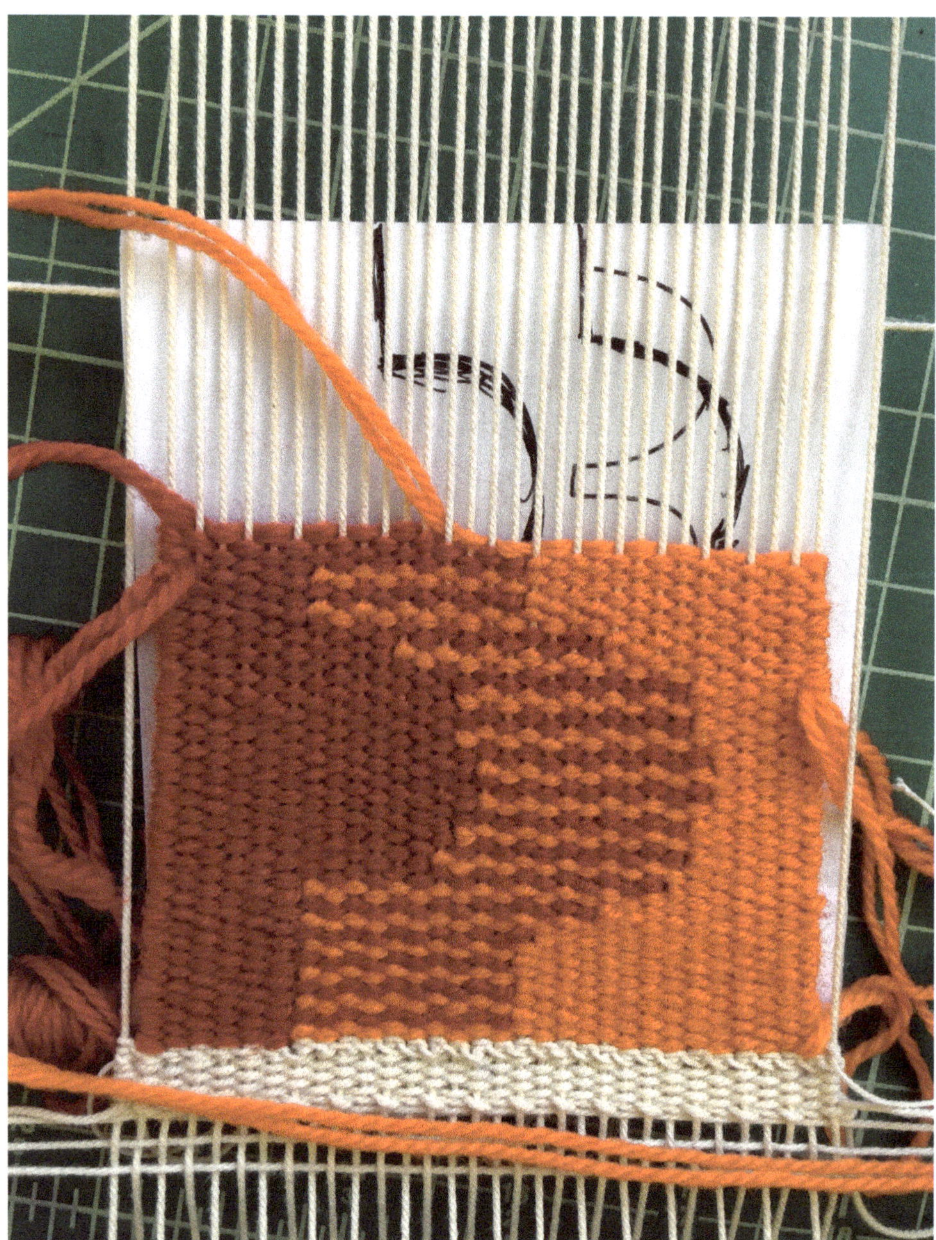

Figure A.15
A student example of two colors with hatching between. Notice how the changing points of return for the meet and separate can create a shape made up of thin horizontal lines that blend the two side colors.

Shape Building:

If you weave shapes independently, rather than changing wefts for the shapes as you go across each pick, they must be done in decreasing or descending ways. This allows new shapes to be built against what's woven. If a diagonal edge is woven, for instance, the angle will slope away and the new shape will be able to weave against it, as the diagram shows. (Fig. A.16)

As you weave a diagonal, the acute angle that is created will depend on the number of times you turn around a warp thread before stepping back to another one for the next turn. The steeper the angle approaches 90 degrees, the more turns at each warp will be made. These steps are necessary to build the angle of the edge. For a lower angle, you'll skip a warp and turn on the second or third back to make the slant.

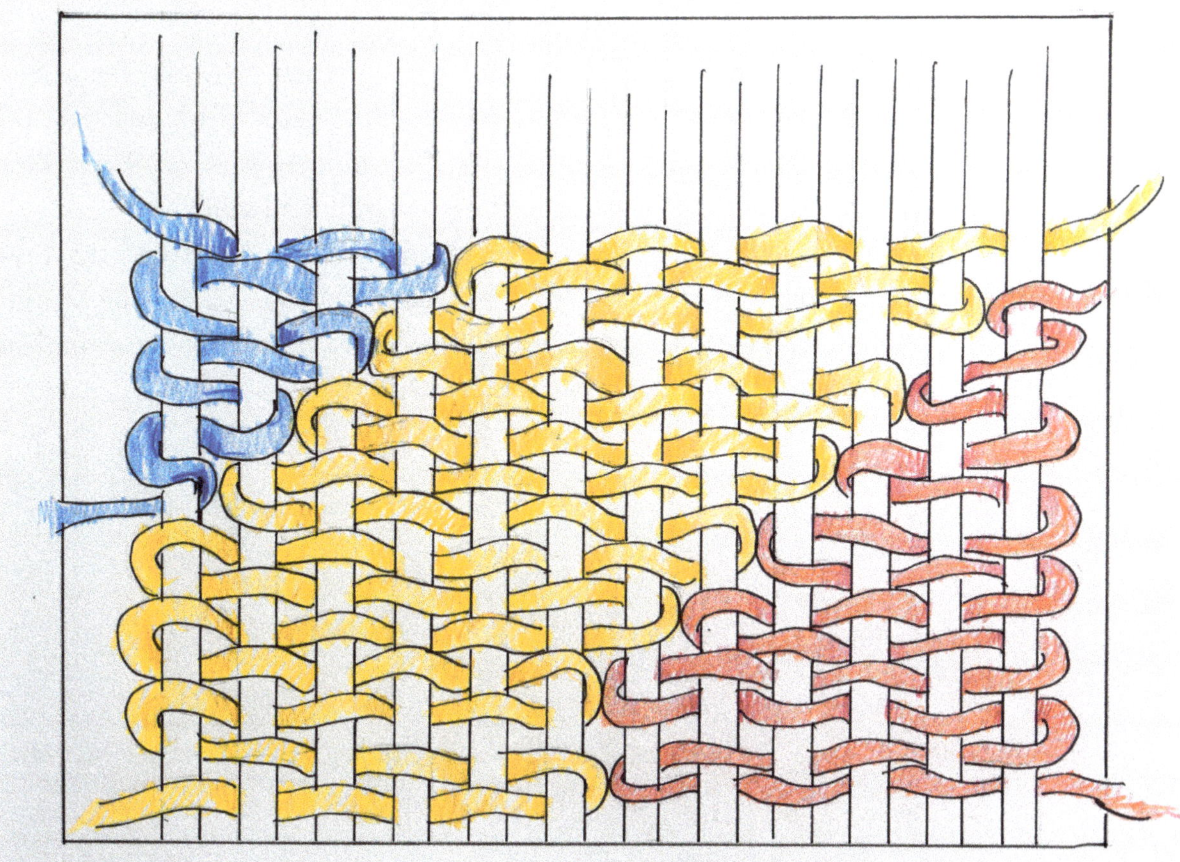

Figure A.16
Shapes may be built individually by weaving the decreasing areas first, then filling in with the next color. If the wefts are set up correctly for meet and separate at the beginning, all will fall into place without weft threads being doubled up.

Geometric shapes with horizontal, vertical, and diagonal edges are all easy and natural to the nature of tapestry. Curving, organic shapes are more challenging to weave. Think about it this way: in tapestry weaving, the curves are really made the same way as the diagonals. For curves, the steps to bring the sides up are done in uneven amounts as you are decreasing or increasing. Sound confusing? But if you remember to acknowledge the nature of the technique and aim for a weaverly way to create the design, all will be well.

Adding a Third Color:

Meet and separate for tapestry is a basic skill to learn. Many wonderful designs may be created using only two colors. However, soon you may want to introduce other colors into the design. Right away you'll notice when you add a third color there is a problem. One of the first two colors will not be able to meet and separate correctly with the new color.

An easy way to make the correction is for one of the original two colors to *change direction*. To do that, cut off and reenter the weft from the opposite side of where it is at the time so that it will meet and separate with the new color in the correct way. Remember to keep it in the correct pick so that the meet and separate will work right for all shapes.

Any other shape/color you want to add can be handled similarly. Check to see if the direction will allow the new weft to meet and separate with the weft that is making the existing shape. If so, weave on! If not, you will usually be able to correct the sequence by restarting one of the existing shapes from the opposite direction. (Fig. A.17)

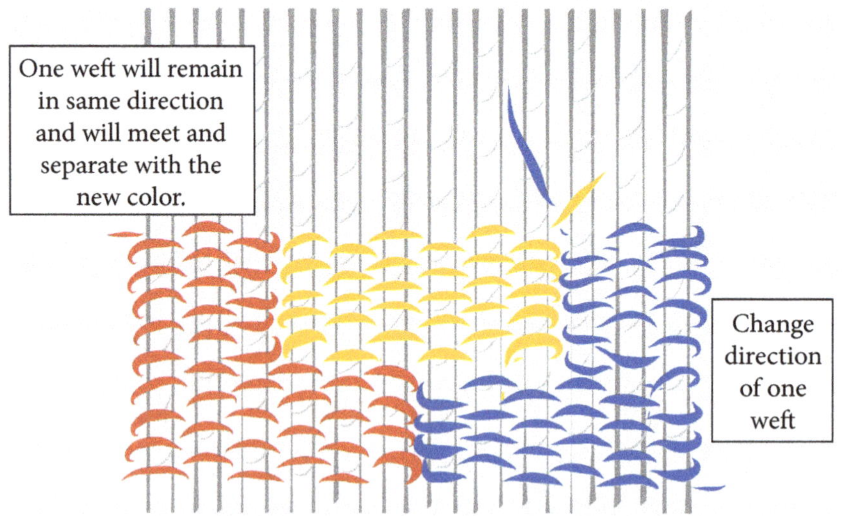

Figure A.17
When adding a third color between meet and separate areas, change the direction in which one of the initial colors moves. Once the third color is finished, the direction of one of the initial colors will have to change again to make the sequence once more correct.

Ending the Tapestry:

You will not be able to weave completely to the top of the frame because the space becomes too narrow to insert the weft yarn. When you have about six-to-eight inches remaining at the top edge, you've reached the end. The inches that are left at the top will be used to tie small groups of four adjacent warps together to secure the weft and keep it from unraveling. (Fig. A.18)

- Cut the warp near the top of the frame, four threads at a time.
- Tie the warps together in an overhand knot as each group of four is cut free.
- When all the warps at the top have been cut off, clip the foundation threads loose from the sides at the bottom of the frame. Remember, those are the three picks that were woven in at the beginning and tied to the frame of the loom at each side.
- Carefully pick loose the knots with which the warp was initially tied to the frame as you were setting up. The tip of a tapestry needle may help with this.
- Notice that the warp loops at the bottom now can be easily found since the tapestry is free at the top.
- Cut the loops of the warp as closely to the very bottom as you can.
- You'll have less length to knot together at the lower end so you may want to carefully unravel the header a few threads at a time, knotting each group of four warp ends as you go.
- Finish your tapestry sampler by trimming both ends of the warp evenly. You may also want to trim any weft tails at the backside to about one inch in length.

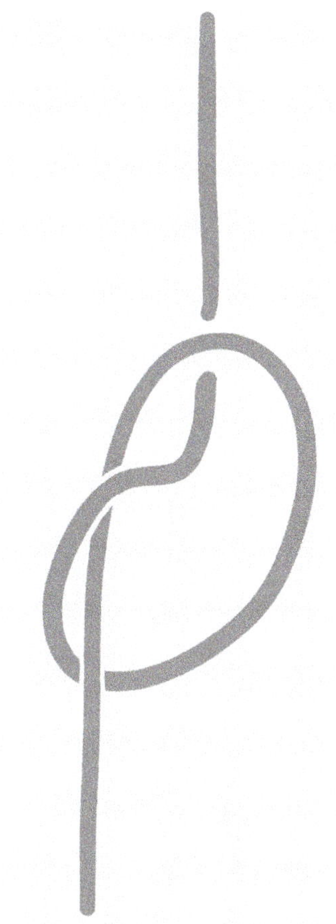

Figure A.18
An overhand knot can be used to group and tie together a few ends at a time for the finishing. The diagram shows a single line as the path to be used. The knot should be pulled snugly against the edge of the tapestry. I'd suggest putting not more than four warps together into each overhand knot so that the woven area won't be pulled in too much.

Troubleshooting:

Here are a few problems that may arise in tapestry and their suggested solutions. Remember, just as with any skill, first attempts are often unsteady. Don't be discouraged. If you really want to have a go at tapestry in a more serious way, warp up the loom again and do another sampler. And a third and a fourth!

Try out ideas that may come to you as you are weaving. If you feel you want to have more control of the warp tension as you weave, so that you can loosen it or tighten it as need be, you might build a pipe loom like the one I've shown at the end. It can be made larger than the dimensions I've given by using longer pipe lengths of larger diameter. The pipe loom design concept is one that master weaver and teacher Archie Brennan has shared with students over many years. This type of frame loom for tapestry is very economical and a quickly-assembled option for exploring tapestry weaving. After all, your nearest hardware store can become your handy loom supplier.

1. *The edges begin to draw in?* This often happens if the warp is not evenly tensioned or is too loose at the edges. When you set up the loom, be as consistent and even as you can be when you wind on the warp threads. If you begin to notice the edges drawing in, right away try to arc or bubble the weft a bit more to give enough slack Remember that there must be sufficient allowance for the weft to really "snake" around the warps to completely cover.

2. *Warps are spreading out too much?* Instead of too much weft tension, you possibly have too little. Try to tighten up the weft slightly. Your weft may also be too large in diameter for the space between the warps. If your warps are spreading apart and the weft also isn't covering the warp completely, your weft is probably too large.

3. *Edge of the weaving or a shape within the tapestry building up too high?* The warp may be too loose and not allowing the weft to be closely packed down. On a frame loom without a tensioning device, you may tighten the warps by weaving a few picks of scrap yarn near the top of the frame within the loose warp threads to take up the slack. Another reason this may happen is if the weft being used is too large or is of different size than other wefts.

4. *Edge of the weaving sloping or falling down?* This can happen if the last few warps at each side are too far apart. Be sure to make the weft turns firm at the edge—not so firm that the warp will draw in but enough so as to keep each of those side threads in the same alignment as the rest of the warp.

5. *Whole surface is buckled or wrinkled?* This effect usually is seen when there are many shapes used, side-by-side, and the wefts at each edge of the shapes aren't pulled snugly enough. Try to make the turn of each adjacent weft take up only half of the space between two adjacent warps.

6. *The shapes are "squashed " and distorted?* When you weave the tapestry, the previous weft rows are continuing to be packed down. If you're weaving a square and you want it to be as high as it is wide, you'll actually have to weave it higher than the width! How much higher? That depends on the closeness of the warps to each other, on the weft size, and on the type of the weft (some wefts are softer than others and will pack down more).

Moving Forward with Tapestry

What's next? This primer has been a very rudimentary description of all of the complexity that is tapestry weaving. However, if you've worked your way through a sampler of these methods, I believe you'll find you have a greater understanding and appreciation for what's involved with this very slow process. If you've become intrigued with the possibilities enough to explore tapestry further, I hope these thoughts and the accompanying resource list will suggest where you may want to go next.

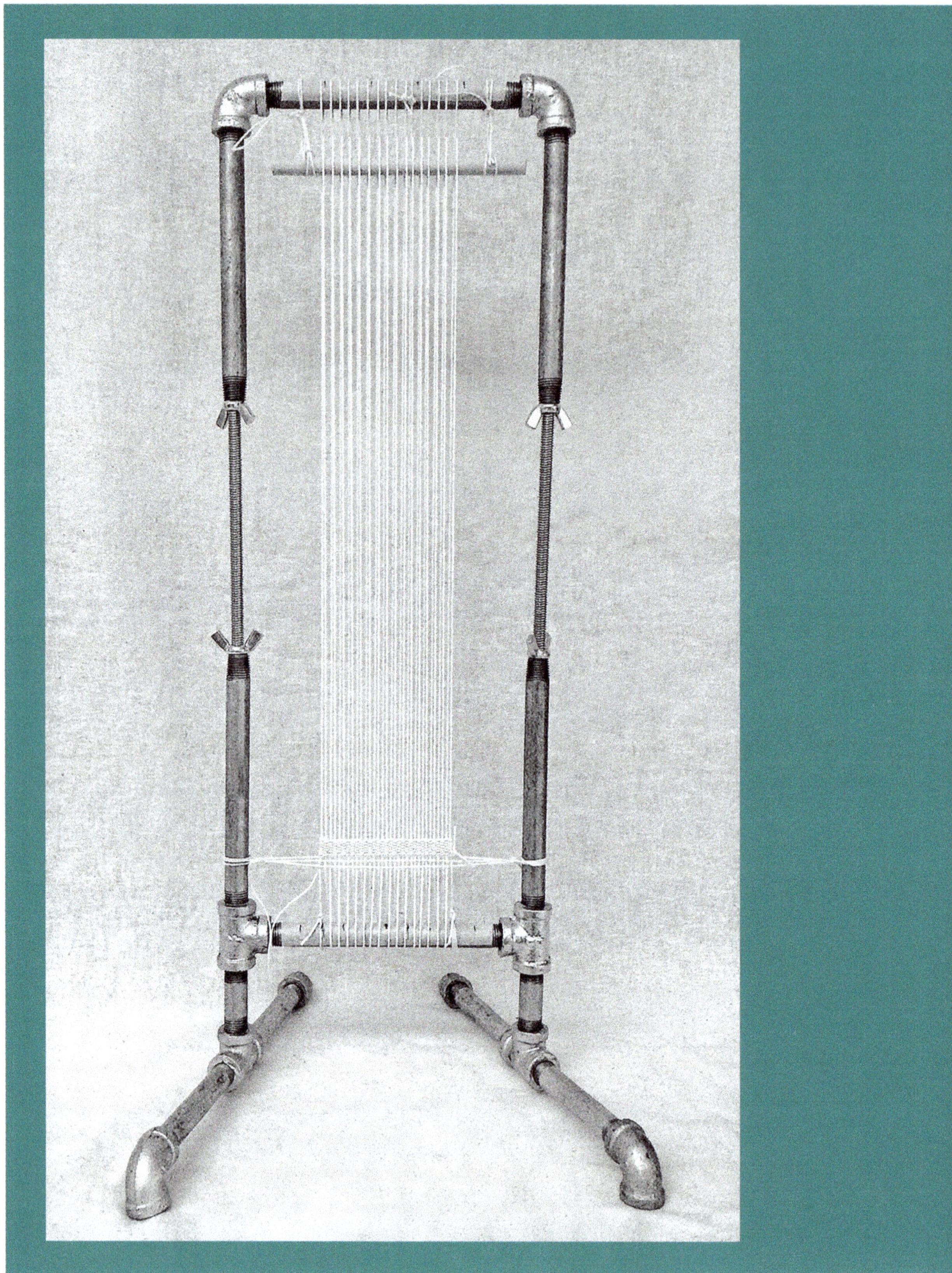

Figure B.1
A small galvanized pipe loom

B

Small Galvanized Pipe Loom[1]

Parts needed:

6 – ¼" diameter threaded pipe (called nipple), 6" long each

4 – ¼" diameter threaded nipple, 4" long each

2 – ¼" diameter threaded nipple, 1" long each

4 – Elbows to fit the ¼" threaded pipes

4 – Tees to fit the ¼" threaded pipes

2 – Caps for the ¼" threaded pipes

2 – Threaded rods, 12" x ¼" diameter

4 – Wingnuts to fit the threaded rod

---

1 Sarah Swett shared her inspirational use of pipe loom parts at her blog: http://www.afieldguidetoneedlework.com/blog/galvanized-pipe-looms

The frame of the loom is built with the 6 pieces of 6" long nipple.

The top has two Elbows joining three of the 6" pieces into a U-shape.

The bottom has two Tees joining the three remaining 6" pieces into another U-shape.

The two 1" long nipples screw into the bottom Tees to make the legs.

Screw two more Tees on the other end of the 1" pieces. These will hold the feet extensions.

Put the 4" nipple at either end of the bottom Tees, placing an Elbow on one end and a cap on the other end.

C

Brief Glossary of Tapestry Terms

Beater—used to pack in weft. A kitchen fork can serve as a beater.

Cartoon—design from which tapestry is woven, often drawn on paper and attached behind the warp.

Foundation picks—these are three picks, each in alternate paths across the warp, firmly woven across the bottom before starting the tapestry.

Hatching—horizontal lines that are made between two areas of weft when two passes (four picks) of each meet and separate in uneven lengths.

Header—beginning area, approximately one-half inch high, used to aid warp spacing. This is removed at the end.

High or Low—the two positions a weft yarn will take as it makes a turn around a warp on the second pick of a pass.

Loom—device to hold warp threads as weft is woven.

Meet and separate—method in which wefts travel in opposite directions in the same row or pick.

Overhand knot—a simple knot used to secure ends of the warps upon finishing the tapestry.

Pass—two pick of weft, each one in successive rows, both needed to complete a sequence of plain weave.

Pick—a single trip of weft in a row. It will alternately go over and then under each warp in turn.

Plain weave—simplest weave in which weft goes over one warp and then under the next in each pick.

Sett—number of warp ends used in each inch of the weaving.

Soumak—a method of adding a supplemental yarn, as the weaving is under way. It may be done horizontally along the rows or may move diagonally or vertically.

Warp—the thread on the loom; needs to be strong for the tension of the warp for tapestry.

Weft—the yarn or thread used for weaving into the warp.

D

Selected Resources for Tapestry

Books and Video:

Glasbrook, Kirsten. *Tapestry Weaving*. Tunbridge Wells, Kent, UK: Search Press Limited, 2002.

Harvey, Nancy. *Tapestry Weaving: A Comprehensive Study Guide*. Fort Collins, Colorado: Interweave Press, 1991.

Mezoff, Rebecca. *The Art of Tapestry Weaving*. North Adams, Massachusetts: Storey Publishing, 2020.

Russell, Carol. *The Tapestry Handbook: The Next Generation*. Atglen, Pennsylvania: Schiffer Publishing, 2007.

Soroka, Joanne. *Tapestry Weaving: Design and Technique*. Ramsbury, Wiltshire, UK: The Crowood Press, 2011.

Todd-Hooker, Kathe. *Tapestry 101*. Albany, Oregon: Fine Fiber Press, 2007.

A Weaverly Path: The Tapestry Life of Silvia Heyden (DVD), a documentary film by Kenny Dalsheimer, http://aweaverlypath.com/

Woven Tapestry Techniques with Archie Brennan and Susan Martin Maffei, instructional videos available for streaming, produced by Gary Benson, http://www.brennan-maffei.com/

Victorian Video Productions, Nancy Harvey tapestry videos, plus many other craft instructional videos and DVDs, http://www.yarnbarn-ks.com/, Yarn Barn, P.O. Box 334, Lawrence, KS 66044

Online:

The American Tapestry Alliance has a website that gives a wide variety of tapestry information, including educational articles, artist pages, information about current and upcoming exhibitions, and excerpts of past ATA newsletters, among other things: http://www.americantapestryalliance.org/

Tapestry artists and teachers, Archie Brennan and Susan Martin Maffei. There are links to diagrams of pipe looms of several sizes at this website: http://www.brennan-maffei.com/

My blogs are *Works in Progress* at http://tapestry13.blogspot.com and *Tapestry Share* http://tapestryshare.blogspot.com. I have links to a number of other tapestry weavers' blogs listed there.

Rebecca Mezoff offers several online learning courses for tapestry: https://rebeccamezoff.com/online-learning

Tapestry Instruction:

The American Tapestry Alliance offers a mentoring program. More information is available at the website: https://americantapestryalliance.org/tapestry-education/tapestry-weaving-instruction-mentoring-program/

Tapestry Organizations:

American Tapestry Alliance (ATA), http://americantapestryalliance.org

Tapestry Weavers South (TWS) membership@tapestryweaverssouth.org

Other regional groups in the USA include: Tapestry Weavers West (TWW) and Tapestry Weavers in New England (TWiNE). Contact information about those may be found at the ATA website: http://americantapestryalliance.org/NandR/Links.html

British Tapestry Group and Canadian Tapestry Network are also open to membership from around the world.

British Tapestry Group: http://www.thebritishtapestrygroup.co.uk/

Canadian Tapestry Network: http://www.canadiantapestrynetwork.com/

www.ingramcontent.com/pod-product-compliance
Lightning Source LLC
LaVergne TN
LVHW060630110826
845147LV00014B/884
* 9 7 8 1 9 4 0 7 7 1 7 2 4 *